Branding and Sustainable Competitive Advantage:

Building Virtual Presence

Avinash Kapoor
Management Development Institute, India

Chinmaya Kulshrestha
Management Development Institute, India

BUSINESS SCIENCE Reference

Senior Editorial Director: Kristin Klinger
Director of Book Publications: Julia Mosemann
Editorial Director: Lindsay Johnston
Acquisitions Editor: Erika Carter
Development Editor: Joel Gamon
Production Editor: Sean Woznicki
Typesetters: Chris Shearer, Jennifer Romanchak
Print Coordinator: Jamie Snavely
Cover Design: Nick Newcomer

Published in the United States of America by
Business Science Reference (an imprint of IGI Global)
701 E. Chocolate Avenue
Hershey PA 17033
Tel: 717-533-8845
Fax: 717-533-8661
E-mail: cust@igi-global.com
Web site: http://www.igi-global.com

Library of Congress Cataloging-in-Publication Data

Branding and sustainable competitive advantage: building virtual presence / Avinash Kapoor and Chinmaya Kulshretha, editors.
p. cm.
Includes bibliographical references and index.
Summary: "This book explores the processes involved in managing brands for long-term sustainable competitive advantage, helping readers better understand the importance of consumers' perceptions in brand management"--Provided by publisher.
ISBN 978-1-61350-171-9 (hbk.) -- ISBN 978-1-61350-172-6 (ebook) -- ISBN 978-1-61350-173-3 (print & perpetual access) 1. Branding (Marketing) 2. Brand name products--Management. 3. Product management. I. Kapoor, Avinash. II. Kulshretha, Chinmaya, 1976-
HF5415.1255.B72 2012
658.8'27--dc23
2011031126

British Cataloguing in Publication Data
A Cataloguing in Publication record for this book is available from the British Library.

To my mother Dr. Gyan Kapoor, my Brother Vivek Kapoor, my wife Namita, and my son Akshat for their continued love and support and encouragement.

Avinash Kapoor

To my beloved parents Mrs. Indira Kulshrestha and Dr. N. K. Kulshrestha for their blessings, and to my husband Shailendra and my son Yashmit for their unflinching support.

Chinmaya Kulshrestha

Editorial Advisory Board

List of Reviewers

Table of Contents

Preface ... viii

Acknowledgment ... x

Section 1
Branding and Sustainable Competitive Advantage

Chapter 1
Is Being Perceived as Sustainable a Means to Achieve a Differential Advantage? ... 1
Avinash Kapoor, Management Development Institute (MDI), India
Chinmaya Kulshrestha, Management Development Institute (MDI), India

Chapter 2
Are Strong Brands a Source of Competitive Advantage in the Virtual World? ... 4
Piyush Sharma, The Hong Kong Polytechnic University, Hong Kong

Chapter 3
Taking Public Health Learning Global through Branding and Identity Management ... 24
Shalin Hai-Jew, Kansas State University, USA

Section 2
Strategic Branding Decisions

Chapter 4
Exploring Key Issues in Destination Branding ... 47
Piyush Nangru, Great India Rural Tours, India
Vaibhav Rustagi, ITC Ltd, India
Manish Makhija, HCL Technologies, India
Lubna Nafees, IMT, India
Omkumar Krishnan, IMT, India

Chapter 5
Branding Strategies for Digital TV Channels 57
Margherita Pagani, Bocconi University, Italy

Chapter 6
Between Physical and Virtual Reality: The Case of Benetton Brand, "A Company that is Born from Ideas" 69
Annamaria Silvana de Rosa, Sapienza University of Rome, Italy
Elena Bocci, Sapienza University of Rome, Italy

Chapter 7
Branding and Sustainable Competitive Advantage in Indian Politics: Brand Rahul Gandhi 96
Avinash Kapoor, Management Development Institute (MDI), India
Chinmaya Kulshrestha, Management Development Institute (MDI), India

Section 3
Consumers and Brands

Chapter 8
Brand Engagement and Brand Loyalty 121
Ronald E. Goldsmith, Florida State University, USA

Chapter 9
The Brand Stakeholder Approach: Broad and Narrow-Based Views to Managing Consumer-Centric Brands 136
Jonathan A. J. Wilson, University of Greenwich, UK

Chapter 10
Brand Obsessed Society: Branding Yoga Guru Baba Ramdev in India 161
Chinmaya Kulshrestha, Management Development Institute (MDI), India
Avinash Kapoor, Management Development Institute (MDI), India

Section 4
Digital and Virtual World

Chapter 11
GeoFree BrandComms: Building and Sustaining Virtual Brand Communities 177
P. Raj Devasagayam, Siena College, USA
Dana A. VanDen Heuvel, Pheedo, Inc., USA

Chapter 12
Enhanced Social Presence Through eBranding the Consumer in Virtual Communities 189
Robert Pennington, Fo Guang University, Taiwan

Chapter 13
E-Branding and Institutional Web Sites: The "Visiting Card" of the Municipalities of Rome and Paris 207
Annamaria Silvana de Rosa, Sapienza University di Rome, Italy
Elena Bocci, Sapienza University di Rome, Italy
Massimiliano Picone, Sapienza University di Rome, Italy

Compilation of References 248

About the Contributors 274

Index 279

Preface

Brands help to build sustained relationships with the consumers. Strong brands lend endurance and permanence to an organization and protect it from the market turbulence and uncertainties. Given its strategic role, the selected chapters examine and develop a critical understanding of the processes involved in building and managing brands for gaining long-term sustainable competitive advantage. The book provides an insight into the world of sustainable and competitive branding through thirteen chapters divided into four sections.

In section one, "Branding and Sustainable Competitive Advantage," the first chapter discusses whether being perceived as sustainable is a means to achieve a differential advantage. Whereas, the second chapter on "Are Strong Brands a Source of Competitive Advantage in the Virtual World?" highlights the importance of customer education and employee training to prevent the erosion of brand image and loyalty on one hand, and improve perceived service quality and customer satisfaction on the other, for companies using offshore outsourcing of customer services.

Finally, the third chapter, "Taking Public Health Learning Global through Branding and Identity Management," explores potential methods for online branding and identity management. This chapter addresses an environmental scan of the global public health environment and work implications of the global branding, along with the engagement and the maintenance of the brand over time.

In section two "Strategic Branding Decisions," the first chapter, "Exploring key issues in Destination Marketing," discusses and presents an analytical framework to effectively communicate the competitive advantage of destinations and market them as brands. The second chapter, "Branding Strategies for digital TV Channels," analyses the impact of digitalization on TV marketing strategies focusing on the role of brand as a loyalty-based resource, available to digital television networks to create a sustainable competitive advantage. The third chapter, entitled "Between Physical and Virtual reality: the case of Benetton Brand," identifies the organizational dynamics of the Benetton Company and presents a perspective theory that seeks to analyze the connections between social representations and corporate communication.

Further, the fourth chapter, "Branding & Sustainable Competitive Advantage in Indian Politics: Brand Rahul Gandhi," discusses and analyses Rahul Gandhi as a brand to find a match between brand identity, brand personality, and consumer perception in terms of benefits sought and influence of activities undertaken by him. The chapter concludes that there should be a sustainable synergy between the leader and the party to avoid brand equity dilution.

In section three, "Consumers and Brands," the first chapter, "Brand Engagement and Brand Loyalty," states brand engagement from theoretical, managerial, and methodological perspectives. The theoretical component describes types and levels of engagement and emphasizes their antecedents and consequences.

The managerial component briefly describes management interests in branding and brand loyalty and the relation of brand engagement to loyalty. Finally, the methodological component briefly describes how to operationalize the engagement concepts. Similarly, the second chapter, "The Brand Stakeholder Approach: Broad and Narrow-based views to managing consumer-centric brands," presents a dynamic collaborative process of creation of brands seeking to engage consumers in new and innovative ways in order to gain authenticity.

Finally, the third chapter, "Brand Obsessed Society: Branding Yoga Guru Baba Ramdev in India," explores the value propositions, and the sustainable key differentiators to analyze the brand status and brand strategy of spiritual beacon Baba Ram Dev. The chapter concludes that, a strong synergy between image and identity of Brand Baba Ramdev results in strong personality that offers him a competitive advantage to get across to the consumers.

In section Four, "Digital And Virtual World," the first chapter, "GeoFree BrandComms: Building and Sustaining Virtual Brand Communities," presents the use of Weblogs (Blogs) and related technologies as strategic tools in building GeoFree BrandComms and posits the applications of GeoFree BrandComms in Web-based marketing strategies that find their basis in strong brands and loyal customers.

Further, the second chapter, "Enhanced Social Presence Through eBranding the Consumer in Virtual Communities," discusses that brands have become an important mode of consumer communication, identifying and distinguishing consumers as social objects within consumer market culture. In addition, eBranding affords consumers the necessary tools to represent themselves by communicating their roles and relationships in virtual consumer culture environments for transfer to actual consumer culture environments.

Finally, the third chapter, "E branding and Institutional Websites: the Visiting Cards of the Municipalities of Rome and Paris," presents the analysis of the municipal web sites of two historical capitals, Rome and Paris, considered as the Visiting Cards these two cities offer citizens and tourists. In sum, the chapter offers guidelines for web professionals and institutional communication managers.

Avinash Kapoor
Management Development Institute, India

Chinmaya Kulshrestha
Management Development Institute, India

Acknowledgment

Our colleagues in both academics and business world have really helped in providing us valuable guidance and insight into Branding and Sustainable Competitive Advantage: Building Virtual Presence, along with intellectual stimulations. We would like to thank everyone who has influenced our thinking directly or indirectly. Our heartfelt thanks to all the contributors for bringing their intellectual insights on branding and sustainable competitive advantage.

We would like to pay our special thanks and regards to Professor VK Gupta, Director, Dr B.S Sahay, Director, IIM Raipur (Former Director MDI) for encouraging us to bring out this the edited book. We acknowledge the support of Marketing Area faculty and the member of the other functional area faculty of MDI.

We place on record our sincere thanks to members of editorial advisory board and reviewers' team who helped us in selecting and screening the chapters.

We acknowledge the tremendous support received from Prof. Ashok Kumar Grand Valley State University, Michigan, Prof. Jaideep Motwani, Grand Valley State University, Michigan, Prof. Ralf Wagner, DMCC Kassel Germany, University of Kassel, Prof. Richard Feinberg, Purdue University, Dr. J. C. Kapoor, Management and IT consultant formerly, Professor and Consultant Indian Institute of Public Administration, New Delhi, Prof. Om Prakash Gupta, University of Texas, Prof. Y. C. Bhatt MNIT, Prof. M. K. Bhargava MNIT, Prof. S. K. Khosla University of Rajasthan, Prof. Ritu Parashar University of Rajasthan, Dr. Ruby Diwedi University of Rajasthan, Professor Adrian Palmer University of Swansea UK, Professor Asha Bhandarkar, MDI Gurgaon, Professor Anjila Saxena, University of Rajasthan, Professor Mukul Gupta, MDI Gurgaon, Dr. Harsh Diwedi University of Rajasthan, Dr. Rajesh Kothari, University of Rajasthan, Dr. Arvind Kalia, National Corporate Head Rajasthan Patrika, Dr. Geetika Kapoor University of Rajasthan, Dr. Ashok Sharma University of Rajasthan, Mr. Yogendra Khare, Project Manager Accenture, Mr. Amit Khare, Consultant, CGI, Sadat Khan Godphrey Philips, Mr. Vivek Kapoor Tata Docomo, Ms. Shefali Chhachi Marketing Director Max Bupa, Mr. Nitin Puri, Tata Docomo, Mr. R. K. Malhotra GM Sahara India Ltd.

We would like to pay our very special thanks and regards to Dr. Pritam Singh, ex-Director and Professor Eminence MDI, who inspired and encouraged us to take up such an endeavour.

We acknowledge with sincere gratitude the encouragement and the support given by our family members, friends, and the Publisher, IGI Global, as well as the entire production staff.

Finally, we owe everything to God Almighty and our dear parents, whose blessings and guidance have always inspired and encouraged us.

Avinash Kapoor
Management Development Institute, India

Chinmaya Kulshrestha
Management Development Institute, India

Section 1
Branding and Sustainable Competitive Advantage

Chapter 1
Is Being Perceived as Sustainable a Means to Achieve a Differential Advantage?

Avinash Kapoor
Management Development Institute (MDI), India

Chinmaya Kulshrestha
Management Development Institute (MDI), India

ABSTRACT

Sustainability has been a concern of activists, organizations, and public officials for several decades. The chapter discusses an important issue: whether consumers purchase sustainable products because they perceive them to be higher in quality or because it makes them feel good. Finally, it submits that the sustained efforts of the organizations can fulfill a brand promise dedicated to enhancing the lives of citizens in the state, nation, and world!

INTRODUCTION

Organizations across all sectors of the economy believe that being perceived as sustainable is a means to achieve a differential advantage. One example of this is BP (formerly British Petroleum), which is one of the top oil and gasoline distributors. BP has shed its old namesake and replaced it with the brand "beyond petroleum." Also, environmentally conscious brochures are available at the pumps that contain embedded seeds so if they are littered they will still benefit the Earth. However, what is missing in both the strategic initiative and the marketing literature is a thorough consideration of how being perceived as sustainable benefits organizations in their marketing efforts.

The literature's scant treatment of sustainability issues is surprising given the growing trend towards positioning organizations as sustainable. This positioning reflects growing need for firms to take into full account their environmental impact when making business decisions (Menon and Menon, 1997). Often associated with terms such as "green business," "going green," and the "green

DOI: 10.4018/978-1-61350-171-9.ch001

movement," sustainability has been a concern of activists, organizations, and public officials for several decades. First widely researched in the 1970's (Ellen, Wiener, and Cobb-Walgren, 1991; Henion and Wilson, 1976; Kinnear, Taylor, and Ahmed, 1974; Murphy, Kangun, and Locander, 1978; Scott, 1977; Webster Jr., 1975), sustainability was dismissed as a "cause" rather than a mainstream concern of either the academic literature or popular press. In recent years, however, sustainability has become a global issue that is viewed as an important concern in every facet of society and business. Today, consumers, managers and government officials, as well as the press, all appear to consider sustainability a timely concern.

In fact, sustainability is now frequently identified as a prescription for long term survival by many businesses and strategic planners (Miles and Covin, 2000), as well as a primary research interest by such organizations as the Marketing Science Institute (MSI) (Osterhus, 1997). Interest in sustainability is growing because of greater social awareness (Roberts, 1996) that appears to have resulted from the media exposure.

In short, exposure to sustainable themes is leading to greater social awareness and concern relative to the issue of sustainability, as well as greater acceptance of sustainability as a viable option in organizational branding and promotional efforts. Sustainability is also an issue of interest to government. As energy costs soar, and sustainability increases in visibility and concern among consumers, public officials are increasingly considering social policies related to conservation incentives, pollution, and sustainable economic development. President Barack Obama has argued that environmental sustainability is not a "someday" issue it is "now" (Obama 2007). This strategy is being pursued by his administration. Recently, it awarded 54 billion dollars to developing renewable energy and technology (Times Online 2008).

ISSUES

In spite of the interest demonstrated by consumers, managers, and public officials in sustainability, there is a gap in the literature concerning the role of sustainability in marketing and branding strategies and the effects of environmental responsiveness on consumers' assessments of brands. However, consumers may also doubt the authenticity of sustainable claims made by firms long associated with products not considered environmentally friendly. An important question that remains is whether consumers purchase sustainable products because they perceive them to be higher in quality or because it makes them feel good. The importance of such information is particularly high for organizations as they assess how to best position and promote their organization's goods and services. Further, it is likely that an emotive effect is also present when a consumer considers an environmentally responsive organization and its effects on quality, satisfaction, and purchase intentions.

The relevant question that remains unanswered is which effect has the greater impact on consumers' product evaluations and purchase decisions. In addition, many consumers are confused about sustainable products, which hurt evaluations and reduce purchasing intentions. Therefore, testing the effects of different branding tools and promotional types on consumer assessments in a sustainable context addresses a timely gap in the literature.

Further, in today's competitive marketplace, it is challenging for an organization to be heard, seen, and remembered. It is important to remember that brand is about much more than logos, colors, and typefaces. In order to deliver messages more consistently and effectively, successful organizations organize their marketing and communications efforts around a brand identity. Ask yourself, as an organization are you committed to developing communications strategies that strengthen your image and build new and sustained loyalty among your audiences. Brand image is reflected in the way people think, feel, and respond when they hear the words about you. Your audiences should be able to associate those words with a mental picture of an organization dedicated to making the world a better place for all of its citizens. Every employee is a brand ambassador. Each time one of them represents the organization when communicating with someone, and thus over a period, employees can build a powerful brand around the concepts of innovation, a can-do spirit, high quality, and making a difference for others.

CONCLUSION

There is a need to investigate and build the relationship between perceived environmental responsiveness and consumer outcomes, and consider possible mediators for this relationship. Organizations should also address the question of how environmentally responsive positioning helps them increase the perceived quality and satisfaction contributed to its products; and, if so, whether such positioning increases intentions to purchase a branded product. Finally, we submit that sustained efforts of the organizations can fulfill a brand promise dedicated to enhancing the lives of citizens in the State, Nation, and World!

REFERENCES

British Petroleum. (n.d.). *Homepage*. Retrieved from www.bp.com/US

Ellen, P., Wiener, J., & Cobb-Walgren, C. (1991). The role of perceived consumer effectiveness in motivating environmentally conscious behaviors. *Journal of Public Policy & Marketing*, *10*(2), 102–117.

Henion, K., & Wilson, W. (1976). *The ecologically concerned consumer and locus of control. Ecological Marketing* (pp. 131–144). Chicago, IL: American Marketing Association.

Kinnear, T., Taylor, J., & Ahmed, S. (1974). Ecologically concerned consumers: Who are they? *Journal of Marketing*, *38*(2), 20–24. doi:10.2307/1250192

Menon, A., & Menon, A. (1997). Enviropreneurial marketing strategy: The emergence of corporate environmentalism as market strategy. *Journal of Marketing*, *61*(7), 51–67. doi:10.2307/1252189

Miles, M., & Covin, J. (2000). Environmental marketing: A source of reputational, competitive, and financial advantage. *Journal of Business Ethics*, *23*(3), 299–311. doi:10.1023/A:1006214509281

Murphy, P., Kangun, N., & Locander, W. (1978). Environmentally concerned consumers-racial variations. *Journal of Marketing*, *42*(4), 61–66. doi:10.2307/1250087

Obama, B. (2007). *The change we need*. Retrieved February 10, 2008, from http://www.barackobama.com/2007 /10/08/remarks_of_ senator _barack_obam_28.php

Osterhus, T. (1997). Pro-social consumer influence strategies: When and how do they work? *Journal of Marketing*, *61*(4), 16–29. doi:10.2307/1252084

Roberts, J. (1996). Green consumers in the 1990s: Profile and implications for advertising. *Journal of Business Research*, *36*(3), 217–231. doi:10.1016/0148-2963(95)00150-6

Scott, C. (1977). Modifying socially-conscious behavior: The foot-in-the-door technique. *The Journal of Consumer Research*, *4*(3), 156–164. doi:10.1086/208691

Times Online. (2008). *Barack Obama looks to green jobs to save the planet and economy*. Retrieved from http://www.timesonline. co.uk /tol/news/world/us_and_americas/article5349809.ece

Webster, F. Jr. (1975). Determining the characteristics of the socially conscious consumer. *The Journal of Consumer Research*, *2*(3), 188–196. doi:10.1086/208631

Chapter 2
Are Strong Brands a Source of Competitive Advantage in the Virtual World?

Piyush Sharma
The Hong Kong Polytechnic University, Hong Kong

ABSTRACT

Offshore outsourcing is a fast-growing trend in the world economy today, and it is changing the way business is done across national boundaries. Specifically, customers are increasingly interacting with service employees located in other countries resulting in many instances of customer backlash due to poor perceived service quality and dissatisfaction. Prior research argues that service firms with strong brands may be less vulnerable to such negative reaction from customers. However, recent studies show that consumer ethnocentrism and unfavorable attitudes towards offshore outsourcing may adversely impact perceived service quality, satisfaction, complaint behavior, brand image, brand loyalty, and repeat purchase intentions. This chapter summarizes these diverse findings and highlights the importance of customer education and employee training to prevent the erosion of brand image and loyalty on one hand, and improve perceived service quality and customer satisfaction on the other, for companies using offshore outsourcing of customer services.

INTRODUCTION

Offshore outsourcing is one of the most controversial yet fast-growing trends in the world economy today; the worldwide spend on global outsourcing of services was estimated at just under US$ 1 trillion in 2006 and is expected to grow by 50% to about US$ 1.5 trillion by end 2010 (Frost & Sullivan, 2007). In an alarming report, Forrester Research estimated that 3.3 million jobs worth about $136 billion in wages will move offshore to countries such as India, China and Russia by 2015, causing wide-spread concern among average Americans (McCartney, 2003; Ross, Temkin, & Herbert, 2003). In fact, Gartner estimated that the global IT outsourcing revenues grew from $184 billion in 2003 to almost $300 billion in 2010 (Blackmore, DeSouza, Young, Goodness,

DOI: 10.4018/978-1-61350-171-9.ch002

& Silliman, 2005) and IDC estimated business process outsourcing (BPO) in Europe to grow from $43 in 2002 to almost $100 billion Euros in 2010 (Corbett, 2002, 2003).

Offshore outsourcing is expected to benefit not only the service companies but also their end-customers by reducing costs and improving productivity in the long run. However, based on their experience in recent years, firms have become cautious about offshore outsourcing of their service because of its 'invisible' costs (Stringfellow, Teagarden, & Nie, 2008), including threats to the firm's reputation, brand image, core skills and intellectual property (Reilly, 1997; Swartz, 2004a, 2004b). Besides these concerns, offshore outsourcing may also lead to lower customer satisfaction, reduced brand loyalty, increase in customer complaints, and lower service standards (Cornell, 2004; Data-Monitor, 2004; Economist, 2001; Kennedy, 2002; Roy, 2003).

A customer survey by American Banker/Gallup (2004) showed that two-thirds (71%) of the respondents were aware of offshore outsourcing to lower-cost countries. Among those aware, a whopping 78% held an unfavorable opinion about it and more than 80% said they would feel better if outsourcing did not take away American jobs and only less than half would feel better if it made American companies more competitive in the global marketplace (51%) or if it improved American companies' profits (46%). Similar results have been reported by market research firms about the consumers in UK (ContactBabel, 2004; Mintel, 2007).

Most of the early research on offshore outsourcing in the management and human resources areas focused on issues such as the labor costs and ethical issues, effects of strategic outsourcing decisions on organizations, and operational issues related to offshore outsourcing (Clott, 2004). Similarly, criticism of outsourcing is restricted to the changes in the employment patterns and the globalization of labor force, and their adverse impact on employees and organizations with little consideration to the end-customers (Briggs, 2005; Cornell, 2004). However, there is now growing research on the impact of offshore outsourcing on the attitudes and behavior of the end-customers (P. Sharma, Mathur, & Dhawan, 2006, 2008a, 2008b, 2009).

For example, Sharma et al. (2006, 2008a, 2008b) show that ethnocentric customers in three developed countries (Australia, UK, and USA) had distinctly less favorable perceptions about service quality, lower customer satisfaction and greater complaint behavior towards firms using offshore outsourcing of customer services. However, the findings on brand image, brand loyalty and repurchase intentions were mixed, with customers in US and Australia showing lower brand image, those in Australia showing lower repurchase intentions and those in UK showing a less favorable brand image for companies using offshore outsourcing (P. Sharma, et al., 2006). Others use the homophily principle and hybrid organization theory to show that customers experience greater satisfaction with the communication skills and problem-solving ability of domestic vs. offshore customer service representative (Bharadwaj & Roggeveen, 2008).

In contrast, recent research using the information integration theory shows that firm reputation may moderate the influence of call center location on customers' pre-encounter expectations and that their beliefs about the training provided by the firm mediates this process (Roggeveen, Bharadwaj, & Hoyer, 2007). Similarly, Sharma et al. (2009) use a field survey-based study show that attitude toward offshore call centers may moderate the link between service quality and customer satisfaction. Moreover, they find that the brand image of the service provider firm may also moderate the influence of customer satisfaction negatively on customer complaints and positively on repeat purchase intentions (P. Sharma, Mathur, et al., 2009).

In view of the above mixed evidence, it is still not clear to what extent is the brand image or reputation of a service firm helps in overcoming the negative attitudes towards offshore outsourcing in general and offshore call centers in particular. Moreover, we do not know to what extent the negative perceptions about the quality of service provided by the offshore customer service representatives (CSRs) can erode the brand image or reputation of the service firm. Recently, Sharma (2010) address this important gap with an empirical study using customers of a large American financial services company. Specifically, they explore the role of customer satisfaction as a mediator in the process by which perceived service quality influences the brand image, brand loyalty, customer complaint behavior and repeat purchase intentions.

This chapter reviews the growing literature in this important area and describes all the major findings to highlight the importance of customer education and employee training for the companies using offshore outsourcing of customer services, in order to prevent the erosion of brand image and loyalty as well as improve perceived service quality and customer satisfaction, to ensure the long-term sustainability of their profitability and competitive advantages.

LITERATURE REVIEW AND THEORETICAL BACKGROUND

Country-of-Origin and Customer Ethnocentrism

Country-of-Origin (COO) effects have drawn much attention from researchers in the last few decades, with different terms being used to describe this important phenomenon – "country image," "product-country image," "country equity," "made in country image" and "origin country image" (Alden, Steenkamp, & Batra, 2006; Russell & Russell, 2006; Verlegh, Steenkamp, & Meulenberg, 2005). The primary thesis of this stream of literature is that the customers in developed markets perceive products from less developed markets to be of inferior quality compared to the products from other developed markets (Gurhan-Canli & Maheswaran, 2000). Hence, there seems to be a significant positive direct effect of COO with products from countries with favorable perceptions being evaluated more favorably (Hong & Wyer Jr., 1990).

Customer ethnocentrism represents a preference for domestic products on the basis of nationalistic feelings and ethnocentric customers tend to be reluctant to buy foreign products due to a strong sense of loyalty towards their home country (Shimp, 1984; Shimp & Sharma, 1987). Customer ethnocentric tendencies may also lead to negative attitudes towards foreign products in general. Prior research has identified several antecedents and moderating factors of customer ethnocentricity in the product-sector, including four socio-psychological antecedents: 'openness to foreign cultures,' 'patriotism,' 'conservatism,' and 'collectivism/individualism'; four demographic factors: 'age,' 'gender,' 'education' and 'income'; along with two moderating factors: 'perceived necessity of the product' and 'perceived economic threat of foreign competition' (S. Sharma, Shimp, & Shin, 1995).

Prior research in COO area has linked it with several psychographic variables including consumer ethnocentrism, patriotism, conservatism, and openness to foreign cultures on one hand and demographic variables such as age, gender, education, occupation, country of birth, residence, and citizenship (Ali-Sulaiti & Baker, 1998; S. Sharma, et al., 1995). Specifically, it is shown that highly ethnocentric, patriotic, conservative and less open to foreign cultures consumers are more likely to have negative perceptions about imported products and services. Similarly, older, female, less educated, blue-collar workers and consumers who are born and brought up in developed countries are shown to be more ethnocentric.

Ruyter et al. (1998) extended the consumer ethnocentrism construct to the services sector using an empirical study with Dutch customers, confirming its generalizability and providing evidence that COO effects play a role in customers perceptions and behaviors towards international service providers. Ruyter et al. (1998) also replicated Sharma et al.'s (1995) findings for all the socio-psychological antecedents of consumer ethnocentrism. Others have also found that customer patriotism, conservatism, and ethnocentrism play a role in the service sector (Ali-Sulaiti & Baker, 1998; Gronroos, 1999; Kaynak, Kucukemiroglu, & Kara, 1994).

Recent research on the offshore outsourcing in the manufacturing industry acknowledges the presence of hybrid products (i.e., products are designed in one country, their components produced in another country and they may be assembled in yet another country) (Chao, 1993a, 2001; Han & Terpstra, 1988; Tse & Lee, 1993). Using Osgood and Tannenbaum's (1955) congruency principle it is argued that the congruency among the different COO elements may influence the overall customer attitudes towards a hybrid product. Hence, COO has now been reconceptualized as a multidimensional construct (e.g. uni- vs. bi-national products) (Han & Terpstra, 1988), country of components vs. assembly (Tse & Lee, 1993), country of design vs. assembly (Sauer, Young, & Unnava, 1991) country of assembly vs. parts vs. design (Chao, 1993b, 2001) and multiple COO facets due to global outsourcing (Li, Murray, & Scott, 2000).

Using a similar approach, others argue that offshore outsourcing of customer services has converted many conventional services into hybrid forms wherein various components of many services are now performed in different countries (Bharadwaj & Roggeveen, 2008; P. Sharma, et al., 2006, 2008a, 2008b; P. Sharma, Mathur, et al., 2009). For example, doctors in the US may examine their patients physically and record their observations into their Dictaphones. Next, these recordings may be digitized and uploaded onto the servers of medical transcription companies based in Indian cities such as Bangalore, Pune, or Gurgaon, where skilled operators may decipher these and complete the documentation such as patient records and billing. Similarly, call center operators based in Philippines or Singapore may handle post-visit queries from these patients. Thus, offshore outsourcing of customer services has dramatically changed the way many services are delivered.

Offshore Outsourcing of Customer Services

Outsourcing is a contractual agreement between the customer and one or more suppliers to provide services or processes that the customer is currently providing internally (Fan, 2000). Thus, outsourcing involves transferring some of the tasks of an organization to an outside supplier (Siems & Ratner, 2003). The well-known benefits of outsourcing include (1) lower cost, (2) better quality, service and delivery, (3) greater organizational focus, (4) more flexibility, and (5) change facilitation. Most studies portray the strategic benefits of offshore outsourcing for firms as a means to reduce costs, improve asset efficiency, and increase profits (Quinn, 1997).

However, in recent years organizations have become more cautious about moving towards outsourcing and conscious of the need to protect their reputation, brand image, core skills and property rights (Reilly, 1997). According to Kennedy (2002) companies risk losing potential customers for the parent brand due to poor customer relationship management by outsourced sub-contractors. Similarly, companies in UK have been warned of a possible customer backlash if they continue to offshore jobs to lower-cost economies, as further domestic job cuts may harm their corporate image (Data-Monitor, 2004). Outsourced services suppliers also play a key role in influencing outsiders' opinions of the organization (Trapp, 1999).

In a famous example, Dell Computers returned its business help desk from India to North America because of an increase in complaints from its customers about the Indian employees' perceived heavy reliance on scripted answers and lack of expertise required for solving complex computer problems (Cornell, 2004). Moreover, due to concerns that Indian call centers may have distinctly lower service standards than the British ones, they mostly deal with simple customer account queries while the more complex enquires are handled in UK (Data-Monitor, 2004). Some American medical-transcription firms even refuse to outsource work to India due to concerns about privacy of information, despite potential savings of up to 50% (Economist, 2001). There are also concerns about how many American medical and financial services firms are shifting information-processing work to low-wage countries that lack tough privacy laws, leaving the most sensitive details of the lives of millions of their customers vulnerable to lax security and in the hands of malicious identity thieves (Swartz, 2004a, 2004b). These examples highlight the need to reexamine the pros and cons of offshore outsourcing of customer services.

In this context, it is important to remember that service organizations may outsource many different types of services to offshore locations and therefore, it is important to clarify which types of services may be most affected by adverse customer attitudes towards offshore outsourcing. Youngdahl and Ramaswamy (2008) categorize offshore outsourced services on the basis of two dimensions: level of embedded knowledge (solutions vs. transactions) and the extent of customer contact (back-office vs. front-office), as shown in Figure 1. Thus, back-office medical services such as interpreting X-ray and lab reports require higher embedded knowledge compared to account services such as bills and payroll processing. In contrast, front-office technical services such as customer support require higher level of knowledge compared to call center services (e.g., in-bound complaint handling and out-bound telesales).

As expected, most research on customer reactions to offshore outsourcing focuses on the front-office services such as customer service hotlines and technical support services, because customers have a direct interaction with the offshore service representatives in such services. Prior research shows that such direct one-on-one interactions are likely to have a greater impact on customers' perceptions about the service quality and their level of satisfaction with the service provided

Figure 1. Offshore outsourcing services typology (Youngdahl and Ramaswamy 2008)

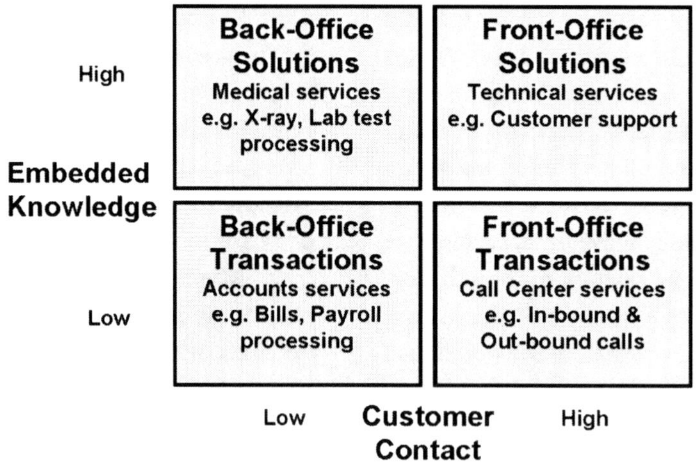

(Bharadwaj & Roggeveen, 2008). Next section reviews the growing evidence about the adverse customer reactions to offshore outsourcing of customer services.

Customer Reactions to Offshore Outsourcing

Customers in most developed countries are increasingly becoming aware about the use of offshore outsourcing by their service providers and many of them are expressing their dissatisfaction with the level of service provided by offshore customer service representatives. A few years ago ICM Research, a big UK market research firm, surveyed 1008 adult UK consumers, to understand their knowledge, attitudes, experience and reactions towards the offshoring of customer contact (ContactBabel, 2004). Some of their key findings are as follows:

1. Almost three-fourth (74%) of those customers who have personally experienced offshore customer contact, now feel more negative towards the company than before.
2. Customers who have experienced offshore customer contact are four and a half times more likely to have changed their supplier than customers who have had no direct experience of offshoring.
3. A little less than half (42%) of customers are less interested in sales calls when they come from outside the UK. Around 70% of customers feel that companies should tell them if they are providing customer service from offshore.
4. Two-thirds of customers prefer speaking with a UK-based agent for both simple and complex enquiries. However, if the UK operation is closed, half of them would prefer to call offshore immediately, rather than wait for the UK operation to re-open.
5. 62% of customers would still prefer to speak with a UK contact centre: even if the offshore operation was providing a similar or better standard of service.
6. A small but significant (7.3%) proportion of customers changed suppliers based on their company's use of offshore contact centers. Telecom and insurance companies suffered the greatest levels of offshore-related customer defection.

In view of these findings, the report suggests that businesses such as banks, insurance companies, and telcos who have committed themselves to moving substantial portions of customer service offshore may find their strategy backfiring as customer dissatisfaction with the concept and reality of offshoring is translated into defection, severely eroding their cost savings. Many more customers may be planning to defect within the next twelve months, and evidence suggests that as more people experience offshore customer contact in its current form, dissatisfaction and defection will grow further (Brown & Chin, 2004).

In fact, a more recent study by another UK-based Market Research firm Mintel (Mintel, 2007) shows that an overwhelming majority of consumers (82%) would rather not speak to someone in an overseas call center up from the 66% shown in the ContactBabel (2004) report. As many as 83% are concerned about account mishandling and about 75% have security fears even though there is no evidence that security problems at offshore customer service centers (OCSC) are any more rife than in their UK counterparts (Mintel, 2007). Some of the major problems with OCSC include amount of time on hold or no response (75%), not understanding what the customer service representative (CSR) is saying (58%), and the inability of the CSR to understand the customers' problem or request (45%).

Even in the US, a customer survey by American Banker/Gallup (2004) showed that two-thirds (71%) of the American respondents were aware of offshore outsourcing to lower-cost countries and among those aware, 78% held an unfavorable opinion about it, and more than 80% said they would feel better if outsourcing did not take away American jobs. Interestingly, only about half of those aware would feel better even if it made American companies more competitive (51%) or if it improved their profits (46%). All these are clearly alarming findings and signify a deep negative undercurrent against offshore outsourcing of customer services.

In view of such strong anecdotal evidence, it is not surprising to note the recent efforts from academic researchers to explore this phenomenon. For example, Sharma et al. (2006) have introduced a conceptual framework (Figure 2) including various demographic variables (e.g., age, gender, education, occupation, country of birth and residence etc) as the antecedents of consumer perceptions about businesses and brands that use offshore outsourcing of customer services. Sharma et al. (2006) also suggested that many psychographic variables (e.g., patriotism, conservatism, ethnocentrism etc) may moderate the influence of these demographic variables on consumer perceptual (e.g., service quality, customer satisfaction, and brand image) and behavioral (e.g., brand loyalty, repeat purchase intentions and complaint behavior) variables. However, they only focus on two of these variables (i.e., home country and consumer ethnocentrism) and examine their influence on consumer perceptions, attitudes and behaviors.

Specifically, using a sample of consumers from three developed countries (Australia, UK, and USA), Sharma et al. (2006, 2008a, 2008b) found that ethnocentric customers in all these countries showed significantly less favorable service quality perceptions, lower customer satisfaction, and greater intentions to complain if their services providers were outsourcing their customer services to offshore locations. Interestingly, other researchers also found that customers may experience greater satisfaction with the communication skills and problem-solving ability of a customer service representative in a call center based in their own country compared to an offshore one (Bharadwaj & Roggeveen, 2008).

Figure 2. Conceptual framework (Sharma, Mathur, and Dhawan 2006, 2008a, 2008b)

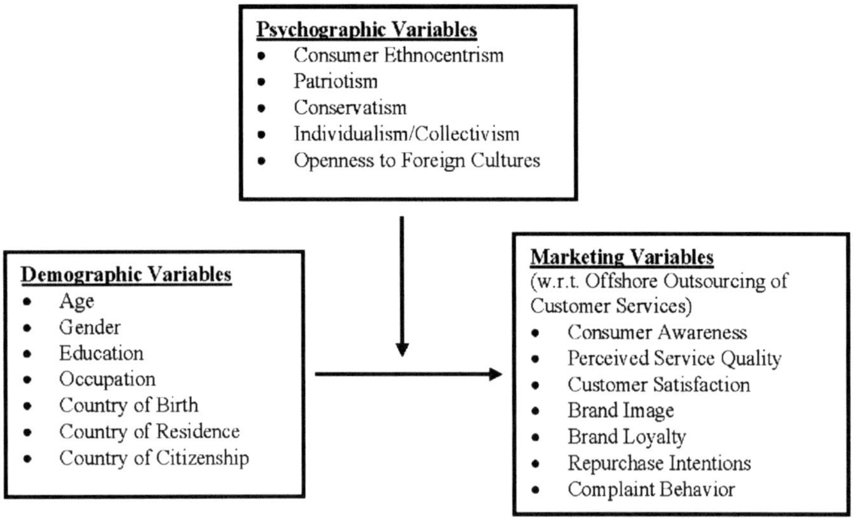

Attitude towards Offshore Outsourcing (AO)

Despite growing evidence that customers in developed countries are becoming concerned about offshore outsourcing of customer services, till recently there was no explicit measure of the attitude towards offshore outsourcing. Based on prior research on country-of-origin effects (Al-Sulaiti & Baker, 1998), Sharma et al. (2009) introduced a new construct called 'attitude towards offshore call centers' (OCC) and also developed a scale based on the consumer ethnocentrism scale, to measure this new construct. This scale uses a Likert-type response format to record the participants' level of agreement with statements representing cognitive, affective and behavioral aspects of the attitude toward offshore outsourcing of call centers (e.g., offshore outsourcing takes jobs away from my country; offshore outsourcing is good for our economy in the long run; and I do not like dealing with offshore customer service representatives).

Sharma et al. (2009) expected the patriotic, conservative and less open to foreign cultures customers to be more ethnocentric and hence more likely to have negative perceptions and a less favorable attitude towards OCC. Sharma et al. (2009) also expected older, female, less educated, blue-color workers and customers in developed countries to have greater negative attitude toward OCC. Interestingly, using a survey-based empirical study, they found that the attitude toward offshore call centers moderates the link between service quality and customer satisfaction; and brand image of the service firm moderates the influence of customer satisfaction negatively on customer complaints and positively on repeat purchase intentions (Figure 3).

These results support prior findings, which showed an interaction between firm reputation and location of call center in their influence on customer expectations, such that the location of a call center impacts customer expectations about anticipated satisfaction only when the firm is not well-reputed (Roggeveen, et al., 2007). Interestingly, Roggeveen et al. (2007) conducted their research with MBA students in the US using imaginary scenarios and did not explicitly measure the attitude toward OCC. In contrast, Sharma et al. (2009) conducted a field survey with adult shoppers using mall-intercept approach in a large mid-Western city in the US, thus not only validating prior findings but also providing them greater generalizability.

The above results seem to go against recent market reports about the increase in customers' intentions to complain and change their service provider because of lower levels of service quality and customer satisfaction (e.g., ContactBabel,

Figure 3. Brand image as a moderator (Sharma, Mathur, and Dhawan 2009)

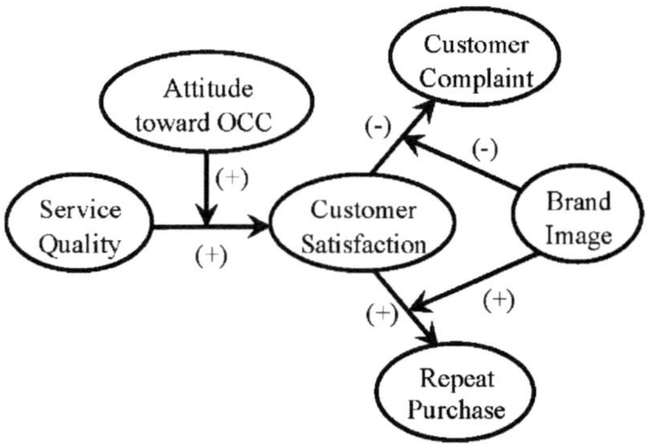

2004; Data-Monitor, 2004; Mintel, 2007). Sharma et al. (2009) explain that one of the reasons for these findings could be that the customers in general are wary of complaining or switching their service firms (Chebat, Davidow, & Codjovi, 2005) and hence, the participants in their study may not have complained or switched even if they were dissatisfied with the service provided by the offshore call centers.

Sharma et al. (2009) also argue that customers may have smaller choice-sets in services (Brand & Cronin, 1997) and associate services with greater perceived risk compared to products (Murray & Schlacter, 1990). Consumers may also be influenced by the exit barriers imposed by their service providers especially in financial (banking, investments etc), healthcare, travel and other such service categories (Mittal & Kamakura, 2001). A combination of all such factors may also reduce the chances of changing the service provider or reducing repeat purchase behavior despite lower perceived service quality and customer satisfaction. Sharma et al. (2009) also caution service firms using offshore outsourcing of customer services that just because the perceived service quality and satisfaction levels may not have yet dropped to levels to trigger greater complaining or switching behaviors, there is no guarantee that it may never happen.

Perceived Service Quality (SQ) and Customer Satisfaction (SAT)

The rapid growth in offshore outsourcing of customer services in recent years has led to a much greater interaction between customers and service providers from diverse cultural and socio-economic backgrounds (Clark, Rajaratnam, & Smith, 1996). Managing inter-cultural interactions is an extremely difficult task because of the differences in the expectations, perceptions, and evaluations of service employees and customers (P. Sharma, Tam, & Kim, 2009). Recent research on inter-cultural service encounters also demonstrates the extremely negative perceptions that many customers have about the quality of service provided by service employees with cultural and ethnic backgrounds different from their own (e.g., Barker & Härtel, 2004; Davis & Thornton, 2005; Paswan & Ganesh, 2005; Sizoo, 2007).

Recent studies by market research firms in the US and UK show that a significantly large proportion of customers do not like to speak to overseas call center executives because of fears about account mishandling and data security fears, and because they do not pick up the call quickly, put them on hold for a long time, are not able to understand them, and take much longer to resolve the problems compared to their local call center agents (American Banker/Gallup, 2004; ContactBabel, 2004; Mintel, 2007). Many customers also find the offshore service agents' accent significantly different from their own making it difficult for them to understand each other.

Communication is an essential element of the service quality provided by offshore customer service agents and they are expected to be attentive, perceptive and responsive in all their interactions with the customers to build trust and provide satisfactory service (Ruyter & Wetzels, 2000), any poor performance on this score reflects in lower perceived service quality. Based on this, Sharma (2010) argues that customers with less (more) favorable attitude towards offshore outsourcing may perceive the quality of service provided by offshore customer services centers to be lower (higher). In contrast, customers' ethnocentric tendencies may negatively affect the perceived quality of service provided by offshore customer service agents. Moreover, according to Sharma (2010), perceived service quality may mediate the influence of consumer ethnocentrism and attitude towards offshore outsourcing on customer satisfaction (Figure 4).

Repeat Purchase and Complaint Intentions

Prior research shows that customer satisfaction is directly and positively related to repeat purchase intentions because satisfied customers are more likely to want to experience the same satisfactory experience again and again (Anderson & Sullivan, 1993; Brown & Chin, 2004; Butcher, Sparks, & O'Callaghan, 2001). Similarly, the customer complaint behavior literature shows that the lack of satisfaction often triggers the process of complaining and this effect is stronger in case of services compared to products (Bearden & Teel, 1983; Crié, 2003; Gronhaug & Gilly, 1991; Singh & Wilkes, 1996). Based on these, Sharma (2010) argues that customers with high scores on consumer ethnocentrism and unfavorable attitudes towards offshore outsourcing may be more likely to attribute the instances of service failure to the offshore customer service representatives (Roggeveen, et al., 2007), resulting in greater amount of complaints and lower repeat purchase intentions.

Brand Image and Brand Loyalty

Customers' perceptions about the quality of service relates closely with the brand image of the service provider across a wide range of industries, including hospitality (Francese & Renaghan, 1990), auto insurance and copy service (Arora & Stoner, 1996), life insurance (Hill, 1996), travel and tourism (Gilbert & Hewlett, 2003), and cruise lines (Ahmed, Johnson, Ling, Fong, & Hui, 2002). Similarly, customer satisfaction is relates positively with brand image (Mayer, Bowen, & Moulton, 2003; Palacio, Meneses, & Perez, 2002; Selnes, 1993). Prior research also shows that highly ethnocentric customers have a poor image about products and services from other countries (Harrison-Walker, 1995; Kaynak & Kara, 2002). Therefore, the poor perceptions about the service quality and level of satisfaction with the service provided by offshore service representatives may influence perceptions about brand image (P. Sharma, 2010).

Service quality relates positively with customer loyalty to a service firm (Wong & Sohal, 2003), and with emotional satisfaction, which is

Figure 4. Conceptual framework and hypotheses (Sharma 2010)

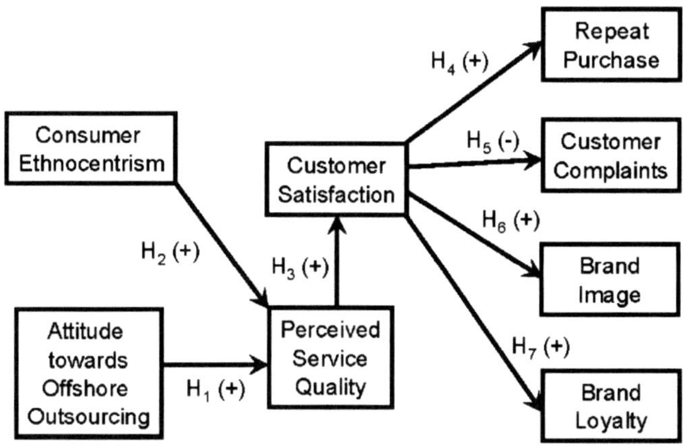

positively associated with both customer loyalty and relationship quality (Wong, 2004). Similarly, there is strong evidence that customer satisfaction may result in brand loyalty across several services including telecom (Kim, Park, & Jeong, 2004), financial services (Chernatony, Harris, & Christodoulides, 2004) and travel services (McCaskey & Symes, 2004). Hence, Sharma (2010) propose that customer satisfaction and perceived service quality may mediate the influence of consumer ethnocentrism and attitude towards offshore outsourcing on brand loyalty as well as brand image.

To test the framework shown in figure 4, Sharma (2010) collaborated with one of the largest Indian offshore outsourcing players with more than 3000 employees located in more than 30 cities. The company helped the author contact customers of one of its large clients, an American financial services firm with a base of over one million customers located all over the US. The client company agreed to share its data on terms of anonymity and a promise to share the findings with them. The author contacted via email a sample of 5000 customers randomly chosen from a database of over 100,000 customers provided by the American financial services company. The author received 548 (about 11%) complete online questionnaires over a four-week period during Jul-Aug 2008, an acceptable response rate for online or email surveys.

The online questionnaire had two parts presented one after the other. First, the participants rated their service provider (the American financial services company) based on their interaction with the offshore customer service representative, on several attributes including service quality, customer satisfaction, repeat purchase intentions, complaint intentions, brand image, and brand loyalty. Next, they completed the scales for attitude towards offshore outsourcing and consumer ethnocentrism followed by some demographic questions including gender, age, education, and occupation.

As expected, consumer ethnocentrism and attitude towards offshore outsourcing negatively correlated with each other ($\Phi = -.38$, $p < .001$). Attitude towards offshore outsourcing associated positively ($\gamma = .33$, $t = 6.18$) and consumer ethnocentrism negatively ($\gamma = -.21$, $t = 3.32$) with perceived service quality, as hypothesized. Perceived service quality mediated the influence of attitude towards offshore outsourcing and consumer ethnocentrism on customer satisfaction; and customer satisfaction mediated the influence of perceived service quality on repeat purchase intentions ($\beta = .17$, $t = 2.78$), customer complaints ($\beta = -.24$, $t = 3.39$), brand image ($\beta = .19$, $t = 2.91$), and brand loyalty ($\beta = .18$, $t = 2.86$), as hypothesized.

To further investigate the influence of these demographic variables, the author also compared the average scores for all the constructs used in this study across the different groups based on gender, age, education, and occupation, and found many significant differences. Specifically, as reported in prior research, males were more ethnocentric ($M = 4.27$ vs. 3.63, $p < .001$), more likely to indulge in complaining ($M = 3.38$ vs. 2.88, $p < .001$), and with a less favorable attitude towards offshore outsourcing ($M = 3.87$ vs. 4.32, $p < .001$) compared to females; whereas females were more likely to repeat purchase ($M = 5.42$ vs. 4.93, $p < .001$), and perceived higher service quality ($M = 5.58$ vs. 5.34, $p < .01$), brand image ($M = 4.74$ vs. 4.41, $p < .01$), and brand loyalty ($M = 4.45$ vs. 4.22, $p < .01$) compared to males.

The younger (≤ 30 years old) consumers perceived higher service quality ($M = 5.59$ vs. 5.38, $p < .01$), customer satisfaction ($M = 4.91$ vs. 4.66, $p < .01$), brand image ($M = 4.67$ vs. 4.50, $p < .05$), and brand loyalty ($M = 4.44$ vs. 4.27, $p < .05$) compared to older (> 30 years old) consumers; whereas, the older consumers were more ethnocentric ($M = 4.15$ vs. 3.65, $p < .001$), and with a less favorable attitude towards offshore outsourcing ($M = 3.92$ vs. 4.37, $p < .001$).

The findings for education and occupation were also similar. Consumers with lower education (≤ High School) and blue collar workers were more ethnocentric and had a less favorable attitude towards offshore outsourcing, compared to those with higher education (≥College) and white collar workers. Moreover, consumers with higher education and white collar occupations also perceived greater service quality, customer satisfaction, brand image and brand loyalty, but interestingly they were also more likely to complain.

Finally, the author also explored the correlations among all the constructs used in this study. As expected, perceived service quality and customer satisfaction were strongly positively correlated ($r = .36$, $p < .001$), whereas consumer ethnocentrism and attitude towards offshore outsourcing were negative correlated ($r = -.38$, $p < .001$). Customer complaint intentions correlated negatively with both perceived service quality ($r = -.24$, $p < .01$) and customer satisfaction ($r = -.23$, $p < .01$). Repeat purchase intentions correlated positively with both perceived service quality ($r = .23$, $p < .01$) and customer satisfaction ($r = .19$, $p < .01$). Finally, consumer ethnocentrism correlated negatively with perceived service quality ($r = -.23$, $p < .01$) and positively with complaint intentions ($r = .12$, $p < .05$). All these findings further validate the findings reported by Sharma (2010) in the context of offshore outsourcing of customer services.

GENERAL DISCUSSION AND IMPLICATIONS

The objective of this chapter was to review the growing literature on the customer perceptions and reactions towards the increasing offshore outsourcing of customer services. While early research on offshore outsourcing focused on management and human resources issues such as the labor costs, ethics, strategic implications, and operational issues related to offshore outsourcing (Clott, 2004). Interestingly, the criticism of outsourcing was also limited to the implications of the changes in the employment patterns due to the globalization of labor force for the employees and organizations with little attention to the perceptions and reactions of the end-customers (P. Sharma, et al., 2006, 2008a, 2008b; P. Sharma, Mathur, et al., 2009).

However, there is growing research now into this important business phenomenon beginning with early studies showing a strong negative influence of consumer ethnocentrism on perceived service quality and customer satisfaction resulting in greater complaint behavior (P. Sharma, et al., 2006, 2008a, 2008b). However, there was mixed evidence about the impact of offshore outsourcing of customer services on the brand image, brand loyalty and repurchase intentions. Others also found that customers experience greater satisfaction with the customer service representative in a domestic vs. an offshore call center (Bharadwaj & Roggeveen, 2008).

Interestingly, the following studies found that firm reputation may moderate the influence of call center location on customers' pre-encounter expectations (Roggeveen, et al., 2007), and the brand image of the service provider firm may moderate the influence of customer satisfaction negatively on customer complaints and positively on repeat purchase intentions (P. Sharma, Mathur, et al., 2009). Similarly, the attitude toward offshore call centers also moderated the association between service quality and customer satisfaction (P. Sharma, Mathur, et al., 2009).

All these studies provided useful insights into the customers' minds in terms of their perceptions and reactions to the offshore outsourcing of customer services, however, they did not examine to what extent the brand image or reputation of a service firm may itself be eroded with the growing negative perceptions about the quality of service provided by offshore customer service representatives. Sharma (2010) address this important gap by exploring the role of customer satisfaction as a mediator in the process by which perceived service quality influences the brand image, brand loyalty, customer complaint behavior and repeat purchase intentions. They found a significant but small effect of offshore outsourcing on brand image and loyalty.

These findings provide first empirical support to the various articles in popular press (e.g., Briggs, 2005; Jain, 2006; Venables, 2006), as well as industry reports (e.g., American Banker/Gallup, 2004; ContactBabel, 2004; Data-Monitor, 2004; Mintel, 2007), which highlight the negative impact of offshore outsourcing of customer services. It seems clear that the customers with higher scores on consumer ethnocentrism tend to have relatively more unfavorable attitude towards offshore outsourcing because of its perceived negative impact on the domestic economy in general and the employment situation in particular. Alarmingly, these ethnocentric feelings also seem to spill over in the inter-personal interactions between the customers and the offshore customer service representatives. Consequently, such customers not only perceive the quality of service provided by these offshore service representatives as inferior compared to their domestic counterparts, and report greater dissatisfaction with their service.

The high levels of dissatisfaction experienced by these ethnocentric customers also seem to have a significant impact on their complaint behavior and repeat purchase intentions. In other words, they may complain more against the offshore service representatives and be less likely to continue with their current service provider. Moreover, this dissatisfaction is also likely to negatively impact their perceptions about the brand image of the service provider and their brand loyalty. Notwithstanding the above, the negative impact of dissatisfaction with offshore service representatives (although statistically significant) does not appear to be very strong on customer perceptions and behavioral intentions, with r^2 values ranging from.13 to.21. One of the reasons for this could be that complaint and repeat purchase intentions, brand image, and brand loyalty may be influenced by many other factors besides perceived service quality and customer satisfaction, such as involvement, perceived risk and high exit barriers that characterize many service relationships. In other words, customer dissatisfaction resulting from higher consumer ethnocentrism and unfavorable attitude towards offshore outsourcing may not be strong enough to have a huge impact on all these constructs at least in the short run.

However, if the customers continue to be dissatisfied with the poor perceived service quality provided by offshore CSRs, it may further erode the brand image and loyalty, especially among those customers with stronger ethnocentric tendencies and unfavorable attitudes towards offshore outsourcing in general. Therefore, these findings should act as a red flag for the service firms rushing indiscriminately to outsource their customer service operations just to save on costs. They need to acknowledge the ethnocentric tendencies among some of their customers and address it with customer education; while trying to improve the quality of service provided by their offshore CSRs by providing them adequate training and support, to improve their perceived service quality. In this respect, the service firms may also need to pay special attention to several demographic groups, which show significantly higher scores for consumer ethnocentrism and unfavorable attitudes toward offshore outsourcing in general, such as males, blue collar workers, older, and less educated individuals. Such customers also tend to have more negative perceptions about the quality of service provided by offshore customer service representatives and report much lower satisfaction levels. Although, many of them do not intend to complain or switch their service provider, if these negative perceptions persist over a period of time, it may well have a negative impact on the image of the service provider and lead to a decline in the brand loyalty and repeat purchase intentions, affecting the service firm's reputation and profitability.

In view of these findings, this line of research should be a timely reminder for managers of firms using offshore outsourcing of customer services, to make them more aware of the need to understand the challenges in managing the fragile relationships between their loyal customers and their offshore customer service representative. Service firms should also keep investing in brand building although it may not continue to protect them forever from the backlash of poor perceived service quality and the feelings of lower customer satisfaction. Hopefully, even more academic researchers would also be drawn to this emerging area with great practical relevance, to develop and test more comprehensive conceptual frameworks with samples drawn from different target populations and using diverse methodologies.

DIRECTIONS FOR FUTURE RESEARCH

While there is some research in this area now, there is still a major scope for future research. First, most of the research in this area focuses on the front office transaction services in the B2C settings characterized by low embedded knowledge and high customer contact such as call center services, as per the 'Outsourced Services Typology' (Youngdahl & Ramaswamy, 2008). Due to the low level of embedded knowledge in such services, it is likely that the customers may focus more on the behavioral aspects of customer service such as language and accent used by the service representative, the extent to which they can comprehend the customers' problems, and the speed of response. However, a large proportion of front-office services especially in B2B settings such as technical support services, may involve high customer contact as well as high embedded knowledge. Hence, it would be useful to examine to what extent the level of embedded knowledge may moderate the roles played by brand image, consumer ethnocentrism, and attitude towards offshore outsourcing (Figures 2, 3 and 4).

Second, the conceptual framework (Figure 2) introduced by Sharma et al. (2006, 2008a, 2008b) includes various demographic variables (e.g., age, gender, education, occupation, country of birth and residence etc) as the antecedents of consumer perceptions and many psychographic variables (e.g., patriotism, conservatism, ethnocentrism, individualism/collectivism, openness to foreign cultures etc) as moderators of the influence of these demographic variables on a wide variety of consumer perceptual (e.g., service quality, customer satisfaction, and brand image) and behavioral (e.g., brand loyalty, repeat purchase intentions and complaint behavior) variables. However, they study only two of these variables (i.e., home country and consumer ethnocentrism). Future research may examine the influence of the other antecedent and moderator variables on the consumer perceptions, attitudes, and behaviors.

Third, Sharma's (2010) conceptual model includes only the direct effects of consumer ethnocentrism and attitude towards offshore outsourcing on customer perceptions about service quality, and indirect effects on customer satisfaction, repeat purchase, complaint behavior, brand image and brand loyalty. Prior research shows that the inter-relationships among all these variables may be quite complex including moderating roles as well. Hence, future research may try to hypothesize alternative conceptual models and attempt to validate those empirically.

Fourth, most research in this area measures the behavioral variables such as repeat purchase and complaint behavior only indirectly (i.e. in terms of behavioral intentions) which raises concerns about external validity and generalizability of their findings. Future studies may use direct measures of actual customer behavior for more realistic results.

Fifth, due to the cross-sectional design of prior studies, they could not estimate the long-term effect of repeated negative experiences with offshore customer service centers on all their dependent variables (complaint behavior, repeat purchase, brand image, and brand loyalty). Future research using a longitudinal design would be able to estimate the extent of this adverse impact of customer dissatisfaction with offshore outsourcing on customer services in the longer run.

Sixth, due to operational limitations prior studies about offshore outsourcing of customer service focus mainly on the US customers and Indian call center representatives. Future research may provide richer insights into this phenomenon by trying to replicate prior findings in other countries that are popular destinations for offshore outsourcing of customer services such as Malaysia, Philippines, and even China.

Finally, most of the research in this area examines the customers' perspective, with little or no attention paid to the service representatives' point of view. Future research may address this limitation, to provide a complete picture of offshore outsourcing, an important worldwide phenomenon and rapidly growing business practice.

REFERENCES

Ahmed, Z. U., Johnson, J. P., Ling, C. P., Fong, T. W., & Hui, A. K. (2002). Country-of-origin and brand effects on consumers' evaluations of cruise lines. *International Marketing Review*, *19*(2/3), 279–302. doi:10.1108/02651330210430703

Al-Sulaiti, K. I., & Baker, M. J. (1998). Country of origin effects: A literature review. *Marketing Intelligence & Planning*, *16*(3), 150–199. doi:10.1108/02634509810217309

Alden, D. L., Steenkamp, J.-B. E. M., & Batra, R. (2006). Consumer attitudes toward marketplace globalization: Structure, antecedents and consequences. *International Journal of Research in Marketing*, *23*(3), 227–239. doi:10.1016/j.ijresmar.2006.01.010

Ali-Sulaiti, K. I., & Baker, M. J. (1998). Country of origin effects: A literature review. *Marketing Intelligence & Planning*, *16*(3), 150–199. doi:10.1108/02634509810217309

American Banker/Gallup. (2004). What Americans think about overseas outsourcing. *Consumer Survey*. Retrieved June 1, 2009, from http://www.americanbanker.com/

Anderson, E. W., & Sullivan, M. W. (1993). The antecedents and consequences of customer satisfaction for firms. *Marketing Science*, *12*(2), 125–143. doi:10.1287/mksc.12.2.125

Arora, R., & Stoner, C. (1996). The effect of perceived service quality and name familiarity on the service selection decision. *Journal of Services Marketing*, *10*(1), 22. doi:10.1108/08876049610106699

Barker, S., & Härtel, C. E. J. (2004). Intercultural service encounters: An exploratory study of customer experiences. *Cross Cultural Management*, *11*(1), 3–14. doi:10.1108/13527600410797710

Bearden, W. O., & Teel, J. E. (1983). Selected determinants of consumer satisfaction and complaint reports. *The Journal of Consumer Research*, *20*(1), 21–28.

Bharadwaj, N., & Roggeveen, A. L. (2008). The impact of offshored and outsourced call service centers on customer appraisals. *Marketing Letters*, *19*(1), 13–23. doi:10.1007/s11002-007-9025-y

Blackmore, D., DeSouza, R., Young, A., Goodness, E., & Silliman, R. (2005). *Forecast: IT outsourcing, worldwide, 2002-2008*. Gartner.

Brand, R. R., & Cronin, J. J. (1997). Consumer-specific determinants of the size of retail choice sets: an empirical comparison of physical goods and service providers. *Journal of Services Marketing*, *11*(1), 19–38. doi:10.1108/08876049710158349

Briggs, B. (2005). Offshore outsourcing poses risks. *Health Data Management*, *13*(2), 68–78.

Brown, S. P., & Chin, W. W. (2004). Satisfying and retaining customers through independent service representatives. *Decision Sciences*, *35*(3), 527–550. doi:10.1111/j.0011-7315.2004.02534.x

Butcher, K., Sparks, B., & O'Callaghan, F. (2001). Evaluative and relational influences on service loyalty. *International Journal of Service Industry Management*, *12*(4), 310–327. doi:10.1108/09564230110405253

Chao, P. (1993a). Partitioning country-of-origin effects: Consumer evaluations of a hybrid product. *Journal of International Business Studies*, *24*(2), 291–306. doi:10.1057/palgrave.jibs.8490851

Chao, P. (1993b). Partitioning country of origin effects. *Journal of International Business Studies*, *24*(2), 291–306. doi:10.1057/palgrave.jibs.8490851

Chao, P. (2001). The moderating effects of country of assembly, country of parts, and country of design on hybrid product evaluations. *Journal of Advertising*, *30*(4), 67–81.

Chebat, J.-C., Davidow, M., & Codjovi, I. (2005). Silent voices: Why some dissatisfied consumers fail to complain. *Journal of Service Research*, *7*(4), 328–342. doi:10.1177/1094670504273965

Chernatony, L. d., Harris, F. J., & Christodoulides, G. (2004). Developing a brand performance measure for financial services brands. *The Service Industries Journal*, *24*(2), 15–33. doi:10.1080/02642060412331301232

Clark, T., Rajaratnam, D., & Smith, T. (1996). Toward a theory of international services: Marketing insights in a world of nations. *Journal of International Marketing*, *4*(2), 9–28.

Clott, C. B. (2004). Perspectives on global outsourcing and the changing nature of work. *Business and Society Review*, *109*(2), 153–170. doi:10.1111/j.0045-3609.2004.00189.x

ContactBabel. (2004). Finding the balance: The effect of offshore customer contact on profit and brand. Retrieved June 1, 2009, from http://www.contactbabel.com/

Corbett, M. F. (2002). *Outsourcing's next wave.*

Corbett, M. F. (2003, June 18). Outsourcing's future. *Fortune*, S1–S6.

Cornell, C. (2004). Offshore options: Outsourcing operations to overseas providers can save you money or cause you pain. The choice is yours. *Profit*, *23*(4), 87–88.

Crié, D. (2003). Consumers' complaint behaviour. Taxonomy, typology and determinants: Towards a unified ontology. *Database Marketing & Customer Strategy Management*, *11*(1), 60–79. doi:10.1057/palgrave.dbm.3240206

Data-Monitor. (2004). *Axa/Abbey: A passage to India.* MarketWatch: Financial Services.

Davis, L., & Thornton, C. (2005, December 11-14). *You are not my type!! The influence of stereotypes in the service encounter.* Paper presented at the 11th Cross-cultural Research Conference, Puerto Rico.

Economist. (2001, May 3). *India, back office to the world.* Retrieved June 1, 2009, from http://www.economist.com/

Fan, Y. (2000). Strategic outsourcing: Evidence from British companies. *Marketing Intelligence & Planning*, *18*(4), 213–219. doi:10.1108/02634500010333398

Francese, P. A., & Renaghan, L. M. (1990). Data-base marketing: Building customer profiles. *The Cornell Hotel and Restaurant Administration Quarterly*, *31*(1), 60–63. doi:10.1177/001088049003100116

Frost & Sullivan. (2007). Global outsourcing market to be worth $1,430bn by 2009. *Computer Business Review*. Retrieved from http://cbr.co.za/article.aspx? pklArticleId=4714&pklCategoryId=404

Gilbert, D., & Hewlett, J. (2003). A method for the assessment of relative brand strength: A UK tour operator example. *The Service Industries Journal*, *23*(2), 166–182. doi:10.1080/02642060412331300942

Gronhaug, K., & Gilly, M. C. (1991). A transaction cost approach to consumer dissatisfaction and complaint actions. *Journal of Economic Psychology*, *12*(1), 156–183. doi:10.1016/0167-4870(91)90048-X

Gronroos, C. (1999). Internationalization strategies for services. *Journal of Services Marketing*, *13*(4/5), 290–297. doi:10.1108/08876049910282547

Gurhan-Canli, Z., & Maheswaran, D. (2000). Cultural variations in country of origin effects. *JMR, Journal of Marketing Research*, *37*(August), 309–317. doi:10.1509/jmkr.37.3.309.18778

Han, C. M., & Terpstra, V. (1988). Country-of-origin effects for uni-national and bi-national products. *Journal of International Business Studies*, *19*(Summer), 235–255. doi:10.1057/palgrave.jibs.8490379

Harrison-Walker, L. J. (1995). The relative effects of national stereotype and advertising information on the selection of a service provider. *Journal of Services Marketing*, *9*(1), 47–59. doi:10.1108/08876049510079880

Hill, J. (1996). Keeping customers loyal at Liverpool Victoria Friendly Society. *Managing Service Quality*, *6*(4), 27–31. doi:10.1108/09604529610120258

Hong, S.-T., & Wyer, R. S. Jr. (1990). Determinants of product evaluations: Effects of the time interval between knowledge of a product's country of origin and information about its specific attributes. *The Journal of Consumer Research*, *17*(December), 277–288. doi:10.1086/208557

Jain, P. (2006). Offshore outsourcing "India vs China:" An empirical investigation. *Business Review (Federal Reserve Bank of Philadelphia)*, *6*(2), 316–324.

Kaynak, E., & Kara, A. (2002). Consumer perceptions of foreign products: An analysis of product-country images and ethnocentrism. *European Journal of Marketing*, *36*(7/8), 928–949. doi:10.1108/03090560210430881

Kaynak, E., Kucukemiroglu, O., & Kara, A. (1994). Consumer perceptions of airlines: A correspondence analysis approach in an airline industry. *Management International Review*, *34*(3), 235–254.

Kennedy, C. (2002). Name and shame: If you outsource, beware. Your brand may be in tatters through appalling customer service - And you may never know it. *Director (Cincinnati, Ohio)*, *56*(5), 23.

Kim, M.-K., Park, M.-C., & Jeong, D.-H. (2004). The effects of customer satisfaction and switching barrier on customer loyalty in Korean mobile telecommunication services. *Telecommunications Policy*, *28*(2), 145. doi:10.1016/j.telpol.2003.12.003

Li, Z. G., Murray, L. W., & Scott, D. (2000). Global sourcing, multiple country-of-origin facets, and consumer reactions. *Journal of Business Research*, *47*, 121–133. doi:10.1016/S0148-2963(98)00061-7

Mayer, K. J., Bowen, J. T., & Moulton, M. R. (2003). A proposed model of the descriptors of service process. *Journal of Services Marketing*, *17*(6), 621–639. doi:10.1108/08876040310495645

McCartney, L. (2003). A shore thing. *CFO-IT Magazine,* Spring, 60–63.

McCaskey, D., & Symes, S. (2004). Travel Inn: Everything you want for a good night's sleep - 100 per cent satisfaction guarantee or your money back. *International Journal of Contemporary Hospitality Management, 16*(3), 166–174. doi:10.1108/09596110410531159

Mintel (2007). Call centres: Offshoring vs onshoring in the United Kingdom. Retrieved June 1, 2009, from http://www.mintel.com/

Mittal, V., & Kamakura, W. A. (2001). Satisfaction, repurchase intent, and repurchase behavior: Investigating the moderating effect of customer characteristics. *JMR, Journal of Marketing Research, 38*(2), 131–142. doi:10.1509/jmkr.38.1.131.18832

Murray, K. B., & Schlacter, J. L. (1990). The impact of services versus goods on consumers' assessment of perceived risk and variability. *Journal of the Academy of Marketing Science, 18*(1), 51–65. doi:10.1007/BF02729762

Osgood, C. E., & Tannenbaum, P. H. (1955). The principle of congruity in the prediction of attitude change. *Psychological Review, 62*(1), 42–55. doi:10.1037/h0048153

Palacio, A. B., Meneses, G. D., & Perez, P. J. (2002). The configuration of the university image and its relationship with the satisfaction of students. *Journal of Educational Administration, 40*(4/5), 486–505. doi:10.1108/09578230210440311

Paswan, A. K., & Ganesh, G. (2005). Cross-cultural interaction comfort and service evaluation. *Journal of International Consumer Marketing, 18*(1/2), 93–115. doi:10.1300/J046v18n01_05

Quinn, J. B. (1997). *Innovation explosion: Using intellect and software to revolutionize growth strategies.* New York, NY: Free Press.

Reilly, P. (1997). Outsourcing: Employers becoming cautious. *Management Services, 41*(6), 9–11.

Roggeveen, A. L., Bharadwaj, N., & Hoyer, W. D. (2007). How call center location impacts expectations of service from reputable versus lesser known firms. *Journal of Retailing, 83*(4), 403–410. doi:10.1016/j.jretai.2007.03.008

Ross, C. F., Temkin, B., & Herbert, L. (2003). *Can outsourcers really transform IT?* Boston, MA: Forrester Research Inc.

Roy, M. (2003, November 7). Outsourced call centres damage long-term effort. *Precision Marketing,* 14.

Russell, D. W., & Russell, C. A. (2006). Explicit and implicit catalysts of consumer resistance: The effects of animosity, cultural salience and country-of-origin on subsequent choice. *International Journal of Research in Marketing, 23*(3), 321–331. doi:10.1016/j.ijresmar.2006.05.003

Ruyter, K. d., Birgelen, M. v., & Wetzels, M. (1998). Consumer ethnocentrism in international services marketing. *International Business Review, 7,* 185–202. doi:10.1016/S0969-5931(98)00005-5

Ruyter, K. d., & Wetzels, M. G. M. (2000). The impact of perceived listening behavior in voice-to-voice service encounters. *Journal of Service Research, 2*(3), 276–284. doi:10.1177/109467050023005

Sauer, P. L., Young, M. A., & Unnava, H. R. (1991). An experimental investigation of the processes behind the country-of-origin effects. *Journal of International Consumer Marketing, 3*(2), 29–59. doi:10.1300/J046v03n02_04

Selnes, F. (1993). An examination of the effect of product performance on brand reputation, satisfaction and loyalty. *European Journal of Marketing, 27*(9), 19–35. doi:10.1108/03090569310043179

Sharma, P. (2010). Offshore outsourcing of customer services - Boon or bane? *Working Paper*.

Sharma, P., Mathur, R., & Dhawan, A. (2006). Understanding consumer reactions to offshore outsourcing of customer services. In Kehal, H., & Singh, V. P. (Eds.), *Outsourcing and offshoring in the 21st century: A socioeconomic perspective* (pp. 326–340). doi:10.4018/978-1-59140-875-8.ch015

Sharma, P., Mathur, R., & Dhawan, A. (2008a). Understanding consumer reactions to offshore outsourcing of customer services (Reprint). In Becker, A. (Ed.), *Electronic commerce: Concepts, methodologies, tools and applications* (*Vol. 1*, pp. 92–104). Hershey, PA: Idea Group Inc.

Sharma, P., Mathur, R., & Dhawan, A. (2008b). Understanding consumer reactions to offshore outsourcing of customer services (Reprint). In Bandyopadhyay, S. (Ed.), *Contemporary research in e-branding* (*Vol. 1*, pp. 228–240). Hershey, PA: Information Science Reference. doi:10.4018/978-1-59904-813-0.ch015

Sharma, P., Mathur, R., & Dhawan, A. (2009). Exploring customer reactions to offshore call centers: Toward a comprehensive conceptual framework. *Journal of Services Marketing*, *23*(5), 289–300. doi:10.1108/08876040910973404

Sharma, P., Tam, J. L. M., & Kim, N. (2009). Demystifying intercultural service encounters: Toward a comprehensive conceptual framework. *Journal of Service Research*, *12*(2), 227–242. doi:10.1177/1094670509338312

Sharma, S., Shimp, T. A., & Shin, J. (1995). Consumer ethnocentrism: A test of antecedents and moderators. *Journal of the Academy of Marketing Science*, *23*(1), 26–37. doi:10.1007/BF02894609

Shimp, T. A. (1984). Consumer ethnocentrism: The concept and a preliminary empirical test. *Advances in Consumer Research. Association for Consumer Research (U. S.)*, *11*, 285–290.

Shimp, T. A., & Sharma, S. (1987). Consumer ethnocentrism: Construction and validation of the CETSCALE. *The Journal of Consumer Research*, *24*(August), 280–289.

Siems, T. F., & Ratner, A. S. (2003). Do what you do best, outsource the rest. *Southwest Economy*, *6*, 13–14.

Singh, J., & Wilkes, R. E. (1996). When consumers complain: A path analysis of the key antecedents of consumer complaint response estimates. *Journal of the Academy of Marketing Science*, *24*(4), 350–365. doi:10.1177/0092070396244006

Sizoo, S. (2007). The effect of intercultural sensitivity on cross-cultural service encounters in selected markets: Hawaii, London, and Florida. *Journal of Applied Management and Entrepreneurship*, *12*(1), 47–66.

Stringfellow, A., Teagarden, M. B., & Nie, W. (2008). Invisible costs in offshoring services work. *Journal of Operations Management*, *26*(2), 164–179. doi:10.1016/j.jom.2007.02.009

Swartz, N. (2004a). Much more than jobs being outsourced. *Information Management Journal*, *38*(3), 3.

Swartz, N. (2004b). Offshoring privacy. *Information Management Journal*, *38*(5), 24–26.

Trapp, R. (1999). Blunder boss. *British Journal of Administrative Management*, (July/August): 12–16.

Tse, D. K., & Lee, W.-N. (1993). Removing negative country images: Effects of decomposition, branding and product experience. *Journal of International Marketing*, *1*(1), 57–75.

Venables, M. (2006). Final say: Outsourcing falls short of expectations. *Manufacturing Engineering*, *85*(3), 48. doi:10.1049/me:20060315

Verlegh, P. W. J., Steenkamp, J.-B. E. M., & Meulenberg, M. T. G. (2005). Country-of-origin effects in consumer processing of advertising claims. *International Journal of Research in Marketing*, *22*(2), 127–139. doi:10.1016/j.ijresmar.2004.05.003

Wong, A. (2004). The role of emotional satisfaction in service encounters. *Managing Service Quality*, *14*(5), 365–376. doi:10.1108/09604520410557976

Wong, A., & Sohal, A. (2003). Service quality and customer loyalty perspectives on two levels of retail relationships. *Journal of Services Marketing*, *17*(4/5), 495–511. doi:10.1108/08876040310486285

Youngdahl, W., & Ramaswamy, K. (2008). Offshoring knowledge and service work: A conceptual model and research agenda. *Journal of Operations Management*, *26*(2), 212–221. doi:10.1016/j.jom.2007.02.007

KEY TERMS AND DEFINITIONS

Brand Image: How the brand owner wants the consumer to perceive a brand, typically in terms of the attributes one associates with that brand.

Brand Loyalty: Consumer commitment to a brand, generally demonstrated by repeat purchase of a product or service, and other positive behaviors such as word of mouth.

Consumer Ethnocentrism: Ethnocentric views held by consumers in one country (in-group), towards products from another country (out-group).

Country-of-Origin: The country where a product or service is developed, produced, or manufactured.

Customer Satisfaction: A measure of the extent to which a product or service satisfies consumers' needs or requirements.

Offshore Outsourcing: Hiring an external organization to perform some business functions in a country other than the one where the products or services are actually developed or manufactured.

Perceived Service Quality: The perception about the quality of service delivered.

Repurchase Intentions: The intention to purchase a product or service again.

Chapter 3
Taking Public Health Learning Global through Branding and Identity Management

Shalin Hai-Jew
Kansas State University, USA

ABSTRACT

"Pathways to Public Health" involves undergraduate and graduate degrees offered fully online through Kansas State University (K-State) to both meet the needs of traditional-age learners and professionals in the public health field who will need formal credentialing. This curriculum offers learning with global implications and has a wide potential to benefit global learners. In light of this, this chapter explores potential methods for online branding and identity management for this course series as a central analytical aspect of the program's development and launch. This chapter will address the following issues: an environmental scan of the global public health environment; the definition of the core identity; a branding strategy using the World Wide Web (WWW), Internet, and Web 2.0 affordances (to reach both internal and external "publics"); an initial risk assessment; legal considerations; work implications of the global branding; the engagement of students and graduates in the branding outreach, and the maintenance of this brand over time.

DOI: 10.4018/978-1-61350-171-9.ch003

INTRODUCTION

Public health is a broad field that involves a breadth of domain-specific and cross-domain fields: human medicine, veterinary medicine, environmentalism, nursing, health inspection, policy-making, epidemiology, agriculture, law enforcement, homeland security, and others. Public health focuses on "herd medicine" or population health. As such, this includes laws, policies, and practices regarding workplace safety, environmental health, product safety, food safety, and overall homeland security. Some aspects of public health are global—such as in cases of environmental pollutions and epidemics—and other aspects are highly localized such as particular diseases.

Online public health courses, designed with both local and globalized perspectives, may benefit the larger learning public. With projections of growing online learning in the US and abroad in the near-term (Adkins, 2009), this learning modality needs to be fully and constructively employed, whether the learning is formal or informal; human-facilitated or self-driven; credit or non-credit; fully immersive, partially immersive or non-immersive; media-rich or lean; collaborative or individualistic, and sequential or stand-alone.

To reach the many local to national to international learners, global branding will be designed and potentially deployed. Branding is not advertising—which focuses on selling particular products or services. It is not marketing—which emphasizes acquiring customers and maintaining a relationship with them. It is not public relations or the maintenance of public image. Branding is about strategic identity creation and communicating that identity to a broader audience—to convert those who may be interested in public health into learners in the program. Branding is about trust-building with various "publics"—those people who are internal (within the same organization) and those who are external (outside the organization). Trust-building may be achieved with some personalizing of information (Luo & Najdawi, 2004).

People need to be able to identify their respective brands (particularly in a competitive marketplace) and to emotionally connect with that experience and representation:

As a customer gets in touch with or lives by any concrete reification of a brand, a brand experience takes place. It consists of all the perceivable elements (communication artifacts, physical products, people, services, events,...) that give to the customer the experiential, comprehensive feeling of the brand. It is everything that creates not only a functional, but also an emotional relationship with a product or service and the brand underneath it. A brand experience should induce brand awareness, i.e., the capability of recognizing "your" brand as "yours", identifying it under different conditions, and understanding the distinctive qualities that make it better than the competition. (Bolchini, Garzotto, & Paolini, 2007, p. 173)

High name recognition and past positive experiences may enhance user trust in a health portal in terms of predicting "the ability, benevolence, and integrity" of that site (Luo & Najdawi, 2004, p. 112). Branding also helps define the full user experience—from the first inquiry to their long-term interactions with the brand and related educational services. All employees and representatives (even temporary ones) are seen as being part of the branding experience.

Accredited state universities do not have a profit motive; their work is to conduct relevant research and to support learners in their learning endeavors and research. They do have an interest in their own public reputations and how they appear, especially to their various stakeholders. Universities do need to replace fast-diminishing federal and state funds for learning and to become more self-supporting through grant funding and public-private partnerships and for-profit endeavors. In a global economic downturn, though, universities tend to be counter-cyclical, which means that universities may be more successful in attracting learners ("Marketing…"). That said, others suggest that difficult economic times mean more direct competition between universities and therefore require academic branding (Wu, Fan, & Wang, 2008). In the realm of global e-learning, without the regional advantages of local learners, the competitive advantages for the learning programs will involve branding—in part.

So while some of the language here relates to business practices, the understandings are a little different in an academic context. If learners perceive the learning experiences to be the same across a particular domain field, they would rationally go to the lowest-cost alternative, so branding and unique value is part of a differentiation policy (Dereli, Ar, & Durmosoğlu, 2006) that may broaden the potential pool of learners for a particular program. Strong brands "are effective substitutes of price competition" (Qiu, Hu, & Zhao, 2007, p. 4181).

Public Health Branding

This branding will involve an environmental scan of the global public health environment, and the competitors in terms of this course in the same tuition price class. This will explore the core identity development and management of the "Pathways to Public Health" learning and the professionals supporting the learning. It will involve the learners' full experiences with the program from first-contact to graduation and evolution into program graduates. This branding strategy will include uses of the World Wide Web (WWW), Internet, and Web 2.0 virtual community affordances—because of the alignment of these technologies with the branding goals. Also, this is where the students are. And lastly, public health relies extensively on various information technologies (IT) for research, information collection, analysis, intercommunications, public consultations, surveillance, simulations, and health promotion. IT is used to model realistic social networks and the spread of disease through a population; technologies are used to model "contact tracing" to identify the paths of disease spread (Zhang, Yan, Chen, Chen, Thurmond, King, Zeng, & Larson, 2008, p. 393). These benefit by providing situational analyses, planning, and preparations for public health experts but also raise public awareness and encourage public cooperation.

INFORMATION TECHNOLOGY (IT) AND PUBLIC HEALTH

Information technology tools may be used to analyze complex datasets to understand "hidden" causal relationships and correlations. Geographic (or Geospatial) information systems (GIS), used with remote sensing devices, are used to map various vector-borne diseases and to understand the trendlining of disease spread and the efficacy of various interventions. These geospatial systems may also be used to identify time-space "hotspots" and anomalies that may be indicative of a particular manifestation of disease for real-time decision-making. IT is also used for studying and visualizing syndromes for the identification of potential bioterrorism attacks. Other systems are used for decision-supports by projecting the effects of certain decisions or analyzing complex datasets of live and archived information.

Electronic health networks connect those working in public health—in offices, in labs, and in the field—for real-time collaboration and decision-making. Information may be collected and shared, often with geolocation metadata reportage.

Socio-technical spaces, like wikis and virtual community websites where people congregate, inter-communicate, and interact, may be used for "participatory sensing" by citizens (who use mobile devices to capture sensor readings, imagery, or sounds) to inform emergency responders and law enforcement of real-time situational realities. Government workers may get a sense from the public about what is important in terms of public health (Jones-Lee & Loomes, 2004). Citizens have an important voice in public health policy and planning (Scutchfield, Ireson, & Hall, 2004).

IT enables partnerships with the general public in combating terrorism (McDonald, 2002) by keeping citizens informed and engaged in every stage—from prevention to detection and verification to early response, a sustained response, and ultimately and optimally, recovery. Real-time communications technologies may involve SMS messaging, one-to-many media channels (podcasting, websites), and co-created wikis, in conjunction with broadcast media like radio and television. These communications channels allow almost real-time immediacy of interactions and sharing (Heitmann, Prykop, & Aschmoneit, 2004).

Many people use the Internet for health information (Luo & Najdawi, 2004). This will also involve an initial risk assessment of going live with an academic brand, given some anti-branding or negative-brand backlash (Krishnamurthy & Kucuk, 2009). This will also examine legal considerations in launching a global brand. This will suggest some ways to work with learners and program graduates in the branding outreach. This will also consider the maintenance of this brand over time.

So-called "persuasive technologies" are used for health monitoring, communications, and behavior modifications. These include computerized dolls that simulate babies and the challenges of parenthood and devices that encourage hand-washing after bathroom use (King & Tester, 1999, p. 32). Other persuasive devices monitor caloric intake, exercise, and dietary habits. There are exertion-based interfaces for exercise-based games (known as "exergames" that promote "physical activity, fitness, and gross motor skill development") (Adams, Marshall, Dillon, Caparosa, Ramirez, Phillips, & Norman, 2009, n.p.). Various haptic interfaces are used for therapy interventions by conveying heat or cold, "therapeutic holding" or "hugging," and controlled infliction of pain for "sensory grounding" (Vaucelle, Bonanni, & Ishii, 2009). These persuasive and therapeutic technologies may be conduits for effective academic branding messages; however, it may be a challenge to brand to the smaller screens of mobile phones, PDAs and smaller devices (Rondeau, 2005).

A Literature Review

The research literature offers little about global branding of online courses or programs. Universities themselves may be too complex "to be encapsulated by one brand or identity definition" (Wæraas & Solbakk, 2009, p. 449), but nevertheless, branding an educational institution involves plenty of complexity. Higher education websites must balance informational updates with institutional marketing and content development (Krause, 2003). Often, on-campus public relations offices will enforce the constraints of house-style web guidelines and designs of the university. A brand is a sign "formed by words, sounds, or graphics that represent or signify the brand and perceptions of the brand as shaped by experience. These perceptions are created by the brand steward, who provides the product and marketing message, and also by the people that experience the brand" (Rondeau, 2005, p. 62). A design may involve the trademark, logos and logotype, recurrent imagery, taglines, design elements, and definitive looks-and-feels. See also Figure 1 and Figure 2.

The move to the Internet suggests quicker uptake of information by people and less friction and noise in conveying the message. Some suggest the advantages of digital branding over more traditional branding in the so-called new economy (Wang, 2009). Branding is not a one-time issue of naming but a continuing endeavor at "brand-building"; techno-branding suggests an alignment of the technologies with the branding aims (Dereli, Ar, & Durmosoğlu, 2006). The need for continuing value is emphasized given that most sites have a lot of return users to a site (Teevan, Cutrell, Fisher, Drucker, Ramos, Andre, & Hu,

Figure 1. The "Pathways to Public Health" brochure cover

Figure 2. The "Pathways to Public Health" logo

PATHWAYS
TO PUBLIC HEALTH

2009). The brand is to lead to "attraction, loyalty and retention" (Heitmann, Prykop, & Aschmoneit, 2004, p. 1).

Global Branding in Academia

To get a sense of global branding strategies, those working in higher education and who have a hand in global branding of trainings, courses, and programs were asked to participate in this survey. People were contacted through the electronic mailing lists: Distance Education Online Symposium (DEOS) at Pennsylvania State University; the Colleague to Colleague (C2C) consortium; the Canadian Institute for Distance Education Research (CIDER); directors' and faculty lists at Washington Online (WAOL); blogs: Instructional Design Open Studio(IDOS), and website postings. However, the responses were insufficient for significance. The survey did find some respondents who used professional advertising agencies for their branding plan.

An Environmental Scan

Environmental scans of an educational program's presence online will the general public footprint and Internet profile of a particular program. This information enables some degree of online reputation management.

A general Web search reveal competing programs with some similar contents. Various search rankings and "alerts" services online may offer real time awareness of competing program's endeavors.

Further situational analysis may reveal insights—as through a SWOT (Strengths, Weaknesses, Opportunities, and Threats) view. For this particular example, public health program, strengths might include unique learning approaches, learner accommodations, the localization of the assignments to the students' respective geographical locales, and the "star power" of various guest speakers who contributed to the course videotapes. Another strength would be the path that learners can take from freshman all the way through a Master's of Public Health, along this designed pathway. The focus on medical science is a strength, but the curriculum does not have cultural sensitivity or tailoring per se—just an objectivist approach. (The "SWOT" does involve some interpretation.) Weaknesses of the program might involve the monolingualism of the coursework or limitations to student scholarship funding. Opportunities for this "Pathways to Public Health" may be the broad institutional access to various professionals in the fields related to public health. Threats to this program may be other centers of excellence for public health and the ever-changing curriculum (and nature of public health) over time.

In terms of fully online degree programs for public health, a cursory look surfaced several dozen. This suggests the need for regional advantages for Kansas State University. This means drawing on the power of its faculty, its students, its learning resources, and its research infrastructure. A deeper analysis may evaluate the degree focuses and courses of other programs, in order to identify unfilled niches. Different public health programs offer different areas of expertise—industrial ecology, toxicology, policy-making, and others. Unique areas of specialty may be highlighted, such as the concentration of world-class experts on food safety and security, biosecurity, and veterinary medicine. The branding of "star" faculty and researchers and epidemiologists may also enhance the program and may attract people to the program. The individual is a brand (Snodgrass & Brucks, 2004), such as in a culmination of publications, public appearances, partnerships with other professionals, and shared public works.

The environmental scan may also surface strategic partners for complementary and mutually supportive relationships. These may involve organizations that support public health endeavors, for example. Existing online learning networks—such as the Great Plains IDEA (Interactive Distance Education Alliance) and KC REACHE—may offer more potential access to groups of local and regional learners.

This scan may also reveal professional electronic mailing lists that may offer channels for connecting with a wider public. It may reveal professional, non-profit, non-governmental, and other organizations that may serve as conduits to various potential learners. So-called third sector organizations ("voluntary organizations, special interest groups, communities and business related support organizations") with aligned goals may help reach a wider audience (Donnelly & Merrick, 2003, p. 9).

An environmental scan defines the various publics for this endeavor (Table 1). The internal publics refer to those who are part of the university and program staff. Collaborative partners, guest speakers, and specialists in the field may be in the outer orbit of the internal publics. The in-between publics are learners and graduates. The external publics may involve potential students, potential public-sector organizational partners, potential private-sector partners in the inner orbit, and then the general public, informal learners, competitors, and non-related specialists in the field, in the outer orbit of the exterrnal publics.

EXAMINING COMPETITOR STRATEGIES

A cursory examination of competitor approaches to global branding of their academic programs may examine their techniques for differentiation, trust-building, multi-cultural connections, and the communications technologies and techniques used.

A Core Identity

In public health, a number of values guide the field. There are issues of social equity—in the many endeavors to create equal access to healthcare and to eliminate health disparities between racial and other demographic groups, including tailoring health messages and outreaches for particular recipients (through different languages, through different culturally-sensitive strategies). There is the value of not doing harm. Public health policies are evolved to maximize health gains for the investments. There's an ethic of sharing resources and research information across national boundaries for the sake of improved global health. Another

Table 1. Internal and external "publics" for Pathways to Public Health

Internal Publics	In-Between Publics	External Publics
Inner Orbit • University Instructors • University Staff • University Administrators • The Public Health Program Staff	**Inner Orbit** • Students	**Inner Orbit** • Potential Students • Potential Public-Sector Organizational Partners (government agencies, non-governmental organizations, educational institutions, and citizen groups) • Potential Private-Sector Partners (corporations)
Outer Orbit • Collaborative Partners • Guest Speakers • Specialists in the Field	**Outer Orbit** • Graduates	**Outer Orbit** • The (Local to Global) General Public • Informal learners • Competitors • Specialists in the Field

core value involves the preventing of premature mortality through tobacco use, substance / alcohol abuse, dietary behaviors, exercise behaviors, injuries, and communicable diseases. There are focuses on stress relief and mental and emotional health. Practitioners adhere to values of "beneficence, nonmaleficence, respect for persons, and justice" as well as "scientific uncertainty, criteria of evidence, practicability, cultural acceptability, and cost" (Weed, 2002/2003, p. 45).

The "one health" and "one medicine" concepts encourage cross-domain sharing of research information for addressing diseases that may be transmissible between animals and humans and which may have negative implications for the environment. Strict guidelines of protections and informed consent for human-based research are followed as basic standards of professionalism. Public health also strives for widespread clarity and transparency—as a critical element of electronic governance, which also deeply values citizen participation in government decision-making.

A core identity for an organization is formed by its defining principles and values, its lived history, its members, and its interrelationships with others. A core identity evolves also from its conscious self-definition and follow-through in terms of actions that are aligned with its professed values (expressed as "lived values"). Such a core identity may help unify an organization and its endeavors (Ackerman, 2000, p. 8). Any part of an identity is a core element of a brand; non-core elements may involve lesser branding decisions such as particular applied strategies such as events.

Partnerships within networks may result in strategic alliances. They may involve co-branding or the alliance of two complementary and synergistic brands (which may also be expressed as shared advertising) (Chang, 2008). Or various endeavors may involve the sharing of a single brand, with the brand "extending" to other learning opportunities. A brand may be strengthened (or diffused) over several partner organizations. Some "partners" may be unsolicited ones that in-link to the particular pages. These organizations should be identified and contacted for more formal linkages where appropriate.

Branding Strategies

A number of communications channels may be used to communicate brand to various publics. Internally, intranets, electronic mail, publications, events, and meetings may communicate the internal brand message. Externally, the technologies may include billboards, print publications, electronic mail, broadcast television, events, Web 2.0 technologies (such as micro-blogging through mobile devices, video-sharing sites, wikis, and blogs), the WWW, and Internet.

The skill sets to effectively develop and sustain sites include website navigation design, visual design, information design, sound design, experience design, and usability analysis, in combination with understandings of human cognition and emotion, and branding strategies. Additional helpful skills would involve cultural models of understanding and decision support.

With the popularization of the so-called Connective Web, interactions are always multi-way and semi-relational; actual communities may be built up around shared interests and learning experiences. Many organizations are creating online communities to promote brands; these virtual communities have an awareness of the brand; engage in "brand-specific behaviors and traditions," and have a sense of moral responsibility for their "shared support in the correct use of a product or service" (Rood & Bruckman, 2009, p. 210). Virtual communities may promote a sense of "strong pleasure" and flow experiences that may lead to higher brand identification attitudinally and behaviorally (Sha, Wen, Gao, & Wang, 2009, n.p.).

Such communities do not offer one-way communications of a brand but rather offer insights into the thinking of their clients; the interactions may generate ideas for product development; these interactions encourage client loyalty and retention, and often increase their satisfaction. Such communities may attract new consumers (Rood & Bruckman, 2009, p. 211). These communities have been found to offer a "relationship benefit" of greater brand loyalty (Li & Zhang, 2008, p. 578). These communities may exist in virtual three-dimensional (3D) spaces. The exhibition of social behaviors from real life are expressed in virtual worlds via human-embodied avatars, and people will co-create social realities in virtual worlds (Junglas, Johnson, Steel, Abraham, & Loughlin, 2007), which suggests the importance of social presences in these spaces for academic brands.

Higher-end types of branding involve the offering of rich information streams through digital repositories, visualizations of complex datasets, designed immersive spaces and virtual ecologies (Lu & Xue, 2008), open decision-support systems, locative place-based resources, digital installations, simulations, and information architectures. Personalization of a site to user needs may lead to greater brand loyalty (Strauss, Schoder, & Gebauer, 2001).

Some ground rules are assumed. One is that there is non-manipulation of imagery of "shiny, happy people" to create particular trust effects, which may be misleading (Riegelsberger, J., Sasse, M.A., & McCarthy, J.D., 2003). However, quality effects (such as an efficient and usable navigational structure, an attractive interface, quality contents, customization, and user engagement) have a "halo effect" on other aspects of a site (Hartmann, Sutcliffe, & De Angeli, 2008). Some cutting-edge approaches to branding involve user experiences through digital storytelling or gaming or interactivity-rich designs to create a sense of excitement (Tobias & Spiegel, 2009).

The design of websites is created to build up trust over time. Website elements that communicate trustworthiness involve "design features, corporate image integrity, business processes transparency, customer support, (information) security features and legal support" (Tsygankov, 2004, p. 265). Other factors include Information about those behind a website and organization, and the partnerships and alliances between the organization and others. Knowledge sharing in virtual communities may enhance consumer trust (Zhu & Chang, 2009). All operational actions and methods should back up the claims on the site.

For locative and situated branding, users have been found to have "a strong implicit association between locative images and trust" (Kostakos & Oakley, 2009, p. 329). Place has deep relevance to people. In a sense a global brand has to create a loyal base in its own locality—based on A. Saxenian's concepts of regional advantage"—from which it can then reach out globally to potential learners there.

Electronic (E-)Marketing Tools

Marketing plans involve a range of modern technologies. While technologies are not pulled out individually independent of an overall plan, various selected technologies may be employed to achieve certain objectives. Besides web sites, electronic marketing (e-marketing or "online marketing") uses a range of technologies to reach out to and engage the various publics. This section highlights some of these tools.

- **Social Media.** Various websites enable people to create virtual communities. With the phenomeno of "homophily," people tend to cluster like-to-like (similar people become friends). This means that electronic marketers can reach a variety of similar individuals if they can find and target opinion leaders who may spark exponential interest in a certain curriculum (viral marketing). Such efforts must avoid even the impression of "astroturfing" or the artificial attempt at the creation of a viral marketing effect. Social media also enable public relations—or the maintenance of "relationships" with various members and groups that comprise the public, particularly given the necessity of real-time information-sharing. Are there events that will be hosted for the students in the program? Fieldtrip opportunities? A digital lab that will be launched? There are many occasions that may be tapped for such publicity.
- **Email Marketing.** Using electronic mail and electronic mailing lists is a common way to communicate with a particular targeted group. Emails, while they're considered a lean form of communications, now may include images, and links to audio and video and simulations.
- **Mobile Marketing.** This endeavor involves the uses of mobile devices to send out text messages (short message service) to those who opt-in to such messages. There are quick response (QR) codes (also known as 2D codes) that can jump users to a website or a video or other contents with a click of their smart phones or enabled mobile devices. There are location-sensitive (geo-targeted) messages delivered to individuals who are in certain locations, such as those next to a public health curriculum booth at a majors fair for those in healthcare. Ads have started moving out to e-readers and e-books, and those may offer other channels to reach a targeted audience interested in a particular field. Marketers are working on ever-more creative outreaches to those in the "handset culture"—who are continually connected and always on the Internet through their mobile devices.
- **Online Advertising.** The current structure of online advertising and e-marketing involves the uses of "search engine advertising," which involves the defining of "key words" that will bring up a certain display ad related to the academic program. The university or college that has put up the ad will have to pay the corporations hosting the search engines for every click-through (when an Internet surfer clicks through an advertisement and to the "landing page" of a certain website). This sort of advertising goes beyond so-called "organic searches" on search engines and actually involves the purchase of space on a search engine site based on user profiles collected by search engine companies. These ads create positive "impressions" by those who see the site, and they offer "click-throughs" and some "conversions" for those who are interested in the information provided by the advertisement.
- **Site Analysis.** Various brand managers use software site analytics tools in order to track the traffic to the site. They learn

what browsers are used to arrive at a site; where site visitors come from; how the site visitors behave on the site, and how many of the site visitors "convert" to the site by offering personally identifiable information (PII) or signing up to be contacted by program administrators or enrolling in a course. More complex programs may track the "return on investment" (ROI) of e-marketing programs to see what lead generation has come from any endeavor. What are site visitor's response rates, and how many site visitors have converted to a university's e-marketing outreach? How many former students have been re-activated or retained? The enablements of site analytics have strengthened the "trackability" of those targeted by various brand messaging and e-marketing outreaches.

- **Company and Site Endorsements.** Further, there are tools that raise the trust of a site. For example, there may be site endorsements that are earned by a site through its technological setup for privacy (TRUSTe), professional business practices (Better Business Bureau Online), authentication services (VeriSign), and others.

An Initial Risk Assessment

Going forward with a global brand is not without risks. Public health touches on highly sensitive issues of worldviews and healthy habits, and the concepts may cross cultural boundaries in provocative ways. For example, the concept of health care as a human right is a controversial idea (Walton, Farmer, Lambert, Leandre, Koenig, & Mukherjee, 2004).

In the Information Age, positive and negative information moves quickly. Risk assessments should consider the speed of word-of-mouth analyses of different products—through the Webosphere, the Internet, and the social networking world—and a lessening ability to control information, disinformation, and misinformation. These messages may be highly influential on consumer behaviors. Some companies track instantaneous micro-blog posts so as to intervene immediately with dissatisfied consumers (Jansen, Zhang, Sobel, & Chowdury, Micro-blogging as online…, 2009). Microblogging is often part of an overall marketing strategy (Jansen, Zhang, Sobel, & Chowdury, "Twitter power…," 2009, p. 2169)

Internal risks include deploying the wrong strategies and offending various publics. There may be miscommunications that offend particular demographic groups. The timing may be off. Choices for action may be made when inaction is desirable, and vice versa. The technologies deployed may be too intrusive, such as in pop-ups (ads that appear over the page that one is viewing), pop-unders (ads that appear under the page that one is viewing), "skyscraper" Web ads (tall ads that run along the side of a web page), interstitial ads ("between" ads that appear the URL and the body of the web page and then minimize after the display has been shown); the multimedia may be too rich or too lean. Raising the profile of a learning program itself involves some risk. Fame—and the amplification of the program's stature—involves both positive and negative press coverage, purposive messages and unintended ones. Other risks involve the degradation of brand messages and endeavors over time if these are not continually reassessed and refreshed.

There may be direct competition from other universities and colleges that offer degrees in public health. Their competing brands may offer various appeals to the same pools of potential learners and partners. Staying aware of the larger environment will be important for maintenance of the academic brand. Direct competitors may enhance the learning, and there is certainly room for professional competitors who offer comparable online learning. Oftentimes, the guidelines for how universities may compete is defined by geographical and population boundaries—in a kind of enforced market segmentation within a state—but the guidelines do not apply for international and global learners, so the brand positioning and competition would apply powerfully there.

Other risks may involve anti-branding or negative brand targeting. Other risks may involve those who would "cyber-squat" on similar uniform resource locators (URLs) or dilute a brand through emulation or misrepresentation or fraud. Brand piracy may involve the misuse of another's trademark and public reputations. Protections against misuses of brands involve close following of intellectual property and trademark laws and guidelines, and keeping these up-to-date. Trademark holders are responsible to prevent brand dilution. Various online technologies may be deployed for online brand protection, such as the tracking of logos through the uses of watermarking and spiders. There are tools that may capture slander messages or campaigns against a particular brand in order to pursue legal remedies.

Still others may spoof emails ostensibly from the educational institution or program. They may use other misrepresentations as part of phishing schemes to try to get passwords or unauthorized access to various educational, IT, ICT or branding and reputational resources. More sophisticated hackers may try to compromise a site's security and use that as a launch-ground for cyber-attacks, email security compromises, and the distribution of malware.

Others may try to compromise the information assurance of the site, particularly if sensitive information is exchanged and archived. Microdata that is released on various databases may be cross-referenced (in "joining attacks") with other databases to surface personal individually identifiable (PII) information. Public health involves potential tensions between personal privacy and population safety (Baker, 2006).

Responsible brand stewardship requires continuing vigilance on a number of internal and external fronts given the easy tarnishment of a brand. Most organizations maintain a crisis management plan which names key crisis management team members, anticipates possible environmental risks, plans and prepares for potential eventualities, and works to have smooth organizational functions and a clear public face and message in the case of a crisis. One of the main goals of a crisis management team is the protection of the brand image and reputation.

Feedback from potential learners and current students will be important for the design brand. After all, they are the desirable target audience. They may have powerful suggestions about the learner experience, ways to improve, and services they would like to have.

Some IT functionalities may be used to early warnings of "brand-switching intentions." These may help faculty and staff conduct more outreach with learners to support their learning and to enable their adjustments so as to continue with the learning program for improved learning retention. Understanding the risk environment is an important part of designing, executing, and maintaining an academic brand.

Some Legal Considerations

Branding endeavors must consider legal issues from the beginning. For example, logos, taglines, and trademarks may already belong to other people. A due diligence search through the US Patent and Trademarks Office (USPTO) will be an important early step in terms of vetting possible marks. Also, open World Wide Web and Internet searches offer very broad views of word meanings and implications as well as extant brands. A check of Network Solutions repositories may surface who owns various URLs that are part of a branding strategy. These searches define limits and parameters to the branding endeavors.

The development team also needs to be aware of privacy protections for all collected information from users, so that they do not incur legal risks with how they proceed. If information is collected from children (13 and under), the Children's Online Privacy Protection Act (COPPA) will be an important law to note. Information that is collected should not be extraneous but used to particular purposes, and they should be handled professionally in protected ways.

Legal counsel should be at the table early on in terms of creating disclaimers and site use policies to protect the university in the branding.

The team should also design some internal self-regulating policies to guide the operations of the site (Luo & Najdawi, 2004). There should be internal policies for the following:

- Content vetting policies (to avoid inaccuracies, defamation, libel or slander, and other risks)
- Guidelines for image use (so as not to communicate stereotypes or bias)
- Information collection, handling, and staff access; privacy policies
- IT security
- Editorial policies
- Crisis management processes

Websites should offer both visual and nonvisual access, sound and non-sound access—based on the Americans with Disabilities Act and Section 508 accessibility guidelines. Well designed sites should consider accessibility from the beginning, so the navigational structure and all contents are appropriately designed for accessibility.

WORK IMPLICATIONS OF BRANDING

Branding strategies are often defined as general concepts or principles, whose expression will differ over time and in different cultural contexts.

The Design Phase

The brand is known as a "design driver," in terms of informing the various aspects of design—of information, look-and-feel, and experience. How a defined brand is expressed depends on various elements of technology (with various affordances and constraints), design aesthetics, language, and raw resources. A concept may be expressed in myriad ways on a number of devices. The conventions of various forms of communications will further shape the message—such as the conventions of short videos, press releases, short messages, podcasts, and micro-blogs.

Wireframes may express the navigational structure of a site. Information may be structured online for easier access. Multimedia projects are usually guided by the use of stylebooks for shared guidelines; templating for consistency; and an aesthetic plan for the look-and-feel. A site may offer support for certain task types—such as academic counseling, schedule or degree planning, course searches, career planning, and other functionalities.

There should be a planned way to collect feedback from the various constituencies to the brand and to use that information to enhance site redesigns and branding iterations. The pace of change on the Web is swift, and some organizations use fast methods to evolve their online brands: "rapid ethnography, cultural probes, rapid prototyping, role playing, scenario development, and 'ideal types' user profiles" (Anderson, 2000, p. 30).

Learner Support

Once a brand identity has been created, it is important to follow-through with all expressed values. If particular information channels are open for human feedback, those should be made and kept live with short turnaround times and accurate information exchanges. If particular promises of service are made, those should be deliverable. If faculty members are branded as responsive and supportive, they should embody that in their interactions with learners. The human touch is a critical element in learner interest and retention. The diversity of the US population may be a point of strength in this global brand endeavor.

A global brand also should involve localized learning, so the international learners may access the resources nearby (in their respective localities) to enhance their learning and their professional connections. The curriculum should address the potential barriers of cultures, languages, worldviews, and the "noise" of stereotypes and political tensions. The learning must be authentic and supportable by the empirical research but also as non-offensive as possible.

Information Streams

Most online endeavors require plenty of valid information to sustain websites, digital repositories, communications channels (like microblogs and social networking sites) and other online endeavors. This may be culled from primary research and reworked for public consumption. It may be drawn from existing secondary research sources, in which case the value then comes from the re-packaging of the contents. It may be purchased from various content providers. It may be collated from various partners. There may also be so-called "grey literature" content or "meeting notes, think-tank reports, policy statements, and data sets" (Turner, Liddy, & Bradley, 2002, p. 411) that are not part of the official record.

Establishing valid information streams and methods for vetting and packaging data will be critical to the maintenance of both a fresh brand identity and a fresh site. A site must add continuing value and service to maintain regular users.

Students and Graduates as Branding Supports

Allies in a continuous global branding endeavor may include the program's students and graduates. They may serve as the eyes and ears in a domain field. They may propose new courses, programs, learning activities, fieldtrips, or learning materials. They may suggest localized resources to expand the public health program, such as local public health offices, wastewater treatment plants, laboratories, public transportation hubs, or other sites with learning value.

Learners' comments and feedback may help the team evolve the brand identity and make it more culturally sensitive or culturally neutral. (Cultural sensitivity targets a particular culture; cultural neutrality strives to remove any cultural elements from the curriculum and brand.)

As students graduate and enter the professional realm, they may expand the program's reach. Their work may also connect professors stateside with their counterparts abroad for potential professional collaborations.

Students and graduates may also be tapped for user testing of various designs and new technology roll-outs, based on their insights. They may also offer domain-specific insights about translated learning objects in foreign languages, for language correctness and tone.

Sustaining the Global Brand

The sustenance of the global brand involves continual awareness of the brand's various impacts; the word-of-mouth in the digital spaces about it; a monitoring of the feedback channels that have been created with both internal and external publics; and environmental changes.

Of special note would be any of the following: new direct competitors, major changes in technologies, changing public health realities, and cultural shifts among the potential learners (with a constant need for "coolhunting" to connect more effectively). The information cycles on the Web are fast and continuous, and the relevance of all WWW assets will need to be maintained. Policies that affect accessibility will need to be heeded.

CONCLUSION

Global branding for academic programs is *de rigueur* for competitive advantage. Falling under the auspices of a university reputation and brand is no longer sufficient for unique online learning sequences, degrees, and training types because of the targeted nature of the learners. With particular internal publics and a wide range of culturally diverse external audiences, a global brand for learning needs to be savvy and nuanced—in its symbology, its language, its use of multimedia for multi-sensory approaches, and its start-to-finish brand experience.

ACKNOWLEDGMENT

Thanks to Drs. Beth Montelone and Lisa Freeman for their encouragement of this project. I appreciate the gentle supervision of Dr. Kimathi Choma. Many talented individuals from multiple colleges and universities contributed to the "Introduction to Public Health" curriculum, but they are too many to name here. Dr. Esther Swilley provided fresh insights on electronic marketing. For R. Max.

REFERENCES

Ackerman, L. D. (2000). *Identity is destiny: Leadership and the roots of value creation* (p. 8). San Francisco, CA: Berrett-Koehler Publishers, Inc.

Adams, M. A., Marshall, S. J., Dillon, L., Caparosa, S., Ramirez, E., Phillips, J., & Norman, G. J. (2009). A theory-based framework for evaluating exergames as persuasive technology. In the *Proceedings of the 4th International Conference on Persuasive Technology*. Association for Computing Machinery.

Adkins, S. S. (2009). *Innovation in educational technology: The virtualization of K-12 and higher education*. Webinar. Elluminate Series.

Anderson, R. I. (2000). Making an e-business conceptualization and design process more user-centered. *Interaction*, 7(4), 27–30. doi:10.1145/345190.345235

Baker, D. B. (2006). Privacy and security in public health: Maintaining the delicate balance between personal privacy and population safety. In the *Proceedings of the 22nd Annual Computer Security Applications Conference* (pp. 3–22). IEEE.

Bolchini, D., Garzotto, F., & Paolini, P. (2007). *Branding and communication goals for content-intensive interactive applications*. 15th IEEE International Requirements Engineering Conference (pp. 173–182). IEEE.

Chang, W.-L. (2008). *Using multi-attribute utility theory to rank and select co-branding partners*. Eighth International Conference on Intelligent Systems Design and Applications (pp. 195–200). IEEE.

Dereli, T., Ar, A. A., & Durmosoğlu, A. (2006). *Branding and technology management* (pp. 1757–1763). PICMET 2006: Istanbul, Turkey. IEEE.

Distance Education Report. (2009). Marketing online programs in a recession. *Distance Education Report, 13*(7), 1 – 3.

Donnelly, V., & Merrick, R. (2003). *Community portals through communitization. CUU '03* (pp. 9–14). Vancouver, British Columbia, Canada: Association for Computing Machinery.

Hartmann, J., Sutcliffe, A., & De Angeli, A. (2008). Towards a theory of user judgment of aesthetics and user interface quality. *ACM Transactions on Computer-Human Interaction,* 15(4), 15:1–15:30.

Heitmann, M., Prykop, C., & Aschmoneit, P. (2004). Using means-end chains to build mobile brand communities. *Proceedings of the 37th Hawaii International Conference on System Sciences* (pp. 1–10). IEEE.

Jansen, B. J., Zhang, M., Sobel, K., & Chowdury, A. (2009). Micro-blogging as online word of mouth branding (pp. 3859–3864). CHI 2009: Boston, Massachusetts. Association for Computing Machinery.

Jansen, B. J., Zhang, M., Sobel, K., & Chowdury, A. (2009). Twitter power: Tweets as electronic word of mouth. *Journal of the American Society for Information Science and Technology, 60*(11), 2169. doi:10.1002/asi.21149

Jones-Lee, M., & Loomes, G. (2004). *Eliciting measures of value for health and safety* (pp. 49–58). 9th Australian Workshop on Safety-Related Programmable Systems, Brisbane, Australia.

Junglas, I. A., Johnson, N. A., Steel, D. J., Abraham, D. C., & Loughlin, P. M. (2007). Identity formation, learning styles and trust in virtual worlds. *The Data Base for Advances in Information Systems, 38*(4), 90–96.

King, P., & Tester, J. (1999). The landscape of persuasive technologies. *Communications of the ACM, 42*(5), 31–38. doi:10.1145/301353.301398

Kostakos, V., & Oakley, I. (2009). *Designing trustworthy situated services: An implicit and explicit assessment of locative images' effect on trust* (pp. 329–332). CHI 2009: Boston, Massachusetts, USA. Association for Computing Machinery.

Krause, R. D. (2003). Managing higher ed web sites: Balancing the need for timely updates, the requirements of institutional marketing, and the development of content. In the *Proceedings of the Special Interest Group on University and College Computing Services* (SIGUCCS '03) (pp. 139–141). San Antonio, Texas, USA. ACM.

Krishnamurthy, S., & Kucuk, S. U. (2009). Anti-branding on the Internet. *Journal of Business Research, 62*(11), 1119. doi:10.1016/j.jbusres.2008.09.003

Li, X.-W., & Zhang, M.-L. (2008). *Relationship benefit in consumer markets and its role in brand image-brand loyalty in chain* (pp. 578–584). 2008 International Conference on Management Science and Engineering, Long Beach, USA. IEEE.

Luo, W., & Najdawi, M. (2004). Trust-building measures: A review of consumer health portals. *Communications of the ACM, 47*(1), 109–113.

Qiu, X., Hu, S., & Zhao, P. (2007). *The effect and strategy of high-priced level premium brand products price reduction: An empirical research to auto industry* (pp. 4181–4184). IEEE.

Riegelsberger, J., Sasse, M. A., & McCarthy, J. D. (2003). Shiny happy people building trust? Photos on e-commerce websites and consumer trust. CHI 2003: Ft. Lauderdale, Florida, USA. *CHI Letters, 5*(1), 121–128.

Rondeau, D. B. (2005). For mobile applications, branding is experience. *Communications of the ACM, 48*(7), 61–66. doi:10.1145/1070838.1070867

Rood, V., & Bruckman, A. (2009). Member behavior in company online communities (pp. 209–218). GROUP '09: Sanibel Island, Florida, USA. Association for Computing Machinery.

Scutchfield, F. D., Ireson, C., & Hall, L. (2004). The voice of the public in public health policy and planning: The role of public judgment. *Journal of Public Health Policy*, *25*(2), 197–205. doi:10.1057/palgrave.jphp.3190018

Sha, Z., Wen, F., Gao, G., & Wang, X. (2009). *Antecedents and consequences of flow experience in virtual brand community*. IEEE.

Snodgrass, R., & Brucks, M. (2004). Branding yourself. *SIGMOD Record*, *33*(2), 117–125. doi:10.1145/1024694.1024722

Strauss, R. E., Schoder, D., & Gebauer, J. (2001). The relevance of brands for electronic commerce results from an empirical study of consumers in Europe. *Proceedings of the 34th Hawaii International Conference on System Sciences* (pp. 7064–7072). IEEE.

Teevan, J., Cutrell, E., Fisher, D., Drucker, S. M., Ramos, G., Andre, P., & Hu, C. (2009). *Visual snippets: Summarizing web pages for search and revisitation* (pp. 2023–2032). CHI 2009: Boston, Massachusetts, USA. Association for Computing Machinery.

Tobias, P., & Spiegel, D. S. (2009). *Is design the preeminent protagonist in user experience? Ubiquity, 10(6)*. Association for Computing Machinery.

Tsygankov, V. (2004). *Evaluation of website trustworthiness from customer perspective, a framework* (pp. 265–271). Sixth International Conference on Electronic Commerce, ICEC '04. Association for Computing Machinery.

Turner, A. M., Liddy, E. D., & Bradley, J. (2002). *Breathing life into digital archives: Use of natural language processing to revitalize the grey literature of public health* (p. 411). JCDL '02: Portland, Oregon, USA. Association for Computing Machinery.

Vaucelle, C., Bonanni, L., & Ishii, H. (2009). Design of haptic interfaces for therapy (pp. 467–470). CHI 2009: Boston, Massachusetts, USA. Association for Computing Machinery.

Wæraas, A., & Solbakk, M. N. (2009). Defining the essence of a university: Lessons from higher education branding. *Higher Education*, *57*, 449–462. doi:10.1007/s10734-008-9155-z

Walton, D. A., Farmer, P. E., Lambert, W., Leandre, F., Koenig, S. P., & Mukherjee, J. S. (2004). Integrated HIV prevention and care strengthen primary health care: Lessons from rural Haiti. *Journal of Public Health Policy*, *25*(2), 137–158. doi:10.1057/palgrave.jphp.3190013

Wang, H. X., Chen, J., Hu, Y. C., & Ye, M. (2008). *The consistency of product design and brand image* (pp. 1142–1144). IEEE.

Wang, M. (2009). *Research on the innovation mechanism of digital brand in enterprise* (pp. 728–732). 2009 International Conference on Networks Security, Wireless Communications and Trusted Computing. IEEE.

Weed, D. L. (2002/2003). Is the precautionary principle a principle? *IEEE Technology and Society Magazine*, *21*(4), 45–48. doi:10.1109/MTAS.2003.1166567

Wu, H., Fan, Q., & Wang, X. (2008). *The design of university image and construction of brand strategy* (pp. 874–876). IEEE.

Zhang, Y., Yan, D., Chen, Y.-D., Chen, H., Thurmond, M., & King, C.-C. … Larson, C. A. (2008). BioPortal infectious disease informatics research: Disease surveillance and situational awareness. *Proceedings of the 9th Annual International Digital Government Research Conference. Association for Computing Machinery* (pp. 393 – 394).

Zhu, D.-H., & Chang, Y.-P. (2009). *The influence of knowledge sharing in virtual communities on consumers' brand trust: An empirical study* (pp. 580–583). 2009 International Conference on Networks Security, Wireless Communications and Trusted Computing. IEEE.

KEY TERMS AND DEFINITIONS

Astroturfing: The artificial attempt at creating a viral marketing campaign which is identified as a superficial and manipulated effort.

Brand: An identity, a mark or a label representing the reputation and quality of a product or organization.

Click-Through: The act of an Internet surfer clicking on a display or text advertisement on a search engine page and going to the landing page of the advertiser.

Conversion: The commitment of a site visitor to offering private information, signing up for a service, or committing to a product or service by the university or college (or business).

Digital Governance: The application of information and communications technologies (ICTs) in the work of communicating with citizenry, providing information, providing services, and supporting transparency and accountability in democratic governance.

Electronic Word of Mouth (EWOM): Online word-of-mouth through electronic channels.

Environmental Scan: A survey of the larger environs in terms of competitors, usually done for situational awareness in a business situation.

Feedback Loop: An information channel to provide the development team with information about user attitudes and responses.

Geoinformatic Hotspot Systems (GHS): Integrated computer systems that combine information datasets and real-world sensor data with analytical tools to identify anomalies and so-called "hotspots," particularly those which may be regionally clustered or patterned (in space-time).

Identity: An original sense of self and character, based on a number of characteristics, as differentiated from others.

Impression: The viewing of a display ad.

Information Architecture: Information design with interactivity.

Microblogging: Micro-sharing, micro-updating.

Persuasive Technology: A technology used to affect people's opinions and behaviors.

Reputation: Public standing or estimation.

Social Networking: The use of socio-technical spaces and communications technologies for social interactions and information- and resource-sharing.

Viral Marketing: The exponential word-of-mouth excitement created around a particular product or service.

APPENDIX 1

Global Branding of Electronic Learning Programs and Courses in Higher Education Survey

The purpose of this online survey is to get a sense of some of the strategies used in global branding of academic learning opportunities (programs, courses, trainings, and so on) in higher education. This survey should take about half an hour.

If you have any questions about this survey, please contact Shalin Hai-Jew at shalin@k-state.edu.

Information about the Respondents

1. Please indicate what best describes your role in the institution of higher education:
   Faculty
   Administration
   Staff
2. How long have you been engaging in global branding of academic e-learning?
   1 year or less
   2-3 years
   4-5 years
   6-7 years
   8-9 years
   10-11 years
3. What e-learning curriculum has been branded globally at your institution of higher education?
4. What are the main purposes of your academic global branding? (Please list these in the order of most important to least important, with #1 as the most important.)
   Advertising
   Marketing
   Public relations / relationship management
   Curricular and program differentiation
   Identity management
   Learner recruitment
   Learner retention
   Learner experience coordination
   Internal processes

5. What communications and information technology (IT) channels do you use for global branding? (Please list these in the order of most important to least important, with #1 as the most important.)
   Email
   Electronic mailing lists
   Telephone
   Podcasts
   Micro-blogging (like Twitter™)
   Broadcast radio
   Broadcast television
   Websites
   Virtual worlds / multiverses
   Digital installations
   Simulations
   Digital repositories
   Wikis
   Blogs
   Mobile devices
6. Who are your most important internal "publics"? (Please list these in the order of most important to least important, with #1 as the most important.)
   University instructors
   University staff
   University administrators
   Program staff
   Collaborative partners
   Guest speakers
   Specialists in the field
7. Who are your most important external "publics"? (Please list these in the order of most important to least important, with #1 as the most important.)
   Potential students
   Potential public-sector partners
   Potential private-sector partners
   The general public
   Informal learners
   Competitors
   Specialists in the field
8. Please describe the core identity that you are defining for your internal and external publics. (These include program and professional values, practices, and goals.)
9. Please describe your logo and slogans / catch phrases. Please also explain them in terms of symbology, tone, and purpose.

10. What is your core competitive advantage in the brand?
    Original curriculum
    Star faculty and researchers
    Innovative e-learning strategies
    Research
    Networking and social connections
    Resources
    Reputation
    The value of the degree or certificate in the field
    Student services and supports
    Other
11. How do you measure the effectiveness of your global brand?
    Quantitative Measures:
    Hits / visits on the site; site analytics
    Numbers of student queries about the program
    Successful student recruitments / enrollments
    Stakeholder surveys
    Qualitative Measures:
    User feedback
    Stakeholder surveys
    Other measures?
12. How do you protect your global brand against mis-use or infringements? Please check all that apply.
    No protections (if you do not use any global brand protections)
    OR
    Brand monitoring (technological and human means):
    Legal interventions (policy-making, cease-and-desist letters, registration with the USPTO):
    Third-party monitoring service:
13. What endeavors do you take to try to keep up with the culture of the various potential learners? Please check all that apply.
    Working with current and former students
    Working with professionals in the field
    Reading media information about various peoples
    Reviewing the research (in the domain field and also in branding)
    Traveling abroad
    "Coolhunting" online (studying what each new generation considers attractive and interesting)
    Monitoring the new social networking and other technologies

14. What efforts do you take to reach a global (vs. local) audience? (Please check all that apply.)
    Foreign language translations
    Geographical / regional, and other studies
    Cultural sensitivity (targeted to a culture)
    Cultural neutrality (cultural scrubbing of contents)
    Diverse user testing of messages, contents, and/or services
    Regional "versioning" of contents
    Other:
15. What efforts do you take to sustain and evolve your global brand?
16. How would you assess the value of your global academic brand?

Thank you for your help. If you have any questions, please feel free to contact Shalin Hai-Jew at shalin@k-state.edu.

The results of this survey may be used in an academic publication.

APPENDIX 2

Survey Outreach Announcement

Hello, all: A number of universities have created strong academic degree programs and courses for online delivery. Their areas of specialty enable many to stand out as global leaders in particular domain-field niches, disciplinary fields, and cross-disciplinary areas of study. How these colleges and universities reach out to a global and local student population is of interest, particularly their global branding strategies.

I am conducting a survey on the global branding of e-learning programs and courses in higher education.

This online survey should take 20-30 minutes to complete. Your insights will be collected anonymously and shared in a forthcoming academic publication.

The survey information is as follows:

Survey Title: Global Branding of E-Learning Programs and Courses in Higher Education

Your survey will be offered **Nov 05, 2009 through Nov 27, 2009**. https://surveys.ksu.edu/TS?offeringId=151186

I sincerely appreciate your help.

Dr. Shalin Hai-Jew
shalin@k-state.edu

Section 2

Strategic Branding Decisions

Chapter 4
Exploring Key Issues in Destination Branding[1]

Piyush Nangru
Great India Rural Tours, India

Vaibhav Rustagi
ITC Ltd, India

Manish Makhija
HCL Technologies, India

Lubna Nafees
IMT, India

Omkumar Krishnan
IMT, India

ABSTRACT

In response to increased competition among destinations, destination marketing organizations (DMO) are required to effectively communicate the competitive advantage of destinations and market them as brands. Destination branding, unlike product branding, is a very recent concept. This chapter aims to study and analyse key issues in destination branding which makes it different from branding a product or a service and also identifies certain areas in destination branding where further research is required. The analytical framework of the chapter was developed by reviewing literature on destination branding and case studies in destination branding.

INTRODUCTION

A destination, by itself, is a very complex and unique product. Branding a destination, therefore, is not guided by a set of clearly laid down rules or frameworks, as in case of most products. To make things simpler for this initial discussion, a destination will be considered as a tangible product.

The travel and tourism industry, which is one of the biggest businesses in the world, is also the biggest purchaser of destination products. However, the destination products are also bought by

DOI: 10.4018/978-1-61350-171-9.ch004

investors, governments (policy-makers) and local residents. Now, the manager of a destination (similar to a product manager) is responsible for branding this unique product in a way so that the brand image is able to attract more visitors/investors/policy-makers.

In the light of above discussion, we can understand destination branding as an exercise that combines all the things associated with a destination in order to influence a customer's decision to visit/develop/invest into a particular destination over the other. However, it's not as simple as it sounds because a destination is an intangible product. Therefore, the brand elements and the positioning plank will differ from that of tangible goods. For example, according to Ritchie and Ritchie (1998) a destination brand should convey a unique travel experience.

Also, with varied group of stakeholders the complexity further increases. It should be added here that travel and tourism industry is the most important stake-holder in this process. Therefore it becomes imperative here to study the unique aspects about this industry.

Travel and Tourism Industry

The travel and tourism industry mainly consists of five sectors. The first is the accommodation sector like hotels, hostels, resorts, camp houses, etc. The second is the attraction sector which includes museums, theme parks, monuments, etc. The third is the transport sector which encompasses airline industry, bus/coach operators, railways, etc. The fourth sector is the destination organization sector. This sector includes countries, states, regions, cities, etc and the last sector is the travel organizers' sector that represents tour operators, booking websites, agents, etc.

The above five sectors cover almost all the travel and tourism related products which are marketed in this industry. However, many a times, there is a combination of two or more products involved. The focus of this chapter will however remain on the branding aspect of the destination organization sector.

The travel and tourism marketing, although a part of the services marketing umbrella, has certain uniqueness attached to it (Middleton and Clarke, 2001). Firstly, there is a problem of seasonality (i.e., there are peaks and troughs). For example, there will be higher demand for family packages during the time when schools are on a break. Secondly, there is high fixed cost involved in the marketing activities of travel and tourism products. Lastly, there is heavy interdependence among different types of tourism products. For example, marketing of a cruise package might involve marketing of products from all the five sectors discussed above.

In travel and tourism marketing, like any other services marketing, the extended marketing mix can not be ignored. With its distinctive nature discussed above, the additional Ps namely people, physical evidence and processes gain further importance (Middleton and Clarke, 2001). These are discussed hereunder:

People

The employees are the most valuable resource to a tourism organization. Their appearance, behaviour, knowledge and attitude can have a powerful impact on customers' perception of the tourism product. Also, from promotion point of view, employees are the walking billboards for an organization (Zeithaml, Bitner and Gremler, 2009). Thus all the organizations should ensure uniform grooming.

Process

In the consumption of a tourism product, various service encounters (or touch points) at each stage form the overall experience. Even a single unsuitable experience may lead to overall negative evaluation by the consumer. A proper feedback system can help rectify this issue.

Physical Evidence

Travel and tourism products are high involvement and high risk products. That is, there is huge amount of money paid for something highly intangible. Therefore, there is a need for something tangible to be produced. This involves the layout, colours, furniture, images, etc at airports or booking offices or in pamphlets, etc.

The above discussion was necessary to introduce certain intrinsic characteristics of travel and tourism marketing as they will help in understanding the complexities related to destination branding in a better way.

Understanding Branding

Understanding of branding will first be developed before applying it to destinations. The most basic definition of a brand can be said to be given by Aaker (1996) as:

The distinguishing name or symbol (such as logo, trademark or packaging design) intended to identify the goods or services of either one seller or a group of sellers and to differentiate those goods and services from those of competitors.

Aaker's definition lays too much stress on constructing a logo. A differentiating logo is definitely a key component of branding, but the process of branding involves much more than that. Moreover, a service brand can not be differentiated with a logo only.

The American Marketing Association (AMA, 2009) defines a brand as:

A brand is a customer experience represented by a collection of images and ideas; often, it refers to a symbol such as a name, logo, slogan, and design scheme. Brand recognition and other reactions are created by the accumulation of experiences with the specific product or service, both directly relating to its use, and through the influence of advertising, design, and media commentary.

This definition is far more exhaustive than the previous one as it recognizes the involvement of 'customer experience' and 'role of advertising, design and media' in overall development of a brand. It is the latter definition of branding that will be referred in the subsequent parts of this chapter. Now the same concept will be applied to destinations.

Destination Branding

Although branding has been there since centuries, destination branding is a relatively newer concept. It refers to activities of creating and sustaining a brand for a destination. A 'destination' may be any geographical area, ranging from small cities to regions to countries. The aim is to produce a logo, image and promise that are accurately perceived by the consumers. Therefore, for tourism destinations, the overall visitor experience must be included in the branding process (Berry, 2000). Based on this concept, Blain, Levy and Ritchie (2005) devised the following definition of destination branding:

The marketing activities (1) that support the creation of a name, symbol, logo, word mark or other graphic that both identifies and differentiates a destination; (2) that convey the promise of a memorable travel experience that is uniquely associated with the destination; and (3) that serve to consolidate and reinforce the recollection of pleasurable memories of the destination experience, all with the intent purpose of creating an image that influences consumers' decisions to visit the destination in question, as opposed to an alternative one.

The definition first discusses about the importance of branding elements. Also, it should be noted that above definition justly addresses the importance of a 'unique experience' in the branding process of a destination. However, the authors do not agree with the last part of the definition as it limits the purpose of destination branding to tourist visitors only, whereas there are far too many stakeholders involved in the branding of a destination.

There's no denying of the fact that tourist visitors are the major stakeholders in the process of destination branding. But, not recognizing other set of stakeholders has been criticised by Kotler, Haider and Rein (1993). Different stakeholders have different interests in the process and hence power and politics come into play and can alter the process.

Controlling the branding process of a destination is a tough task and is affected by various factors which are at times beyond a marketer's control (Hankinson, 2004). This and other key issues are discussed in the next section.

CURRENT KEY ISSUES IN DESTINATION BRANDING

Destination branding has a lot of complexity involved with it. It is far more challenging than branding of other goods and services. Following are some of the key issues in this context which are of importance to a destination marketer:

Branding Elements

Referring to the definitions discussed in the previous section, the name of the product is an important element of branding. Now, the marketers have little choice here because they can't change the name of the destination as there is a risk of loss of identity. Hence the destination name does not provide any differentiation (Pike, 2005).

Further, in a research conducted on tourism directors, which have publicly announced the use of branding, across the globe (Park and Petrick, 2006) it was found that a logo and the slogan are the two most important elements in a destination's branding strategy. But, destinations are far more multi dimensional than consumer goods and other services. It is not always possible to encapsulate the diversity offered by a destination in a slogan. In other words, slogan alone too fails to differentiate between destinations (Gold and Ward, 1994).

So, when name and slogan fail to substantially differentiate a destination, destination branding should include some other differentiating element. Thus, the destination branding process should also be looking to deliver impactful experiences, as discussed in the second part of the definition, apart from constructing a brand identity on paper with logos and slogans (Morgan, Pritchard and Pride, 2001). This highlights the concept of experiential branding. It means beneficially differentiating a product or service in somebody's mind by focusing on the totality of the experience, rather than focusing on the features, attributes or benefits of the product (The Bay Charles Consulting Company, 2009).

In practice, this can vary depending upon the destination. If the destination under question represents a diverse geographical area, it will be tough to encapsulate everything in a slogan. Therefore, slogans of nations are more focussed on experiential or emotional attributes. Example: 'Incredible India!', 'Malaysia–Truly Asia'. On the other hand regions and cities, not being as multi faceted as nations, can focus more on functional features (Caldwell and Friere, 2004). Take for instance 'Arizona: Grand Canyon State'.

Number of Stakeholders Involved

Destination marketing organisations (DMOs), often with government support, have traditionally been responsible for promoting their respective locations. However, there is a criticism that these organisations have a limitation of being tourism focused only. That is, destination branding has only been studied from demand side, and supply side has often been ignored (Prideaux and Cooper, 2002). For this, Kotler, Haider and Rein (1993) suggested five target markets for a destination. They are goods and service producers; corporate headquarters and regional head offices; outside investment and export markets; tourism and hospitality business and new residents.

One of the best examples here could be Edinburgh in Scotland. In 2001, Edinburgh Tourism Action Group (ETAG) was setup, as the first public private tourism partnership. Its members included the Edinburgh City Council (responsible for major funding and support for tourism within the city), Edinburgh City Chamber of Commerce (responsible for attracting inward investment), and Scottish Enterprise Edinburgh and Lothians (SEE & L: responsible for the economic prosperity of the Lothians) (Fyall and Leask, 2006)

This involvement by so many organizations at destination level means that for making any tourism decision, ETAG needs to consider variety of aims, policies etc. At times, a consensus may not even be possible.

To overcome this issue, in April 2005, via the integration of regional tourist boards and existing national tourism organization VisitScotland, a single national tourism network was formed. Its objective as stated on the website (www.scotexchange.net, 2009) is:

To contribute significantly to the advancement of Scottish tourism by giving it a real presence in the global marketplace and benefiting the whole of Scotland.

Now, this new network was not a membership body. So, the local voices were not heard. The argument presented was that tourism businesses need to take a long-term view, placing the need to bring visitors to Scotland and then Edinburgh before the need to attract them to individual businesses (Fyall and Leask, 2006).

There exists another set of stakeholders, not discussed in the above example and that is the local residents. They are also stakeholders in the branding process. They can only be persuaded to embrace the official destination branding. They are not obliged to accept the macroscopic level branding.

Now each stakeholder may have a different agenda. Besides, the DMOs have an offering (i.e., the destination), which is rigid in most ways. The DMOs can only change the way a destination is marketed to different segments (Pike, 2005). The DMOs try to attract wide range of stakeholders during this process. Having said this, is it possible that the same set of brand elements appeal to the diverse set of stakeholders involved? Each of the stakeholders tries to influence the functioning of DMOs to suit their interests. This is where power and politics come into play.

Power and Politics

The politics of decision making hampers the branding process of destinations (Ooi, 2004). Various issues like 'selection of the board members', 'who decides the brand elements' and 'who is responsible for it' are critical. Trying to keep all the internal and external stakeholders happy without confusing the brand message is the biggest political challenge for DMOs (Zahra and Ryan, 2007). Power is exerted in two forms: persuasion and authority (Marzano and Scott, 2009). However it is also argued that there is a thin line between considering power to be a managerial tool or to be a tool to influence DMOs.

For example, the Ministry of Tourism (Govt. of India), with the help of UNDP during 2003-2007 executed Endogenous Tourism Projects (ETP) at selected rural sites across India. The ministry involved the Panchayat Raj Institutions (PRI), a rural governing body, to enhance participation of local community and to develop sustainable rural tourism products (Mott MacDonald Report, 2007). Therefore, the Ministry of Tourism was able to use rural political structure as a managerial tool.

However in another example, Pike (2005) cites an example where a domineering attraction manager influenced the regional tourism board to change a destination brand of five years, for a simple reason that he had grown tired of it. This was done at a time when research indicated that the brand elements were gaining popularity in its targeted market.

Marzano and Scott (2009) have clearly figured out the role of power and politics in a destination branding process. They studied the branding process of Gold Coast, Australia and found that power and politics are more than evident in a destination branding process.

Persuasion was used by different stakeholders, to put forward their interests. The chairman of the board being from GCA (Gold Coast Airport) was able to get a lot of decisions in his favour. Also, the Gold Coast City Council, being the major fund provider to the Gold Coast Tourism (GCT), was able to pitch lot of its interests.

However, an interesting point made in the above research is that the GCT was particularly happy about the branding process because it recognized the real sources of power and was able to negotiate with them. So, there is a point here for the destination marketers. They should try not to be on the other side of the most powerful stakeholder.

Importance of Supply Side

There are two broad categories of stakeholders. One the place sellers (local businesses, government, local residents) and the other place buyers (tourists, investors, new residents). These are commonly referred as supply side and demand side respectively.

Till now there has been a unidimensional approach towards destination branding as it is a relatively nascent concept. The major quantum of research has been primarily from the consumer's perspective. This perspective talks only about the perceived image of any destination as a brand. But what it neglects is the brand identity of any destination, that is, what the brand aspires to stand for (Konecnik and Go, 2008).

The brand identity is derived from the projected image by various place-sellers and the perceived image is equivalent to the brand image of a destination as perceived by place buyers. Detailed study of the brand identity of any destination would enable in assessment of gaps between the projected and perceived image if any (Govers and Go, 2004). The assessment helps in deciding on appropriate inputs for building the desired image that is consistent with the brand identity.

The Ministry of Tourism (Govt. of India), since the inception of the 'Incredible India' campaign, has been constantly interacting with travellers and journalists. The importance of this feedback has been emphasized by Mr. Amitabh Kant (2009), joint secretary, Ministry of Tourism, in following words:

Most travellers perceive a destination in their own unique, emotional terms. It was therefore essential as a brand manager to constantly and relentlessly monitor how India as a destination was being perceived. It was necessary to regularly respond to mails, spend time with tour operators and writers and interact with the editors of leading international journals at WTM and ITB. This enabled us to monitor the evolution of the brand and close the gaps that existed between the conceived and perceived positioning of the brand.

In the same context, Curtis (2001), taking example of Oregon as a case in point, explained why a DMO strategy will fail if there's difference between projected and perceived brand image for a destination. For instance, the local residents also interact with the visitors and therefore the destination brand should resonate with both.

A major problem in achieving the above mentioned fit could be the internet. Increased penetration levels of internet have become a concern for DMOs. It offers both opportunity and threat to the destination marketers. It's an opportunity because information (brand message) can be easily updated and made available to millions of people across the globe. However, this advantage of reach ability is also a threat to the DMOs because individual businesses such as hotels, tour operators, etc. can easily bypass the DMO and create a different brand image for the destination. This may result in brand confusion.

It therefore becomes crucial that there should be co-operation between DMOs and individual businesses. This way, the internet will not only cease to be a disturbance, but will also complement DMOs in its branding activities. A single message by all the major stakeholders of the destination will attract more visitors and investors to the destination.

Control and Evaluation

The DMOs, sometimes, have little control over the destination branding activities. This is mainly because of two reasons. Firstly, as discussed above, destinations are complex products involving lot of stakeholders. The marketing manager has therefore very little control over the branding of the destination. Secondly, certain unfavourable events like acts of terrorism, natural calamities, etc. may cause negative attitudes about the destination (Hankinson, 2004). This gets further aggravated by negative global publicity.

Singapore is an epitome of what a small country, with very little scope for domestic movement, can achieve in terms of tourism. This success is attributed to the effective branding of a country with low cultural and natural wealth. Singapore has been continuously re-inventing itself over the years. However, when the international arrival figures from 2001 to 2005 are scrutinized, there is a dip in 2003. (Refer to Table 1)

This is because of the outbreak of Severe Acute Respiratory Syndrome (SARS) in 2003 (Henderson, 2007). Events like these have been known to affect the tourism industry. In the last decade, terrorism has been a major culprit for rendering the destination branding theories as ineffective for multiple times. It is then that the marketers should try to invoke that trust again. The case of South Africa stands apt to this.

The DMOs need to evaluate their efforts through some monitoring system. There can be various indicators like awareness, response, number of visitors, money spent, days spent, market share, etc. Some of the factors will obviously be more reflective of the success of the branding campaign than others. The Anholt-GfK Roper Nation Brands Index is the only analytical ranking of the world's nation brands (gfkamerica.com, 2009).

The branding process should be able to create brand loyalty among visitors. Measuring brand loyalty for a destination is a tricky thing because of the nature of the product. Unlike, other goods and services, one is less likely to visit a destination more than once. Having said this, if brand loyalty can be generated, it can help the destination in two ways. Firstly, certain destinations, especially the weekend getaways, do attract people more than once. For instance, Las Vegas attracts many US residents more than once a year. Secondly, and most importantly, a loyal customer will always promote the destination through word of mouth. Word of mouth is one of the most important elements for creating a powerful destination image.

The above discussion can be summed up in Figure 1.

CONCLUSION

The discussion above explored the differentiating features of travel and tourism marketing. Because of its uniqueness, the extended marketing mix becomes very important in travel and tourism marketing. Definitions of branding and destination

Figure 1. Framework

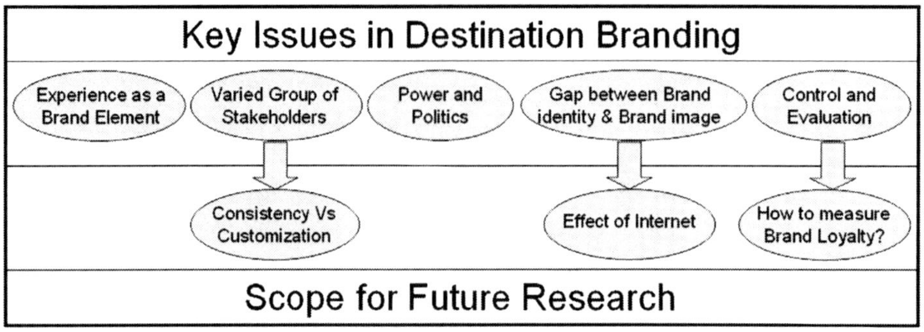

Table 1. Singapore's international tourist arrivals from 2001 to 2005

Year	No. of Arrivals
2001	7,522,000
2002	7,570,000
2003	6,126,569
2004	8,328,118
2005	8,940,000

branding were critically analysed, and it was found that the element of experience is an inseparable part of destination branding.

Various key issues in destination branding were then discussed. The relevance of name and slogan as branding elements was questioned by the authors. Importance of varied group of stake holders was highlighted. The DMOs face the difficulty of addressing the needs of varied group of stakeholders with a single consistent brand image. Role of power and politics was discussed and it was discovered that stakeholders with more power can influence decisions related to branding process.

There is a dearth of research in destination branding from place-sellers' perspective. There is a need to bridge the gap between brand identity and perceived brand image. A major hindrance to this could be the internet. The authors encourage further research on how does internet affect the destination branding process and how can internet be used to reinforce the branding efforts of the DMOs. Next, the chapter highlighted the negative effect of unfavourable events like acts of terrorism, natural calamities, etc on outcome of destination branding. The importance of evaluation methods for destination branding process was discussed. There should be some research effort spent in developing evaluation methods. Brand loyalty should be one of the important parameters while evaluating a destination branding process. The authors encourage further research on what does brand loyalty for a destination mean and what are the ways to achieve it.

REFERENCES

Aaker, D. A. (1996). *Building strong brands*. New York, NY: Free Press.

American Marketing Association. (2009). Resource library: Definitions. Retrieved July 2, 2009, from http://www.marketingpower.com/_layouts/Dictionary.aspx?dLetter=B

Berry, L. L. (2000). Cultivating service brand equity. *Journal of the Academy of Marketing Science, 28*(1), 128–137. doi:10.1177/0092070300281012

Blain, C., Levy, S. E., & Ritchie, J. R. B. (2005). Destination branding: Insights and practices from destination management organizations. *Journal of Travel Research, 43*(4), 328–338. doi:10.1177/0047287505274646

Caldwell, N., & Friere, J. R. (2004). The differences between branding a country, a region and a city: Applying the brand box model. *Journal of Brand Management, 12*(1), 50. doi:10.1057/palgrave.bm.2540201

Curtis, J. (2001). Branding a dtate: The evolution of brand Oregon. *Journal of Vacation Marketing, 7*(1), 75–81. doi:10.1177/135676670100700107

Fyall, A., & Leask, A. (2006). Destination marketing: Future issues — Strategic challenges. *Tourism and Hospitality Research, 7*(1), 50–63. doi:10.1057/palgrave.thr.6050029

GfkAmerica.com. (2009). *The Anholt-GfK Roper nation brands index*. Retrieved July 19, 2009, from http://www.gfkamerica.com/practice_areas/roper_pam/nbi_index/index.en.html/

Gold, J. R., & Ward, S. V. (1994). *Place promotion: The use of publicity and marketing to sell towns*. Chichester, UK: Wiley.

Govers, R., & Go, F. M. (2004). Cultural identities constructed, imagined and experienced: A 3-gap tourism destination image model. *Tourism Interdisciplinary Journal, 52*(2), 165–182.

Hankinson, G. (2004). The brand images of tourism destinations: A study of the saliency of the organic images. *Journal of Product and Brand Management, 13*(1), 6–14. doi:10.1108/10610420410523803

Henderson, J. C. (2007). Uniquely Singapore? A case study in destination branding. *Journal of Vacation Marketing, 13*(3), 261. doi:10.1177/1356766707077695

Kant, A. (2009). *Branding India: An incredible story*. Noida, India: Collins-Business.

Konecnik, M., & Go, F. (2008). Tourism destination brand identity: The case of Slovenia. *Journal of Brand Management, 15*(3), 177–189. doi:10.1057/palgrave.bm.2550114

Kotler, P., Haider, D., & Rein, I. (1993). *Marketing places: Attracting investment, industry, and tourism to cities, states and nations*. Oxford, UK: Free Press.

MacDonald Report, M. (2007). *Evaluation study of rural tourism scheme*. Retrieved October 18, 2009, from www.tourism.gov.in/survey /RuralTourism.pdf

Marzano, G., & Scott, N. (2009). Power in destination branding. *Annals of Tourism Research, 36*(2), 247–267. doi:10.1016/j.annals.2009.01.004

Middleton, V. T. C., & Clarke, J. R. (2001). *Marketing in travel and tourism*. Oxford, UK: Butterworth-Heinemann.

Morgan, N., Pritchard, A., & Pride, R. (2001). *Destination branding: Creating the unique destination proposition*. Oxford, UK: Butterworth-Heinemann.

Ooi, C. (2004). Poetics and politics of destination branding: Denmark. *Scandinavian Journal of Hospitality and Tourism, 4*(2), 107–128. doi:10.1080/15022250410003898

Park, S., & Petrick, J. F. (2006). Destinations' perspective of branding. *Annals of Tourism Research, 33*(1), 262–265. doi:10.1016/j.annals.2005.10.007

Pike, S. (2005). Tourism destination branding complexity. *Journal of Product and Brand Management*, *14*(4), 258. doi:10.1108/10610420510609267

Prideaux, B., & Cooper, C. (2002). Marketing and destination growth: A symbiotic relationship or simple coincidence. *Journal of Vacation Marketing*, *9*(1), 35–51. doi:10.1177/135676670200900103

Ritchie, J. R. B., & Ritchie, J. B. R. (1998). The branding of tourism destinations: Past achievements and future challenges. *Proceedings of the Annual Congress of the International Association of Scientific Experts in Tourism (AIEST)*. Marrakesh, Morocco, (pp. 89-116).

Scotexchange.net. (2009). *About us.* Retrieved June 21, 2009, from http://www.scotexchange.net/about_us /vision_priorities_and_objectives.htm

The Bay Charles Consulting Company. (2009). *Experiential branding: An introduction*. Retrieved July 16, 2009, from http://www.baycharles.com/images/ BC3%20%20Experiential%20Branding %20White%20Paper.pdf

Zahra, A., & Ryan, C. (2007). From chaos to cohesion - Complexity in tourism structures: An analysis of New Zealand's regional tourism organizations. *Tourism Management*, *28*(3), 854–862. doi:10.1016/j.tourman.2006.06.004

Ziethaml, V. A., Bitner, M. J., & Gremler, D. D. (2006). *Services marketing: Integrating customer focus across the firm*. London, UK: McGraw-Hill.

ENDNOTE

1 This chapter is based on the paper "Exploring Key Issues in Destination Branding" that was presented by Piyush Nangru, Vaibhav Rustagi and Manish Makhija at the 2nd International Conference on Brand Management hosted by Institute of Management Technology (IMT), Ghaziabad in January 2010.

Chapter 5
Branding Strategies for Digital TV Channels

Margherita Pagani
Bocconi University, Italy

ABSTRACT

This chapter analyses the impact of digitalization on TV marketing strategies focusing on the role of brand as a loyalty-based resource, available to digital television networks to create a sustainable competitive advantage. We analyze the cognitive process adopted by a viewer in the selection process of a TV channel and provide managerial implications for branding strategy and the tools that a television network and an iTV portal need to adopt to communicate values connected with their brand. The goal of this analysis is to offer insights on how a digital television network may create a channel experience leveraging on brand to increase viewers' loyalty and competitive advantage.

INTRODUCTION

The advent of the new digital technologies and the convergence process within the Information Communication Technology (ICT) are causing progressive hyper-competition which is forcing each single broadcaster as well as digital TV platforms to create strong brand indentities.

Broadcasters are increasingly gaining control over the personality of their networks and on viewers' perception of underlying brand values.

This chapter aims to analyze the impact of digitalization on marketing strategies through an investigation on the growing importance of the brand as a loyalty-based resource, available to digital television networks to aggregate and make loyalty vis-à-vis television viewers more concrete.

DOI: 10.4018/978-1-61350-171-9.ch005

Special attention is being paid to branding policies adopted by digital television networks through a better knowledge of the reasons why brand equity is important in the digital television industry.

The trend towards a progressive worsening of the competition pressure in the television industry results from a number of interconnected causal factors which can generally be reconciled based upon the huge technological and competitive changes in this industry.

The remainder of the chapter is organized as follows. First, a brief review of the brand equity and digital TV industry literatures will provide the theoretical background on the use of equity transfer to facilitate TV marketing strategies. Second, we focus on the cognitive process adopted by a viewer when selecting a TV channel. Third we analyze branding strategies and tools that a television network and an iTV portal adopt to communicate values connected with their brand.

The goal of this analysis is to understand how a digital television network may create a channel experience through increasing viewers' loyalty as the source of the competitive advantage.

BACKGROUND

Customer-Based Brand Equity

A brand is one signal that provides information about the product's expected quality (Rao and Ruekert, 1994; Baker et al. 2010). Customer-based brand equity refers to the ability of a brand to endow added value to a product and, hence, influence customer confidence in the ability of the product to meet or exceed performance expectations. Or as stated by Ailawadi et al. (2003, p. 1):

Brand equity is defined as the marketing effects or outcomes that accrue to a product with its brand name compared with those that would accrue if the same product did not have the brand name (Aaker, 1991, Dubin, 1998; Farquhar, 1989; Keller, 2003; Leuthesser, 1988).

Customer-based brand equity is often conceptualized as having two general components: awareness and image (Aaker, 1991; Keller, 1993). Awareness can be operationalized through measures of recall and recognition; image is more complex and involves assessing the attributes, benefit and value-based associations to the brand (Na et al., 1999). Efforts to develop and validate measures of brand equity have produced fairly similar results. Yoo and Donthu (2001) constructed a three dimensional brand equity scale defined by brand loyalty, perceived quality and brand awareness/associations. Washburn and Plank (2002) reported general support for branding of ancillary products both a three and four factor model, while Yoo and Donthu (2001) posited a four factor version disaggregating awareness and associations. Netemeyer et al. (2004) identified four facets of customer based brand equity: perceived quality, perceived value for the cost, uniqueness and willingness to pay a price premium for the brand.

In this study we consider three main components of brand equity:

- brand identity;
- brand awareness;
- brand image.

Brand identity includes entrepreneurial values which are the basis for the existence of the brand as well as all the elements to ease its recognition and memory (name, logo, symbols, jingles, slogans, etc.).

Brand awareness refers to the strength of brand knowledge. This strength is expressed by how easily a consumer identifies the brand whenever he/she is exposed to prompts represented by the brand itself (brand recognition), or by a product category, by the needs met by that category and by brand recall.

Brand image is made up by the bulk of cognitive associations into one's own memory. Such associations have a meaning attributed to the brand by consumers and are a summary of the following:

- product knowledge
- self-knowledge
- relation knowledge

TV Networks differentiate themselves by offering different genres of programming at different times to different demographic groups. In addition to its unique blend of programming, each TV network also has a distinct logo, jingle, style of promotion, and set of on-air personalities that make up what is known as its interstitial programming (Todreas, 1999). Together, carefully blended programming and interstitials give networks a particular look and feel. Market researchers often test this concept with viewers, who unfailingly identify networks from images or descriptions.

Digital Television Channels Types

Based upon choices made by television networks in terms of differentiation, clusters of viewers reached and types of programs offered, a number of business areas can be identified in the television industry.

A first option is an *undifferentiated strategy* vis-à-vis the audience and types of programs offered. This is the case of the general TV channel offering general programming made of different types of programs and addressing all categories of audience (for example, BBC and Anglia Television in the UK, RAI and Mediaset in Italy, France 2 and 3 in France).

A second option is that of a *concentrated strategy*: the channel focuses on a specific target audience or genre of broadcasts. This means a segmentation according to one or both of these elements as well as a limited choice—narrow scope—to a very limited number of segments to serve with ad-hoc programs. There are several examples of concentrated strategy, such as themed digital channels broadcasting a specific type of program (e.g., National Geographic, BBC News, Disney Channel, MTV, Sky Sport). There are also several examples of channels for specific target viewers offering specifically conceived programs (e.g., Dazed Television and Bravo are addressed to a young audience).

If this strategy is pushed forward to the point of identifying a single genre of broadcasts for a single segment, then a *niche strategy* exists. This strategy is indeed adopted by those channels having a single programming genre for a specific audience (e.g., Cartoon Network).

Based upon Figure 1, the following types of television channels can be identified:

- *general channels,* featuring general programming made by several genres (news, entertainment, films, etc.) and addressing all viewers' categories to satisfy their interests and meet their needs. They target audience maximization and, for this reason, programming is increasingly homogeneous and convergent, made by programs which can attract the highest number of viewers (a blend of comedy and drama series, movies, sports, news and special programming);
- *themed channels* achieve differentiation by filling their entire schedule with programming from a single genre (i.e., Sky News, Sky Sport, RAI News 24, BBC News, MTV, National Geographic). Addressed to all categories of viewers interested in a specific theme, they tend to concentrate on those genres, such as sports, music, news or education which can horizontally aggregate as many viewers as possible;
- *channels for specific viewer-groups* which focus their programmes on a specific audience segment (Diesel Channel or Dazed

Figure 1. Digital television channels breakdown

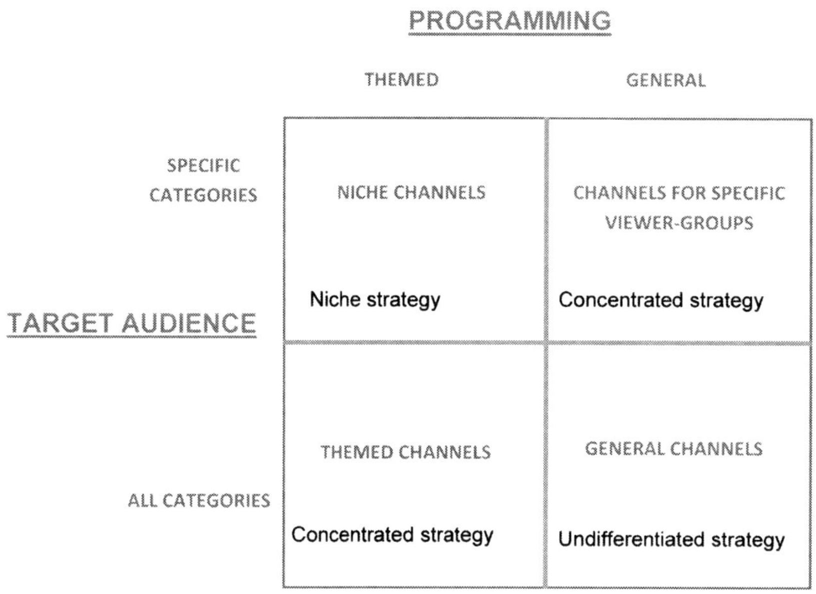

Channel in the UK for teen-agers and young viewers, or Nick Jr. and Disney Channel for children);

- *niche channels* addressing specific audience segments, they offer a single genre (ie., Cartoon Network or Nick J.).

The television market is characterized by an increasing number of themed channels for specific viewer groups. Many of them try to differentiate by adding on to their programming some interactive functionalities (i.e., for music channels, options of music on demand, interactive advertising with purchase of CDs from the channel), or becoming increasingly specialized and focused (i.e., a specific sport, or a single soccer team as in the case of MilanChannel or InterChannel in Italy).

The fragmentation of the audience and the abundance of niche channels cause an increase in the advertising space value of those channels, since the efficacy and quality of the contacts made is enhanced.

A critical success factor for these channels is the ability to pass their values onto their audience to allow for self-identification.

Digital TV Competitive Strategies

The layout adopted to define television businesses can also be used when analyzing competition and assessing each single competitor's strategy. Therefore, it is worth analyzing each competitor according to the audience groups reached and broadcasts.

A first category of competitors is made of those who define their businesses in practically the same way, reaching the same market segments with the same programming genres. For a general domestic channel, a competitor would be another general domestic channel.

A second category of competitors can also be identified grouping those channels which define their businesses in a partially different way. Differences may involve segments of viewers reached, or genres of broadcasts.

The third and last category is made by the new potential competitors who, at least in theory, might be granted market access.

Circumstances may of course vary; yet, three fundamental competitive mechanisms can be evidenced.

1. *Crossover competition:* Many existing general TV channels enter into new business areas through the launching of new themed television channels (BBC with BBCnews24, RAI with RAInews24, or SKY with Sky News and Sky Sport), or of new channels for niche viewers (in the UK, Nickelodeon UK launched Nick Jr, a channel for children only). They can therefore exploit skills and competitive advantages connected with brand knowledge and loyalty already achieved with the viewers.
2. *Chain Competition:* Organizations active in other phases of the value chain enter the television market. In particular, the digital convergence process and the development of interactive technologies has prompted many organizations specialized in interactivity to enter the television market, such as in the case of Microsoft, Playstation and Sega. A lot of publishers launch their own channels, such as RCS and Il Sole 24 Ore in Italy.
3. *Intersectorial competition:* Organisations belonging to different markets and with no previous television experience set up their television channels which make the most of brand knowledge and image already achieved in other areas (this is the case of Pepsi with Pepsi Music Channel or Sport Crazy Channel, and of Disney with Disney Channel).

Several are the reasons behind the entry of these non-television brands into this business, some are listed below:

- low entry barriers in the TV business (especially at technological level);
- further strengthening of the brand;
- chances to increase advertising money.

Following the present evolution trends, image brand takes on an increasingly central role and must perform a relevant mediation role allowing viewers to understand personality, corporation and privileged values in doing the business and to connect both tangible and intangible attributes offered with the socio-psychological benefits they are looking for.

Within this perspective, both TV and non-TV brands existing on the market have a greater advantage during start-up. A strong corporate brand is made of the following items:

- plays a differentiation role;
- represents a strong indicator for basic skills available to an organization and benefits obtainable by viewers;
- represents a strong credibility and identity element.

Within this new competitive scenario, the following are the most successful brands:

- TV and non-TV brands existing on the market;
- brands having previously accumulated a strong credibility vis-à-vis viewers, also being active in different businesses (i.e., Nike and Virgin), or which have distinct programming features (BBC and SKY), or interactive level offered (Sega or Playstation);
- first entries.

VIEWERS' COGNITIVE SYSTEM

In order to understand the way processes triggering loyalty resources by the TV broadcaster work, one must analyze in detail the rationale connected with viewers' behaviors in making use of a television program. The fruition process and viewers' analysis become central in the process of achieving an understanding about a suitable management of the relationships with the market. More specifically, we distinguish the following elements influencing its complexity:

- motivational system, given that the nature of the benefits achievable within the programs depends upon it;
- perceptive system which, through categorizing data of different nature from different information sources, provides an orientation to comparison processes as well as on suitability of choices made;
- sequences and evaluation procedures essential to create the above approaches both before and after viewing experiences.

A user's cognitive process can be broken down into a series of logically sequential phases (Busacca 1994) defining its layout as well as its morphologic and dynamic complexity (Figure 2):

- perception of a general need (the need to watch TV), or a specific need (a specific genre or program);
- information production suitable to give an orientation to comparisons and choices;
- assessment on optional offerings on the market;
- decision to watch;
- assessment on the basis of one's own watching experience of the matching between expectations developed during the previous phases and the actual benefits offered by the program of choice.

Before analyzing each single phase, one needs to know that the program and the channel play different roles within the different phases of the user's cognitive process and one needs to start from the television viewing *basics* in order to fully understand this role.

An individual stays tuned and enjoys a specific program in order to satisfy a generic need for television watching or a specific need to watch a specific program («watching date»). During this first phase, the user's goal is his/her research for a program, or a much looked forward time to deciding how to spend his/her time. During this

Figure 2. User's cognitive process phases

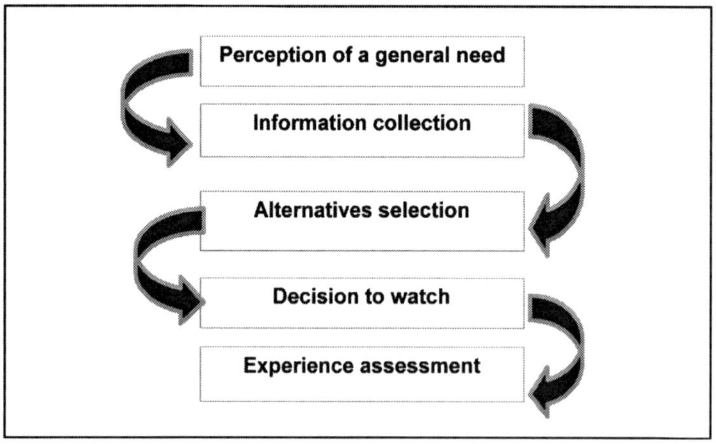

first phase, the program is the final element of choice. The relationship with the channel is limited to simply browsing through and no specific attention is being paid to it. Furthermore, viewers can express an opinion on the program watched; yet, they have trouble in remembering the channel where the program of choice was broadcast, except for a few specific times (i.e. between 6 p.m. and 11 p.m.), and some specific genres (i.e. news) where they can accurately tell the channel and broadcasting times.

The assessment of optional choices (third phase of the cognitive process) is instead made based upon the channel (figure 3). In a television environment characterized by hyper-competition, viewers have problems in checking out all the channels which indeed are offering options (*awareness aggregate*), thus driving the choice process. Therefore, a buffering process is activated only among a given number of channels visited regularly (*evoked aggregate*). On average, each viewer makes a choice between 7 to 9 channels which are being watched on a regular basis. This set of channels is made of those meeting the viewer's expectations in terms of genre type offered, type of programming and ability to satisfy a number of perceived needs by viewers in the different time brackets.

The channel goal is therefore viewers' loyalty development as well as strong reputation achievement in terms of being a competitive source.

The evoked aggregate by channel brands has a steady trend and previous learning is the most meaningful influencing factor in determining behavioral orientations (Aaker 1991). The danger for those channels which are not part of the set of favorites (negative group) is to be connected in the viewers' minds with past prejudices developed by them.

Channel-Watching Motivation Trigger

The factors responsible for the triggering of cognitive processes at the basis for the use of a specific channel or program and assessment of the satisfaction level achieved (Lazarsfeld, 1934, 1935; Lazarsfeld & Rosemberg 1955) can be summarized in the following:

- Exposure variables:
    - *titles* bradcast following advertising breaks to convey useful information in a non-intrusive fashion for the purpose of setting up a long-lasting relationship with users and lead them to place the channel within their choices;
- *Electronic Programme Guide* or Electronic Guide allows users to achieve the following:
    - find titles and timetables of the events in compliance with specific criteria

Figure 3. Options selection

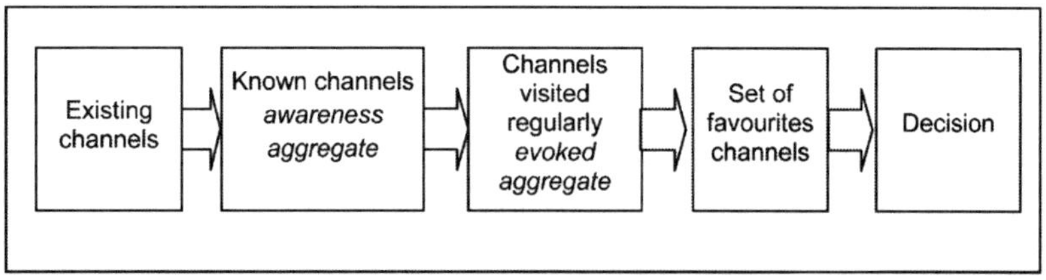

    - (selectable), such as time, program type, subjects, promotional adverts;
    - automatic access to the selected program;
    - set terminal for recording purposes;
    - send pay-per-view request;
    - access to further information.
- Influencing variables:
    - *programme title* as a means to attract audience. A good title raises feelings (suspence, tension, interest, curiosity) and gives an idea to viewers about what they can get in exchange for their attention;
    - *channel logo* is as relevant as the programme since it is a clear-cut invitation and conveys the key message to the market segment addressed.
    - Single user's attitude: a new channel is often found through zapping which has no basic rationale but rather is a casual search for a program, with no specific attention to the channel broadcasting the program. Zapping is a totally random exercise and is not guided by the channel but by the viewer. In a multi-channel environment, a great number of channels and similar options are available.

Audience loyalty to the channel depends upon the chance of finding one's own favorite programs. A positive assessment based upon a watching experience on the matching between expectations from previous stages and benefits actually found in the program of choice allows to have a positive channel experience which develops and gets consolidated through repeated contacts over time. Therefore, it is important that values to be communicated by the brand and channel identity be daily reflected by the programs schedule. The decision of tuning into a channel is only being made in the event the viewer had a positive past channel experience and is aware that his/her expectations can be met by a specific brand.

Meeting audience expectations means developing the viewer's confidence vis-à-vis a specific brand (channel) and all this allows for channel loyalty growth.

Development of channel loyalty is based upon the following four criteria:

1. **knowledge:** the channel brand must be known to viewers who must be able to understand its key values and differences from competitors in order to be able to select it against competing channels;
2. **experience:** each TV program selected by a viewer on a given channel must meet, within a competitive environment, the user's expectations so that through a positive experience made he/she can select once again that specific channel;
3. **relationship:** regular and frequent contacts between the consumer and the brand help building up a relationship so that, also in a competitive environment, the viewer is able to recognize the channel brand and can put it in the core-group of his/her selected channels;
4. **trust:** if the relationship between channel and viewer is strong and frequent and the user has made a positive channel experience, trust is built originating in the viewer an expectation whereby that specific channel brand will keep a promise and confirm his/her positive past experience.

When a viewer makes a positive experience in all four phases, channel brand loyalty is built and made stronger.

BRANDING STRATEGIES FOR DIGITAL TV CHANNELS

A brand is a product that is differentiated from its competition by means of design, name, mark, imagery, or a combination of any or all these (Todreas 1999). Firms trying to sell their products and build loyalty with their customers in a crowded field of competitors use branding to distinguish their products.

At a minimum, brands identify products as different. But, brands can go further, to identify products with positive attributes. Well-liked brands can give consumers trust and confidence in products. In this way, consumers pressed for time can quickly make difficult choices by selecting a known brand with an established reputation.

Creating a successful brand is quite difficult. Branding requires significant and repeated investment.

As it happens for services and consumption products, branding is becoming an increasingly interesting and wider element, also with reference to the media industry (TV, press, radio, etc.).

The broadcast networks are now trying to build on their brands to retain and increase viewership. Instead of using their valuable time between programming to sell advertisers' products, they are using it to promote themselves (Todreas 1999). The time is used to promote both individual shows and entire evening schedules.

With reference to television, the following three brand levels can be devised:

- *corporate* with reference to the broadcaster (ie., ABC, CBS, BBC);
- *channel* (ie., Disney Channel);
- *program* (ie., Beverly Hills 90210).

Each of these brands has its specific life-cycle (Figure 4).

While corporate brand gets consolidated over time, at channel level a brand development stage can be broken down into the four following different phases: launch, growth, maturity and decline.

Single programs have definitely shorter life-cycles.

The countless number of channels and programs on offer forces television networks to consider branding as one of the relevant factor within a new competitive concept.

Brand indeed allows for the following:

- differentiation vis-à-vis competitors as a primary element within corporate market policies;
- immediate recognition of the channel and program by the viewer;

Figure 4. Brand life-cycle

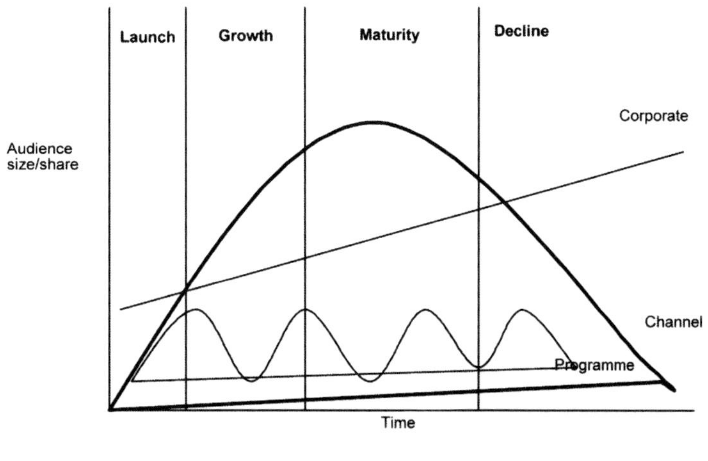

- an important reference point, a form of help, an active guarantee for the user (loyalty);
- an immediate recognition of the quality level of the offer.

Last but not least, it may be useful to bear in mind that a correct management and an on-going development of a brand policy allows the broadcaster to achieve and maintain audience loyalty and, as a consequence, make viewers an «asset» through repetitive and loyalty-oriented behaviours (Busacca, 1994). The four factors mentioned above (differentiation, recognition, quality and loyalty) seem to be central in order to obtain a competitive advantage.

Brand Communication Tools

Tools available to digital television channels for brand communication purposes may either be *on-air* or *off air*.

On-air tools are the programming schedule offered, that is the bulk of programmes, style, atmosphere and the energy reflecting what the brand needs to communicate.

Such tools, day in day out, contribute to make the relationship between a channel and its viewers stronger.

At a time when the branding experience is broadcast «*on air*», it can be switched into an outer «*off air*» environment, making sure that key values do not get lost or altered, but rather made stronger.

For the purpose of developing an «*off air*» awareness, it is important that the following be defined by the television channel:

- who is to be addressed (target audience);
- why targeting that specific group of viewers;
- previous expectations by the target audience;
- where the target audience can be reached;
- the best possible way to convey an actual «branding experience» to a specific market segment.

The choice of the available *off-air* tools depends upon the type of brand and by its very nature.

The following are the tools to make a stronger «*off air*» branding awareness:

- *Live Interactive Road Shows* allow for brand accessibility and «interaction» with viewers. This is a tool which may not be relevant and appropriate for all types of brands, but it works very well with television;
- *Press* (magazines/press) may strictly be oriented to the target audience. Very good from an economic standpoint;
- *Outdoor* has a strong impact according to sizes and positioning of the communication tool. As it happens with the press, it is a static medium and has a greater difficulty in the attempt of conveying an actual branding experience.
- *Direct Mail* can strictly be oriented to the target audience with minimum losses and great economic impact; yet, it runs the risk of being considered as one of the many «advertising brochures» and not be read.
- *Movies*: gives a strong branding experience; yet, one needs to ensure that key values connected to the channel by viewers may be present within the creative performance.
- *Promotional business* provides access to a wide audience.
- *Other tools* such as *merchandise*, consumption products, entertainment, websites and sponsorships.

In communicating a brand, both *on air* as well as *off air,* the channel must greatly focus on what must be communicated and how to do it in order to be coherent with promises made and expectations raised in the viewers' minds.

CONCLUSION

How to create a channel experience by getting hold of viewers to the detriment of one's own competitors? The results achieved, which are the outcome of interviews made to some digital television channels, highlight on the central role of marketing policies adopted.

The marketing function must control marketing services offered, the communication policy on the air, advertising as well as research and planning. For the purpose of making the marketing strategy stronger, new off-air communication tools must be introduced, a steady *breakthrough* level must be achieved and a focus on other media, such as the press and radio, must be made.

Independently from the vehicle of choice, brand personality, values and philosophy must be reflected in the contents offered by trying to meet the expectations raised in the viewers' minds, based upon promises made and previous experiences.

A positive channel awareness and experience made allow the viewer to increase his/her confidence in the brand, select a channel again, or have access again to the interactive portal.

REFERENCES

Aaker, D. A. (1991). *Managing brand equity.* New York, NY: Free Press.

Ailawadi, K. L., Baker, W. E., Sciglimpaglia, D., & Saghafi, M. (2010). Branding of post-purchase ancillary products and services: An application in the mobile communications industry. *European Journal of Marketing, 44*(5), 547–566. doi:10.1108/03090561011032261

Busacca, B. (1994). *Le risorse di fiducia dell'impresa* (pp. 73–74). Turin, Italy: UTET.

Dubin, J. A. (1998). The demand for branded and unbranded products: An econometric method for valuing intangible assets. In Dubin, J. A. (Ed.), *Studies in consumer demand: Econometric methods applied to market data* (pp. 77–127). Norwell, MA: Kluwer Academic Publishers. doi:10.1007/978-1-4615-5665-7_4

Farquhar, P. (1989). Managing brand equity. *Marketing Research, 1*(3), 24–33.

Fiocca, R., & Corvi, E. (1996). *Comunicazione e valore nelle relazioni d'impresa.* Milan, Italy: EGEA.

Keller, K. L. (2003). *Strategic brand management: Building, measuring and managing brand equity.* Upper Saddle River, NJ: Prentice-Hall.

Lehmann, D. R., & Meslin, S. A. (2003). Revenue premium as an outcome measure of brand equity. *Journal of Marketing, 67*(3), 1–17.

Leuthesser, L. (1988). *Defining, measuring and managing brand equity.* (Working Paper No. 88-104). Cambridge, MA: Marketing Science Institute.

Netemeyer, R. G., Krishnan, B., Pullig, C., Wang, G., Yagci, M., & Dean, D. (2004). Developing and validating measures of facets of customer-based brand equity. *Journal of Business Research, 57*, 209–224. doi:10.1016/S0148-2963(01)00303-4

Rao, A. R., & Ruekert, R. W. (1994). Brand alliances as signals of product quality. *Sloan Management Review, 36*(3), 87–97.

Todreas, T. M. (1999). *Value creation and branding in television's digital age* (p. 175). Westport, CT: Quorum Book.

Washburn, J. H., Hill, B. D., & Priluck, R. (2004). Co-branding: Brand equity and trial effects. *Journal of Consumer Marketing*, *17*(7), 591–604. doi:10.1108/07363760010357796

Yoo, B., & Donthu, N. (2001). Developing and validating a multidimensional consumer-based brand equity scale. *Journal of Business Research*, *52*(1), 1–14. doi:10.1016/S0148-2963(99)00098-3

KEY TERMS AND DEFINITIONS

Brand Awareness: Refers to the strength of brand knowledge. This strength is expressed by how easily a consumer identifies the brand whenever he/she is exposed to prompts represented by the brand itself (brand recognition), or by a product category, by the needs met by that category and by brand recall.

Brand Communication Tools: Tools available to digital television channels for brand communication purposes may either be *on-air* or *off air*.

Brand Identity: Includes entrepreneurial values which are the basis for the existence of the brand as well as all the elements to ease its recognition and memory (name, logo, symbols, jingles, slogans, etc.).

Brand Image: Is made up by the bulk of cognitive associations into one's own memory. Such associations have a meaning attributed to the brand by consumers and are a summary of product knowledge, self-knowledge and relation knowledge.

Customer-Based Brand Equity: Ability of a brand to endow added value to a product and, hence, influence customer confidence in the ability of the product to meet or exceed performance expectations.

TV Branding Channel Strategy: Strategy adopted by the digital channel trying to build on their brands to retain and increase viewership.

TV Channel Logo: Is a clear-cut invitation and conveys the key message to the market segment addressed.

Chapter 6
Between Physical and Virtual Reality:
The Case of Benetton Brand, "A Company that is Born from Ideas"

Annamaria Silvana de Rosa
Sapienza University of Rome, Italy

Elena Bocci
Sapienza University of Rome, Italy

ABSTRACT

This chapter presents a perspective theory, not yet fully developed, that seeks to analyze the connections between "Social Representations and Corporate Communication" (Penz, 2006; Usunier & Lee, 2009). It is divided into two sections. In the first, descriptive section we identified the organizational dynamics of the Benetton Company utilizing structural elements found in the enterprise's literature and documents. The objective was to understand Benetton galaxy's role in globalization and its complex market strategies. Since this was an internal view of the company, data was obtained from internal documents, including the company's publications, such as Global Vision and Colors publications. In order to understand the company from an external perspective, we consulted studies conducted on the Benetton universe that considered the marketing element as interaction between the company and the market (Kotler, 1997; Nardin, 1987; Semprini, 1996; Moliner, 1996; Tafani, 2006). In the second, empirical section, the social representation of the Benetton brand is analyzed using a large sample of Benetton's advertisements, selected as the basis for research to identify the perceptive modalities of advertising messages and attitudes in Benetton's communication strategies (de Rosa, 1998, 2001; de Rosa & Losito, 1996; de Rosa & Bocci, 2009). In this second section the relationship between social representations and corporate communication will be presented in a dialogical perspective that examines the social discourse "of"

DOI: 10.4018/978-1-61350-171-9.ch006

Benetton in regard to social issues. We will look at the different phases of advertising campaigns (1992-2008, with special focus on one of the controversial campaigns: Autumn-Winter 1992\1993) and the discourse "about" Benetton. The targets of reference for our research program are considered to be not only recipients of the company's advertising campaigns, but also potential buyers.

SOME STRUCTURAL DATA ON THE COMPANY: FROM A FAMILY BUSINESS, TO AN INDUSTRY, TO A "CULTURAL PHENOMENON"

Established in 1965 as a family business called "*Maglieria di Ponzano Veneto dei Fratelli Benetton,*" the Benetton Group transformed rapidly into an industry that reached far beyond Italy's borders. After initially launching itself on the international market, it then positioned its brand globally, not just in terms of financial markets but also in terms of cultural horizons. The Company itself became a "cultural" phenomenon, in fact, a true "case study."

The Benetton Company's adventures were summed up by Luciano Benetton[1] himself in an interview published on July 28, 1992 in United Colors of Benetton: A Global Vision:

"A company that is born of ideas: this is both the Benetton reality and its legend, as recounted on the pages of newspapers and magazines in America, China, Egypt, France, Japan, India, England, Italy, Poland, Spain and Turkey. Yet in an ever more global and competitive market, every new idea must serve as a solid base for further innovation" (Yagi, 1993:10)

The brand's global position was obtained by flexibly combining centralized planning, mar-

Figure 1. www.benetton.it

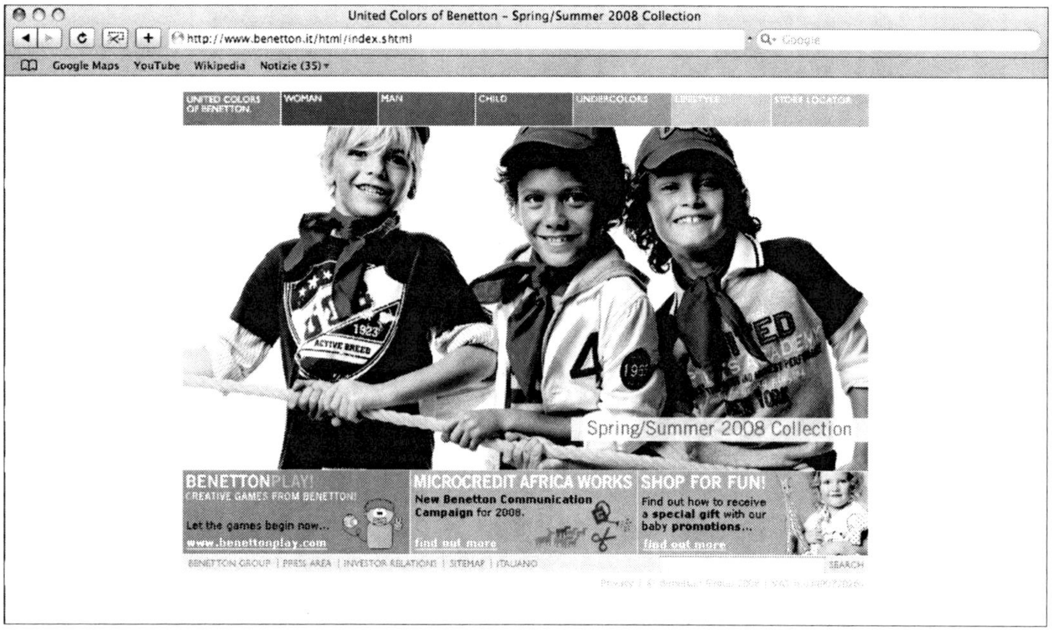

keting, production management and distribution systems with the extensive use of information technology.

In step with an economy increasingly oriented towards a globalizing marketplace, on its very interactive website (Figure 1), the company presents a representation of itself as a "global business" based on the following aspects:

- Global product;
- Common approach to the market;
- Standardized image of stores on a world scale via the "select a country" option;
- Global financial management;
- Global communication strategies.

In line with its philosophy of flexible organization (Kotler, 1997), Benetton did not hesitate to modify its corporate choices and, intent on optimizing results, quickly changed course when necessary.

In retracing the company's principal steps from the very beginning, one can see the particularly dynamic character of this manufacturing company that by offering a colorful and economical product in its own casual clothing stores became a point of reference for young people "of all ages" and from around the world.

At the beginning of the 1970s, the company developed one of the most important keys to its success: "*decentralization*" (Kotler, 1997), which for the company meant a reduction in production risks and costs, and in terms of distribution allowed them to meet clients' needs and trends.

From the very beginning, the name "My Market," still used for numerous sales outlets, targeted young people... of all ages. With products clearly displayed in shop windows and easily reachable on open shelves and music playing at high volume, the sales outlets, initially small and located in central and high traffic areas of cities, were able to pick up on the most up-to-date trends and fulfill purchasers' aspirations.

In the 1980s, the company played the card of *breaking into international markets*. The goal was to reduce costs and escape protectionist problems, making the Benetton organization less dependent on currency fluctuations.

The changes in the company logo (from "*Maglieria di Ponzano Veneto dei Fratelli Benetton*" to "Benetton" and then "United Colors of Benetton") by themselves describe Benetton's structural transformation from a family business, to an industry that was national, international, and finally, global.

Information technology was another tool used to promote the company's growth. In the beginning of the 1980s they developed an internal information system which, by linking design production and distribution flows, gave Benetton an advantage that was practically unknown at that time in the clothing/textile world: receiving orders for garments during the same season and guaranteeing delivery to sales outlets within three weeks.

At the same time, the company adopted a policy to consolidate its image at the international level. In addition to a qualitative boost in product quality, there was a corresponding price rise sustained by an appropriate *market repositioning*. In that regard, the choice of an international advertising medium in the form of Formula 1 racing became one of the company's many sponsorship activities.

Under the banner of dynamism and color, Benetton inaugurated sports centers, financed volleyball, basketball and rugby teams:

"The characteristics of racing car competitions; speed, color, cross-culture glamour, as well as the integration of high technology and human creativity, all have their counterparts in Benetton's philosophy. The Benetton adventure with Formula 1 began in 1983 with the sponsorship

of the Tyrell Team. But Luciano Benetton grew so passionate about car racing, that by 1985 he bought the Toleman Racing Team" (Yagi 1993:16).

The affair that began in 1983 with the sponsorship of "Team Tyrrell," ended with the Benetton family purchasing the "Toleman Team" in 1985. The dynamism and international image of Formula 1 racing progressively was merged with Benetton's image, guaranteeing the company yet another tool for globalization.

However, the element that typified Benetton's new brand positioning was their gamble in investing in *advertising posters,* a medium that had fallen into disuse (Kotler, 1997). The billboards gave the brand a new visibility, allowing it to be present in the most crowded squares and streets around the world. These were giant poster "murals" that carried sophisticated messages that were an invitation to overcome all barriers under the banner "United Colors of Benetton." That choice, which from the company's point of view represented a low cost strategic option to obtain wide social visibility, on the contrary, was considered an act of "ingenuousness" by Semprini (1996)[2] in his socio-semiotic analysis. In his opinion, it contributed to amplify the conflictual and controversial discursive space that for years had marked the Benetton brand in the social arena.

Communication strategies played a primary role in the establishment of this economic empire, which went hand in hand with the creation of a cultural "issue." The communication "change in direction" from traditional advertising canons coincided with Oliviero Toscani's encounter with the Benetton Company. Since 1984 the well-known and controversial photographer has submitted his pictures directly to Luciano Benetton for approval, to the satisfaction of both parties, at least as can judged by the numerous interviews given by these two personalities who have become a recurring figures in the daily press and the subject of biographical accounts. (Toscani, 1995). Toscani swept away the canons of traditional advertising from Benetton's campaigns, which, based on the famous "connotative transfer" model (Barthes, 1964; Semprini, 1996), were present in the company's advertising until 1983 and were centered on the product and positive social values (beauty, wealth, power, beautiful scenery, etc.).

Although with a more graphic than "photographic" expressive style (cf. Semprini, 1996), although remaining anchored to the product, in the initial phase of the various campaigns the advertisements transmitted messages in a style totally different from campaigns prior to 1984. With joy and vitality they expressed a philosophy inspired by "universal harmony," different peoples, races and cultures embracing each other, and by the rainbow of colors representing the chromatic metaphor while at the same time referring to the Benetton's polychromic products that were progressively conquering overseas markets.

From 1989 on, there was a definitive passage from product advertising to corporate advertising. From 1989-1991 there was a transitional phase, that we like to define as 'contrastive' (cf. de Rosa, 1998), which was characterized by the presence of opposites, generally portrayed by couples (no longer by groups, or collective subjects), contrastively connotated by their chromatic dimension (white-black), a whole/part contrast ("hands-body"), symbolism ('angel-devil'), metaphors ('wolf and lamb', 'dog and cat') or shock value (the famous kiss between a priest and nun, toilet paper, the *Pinocchios*, etc.).

The "*Denouncing the Evils of the World*" campaigns, launched beginning Spring/Summer 1992 (there was a preview a year earlier with the ad 'war cemetery and condoms'), began to include images with notable social impact that generated strong conflictual and controversial opinions. Such negative reactions were justified loudly in the name of the illegitimacy of a company to appropriate the right to intervene in that kind of discursive space (traditionally the realm of medical-scientific, legislative, political, etc. specialists, cf. Semprini, 1996). Benetton's communications section, with Oliviero Toscani in the forefront, responded to these with a progressive escalation of increasingly strong messages, claiming their right to distinguish themselves from the grayness of the kind of conformist commercial advertising that sells a sweetened, deceptive and falsified image of reality. The right to denounce "reality" in its pervasive "crudeness" of violence, abuse, sickness, social and natural scourges (immigration, racism, terrorism, mafia, death penalty, ecological catastrophes, etc.) in all corners of the world and to lay claim to themes previously allowed only for non-profit advertising (i.e. AIDS) was reaffirmed, not only abstractly in the name of an enlightened right to knowledge of the "truth or an almost "messianic" desire for communication.[3] The right and desire to speak to the world on universal themes ("sex, religion, race, life and death" Toscani, 1998) was supported by a commercial rationale in which, despite judicial, political and scientific controversies, sales always increased after the ad campaigns. This was true to the extent that the company, confident in its communication success, decided not to finance market studies on the results of its advertising campaigns.

In fact, the results from an extensive research program that we conducted confirmed the success of the strategy that, departing from a social discourse "of" Benetton "on social issues," triggered a social discourse "on" Benetton that ended with the creation of a meta-representation for the brand. The meta-representation turned out to be expanded and played up in auto reverberating circuits fueled by the same contrastive drives that the messages' source had set into motion. This confirms that this strategy, designed with the objective of triggering a process of attitude polarization, was guided less by ingenuousness, as Semprini believes than by a more or less intuitive or intentional choice to stand out in terms of "social visibility," taking their place as an "active minority in the world of advertising" (cf. de Rosa, 1998; de Rosa & Smith, 1997a, 1997b, 1998a 1998b).

Beyond opinions on the mode of communication adopted by the Toscani-Benetton advertisements, their moral, esthetic and deontological criteria and the political and discursive legitimacy that inspired them, it is undeniable that they were able to create a kind of *world-wide virtual conference or debate* on the world's current burning issues. They created a symbolic space for discursive interactivity that played out not only at the level of images (advertisements), texts (Colors) and words (interviews and press releases), but also by direct social intervention. Another means by which Benetton was able to communicate to the entire world was via *actions on, in and towards social issues*, intervening on AIDS issues (distributing condoms in their stores and in schools, financing research, sponsoring publications on prevention, etc.), world peace (distributing 'multicultural passport notebooks' in schools, etc.), poverty (collection and distribution of clothing for people in the Third World with the assistance of Caritas and the Red Cross), etc. If on one hand this change in course from *denunciation to action* can be interpreted as a counter attack to respond to criticism that they had exploited painful public and private human tragedies for commercial purposes[4]. On the other hand, beyond results and the ability to contribute to the resolution of real problems, these organized interventions certainly had the power to communicate to the world that the Benetton company had the tools necessary to intervene in areas and contexts that had always been the prerogative of other forces: political powers through their Ministries of Health, Education and Scientific Research, religious powers and their humanitarian organizations, etc.

If on the whole, from an ideological point of view, the choice of heavily connotated themes seemed to respond to the need to challenge the young people of the 1990s to be drawn closer to themes of social engagement, Benetton's advertising campaigns and social interventions seemed to be seeking to reach a much wider range of interlocutors among "young people of all ages."

The Benetton company's final gamble was to make the transition from *"international" to "global,"* as stated by Aldo Palmeri in an interview given to the editors of News:

"Above all it means to be strongly rooted in the territory. To be everywhere in order to be, above all, local."[5]

Being global in terms of production and distribution is a goal that was only half attained. Benetton wants to be global in terms of *image* as well. The company has always tried to transmit a unified message via the integration of all elements of marketing.

"Our products gradually came to be enriched by certain intangible elements, such us our corporate philosophy and style, our image, and the product displays at points of sale. A simple marketing technique thus contributed to the notion of a global "package" which encompassed, along with our clothing, the idea of a world based on youth and universality" (Yagi, 1993:8).

In contrast with the style of advertising that in the last decade seems to have followed a strategy of "*attracting by dividing'*, their stores were conceived for '*attracting by unifying'* and appear to be offering themselves as symbolic places for social reconciliation, where one can feel at home while celebrating the daily rite of mass consumption. It is not by chance that one never saw posters from the very controversial ad campaigns displayed in Benetton stores, even in periods when they were at their most reckless and were widely distributed. Instead, usually large posters of pictures from the Benetton fashion catalog were displayed, preserving the cheerful graphic style that characterized the cycle we called "universal harmony" that is found in Toscani's first ad campaigns for Benetton.

The commercial network's evolution and updating continued throughout the 1990s, primarily via an expansion in the size of sales outlets, which led to opening multi-purpose megastores, like those in London, New York, San Francisco, Barcelona, Moscow, and Riyadh and the multilevel store opened on Piazza Venezia in Rome in 1998. These were able to offer the entire range of Benetton brand clothing and accessories and to consolidate the prestige and global image of the group.

During these years the company experienced an important growth in terms of dividends and a worldwide increase in sales that brought its debt down to zero.

The 1996 record results were obtained thanks to a program of constant innovation in the corporate system, in later years integrated with incisive plans for containing management costs. Investments for innovation were used to update central processing and applications systems with the latest generation of technologies, and, above all, for continuous improvement in integrated logistics. In this area, new automated systems made possible a notable improvement in efficiency and speed for customer services, while greatly reducing costs.

To have an idea how the group has continued to grow during the third millennium, one can consult the Interactive Value Chain (Figure 2) found on Benetton's corporate website. This growth was predicated on an increase in speed for the entire system and was based on consumer confidence built and consolidated over more than forty years of activity.

Thanks to ample multimedia content, this tool allows the user to discover the world of the Benetton group via the various entries dedicated to the brands and to in-depth studies concerning "Products," "Corporate Governance," and "Communication" that provide users with a 360° view of the Benetton Company.

There is a description of a:

- Global brand (United Colors of Benetton) to which four other specialized brands

Figure 2. The interactive value chain

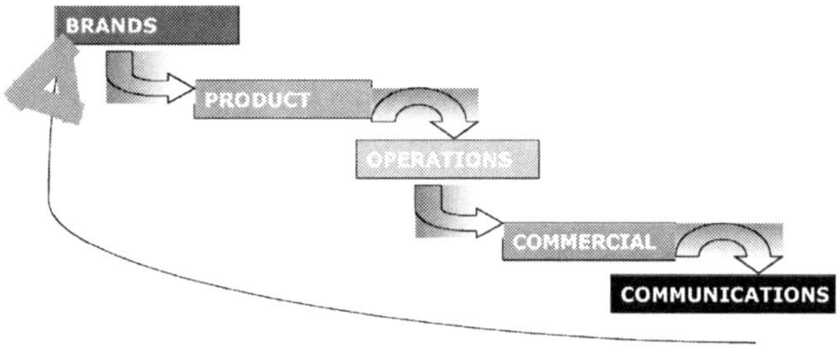

were added (Undercolors, Sisley, Playlife, Killer Loop);
- High-quality creative product that responds to fashion needs in real time;
- Industrial structure based on speed and efficiency;
- Network of 5,800 stores in 120 countries;
- Attention to communication via various instruments.

Alongside *Colors* (the "ideological manifesto," published by Benetton in seven bilingual editions distributed simultaneously around the world) and as part of the global flow of communication, in 1994 a research center for communication development was born: *Fabrica* (Figure 3).

Fabrica is a center for the study of communication that seeks to set itself off from the conventional directives and rhetoric of traditional mass media. *Fabrica* (which in Latin means "workshop") places emphasis on the principle of learning by doing, rather than on didactics; a voyage within experience. *Fabrica* is a production facility where experienced students/ co-workers participate in workshops to study production in publishing, graphics, photography, sound, video and design.

Figure 3. Fabrica

As described to this point, Benetton's corporate profile seems to go well beyond a simple industrial organization and instead represents a "cultural phenomenon."[6]

Luciano Benetton is an enlightened, postmodern patron of the arts who has embraced the attractiveness of a productive and cultural binomial world. To consolidate the company's ties to the cultural dimension, his *Foundation* is involved in historic research and in preservation of cultural patrimony. Research activities include education (courses, seminars and conferences) and publication and dissemination of findings. In fact, the *Benetton Foundation* promotes and directs studies, research and projects aimed at the preserving places, historical memory and other aspects of the area that surrounds the city of Treviso, Italy. This deepening of historic and cultural roots in the area from which the Benetton Group comes produces a double effect in terms on enriching the artistic patrimony of the culture of the Veneto Region while also consolidating the brand name "Benetton," that in terms of image needed strong stability to move from "international" to "global."

In 1993, the Japanese publisher *Robundo* distributed worldwide Tamotsu Yagi's book, *United Colors of Benetton: a Global Vision.* As Tamotsu Yagi explicitly acknowledged in an interview published in *News di Colors*, this book "*shows an industry in constant evolution, and engaged in many things in different areas, from the development of architectural projects and new products, to establishing a kind of experimental school.*"[7]

Global Vision contains clips from an imaginary film, able to encapsulate this large company's communication mix, which leans towards globality in terms of production as well as image. It is clear that when the product's various components are harmonious in expressing a single message, that is, when the name, price, the "made in," and the sales outlet all transmit the same concept, speak one language, and carry the same message, the media's job, and especially that of advertising which acts as a loudspeaker amplifying the company's image, will be much easier.

In fact, with its ad campaigns, Benetton was able to incite debates and continuous confrontations between journalists, writers and scholars in mass communication as well as among the individuals that constitute the company's target of reference: "buyers" and "potential buyers."

The photographs that Oliviero Toscani took personally or chose for advertising campaigns have been exhibited in museums and galleries in many countries and imitated or parodied by many advertising agencies.[8]

Since the end of the 1980s there have been many complaints, legal cases and acts of censorship as well as many positive opinions and expressions of solidarity. As has already been mentioned,

Figure 4. "Tribe"

each new advertising campaign marked a deeper divide and a more radical polarization in attitudes among those who were in favor and those against the communication strategies offered by Benetton.

In the second part of this article we will seek to highlight the social representations of the Benetton Company as expressed by young people, the target of the company's products and its advertising campaigns. We will also explore the possible links between the various global communication strategies implemented by the company and its production goals as well as the role that in the construction of that representation was mediated by the kind of social "meta-communication" that the company was able to create about itself and its own 'discourse' (the Benetton "case," as a cultural phenomenon).

THE BENETTON COMPANY SEEN THROUGH THE EYES OF THE TARGET: YOUTH

This study is part of a much larger product designed to examine social representations and corporate communication. We chose Benetton's 1992/1993 Autumn-Winter ad campaign precisely because of its ability to provoke extreme and clashing reactions in public opinion. Our hypothesis is that the Benetton ad campaigns that denounced the 'evils of the world' activated representations that were expressed in highly polarized evaluative attitudes because of the strong "ideological" connotations

Figure 5. "Interview"

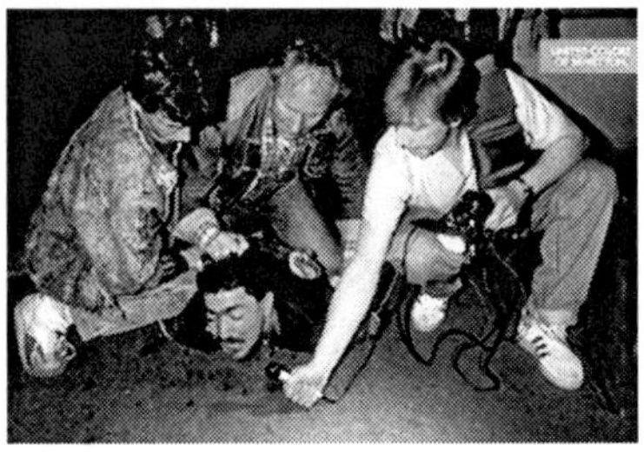

Figure 6. Cormorant

Figure 7. "Pigs in a dump"

Figure 8. "Bricklayers mate"

Figure 9. "Dirty white doll"

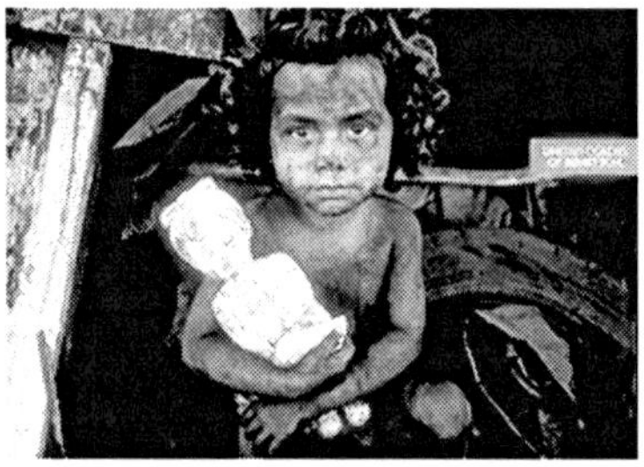

Figure 10. "Dealth penalty"

of these ads that spoke out against various social problems and the implicit request to "choose " a pro or contra position (Figures 4 to 10).

The 1992/93 Autumn/Winter campaign consisted of seven images, all focused on important social topics, each with a strong indictment of "the world's evils." It was a pessimistic progression of the narrative in previous campaigns, which had been more oriented towards an ideology of "fraternity" in the name of "The United Colors of Benetton."

First in Italy and later in other European countries (Austria, France and Portugal), we already have published the methodological plan for this extensive research project as well as results concerning the social representations that emerged from using the campaign ads as research material/ stimulus (cf. de Rosa, 1998; de Rosa & Losito, 1996; de Rosa & Smith, 1997a, 1997b, 1998a 1998b; de Rosa & Bocci, 2009)

Presented in all its aspects (cf. de Rosa, 1998), the methodological plan in particular was designed to reconstruct the representational dynamic in the links between social discourse "of" Benetton in its various expressions (*Colors*, social intervention experiences, etc.) and "on" Benetton. The latter was reconstructed on the basis of textual documents produced by experts and non-experts in scientific publications, interviews and articles published in the press, letters sent to newspapers or directly to the company as well as on responses from subjects in later phases of our study under the experimental conditions described below.

In this article we only will present and discuss some of the results obtained concerning the Benetton brand's social representations and, in particular, the discursive dynamic clearly explained by the associative network produced in reaction to the stimulus "Benetton." We will refer to reactions to the display of the campaign ads only to compare the polarization of the representational field relative to the ads themselves with that of the representations of the Benetton brand in function of the two hypotheses described below.

Hypotheses:

1. Alongside highly opposing reactions to the advertising campaign, the target would have a relatively positive representation of the company and that, paradoxically, the controversy caused by the "provocative" style of the campaign would be associated with a kind of meta-communication that reinforced positive connotations of the brand name.
2. Within the discourse dynamics of the associative networks (stimulus word "Benetton"), the social representation of the Benetton brand name would mediate between the company's advertisements (and other communicative strategies) and its industrial production and activities (goods and attributes).

RESEARCH METHODOLOGY PLAN

Experimental Conditions and Population

The stimuli (i.e. images from the 1992/93 Benetton Autumn/Winter campaign) were presented under two different conditions to two groups of subjects (one condition per group).

Condition A

In experimental condition A, 64 students, representative of the social psychology student population, were exposed to two stimulus images (Tribe and Interview) chosen from 7 images belonging to the previously mentioned ad campaign. These were chosen because of their elevated semantic ambiguity. The two slides were projected and the research tools administered under controlled conditions in the Faculty of Psychology 2 laboratory-classroom at the University of Rome "Sapienza."

Condition B

In condition B, we recreated a situation that produced stimuli that were as close as possible to reality. In order to simulate a condition of normal daily exposure, in contrast to laboratory conditions, and permit the formulation of more spontaneous answers, we gave the subjects magazines classified by type of readership (women, young people, family magazines, etc.) in which one of the seven ads were found.

960 subjects were selected for this second condition, equally distributed in terms of the variables sex, age (14-15; 18-19; 21-25), and profession (students or workers).

Table 1 illustrates the number of subject samples that produced the associative networks starting with the stimulus word "Benetton," the results of which are being presented and discussed in this article. In addition, the table illustrates how the subjects were divided into sub-samples in function of being exposed to the seven images from the Autumn/Winter 1992-93 ad campaign.

This second phase entailed creating a *condition of normal daily exposure* (the most natural possible condition for exposure) to all the seven stimulus images that were part of the 1992/93 Autumn/Winter ad campaign. To this end, each of the experiment subjects was presented with different magazines that had previously been classified by type in function of their typical

Table 1. Number of subjects interviewed and different kinds of exposure to the images in the two different experimental contexts

Benetton Autumn-Winter 1992\1993 Campaign	Number of Subjects and Conditions	
Image	**Condition A**	**Condition B**
Tribe	64 subjects	120 subjects
Interview	64 subjects	120 subjects
Pigs in a dump		120 subjects
Cormorant		120 subjects
Dirty white doll		120 subjects
Bricklayer's mate		120 subjects
Death penalty		240 subjects
TOTAL	**64 subjects**	**960 subjects**

readership (women, young people, families, etc.). The subjects were allowed to browse the magazines (one per subject) for 10 minutes. The objective was to study the type of strategy that guided the selection of ads, how attention was allocated, message comprehension and interpretation and memory of previous exposure to the same image.

Other intervening variables inherent to familiarization with the image and the mnemonic and cognitive processes tied to them were taken into consideration in the *condition of normal daily exposure:*

- prior knowledge of the message;
- familiarization with the image and linked memory and cognitive processes;
- intensity of the memory (how many times the subject had previously seen the ad);
- the location (where it was seen);
- contexts of eventual conversations concerning the message;
- the typology of interlocutors (if and with whom it was the subject of discussion).

The Techniques

The goal of the techniques used to collect the data for this study was to identify possible connections between the dependent variables linked to the message/advertisement (descriptions of the image; interpretation of the message; interpretation of the meaning attributed to the message by the source; memory reactivation processes; evaluation of the message's effectiveness; evaluation of the message's moral acceptability; identification of the message's topic) and variables outside the message (attitude to message's topic; purchasing behavior concerning Benetton products; socio-demographic data).

A series of tools were created and administered to carry out these surveys. They are listed below in the order in which they were administered to the sample subjects:

1. Associative network (for the stimulus words: image, Benetton, I);
2. Description of the image (free texts);
3. The subject's interpretation of the message (free texts);
4. The subject's interpretation of the meaning attributed to the message by the source (free texts);
5. Analysis of mnemonic reactivation processes (questionnaire);
6. Evaluation of the message's efficacy (questionnaire);

Equation 1.

$$\text{Polarity Index (P)} = \frac{\text{No. of positive words - No. of negative words}}{\text{Total No. of associated words}}$$

Equation 2.

$$\text{Neutrality Index (N)} = \frac{\text{No. of neutral words - (No. of positive words + No. of negative words)}}{\text{Total No. of associated words}}$$

7. Identification of the message/denunciation subject (questionnaire);
8. Attitude towards the message/denunciation subject (questionnaire);
9. Purchasing behavior for Benetton products (questionnaire);
10. Socio-demographic data concerning the research subjects (questionnaire).

Concerning the present discussion, the *associative network* was the most important technique used (see de Rosa, 1995, for a complete description of this projective technique). It was the used first in order to prevent responses being anchored by information from the questionnaire that could bias word elicitation. The technique requires participants first to associate words with stimulus words and then to establish connections and branching patterns between the elicited words that are written around the stimulus word found in the center of the page. It enables respondents to specify the structure of a semantic field by themselves. Therefore, starting from a free association test, you obtain a textual web. The associative network also provides information about the order in which words come to mind. This order indicates both their saliency and the level of stereotyping of the elicited representations. Because of their high level of accessibility, participants' first words may be their most salient as well as the most socially shared).

The associative network requires people to attribute a particular polarity to each word (positive, negative or neutral) to describe its connotations. This enables not only the structure and content of a social representation to be revealed, but also the "polarization of the semantic field' (i.e. the evaluative and attitudinal aspects of the representation). A polarity index calculates the positive, negative, or neutral connotations of the free associations evoked by each of the stimulus words used in this study: image, brand name. This index, which varies from +1 to -1 is calculated using Equation 1.

A second "neutrality" control index, which also varies between -1 and +1, is also calculated. In this way the structure, content, and polarity of particular representations are established (Equation 2).

Associative network processing has two objectives in terms of data analysis,: the first is to describe the structure and content of the representational fields associated with the stimuli, achieved by lexical correspondence analysis: SPAD-T (see Lebart, Morineau, & Beçue, 1989). The second is to reconstruct the discourse dynamics implicit in the structure of the associative network by applying a content analysis program DISCAN to the corpus of elicited words (see Maranda, 1990). Technical details of these analyses are described elsewhere.

Data Analysis Procedures

Filemaker memorized words in their order of appearance, branching patterns and connections and then transferred them to Word.

Having two different objectives, the data was analysed using two different procedures. The first described the structure and content of the representational fields associated with the different stimuli; the second reconstructed the discourse dynamics implicit in the associative network's structure.

1. *Analysis of lexical correspondence* (ACL) using the SPAD.T program[9]. The objective was to *identify the structure and content of the representational field* associated with the various stimulus words. Once distinct data bases containing all the *associated words* (active variables) were available and all the *ramifications* and *connections* had been identified by the associative network, the necessary procedures to prepare the files of *illustrative variables* were performed. A cross-analysis of the variables identified by the different survey techniques was conducted, including those identified via questionnaire and those concerning the polarity indices identified by the associative networks. Among the many procedures offered by the SPAD-T program, as analysis strategies we used: Artex, Selox, Numer, and Aspar for active variables (words) and Ardic, Selec and Posit for illustrative variables.
2. To achieve our second goal focused on *content and discursive analysis* we used the DiscAn program[10] that allowed us to identify the organization of the functional roles of the texts' associative dynamic.

The data obtained via questionnaires was organized into contingency tables and then treated with the usual cross-referencing procedures (CHI^2) using the S.P.S.S. program. After appropriate re-categorization, the resulting balanced variables were then extracted as illustrative variables using a SPAD-T analysis of the associative networks.

Following this, a final analysis using the ALCESTE. program[11] was conducted on the textual data (free text) related to the three open questions on the questionnaire (description of the image, the subject's attribution of meaning and in the subject's opinion, the meaning the source attributed to the image).

Given the massive quantity of data and the complex picture of the results that emerge from it, we decided to choose the results concerning the "*discursive dynamic*" related to the stimulus word "Benetton" for presentation in this article. Before continuing, we believe it will be helpful to first provide some information necessary to understand the analysis conducted using the DiscAn program, which is not yet well known. We will refer briefly to a previous article (de Rosa & Losito, 1996).

The DiscAn program was used to show the structure of the functional roles of the associative dynamics of texts.

Like most content analysis programs, DiscAn analyses language corpora into alphabetical and frequency-based lists of lexical units (words, syntagmas, etc.) as well as providing other options such as collocation research and dictionary and thesaurus construction. Once lexical units from a corpus have been organized into a thesaurus according to the researcher's specifications, discourse analysis processes can be applied to this "meta-text."

A single categorization system was used to obtain the DiscAn results. The categories used for the "Benetton" and "image" associative networks included:

- product;
- brand name;
- economic/commercial aspects;
- company leaders and source of the advertisements;
- advertising in general;
- Benetton advertising;
- image;
- message;
- advertisement content;
- advertisement characters;
- context.

Each of the 11 categories included several modalities (43 in total).

This corpus content categorization system was used to organize the lexical units. Classification (thesaurus creation) of associative networks produced "meta-texts" for discourse analysis at a semantic level.

In DiscAn the categories are treated as semantic nodes. DiscAn calculates the contribution of each category to the map for each node of the semantic network (level of activity). A node might therefore generate a wide network of semantic flow, but be relatively inactive, while another might be very active but at the same time hinder semantic flow.

DiscAn calculates the probability of transition from one category to a previous or subsequent one (first level Markov chains). In this way probabilistic chains of semantic nodes represented in the thesaurus categories can be constructed; the degree of reception (input) and emission (output) for each of these can also be calculated and their role in the semantic map defined.

The degree of reception of a node (d-) is termed "internal semigrade" and the degree of emission (d+) "external semigrade." When the internal semigrade of a node is greater than the external semigrade, we have an attractor or "absorber" node, whose input number is higher than its output. If the internal semigrade is lower than the external semigrade, we have a diffractor or "source" node, whose output number is higher than its input. When the internal semigrade is equal to the external semigrade, we have a transmitter or "relay" node, which neither reduces nor expands the discourse dynamics of the corpus but simply acts as a connector. A high number of relays, however, indicates the presence of stereotypes.

This data enables the semantic "activity" of a corpus to be described. Its internal dynamics depend on the intensity with which each node absorbs, diffracts or transmits. DiscAn calculates the d+/d- score for each node A score of 1 means that it is a relay node, if it is greater than 1, it is a source node and if it is less than 1, it is an absorber node. The total of the internal and external semigrade scores for the respective frequencies (d- f) + (d+ f) shows each node's contribution to the global activity of the corpus and its relevance in terms of discourse as well as semantics. A map of this activity can also be produced from this data (de Rosa & Losito, 1996).

DiscAn was used in this research because of the similarity between the dynamics of the elicited words and the dynamics of discourse: they both have a morphological structure that can be analyzed overall in terms of internal relations.

Textual Analysis Categories

Below is found the list of the principle analysis categories used to transform the list of the 9465 words (complete associated dictionary) elicited in response to the stimulus "Benetton" in a meta-text that can be analyzed using DiscAN.

To guarantee that the DiscAn results could be compared to each other, even if derived from associative networks that sometimes referred to advertisements and sometimes to the brand, in order to identify categories that could be generalized as well as being inclusive of the elements present in the entire corpus, we established a single categorization plan which was based on all the associated dictionaries.

Categorization plan for the networks "Benetton" and "image."

- Product
  - -as such (ex. sweaters, pants, wristwatches, look)=1
  - their attributes (ex. warm, expensive, fashionable, appealing to the masses, national-popular, etc.)=2
  - consumers (ex. children, young people, etc.)=3
- Brand Name
  - (ex. O12, brand)=4
  - their attributes (ex. Maletton (play on company name, in Italian bene = good, male =bad), international, etc.)=5
- Economic\Commercial Aspects
  - entrepreneurial activities (ex. stores, franchising, company, sector, fashion)=6
  - entrepreneurial objectives (ex. money, success economics, business, etc.)=7
  - sponsorship (ex. Formula 1, sports teams)=8
- Company Learders And Advertisement Source
  - protagonists (ex. Toscani, Benetton, Luciano...)=9
  - their attributes (senator, La Malfa, clever, from the Veneto..)=10
- Advertising In General
  - communication (ex. publicity, advertising, image)=11
  - channels and tools (ex. photographs, magazine, billboard, technique)=12
- Benetton Advertising
  - communication (ex. publicity concerning Benetton)=13
  - its attributes (current, shocking, strong, rule breaking, colorful, surprising, etc.)=14
  - target audience (ex. young people, women, etc.)=15
- Image
  - visual/perceptive aspects (ex. color, green, white, light blue)=16
  - their attributes (ex. original, imagination, interesting, innovative, stimulating)=17
- Message
  - intention (ex. denunciation...)=18
  - message results (ex. scandal, clamor)=19
  - emotional correlations for the user (ex. pain, tenderness, emotion, crudeness)=20
  - attributes referring to message content (ex. rhetorical, serious, connotation...)=21
- Advertisement Content
  - specific topic (ex. mafia, racism, work, races, death penalty)=22
  - values (ex. liberty, transgression, courage, truth; joy, peace..)=23
  - negative values (ex. violence, abuse, cruelty, indifference...)=24
  - non specific macro issue (ex. social reality, current events, politics, social problems...)=25
  - content elements and details
    - present (ex. electric chair, cormorant, asphalt...)=26
    - absent (ex. arrows, drum, camera..)=27
    - external elements evoked in the associative network for the stimulus (ex. Sofia Loren, Clinton etc.)=28
- Advertisement Characters
  - Individual protagonists:
    - present (policeman, journalist, non-European immigrant)=29
    - absent (photographer...)=30
  - Collective/institutional protagonists:
    - present (tribe, young people, journalism, police...)=31
    - absent 32

- Ethnic/racial identity:
    - (ex. Israeli, Moroccan, Indian)=33
    - physical/external attributes (ex. fat, tall)=34
    - personality traits (ex. shy, introverted, extroverted)=35
    - psychological condition (ex. uncomfortable, embarrassed, afraid, etc.)=36
    - behavioral qualifiers (absurd, boss, cynical)=37
    - verbal or gestural actions represented or presumed (help, murder, etc.)=38
- Context
  - Circumstantial and relational context:
    - present (arrest, environment, dark, closing)=39
    - absent (friendship, community)=40
    - socio-geographic context (USA, London, Italy, United States)=41
    - setting for administration (ex. supervised practical experience program, university)=42
    - other=43

PRESENTATION AND DISCUSSION OF RESULTS

In order to quickly and efficiently verify the first of the two hypotheses presented in this article, we selected the most synthetic and illustrative results from the many that emerged from the various analysis procedures available on the tools mentioned above. We compared polarity indices of the representational fields associated to the various ads from the advertising campaign under examination and the polarity indices relative to the semantic fields created by the subjects for the stimulus word "Benetton."

With a glance at the graph that illustrates the results (cf. Figure 11) it is possible to confirm the hypothesis relative to the company's prevalently positive representation compared to the prevalently negative, or at least ambivalent and contrastive, polarization of the representations evoked by the advertisements under study. Further analyzed in other articles, (de Rosa, 1998; de Rosa & Smith, 1997a, 1997b, 1998a 1998b; Kirchler & de Rosa, 1996; de Rosa & Bocci, 2009) the results confirm that the "confrontational" style of the company's communications, which aim to provoke a particularly animated and contrastive discussion, paradoxically have contributed to the creation of a kind of functional meta-communication that reinforces a positive connotation for the 'brand name'.

The graph highlights that the average polarity index relative to individual images is tendentially negative for almost all of them, in particular for the photographs *Interview* and *Electric chair*. The negative reaction to photographs in which children figure (as in *Tribe* and *Child labor)* was more attenuated, probably because of the effect of the "tenderness" evoked by the little protagonists. Conducted using the content of the images as an independent variable and the average polarity indexes relative to each individual image as a dependent variable, analysis of the variance shows that when the kind of photograph administered is changed, the evaluative reaction expressed about it also significantly varies ($F= 12.58$; $p < 0.001$).

The difference between the prevalently negative evaluation vis-à-vis the seven stimuli advertisements and the positive evaluation concerning the Benetton brand is shown in the figure below. It illustrates the notable "disproportion" between the average polarity indices relative to each individual image (which as you can see are almost always negative) and the average polarity indices concerning the brand name (which are always positive).

Figure 11. Indexes of polarity relating to the seven images (campaign 1992/93) and to Benneton brand

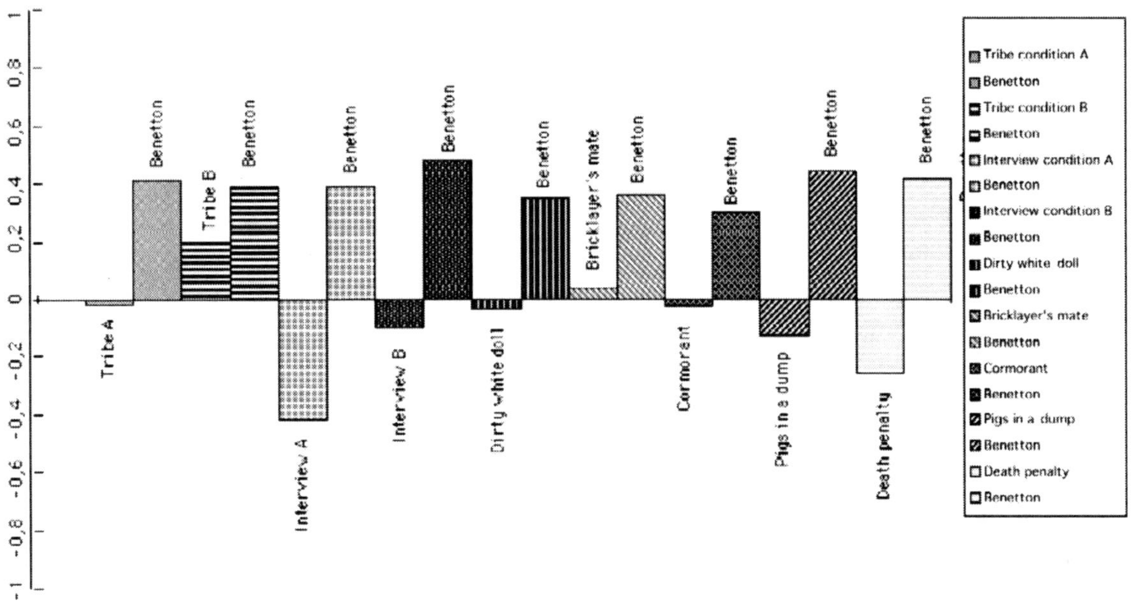

These results were also supported by the significant differences between the average values were obtained via T di student. As far as concerns condition B, the difference between the average polarity indices relative to the brand (X = 0.40) and to the seven images (X = -0.07) is extremely significant (t=-21.73; p<0.001). Analogous results were obtained in condition A. In fact, the difference between the average polarity indices relative to the brand (X = 0.39) and the two images (X = -0.23) is highly significant in this case as well (t = -14.46; p < 0.001).

The average neutrality indices highlighted a strong inclination towards expressing a "clear" stance, sometimes positive (in the case of the brand), sometimes bipolarized but tendentially negative in the case of the seven images. In condition B, the average neutrality indices relative to the brand (X = - 0.54) and to the images (X = -0.63) are, in fact, both highly negative. This shows that there were few neutral associations. However, a comparison between the averages highlights the existence of a significant difference between the two neutrality indices. The evaluative responses vis-à-vis the brand are more neutral than those expressed concerning the seven images (t=-5.26; p< 0.001). In condition A, the neutrality indices relative to the brand (X = -0.46) and to the two images (X = -0.9) are, as in the previous case, both negative even if in the second condition the difference between the averages is not significant (t = -0.76).

As regards the second hypothesis, Figure 12 shows the DiscAn results for the associative networks in terms of the discourse dynamics activated by the stimulus word "Benetton." It shows the links between the categories of words elicited from subjects in response to the brand name[16] and illustrates the semantic connections of the "Benetton" representation in terms of all its advertising, marketing, and production activities. This network seems to occur despite the contrasting polarity indexes for the advertising and brand name representations and confirms the effectiveness of the company's communicative strategies.

The most obvious result is the central role of "goods," which seems to act as the organizing nucleus for all the other source/relay elements.

Figure 12. Semantic map: graphic visualization of DiscAn results

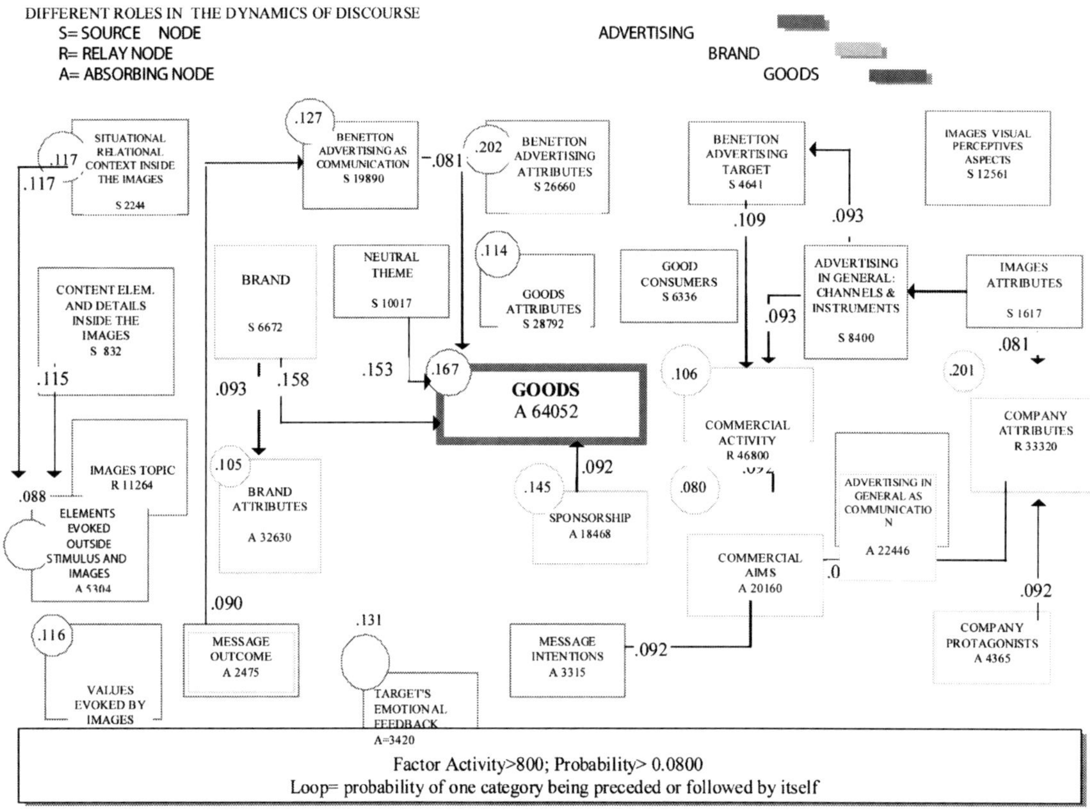

"Sources," "goods attributes" and "Benetton advertising attributes" have the highest level of activity. "Goods" is the biggest "absorber" and has the highest level of activity. The role of "goods" is central: all the other categories on the map (advertising, brand name, economic/commercial aspects) revolve around it.

Associations produced in response to the stimulus "Benetton" refer to different areas. The area relating to "production" was described first, then the area relating to Benetton advertising, specific Benetton campaign images used in the research, advertising in general, economic/commercial activity, the source and its attributes and the campaign message. This semantic route can be traced on the map via source categories in the upper half and absorber categories in the lower half.

The dual role played by advertising in the semantic dynamics is particularly interesting. It acts as a source (i.e., it is greater than 1) for the Benetton stimulus, particularly for the "message outcome," "emotional correlates" and "message intention" categories, and as an absorber (i.e., it is less than 1) for advertising in general. This highlights the more active role Benetton advertising played in activating sources for semantic routes compared with advertising in general, which seems to have had a more receptive/passive role.

The results for the advertising images show links between the descriptive level ("context elements" and "details present in the images" are both source nodes.), the interpretative level ("topic" is a mediator and relay), and the evaluative level (values evoked from the images is an absorber node). As regards links between advertising and company production aspects, "Benetton advertising" seems to open up a discourse about the "product." This was a surprising result since this discourse had been removed or denied during the advertising campaigns. Benetton advertising seems to play a diffracting role in the associative dynamics as if, starting from the advertising message, the associative discourse was able to act as a source for a number of semantic paths. These are clearly more complex links than those that start from the brand name and its attributes or from "product attributes" and "consumers," all of which tend to revolve around the product.

In conclusion, in the description, interpretation, and evaluation of Benetton advertising, the associative discourse expands in the direction of economic/commercial aspects and source attributes and eventually focuses on the Group's "product" and "protagonists."

This link seems to stand out despite the negative attitude registered when the polarity indices associated to the representations of the advertisements related were compared to those of the brand and offers another confirmation of the efficacy of the company's communication strategies despite the numerous controversies.

Is the key to the success of Benetton's communication formula that it follows the path of the discursive dynamic, starting from the world of communications, then moving to that of the company and its marking strategies and finally concentrating on production and assets?

In the final analysis, does the company increase its sales by provoking fierce controversies and rejecting the product that is found at the center of the representational field?

This company "born from ideas" never ceases to surprise. Once the brand had been enriched by the value added by the shock ad campaigns, it did not hesitate to change course and return to themes that are apparently twenty years old but are once again current. This is true not only in Italy, but also in the rest of the world.

CONCLUSION

While it is clear that the results of this research are limited to one case and the population we studied, it does confirm the success of Benetton's communication strategy. Social discourse "by" Benetton "about" social issues set off a social discourse "about Benetton" which then set up a meta representation of the brand name: the brand name is expanded and emphasized within self-reflecting circuits which feed off the contrasting forces activated by the source of the message. This process suggests a paradoxical effect (as shown in the graph) that despite powerful resistance to accepting Benetton's communicative style by a large portion of the target audience, a positive

Figure 13. F=f(C,Rs): fashion as a function of communication and social representations

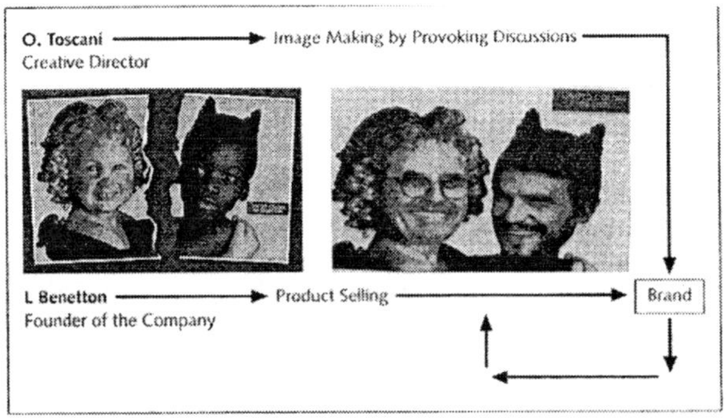

Figure 14. Two strategies, two processes

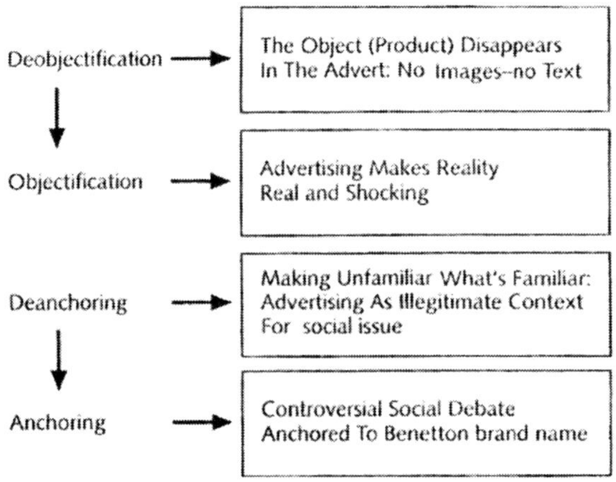

Figure 15. Face to the death

Figure 16. Undercolors collection 2008

representation of the brand name was still created by communicative strategies capable of arousing controversial attitudes to ad campaigns anchored in controversial social representations (Figure 13).

However, is it possible to explain this phenomenon more completely? What did these advertisements change? From what we have seen, what in their character enables them to be certain of success? One way of answering these questions is the connection between Benetton's advertising style and the behavior of an active minority with the fashion world.

As we know, consistency creates conflict through a "virtual" worldwide debate. This conflict or controversy is amplified by the multiple communication genres, including advertisements (icons), interviews and press releases (texts), texts with images (*Global Vision*, *Colors*, the Benetton website), and social actions. As is known, this may be a deliberate attempt to be considered an "active minority," at least in the advertising community. Achieving social visibility (de Rosa, 1998, de Rosa & Smith, 1997a, 1997b, 1998a) is linked to favorable evaluation of the brand. Other observers have commented that Benetton's advertisements have the merit of being noticed and being talked about (Kotler, 1997; Semprini, 1996). We will examine the character of these messages and why they have succeeded in changing advertising practices. It is a critical practice in the sense that it is normal practice for an "active minority" and just a means towards an end. That end is to innovate and to generate a new social representation of the company that chooses to adopt such a strategy. Put in more "commercial" terms, "the goal is to sell" the brand.

If we were to summarize how social representations are shaped during communication, we would say that the two processes (defamiliarization and decontextualization) observed in Benetton's advertisements work alongside the processes of anchoring and objectification that makes the familiar unfamiliar. They create a code for distinguishing and recognizing Benetton's messages as advertisements. Rather than being noise or redundancies, they become events or "happenings" (Figure 14).

Negative reactions were based on the presumed illegitimacy a commercial company intruding in a discourse space traditionally the domain of medical/scientific, legislative, and political discourse communities (Semprini, 1996). Toscani's response to these criticisms was to claim the right to take a different, more colorful approach to traditional commercial advertising, whose images were illusory and falsified reality. Toscani claimed that his portrayal of worldwide "reality" with its full horror of violence, illness, social and natural disasters (e.g., immigration, racism, terrorism, mafia, death penalty, ecological disasters), and his use of issues which previously had only been used in nonprofit advertising was justified not only in terms of an abstract right to "know the truth,"[10] but also commercial logic---sales figures invariably increased after each campaign. Indeed, because of the success of advertising campaigns based on the use of universal issues like sex, religion, race, life and death[11] Benetton decided not to conduct market research on the results of these ad campaigns.

Benetton's use of the HIV issue is one of the best illustrations of its strategic change towards social action. HIV is a topic which has appeared consistently in Benetton ads since 1991, for example, "Condoms" (1991) and "dying AIDS patient with family" (1992). Later, however, Benetton did not simply use the AIDS issue in a message/accusation format. It also supported programs for AIDS prevention among young people by distributing condoms in schools, donating money for AIDS research, exhibiting a huge condom shaped monument in public, and devoting a special issue of *Colors* to AIDS.

In using its advertising to try to demonstrate that it was not an enterprise that profited from human suffering, and that it was genuinely concerned with social issues, Benetton's strategy was clearly an attempt to respond to criticism provoked by Benetton's previous ad campaigns. Their goal was to re-establish a dialogue with those who, after the shock campaigns, had become extremely negative towards the company, including recognized humanitarian institutions. It seems that this dialogue, which for many years has been modulated by alternating the rhetoric between hard and soft messages, was broken off definitively after the 2000 "Looking Death in the Face" campaign (Figure 15).

Benetton's recent history and its communication strategies after the shock campaign on the death penalty, which caused Benetton's "divorce" with Toscani, confirms the hypothesis in de Rosa's (2001) chapter on the need for a new formula after the Benetton\Toscani breakup which consists of a return to the past. This future/past strategy has as its goal to re-establish a brand image of "universal harmony," as demonstrated by the advertising campaign found in Figure 16.

REFERENCES

Baldini, M. (2003). *Popper e Benetton: Epistemologia per gli imprenditori e gli economisti.* Roma, Italy: Armando.

Barthes, R. (1964). Rhétorique de l'image. *Communications.*

Barthes, R. (1964). Eléments de sémiologie. *Communications.*

Brunetti, G. (2004). *Benetton: da United Colors a edizione holding*. Torino, Italy: Utet.

de Rosa, A. S. (1990). Per un approccio multimetodo allo studio delle Rappresentazioni Sociali. *Rassegna di Psicologia, 3*, 101–152.

de Rosa, A. S. (1993). Social representations and attitudes: Problems of coherence between the theoretical definition and procedure of research. *Papers on Social Representations, 2*(3), 178–192.

de Rosa, A. S. (1995). Le "réseau d'associations" comme méthode d'étude dans la recherche sur les représentations sociales. *Cahiers Internationaux de Psychologie Sociale, 28*, 96–122.

de Rosa, A. S. (1998). How to sell pullovers by provoking discussion on social issues. The role of the advertising for activating and diffusing controversial social representations. In Rigas, V. (Ed.), *S.R. and contemporary social problems* (pp. 228–277). Athens, Greece: Ellinika Grammata Publisher.

de Rosa, A. S. (2000). North-South-East-West: The four points of the compass in the European skies. A comparison of views from different latitudes in the social representations of young people in ten European Countries. In Chaib, M., & Orfali, B. (Eds.), *Social representations and communicative processes* (pp. 51–91). Jönköping, Sweden: Jönköping University Press.

de Rosa, A. S. (2001). The king is naked. Critical advertisement and fashion: The Benetton phenomenon. In Deaux, K., & Philogène, G. (Eds.), *Representations of the social* (pp. 48–82). Oxford, UK: Blackwell.

de Rosa, A. S. (2002). The associative network: A technique for detecting structure, contents, polarity and stereotyping index of the semantic fields. *European Review of Applied Psychology*, 181–200.

de Rosa, A. S. (2003). Le réseau d'association. Une technique pour détecter la structure, les contenus, les indices de polarité, de neutralité et de stéréotypie du champ sémantique liés aux représentations sociales. In Abric, J. C. (Ed.), *Méthodes d'étude des Représentations Sociales* (pp. 81–117). Ramonville Saint Agne, France: Erès.

de Rosa, A. S. (2003). The social representations "of" and "within" the changing organizational contexts: The case of the Italian National Institute for Social Provisions and Pensions (INPS). In M. Lavallée, S. Vincent, C. Ouellet & C. Garnier (Eds.), *Les représentations sociales. Constructions nouvelles* (pp. 683-715). Montréal, Canada: Groupe d'étude sur l'interdisciplinarité et les representations socials. Retrieved from http://www.unites.uqam.ca/ geirso/livre_repres_sociales/index_livre.htm

de Rosa, A. S. (2005). A Rede Associativa: Uma técnica para captar a estrutura, os conteùdos, e os ìndices de polaridade, neutralidade e estereotipia dos campos semànticos relacionados com a Representações Sociais. In Paredes Moreira, A. S. (Ed.), *Perspectivas Teorico-metodològicas em Representações Sociais* (pp. 61–127). João Pessoa, Brazil: Editora Universitária – UFPB.

de Rosa, A. S. (2006). The boomerang effect of radicalism in discursive psychology: A critical overview of the controversy with the Social Representations Theory. *Journal for the Theory of Social Behaviour, 36*(2), 161–201. doi:10.1111/j.1468-5914.2006.00302.x de Rosa, A. S. (2006). From September 11 to the Iraq War. Shocking images and the polarization of individual and socially negotiated emotions in the construction of mass flashbulb memory. In Gertz, S., Breaux, J.-P., & Valsiner, J. (Eds.), *Semiotic rotations: Modes of meaning in cultural worlds* (pp. 137–168). Greenwich, CT: Information Age Press.

de Rosa, A. S. (Ed.). (2012forthcoming). *Social Representations in the "social arena."*. New York, London: Routledge.

de Rosa, A. S., & Bocci, E. (2002). E-branding strategies and development of the e-commerce and tourism: The case of Italian tour operators. *International Business & Economics Research Journal, 1*(10), 11–24.

de Rosa, A. S., & Bocci, E. (2006). Social representations and enterprise communication: Profile of the Benetton galaxy between organizational dynamics and featured representations in the target sample. In A. S. de Rosa (Ed.), *8th I.C.S.R. Proceedings, Rome: Rocografica, 2006*, (p. 115).

de Rosa, A. S., & Bocci, E. (2009). Représentations sociales et communication de l'entreprise: Profil de la galaxie Benetton entre la dynamique organisationnelle et les représentations présentes dans l'échantillon cible. *Special Issue of Revue leti im on Les Représentations Sociales et Communication*, 301-342.

de Rosa, A. S., Bocci, E., & Saurini, S. (2006). Risk perception as a motivational barrier for online purchasing. In Zappalà, S., & Gray, C. (Eds.), *Impact of e-commerce on consumers and small firms* (pp. 235–248). London, UK: Ashgate.

de Rosa, A. S., & D'Ambrosio, M. (2005). L'Union Européenne de 15 à 25: Représentations, projections et previsions des jeunes étudiants de neuf nationalités un an avant l'Elargissement. *Connexion, 84*(2), 129–146. doi:10.3917/cnx.084.0129

de Rosa, A. S., D'Ambrosio, M., & Bocci, E. (2005). EuroSKYcompass: Nation, Europe, world, social representations systems in action and construction. *Psihologia Sociala. Buletinul Laboratorului Psicologia câmpului social, 15*, 47-81.

de Rosa, A. S., & Farr, R. (2001). Icon and symbol: Two sides of the coin in the investigation of social representations. In Buschini, F., & Kalampalikis, N. (Eds.), *Penser la vie, le social, la nature. Mélanges en hommage à Serge Moscovici* (pp. 237–256). Paris, France: Les Editions de la Maison des Sciences de l'Homme.

de Rosa, A. S., & Losito, G. (1996). E' bianca o nera? Interpretazioni conflittuali e atteggiamenti contrastanti nei confronti della comunicazione pubblicitaria "ambigua" di Benetton. *Rassegna di Psicologia, 2*(13), 75–117.

de Rosa, A. S., & Mormino, C. (2002). Au confluent de la mémoire sociale: Etude sur l'identité nationale et européenne. In Laurens, S., & Roussiau, N. (Eds.), *La mémoire sociale. Identités et Représentations Sociales* (pp. 119–137). Rennes, France: Les Presses Universitaires de Rennes.

de Rosa, A. S., & Smith, A. (1996a). Tecnica retorica e pubblicità: il caso Benetton. *Informazione Radio TV*, 2.

de Rosa, A. S., & Smith, A. (1996b). Discourse and image: Two sources and ways for expressing social representations. In J. C. Abric (Ed.), *Acts of the 3rd International Conference on Social Representations* (Aix-en-Provence, France 27-30 September 1996). Paris, France: Harmattan.

de Rosa, A. S., & Smith, A. (1997a). Strategie comunicative da minoranza attiva nello scenario dei pubblicitari: il caso Benetton-Toscani. *Micro & Macromarketing, 1*, 99–126.

de Rosa, A. S., & Smith, A. (1997b). Cmpameruu obujehuk akmubhoro mehumuhcmba b peknamhon cujehapuu: Benetton-Toscani. *Psychological Review, 1*(4), 39–55.

de Rosa, A. S., & Smith, A. (1998a). Retorica pubblicitaria e rappresentazioni sociali. La comunicazione Benetton come caso esemplificativo. *Ikon, Forme e processi del comunicare, 37*, 173-208.

de Rosa, A. S., & Smith, A. (1998b). Représentations sociales polémiques et styles d'influence minoritaire: Le cas Benetton-Toscani en tant que 'minorité active' dans le scenario des publicitaires. *Bulletin de Psychologie, 51*(436), 399–416.

Eco, U. (1975). *Trattato di semiotica generale*. Milano, Italy: Bompiani.

Eco, U. (1990). *I limiti dell'interpretazione*. Milano, Italy: Bompiani.

Farr, R. (1993). The theory of social representations: Whence and whither? *Textes sur les Représentations Sociales, 2*(3), 130-138.

Favero, G. (2005). *I colori del successo*. Milano, Italy: EGEA.

Gioiosa, C., de Rosa, A. S., & D'Ambrosio, M. (2005). Exploring the structure of social representations of the Euro via facet theory approach and WSSA1. In Bilsky, W., & Elizur, D. (Eds.), *Facet theory: Design, analysis and applications* (pp. 57–64). Prague, Czech Republic: Agentura Action M.

Kirchler, E., & de Rosa, A. S. (1996). Wirkungsanalyse von Werbebotschaften mittels Assoziationsgeflecht. Spontane Reaktionen auf und überlegte Beschreibung von Benetton-Werbebildern. *Jahrbuch der Absatz und Verbrauchsforschung, 1*, 67–89.

Kotler, P. (1997). *Marketing management casi*. Torino, Italy: ISEDI.

Landi, P. (1993). *News*. Treviso, Italy: Colors Pubblications.

Landi, P., & Pollini, L. (1993). *Cosa c'entra l'aids con i maglioni?* Milano, Italy: Arnoldo Mondadori Editore.

Lebart, L., Morineau, A., & Becue, M. (1989). *SPADT: Système portable pour l'analyse des Données textuelles, Manuel de l'utilisateur*. Paris, France: Cisia.

Lorusso, M. (2007). *Italia in svendita: la privatizzazione delle aziende statali: politica, impresa, etica*. Milano, Italy: Il sole 24 ore.

Losito, G. (1993). *L'analisi del contenuto nella ricerca sociale*. Milano, Italy: Franco Angeli.

Losito, G. (1994). *Il potere dei media*. Roma, Italy: Nuova Italia Scientifica.

Mantle, J. (2000). *Benetton: The family, the business and the brand*. London, UK: Little Brown & C.

Mantle, J. (2002). *Benetton*. London, UK: Penguin Books.

Maranda, P. (1990). *DiscaAn: Users manual*. Quebec, Canada: Nadeau Caron Informatique.

Moliner, P. (1996). *Images et représentations sociales*. Grenoble, France: Presses.

Moscovici, S. (1984). The phenomenon of social representations. In Farr, R., & Moscovici, S. (Eds.), *Social representations*. Paris, France & Cambridge, UK: M.S.H. & Cambridge University Press.

Mulas, A. (2004). *Architettura per Benetton*. Milano, Italy: Skira.

Nardin, G. (1987). *La Benetton Strategia e struttura di un'impresa di successo*. Roma, Italy: Edizioni Lavoro.

Pagnucco Salvemini, L. (2003). *Benetton/Toscani. Storia di una avventura, 1984-2000*. Azzano San Paolo, Italy: Bolis.

Penz, E. (2006). Researching the socio-cultural context: Putting social representations theory into action. *International Marketing Review, 23*(4), 418–437. doi:10.1108/02651330610678985

Petrillo, G., & Lionetto, S. (1996). Spot anti-Aids e rappresentazioni sociali. *Ikon, 32*, 289–320.

Reinert, M. (1992). *Logiciel ALCESTE pour l'analyse des données textuelles (version 2.0)*. Université de Toulouse-Le Mirail C.N.R.S.

Romano, D. (1988).*Immagine Marketing e Comunicazione*. Bologna, Italy: Il Mulino.

Sabbadin, E. (1997). *Marketing della distribuzione e marketing integrato: I casi Marks & Spencer e Benetton*. Milano, Italy: Egea.

Saviane, S. (1998). *Il miliardario: La vita segreta di Luciano Benetton*. Venezia, Italy: Marsilio.

Semprini, A. (1993). *Lo sguardo semiotico*. Milano, Italy: Franco Angeli.

Semprini, A. (1994a). *Marche e mondi possibili*. Milano, Italy: Franco Angeli.

Semprini, A. (1994b). Benetton: dalla missione all' azione. *Micro & Macro Marketing, 2*, 157–173.

Semprini, A. (1997). *Analyser la communication. Comment analyser les images, les médias, la publicité. Paris, France: L'Harmattan, 1996; tr. it. Analizzare la comunicazione. Come analizzare la pubblicità, le immagini, i media*. Milano, Italy: F. Angeli.

Tafani, E. (2006). Image and social representations: Conceptualization and perspectives of application in the fields of marketing, advertising and communication. In A. S. de Rosa, (Ed.), *8th I.C.S.R. Proceedings,* Rome: Rocografica, (pp. 112-115).

Toscani, O. (1995). *Ciao Mamma*. Milano, Italy: Mondadori.

Usunier, J.-C., & Lee, J. (2009). *Marketing across cultures*. Canada: Financial Time Prentice Hall.

Yagy, T. (1993). *United colors of Benetton: A global vision*. Japan: Robundo.

ENDNOTES

1. Luciano Benetton has been in charge of sales since the company was established in 1965. Although there was a clear division of labor among the Benettons (Luciano – sales, Giuliana - production, Gilberto - management, Carlo – physical plant), because of his status as the older brother and his character, it was Luciano who became the charismatic figure of the group (cf Kotler, 1997).
2. According to Semprini, that ingenuousness was determined by the impossibility for the poster medium to segment the *target,* which therefore becomes indiscriminately exposed to messages without the ability to be selectively verified by the message's source. "*Because of their maximum visibility and position in public spaces, posters constitute a particularily direct form of address. It is a form of communication from which we cannot protect ourselves and that cannot avoid seeing. In plain view on billboards, brand messages therefore not only obtain more visibility but also amplify the drawbacks mentioned above in terms of both interpretation and reactions. Not only can a poster not be "turned off" like a television, or "closed" like a magazine, it is also "indiscriminate" communication. Placed on public streets, by definition it is directed to a public of all ages, sexes, and social conditions. This characteristic makes the reception mechanisms of a poster*

campaign less controlable and predictable than if the ads had beeen disseminated in a more targeted way in a magazine. The flow of images and messages that circulates in our societies, even if apparently chaotic and omnipresent, is, in reality, analysed, channeled, specialized and subdivided in order to reach a public that is equally segmented. From this point of view, poster campaigns are perhaps the least discriminating media tool. As a consequence they amplifie the controversial effects of all non-conformist communication." (Semprini, 1996, Italian translation 1997:80-81)

3 This deals with what Semprini considers another form of ingenuousness, critisizing Benetton for its communicative arrogance in deciding to unilaterally break the rules of the discursive space game, ignoring the fact that in "speaking" one does not only pay attention to "what to say," but also selectively to "whom," in "what contexts," in "what ways," to "what ends" and "in the name of what and whom." "*There is another aspect that Benetton seems to ignore in its responses to criticism: the interpretation and reception conditions of a message are inscribed in a socio-cultural space that cannot be disregarded. To consider messages as absolute objects that do not entail proeedures of interpretative cooperation and filtering signifies disregarding one of the most fundamental principles of the functioning of social discourse. (Debray, 1994b)...Benetton's discourse seems therefore to forget that each act of communication sets into motion a network of extremely complex actors which alow us to highlight a second aspect of the "ingenuousness" of this discourse. Just as the awareness of a segment of the public cannot be achieved at the expense of another segment of the same public, one cannot ignore the fact that social discourse is subject to multiple reception phenomena and that the meaning of a message never entirely belongs to the person who enunciates it. Excusing oneself by saying that that you were misunderstood and that you had wanted to say something other that the public, or a segment of the public, understood is not an admissible justification in a mass communication context*" (Semprini, 1996, Italian translation 1997:79-80).

4 cf. concerning Semprini's (1996, Italian translation 1997:57-70) interpretations of the 'Clothing Redistibution Project" linked to the 1993 ad campaign, which he called the "cycle of truth." The character of this campaign as a counter response to the controversies triggered by previous ad campaigns was marked by three breaks in communication style: 1) Explicit consultation and dialog between the leader of the Benetton company and all possible interlocutors receptive to his call to donate used clothing; 2) abandoning the use of color for the chromatic sobriety and seriousness of black and white; 3) legitimization and external guarantee via collaboration with non-profit organizations, such as Caritas and the Red Cross, to neutralize criticism of "using-abusing" the world's ills. If this analysis is interpretively attractive (especially as it explains the element of symbolic reappropriation of the "product," clothing, which for years had been absent from the company's advertising), whether you like it or not, the element of criticism that it involves can be put into perspective by remembering that Benetton's social interventions for the prevention of AIDS began in 1991, parallel with its first poster on the issue ('Condoms'), before their later ads ("Terminal AIDS patient" 1992 and HIV, 1993) unleashed a high-pitched controversy, even with direct interlocutors (AIDS patients) and the organizations that represent their interests.

5 cf interview with Aldo Palmieri published in *News di Colors* (1993:2).

6 It was Palmieri himself who said so. This information came from News di Colors (1993:11)

7 taken from News di Colors (1993:11)

8 "One of the most imitated advertising campaigns is without a doubt that of the United Colors of Benetton. From parodies of famous photographs, to paraphrasing the brand name and different renditions of the graphics, Oliviero Toscani's photographs are ransacked around the world. Sometimes the results are really funny, sometimes dismaying." *(News di Colors, 1993:12).*

9 SPAD-T is the acronym for *Syteme portable d'analyse des donnes textuelle*. The software is availble for PCs and MAC (Lebart, L. Morineau A. & Bécue, M. 1989).

10 DISCAN is the acronym for Discourse Analysis, a program designed by P. Maranda (1990/1992).

11 ALCESTE is the acronym for *Analyse Lexicale par Context d'un Ensemble de Segments de Text*, a program designed by Max Reinert (version 2.0, 1992, for MAC). Four versions currently exist for both PCs and MAC and are available with multilingual dictionaries (French, Portugese, English, Italian and Spanish).

Chapter 7
Branding and Sustainable Competitive Advantage in Indian Politics:
Brand Rahul Gandhi

Avinash Kapoor
Management Development Institute (MDI), India

Chinmaya Kulshrestha
Management Development Institute (MDI), India

ABSTRACT

Political marketing has grown leaps and bounds in India over the last two elections. The purpose of this chapter is to analyze as to how politicians have built their personal brands and how successful they have been at it. More specifically, we study Rahul Gandhi as a brand in order to find a match between brand identity, brand personality, and consumer perception in terms of benefits sought and influence of activities undertaken by him. The chapter concludes personality brands in politics work well when the brand personality matches with the party's ideology, and stays strong through right activities and image building choices. There should be a sustainable synergy between the leader and the party to avoid brand equity dilution.

INTRODUCTION

The recent elections saw many eminent politicians pitching themselves directly or indirectly as the next Prime Minister of India. While Congress and Bhartiya Janta Party clearly declared there PM candidates, BSP's leader Mayawati also emerged as the so called proverbial dark horse for the prime minister's chair. We also saw name of two big leaders, Narendra Modi and Lalu Prasad

DOI: 10.4018/978-1-61350-171-9.ch007

Yadav, being used by the media as the probable candidates for PM if not in this election may be in the near future.

Riding on the wave of victory, Congress supporters gave the credit of the phenomenal victory to the young face of Congress led by Rahul Gandhi. Seen as the prime minister of the future, carrying the legacy of the great Indian political family, he was believed to take a cabinet position in the present government. But as a surprise to all and disappointment to the supporters he refused citing the reason of being too young and inexperienced to take any responsible position in the government. Projected as the face Congress during election campaign "Brand Rahul" is a clear winner. The 'good old' countrymen have accepted his leadership. Nevertheless, why he is reluctant to take the responsibilities? Does "Brand Rahul" needs further refinement and clear positioning among the fellow citizens?

Further, in today's context, political marketing is gaining relevance as media spends for political parties increase during campaigns; strong brands emerge from the ranks of political leaders with each party building a larger than life image of its leaders. Thus, we begin by understanding marketing in the context of politics. In this we look at a very interesting conceptual model proposed by Lees-Marshment (2001) of the way political parties have evolved over time from a product orientation through a sales orientation, and finally to a market orientation. Further, we also study critique of political marketing through a framework put forth by Henneberg (2002). In Addition, a personality brand can be defined in simple terms as a brand based around a single human being. It is a trust relationship between an individual and consumers that bypasses the normal purchase decision-making process. Personality Branding means strategically planning and developing the trust relationship between individual and consumer (Stockman, 2009). In order to understand the concept of developing a brand for a personality in the context of political marketing, we have adopted a framework from the field of human Resources and organizational Behaviour and applied it to marketing. As, personality branding essentially involves stimulating meaningful perceptions about the value and qualities that the personality stand for, we hypothesize that developing personality brands within an organization, humanizes the corporate brand and makes it more relatable.

This chapter tries to draw a parallel between Rahul Gandhi, the future of Indian political scenario, and other probable candidates of prime ministerial post. We have identified following leaders which we believe have strong brand image, to be the PM of the great Indian democracy.

1. **Rahul Gandhi:** He is the heart of our study to understand the status of his brand.
2. **Dr. Manmohan Singh:** The current prime minister of India. Was the decision to make him the PM again was taken by looking into his image? Or having an economist was the need of the hour?
3. **L.K. Advani:** The leader of opposition and the 2nd biggest face of Bhartiya Janta Party after Vajpayee, he was the clear favorite among BJP supporters.
4. **Narendra Modi:** Although he denied being in the race of PM, but had some support from inside the party especially after the victory in Gujarat elections. He is seen as the leader of the next saffron brigade.
5. **Lalu Prasad Yadav:** The party spoiler for the Congress, riding on the image of being a very full-of-beans politician and MBA school friendly politician, he moved away from Congress to form the 4lh front. Realistic or not his supporters started promoting him as the next PM of the country.
6. **Mayawati:** "Parda" loving "Behenji" clearly portrayed herself as a very strong contender for the most lucrative post of the IPS (Indian Political System).

In fact, today, every famous person has some brand value attached to him/her, and modern companies are in a mad race to encash this brand value. It takes a fair amount of effort to convert mere celebrity into brand equity. Entertainers, athletes, authors, and politicians work pretty hard at it, but without competent specialists, they can often be tempted to accept every proposal of endorsement and, thus, their brand image can suffer.

Further, choosing a person to act as a brand enables to look at brand management from different, non-standard perspective. Could a person be treated and managed equally to a consumer good brand? Are theories as Brand Life Cycle or concepts as Brand Personality and Brand Rejuvenation applicable to a human being? Could a celebrity brand be extended? Could a dilution threaten a personality brand? The challenge is how to convert the politician's short-term fame (the once in five years rule!!!) into long-term brand and turn fame into political success.

Therefore, after looking at the literature from political marketing and personality branding perspective we map out the brand identity of Rahul Gandhi using Kapferer's Brand Identity Prism to understand what the voter's perception of Brand Rahul Gandhi is. We also used Aaker's brand Personality Model to understand the facets of personality of Brand Rahul Gandhi. We conducted primary research to develop these frameworks and to understand how the voter as a consumer views brand Rahul Gandhi and how she relates to him.

LITERATURE REVIEW

Political Marketing

Political marketing has grown leaps and bounds in India over the last two elections. In the central government elections earlier this year, ad agencies were one of the major beneficiaries of this election for which ads spend is pegged at around Rs 800 crore. The Congress and the BJP alone spent over Rs 400 crore on ads on television, radio, newspapers, and Internet (Hussaini, 2009).

The thought behind this approach is that if commercial brands are assuming increasing power in consumer lives, then it is possible that the way and nature that people make choices about political parties is akin to how they make choices about their commercial brands (Reeves, P. and de Chematony, L. 2003). Which is why political parties are now working and spending like corporate firms: they are trying to reach out to the youth of India as their target audience. Their long-term goal seems to be in making the youth a loyalist to these political conglomerates as they might be to any other brand (Hussaini, 2009).

The activities in political marketing might comprise developing a strategic political posture for a party, micro-managing an election campaign, coordinating the spin on certain communications with 'parallel' organizations and using political marketing research to focus marketing spend resources, among others (Butler and Collins 1999; Henneberg 2002). Similarly, Lees-Marshment, J., (2001) presents a three-level conceptual model of the way political parties have evolved over time from a product orientation through a sales orientation, and finally to a market orientation (Figure 1).

From Figure 1, it can be suggested that in the political marketplace, there is currently a move towards a market-driven standpoint in that the political parties attempt to design their brand based on the needs of the electorate through market research and polling evidence. However, this market-driven strategy may not be beneficial for political parties in the long term given that the political marketplace is likely to evolve. Political parties therefore also need to be 'market drivers' in predicting and taking action on longer-term programmes, which are not immediately important, but will have longer-term consequences (Reeves et al., 2006).

Despite many points of view on whether marketing in politics is a good or a bad thing, there is a body of political marketing literature which

Figure 1. Three-level conceptual model of political parties

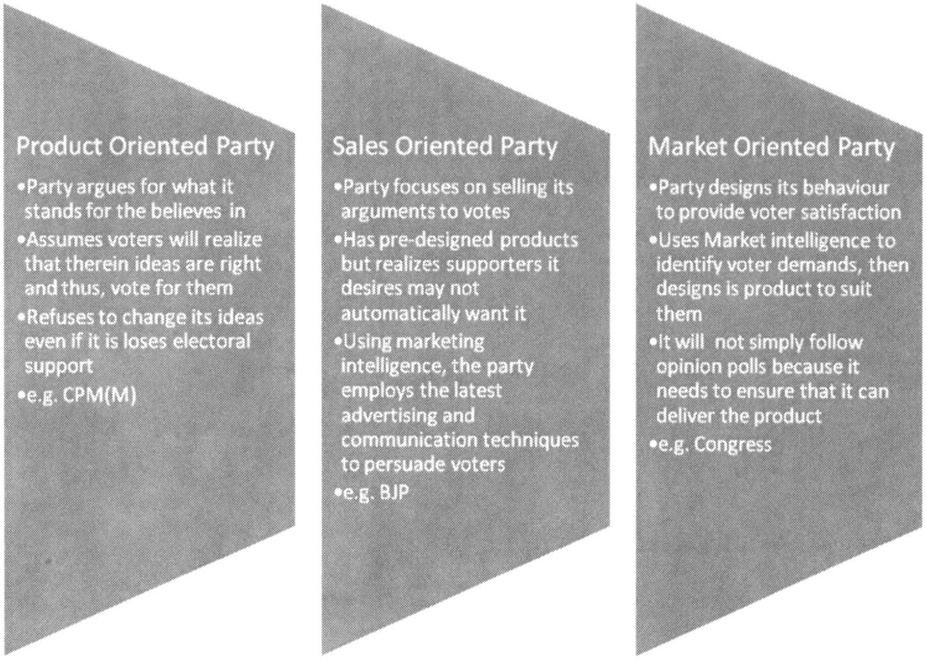

views the concept of marketing being applied to politics as to some extent inappropriate. This stems from the belief that the application of marketing produces negative connotations which damages the political process (O'Shaughnessy, 2002). A second view is that the daily "spin" and constant effort to make one individual "look good" required in politician branding does not resemble how businesses and organizations need to communicate every day (Freidman, 2009). At the other end of the spectrum, it is held that political marketing is, in general, a force for good within society, given that political marketing is concerned with the satisfaction of the electorate. Brand marketing techniques therefore offer an approach that if used effectively, can improve the political process (Reeves et at, 2006).

In addition to these, there are other criticisms of political marketing as well. To understand these, we first classify political marketing under two axes;

1. **Levels of Involvement**
   - **The Theory of Political Marketing Management:** This encompasses the operational management issues of political exchanges. It consists of a theoretical and analytical examination of managerial behaviour. Questions answered on this level are, for example: What do political actors do to manage the political exchange? Which instruments and concepts are successful, and under what circumstances? This operational and managerial focus, however, means that certain elements are not covered by the theory of political marketing management. Those are the more fundamental questions without direct managerial relevance and are covered in the second theory.
   - **The Theory of Political Marketing:** This answers fundamental questions like: What about the wider impact of

Figure 2. Categorization scheme of political marketing

Levels of Focus		Levels of involvement: *Theory of Political Marketing*	Levels of involvement: *Theory of Politics/ Marketing*
	Descriptive		
	Normative		

Figure 3. Criticism of political marketing

Levels of Focus		Levels of involvement: *Theory of Political Marketing*	Levels of involvement: *Theory of Politics/ Marketing*
	Descriptive	Political arena not part of marketing domain and should not be researched with marketing concepts (M)	- Research focussing on peripheral activities like campaigning and communication (M/P) - Research In Political Marketing is not sophisticated or cutting-edge (M/P)
	Normative	No theoretical and ethical framework exists to have value discussion about political marketing (M)	Same as above

political marketing activities on democracy, or the interplay with different party or electoral systems? Or the understanding of how voters perceive political actors in an electoral market system?

2. **Levels of Focus**
   - **Descriptive argument**
   - **Prescriptive (normative) argument**

These levels are shown in Figure 2.

Now, the criticism of Political Marketing comes from two quarters: marketers and political scientists. It comes in the following ways shown in Figure 3.

Despite this criticism (mainly from M: marketers, P: political scientists, or M/P: both [see Figure 3]), political marketing is here to stay. In the next section, we take a look at personality branding in political marketing.

Personality Branding

For consumers the buying decision is based on trust, confidence and the feeling of connection or emotions they relate to a product, service or many times a person. Branding is an activity by which we extend a product beyond its functional benefits. It the changing world where world is moving towards a very dynamic market conditioning, branding has become a more important activity then just selling or marketing.

Branding is not just for corporations anymore. There is a new trend called personality branding. People tend to attach themselves more with a person than to a corporation. They find a person to be more authentic, trust worthy and approachable than a corporation. Couple of reasons stated by Jane Tabachnick, (2007) are:

1. Personality branding is looked as a very essential element for career development. A career can be in any field say politics, big corporations, film industry, social circuit works etc. personality branding helps by providing a tool by which a person is able to define himself in terms of who I am?, what do I stand for, what makes me special, what makes me so unique?
2. It also helps in business development. With the advent of online newsletters, blogs, internet sites, social networking, the information seeking duration about a particular person or organization has reduced drastically. To attract attention of the right kind of people is very important. And with the increased resources to do so personality branding becomes more important. People want to do business with whom they can associate easily. Where they feel some sort of connection.

There are many definitions of personality branding given by various authors such as (Peters, 2007; Hansen, 2007; Montoya, 2005a; McNally & Speak, 2003; Arruda, 2007):

- A perception or emotion maintained by somebody else about you.
- A reflection of who you are and what you believe, expressed by what you do and how you do it.
- Stimulating meaningful perceptions about the value and qualities that you stand for
- Influencing how others perceive you
- The sum of expectations and associations it creates in the mind of its target audience
- An image of yourself that you want to project in everything you do.
- Eliminating the competition and making you unique and better than all your competition in the market.

Having a strong personality brand has benefits, It:

- Stimulates meaningful perceptions about the values and qualities that you stand for.
- Tells others who you are, what you stand for, what are you capable of achieving, what makes you different, what set of values you associate etc
- Influences how others perceive you
- Creates expectations in the mind of others of what they will get when they work with you
- Gets your prospects to see you as the only solution to their problems
- Creates an image of a leader

Therefore, personality branding is more than just marketing and promoting yourself. The image of your personality brand is a perception held in someone else's mind. We have adopted the personal branding model from field of organizational behaviour and studied its application in field of political marketing.

Personal Branding Model

Developed by Dr. Hubert K Rampersad, the personal branding model helps in formulating and implementing an authentic personal brand identity. This organic model consists of the following four phases which are the building blocks of a strong authentic personal brand:

1. **Define and formulate your personal ambition:** This phase involves defining and formulating the personal ambition. It is the core of formulating a personal brand and drives a person forward in achieving the goal. It encompasses;
   - Personal vision: It actually is the ever driving force for a person
   - Personal mission
   - Personal key rotes: that a person wants to take in life or wants others to perceive that he/she is capable of taking.

Formulation is critical to building a strong brand as it helps in providing the fuel to translate personal ambition into actions. In sum, it is all about identifying yourself and figuring out what are my dreams and what I want to achieve finally in life, what is the ultimate motivation of my life? It is like exploring oneself to the core.

2. **Define and formulate your personal brand:** It involves defining and formulating an authentic, distinctive, relevant, consistent, concise, meaningful, exciting, inspiring, compelling, enduring crystal clear, ambitious, persuasive and memorable personal brand promise and to use it as the focal point of the behaviour and actions. It also involves:
   - SWOT analysis to analyze the current situation and understand the points which can be leveraged upon
   - Determine specialization to a particular field
   - Defining main specific services, key characteristics, single leading and most powerful attribute to actually concentrate all the energy on that particular item
   - Determine the target audience and their needs
   - Defining the personal brand story which helps audience in understanding what a person wants to say.
   - Last step could be to develop a personal brand statement or a logo that is visible to the audience.
3. **Formulating Personal Balance Scorecard (PBSC):** The above two phases are restricted to yourself. They are essential but of no use if you do not act upon them. This phase is exactly what it is. It puts emphasis on developing an integrated and well balanced action based on your personal ambition (phase1) and personal brand (phase 2). PBSC entails your personal critical success factors that are related to the above two phases. It translates personal ambition and personal brand into manageable and measurable personal objectives, milestones and improvement actions in a holistic and balanced way. It can be used to develop improvement actions to achieve the objectives, keep track of the progress, record key performance and brand information, build network of contacts, quantify and report key accomplishments.
4. **Implement and cultivate your personal ambition, personal brand and personal balanced scorecard:** Personal ambition, personal brand and the PBSC have no values unless you implement them to make it a reality. Therefore the next step is to implement, maintain, and cultivate the ambitions, brand and PBSC effectively.

Figure 4. Authentic personal branding model

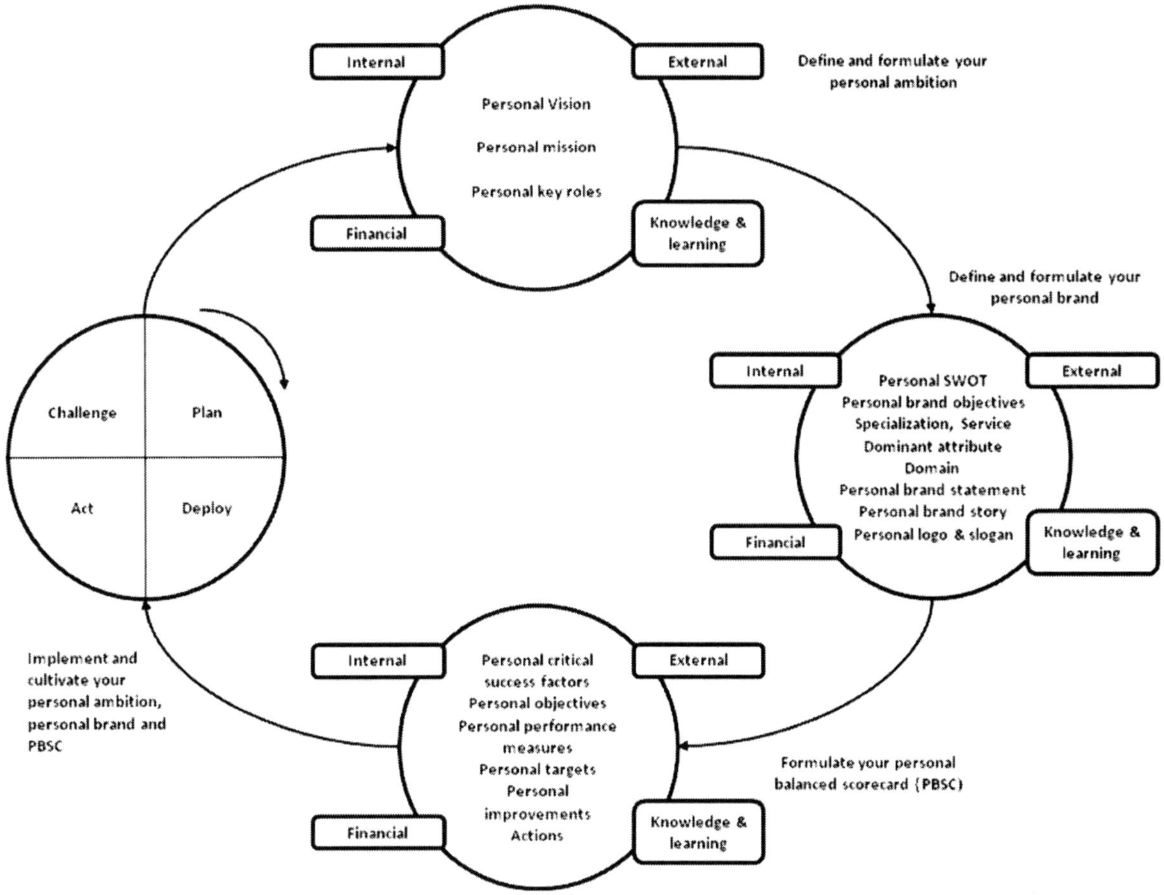

Politics and Personality Branding

As shown in Figure 4, a person could be the hardest worker and have the most intellect in your selected field, but without strategic politics, he/she will not achieve the full potential. Politics is relationship-centric career. Politics is strategic and must be learned by experience in a work setting[1]. "Politics is the best and most fertile ground for creating celebrity status"[2]. As the politicians gain experience they tend to create an image in the minds of the people. Personal branding finds extensive use in this kind of scenario when the face to face interaction with the people is involved and it's a high involvement situation. As people are becoming more knowledge seeker they tend to see their own image in the kind of leader they want to choose. Personal branding thus helps in achieving a distinct image with the people for example, Sonia Gandhi is looked as the great Indian women.

BRAND: RAHUL

Brand Status

Rahul Gandhi is seen as the brand of:

- Youth
- New energy
- Knowledge

Figure 5. Rahul Gandhi

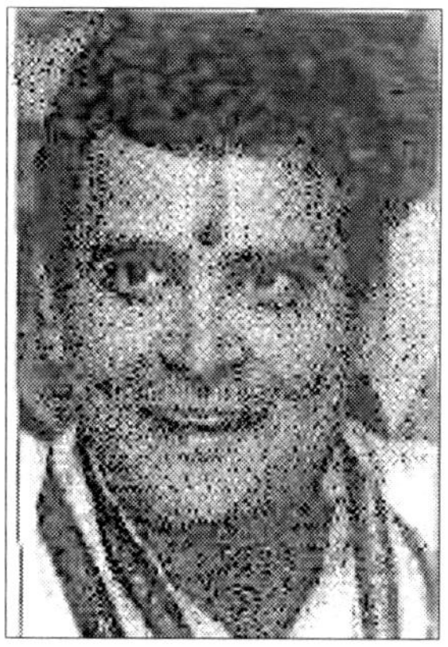

He is perceived by many as the 'new change' in the Indian political system which in many decades has crumbled under the many faces of corruption. Many see the image of Rajiv Gandhi in him and believe that he carries the charisma and energy of his parents (Figure 5). He is believed to carry the legacy of "Gandhi" forward.

Brand Strategies and Activities

1. **Youth Focus:** Rahul Gandhi has actively campaigned on the theme called Generational Revolution: a belief that if more young educated people will join the politics, system would move away from the biases of caste, religion, region etc. He is the chief of the youth wing of Congress and has a strong say in the overall scheme of things of the Indian National Congress. He has set the goal for Congress that 30% of the parliamentary candidates should be young.
2. **Future Prime Minister:** Congress has repeatedly projected him as the future Prime Minister. Congress, in the general elections held in April-May, 2009, had campaigns like "Bhavishya ka saath dein, Congress ka saath dein" with pictures of Rahul Gandhi.
3. **Work-oriented:** Rahul Gandhi has repeatedly through his actions and quotes created an image of a person who is interested in doing work at the grass root level rather than going for the limelight by taking up a ministerial position. For the next two years, he says, his mission is to introduce direct elections for the Youth Congress, the party wing for members 35 and under, so local chapters choose their leaders. He is focussed on strengthening the Congress party with young blood and will take up a position in the cabinet only when he finds the time ripe.
4. **Rural Focus:** With his numerous campaigns in the villages all across India, Rahul Gandhi has tried to portray himself as the messiah of the Rural India. He also championed the idea of NREG (National Rural Employment Guarantee Scheme), which has been successfully implemented in over 200 districts.

SWOT Analysis

In this section we conduct a SWOT analysis of brand Rahul Gandhi to understand the strengths of the brand that can be leveraged towards opportunities and to overcome threats (Figure 6).

Strengths

- **Comes from an iconic family background:** The Nehru-Gandhi family is often touted as the first family of Indian politics. Rahul Gandhi, thus, has a very strong lineage to invoke inspiration amongst the masses. The Nehru-Gandhi family is in politics, or even bigger, what the Bachchan family is in the Indian film industry. They have already given India Prime Ministers in the form of Jawahar Lai Nehru, Indira Gandhi and Rajeev Gandhi. Gandhi name is in itself sufficient to command a huge follower base, and thus Rahul Gandhi has his work cut out, when it comes to creating his Brand Awareness.

Figure 6. SWOT analysis

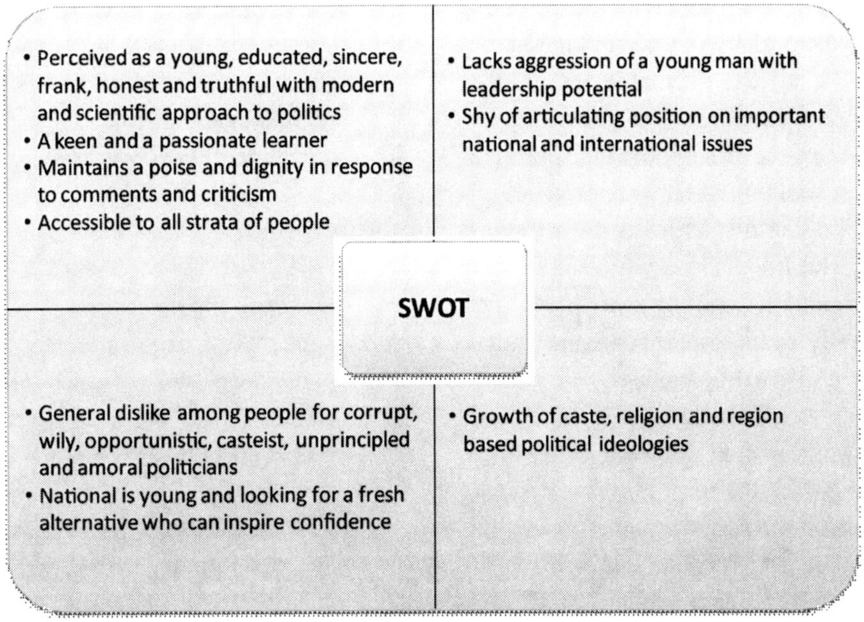

- **Backing of the oldest and largest political party:** Just like having the Gandhi tag, another factor which weighs in heavily in favor of Rahul Gandhi is the party he works for, 'Congress.' Congress is the oldest and the largest political party, involved in active politics since the time of freedom struggle. They have successfully positioned themselves as a nationalist secular party working in the interest of minorities, unlike their other political competitors, which have undertaken either a regional or a communal overtone. Thus Brand Rahul is suitably supported by the brand Congress, as a lot of synergy is seen between the two.
- **Perceived to be a young, educated, sincere, frank, honest and truthful with modern and scientific approach to politics:** Rahul Gandhi has studied in top universities like Cambridge and Rollins, and has even worked for Strategy Guru Michael Porter's firm, Monitor Group for three years. Being one of the most prominent torch bearers of the next generation of political leaders, he is constantly looked upon as frank, honest, logical and educated. All these attributes have been mostly found missing in most of the political leaders of yester years. Thus all these qualities rolled into one gives a great push to Brand Rahul Gandhi.
- **A keen and a passionate learner:** Rahul has proven time and again that he is a keen and passionate learner. He announced his entry into politics in May, 2004, and soon enough he graduated to the post of General Secretary of Congress by September, 2007. He introduced game changing tactics in the scheme of things of Congress when he laid out the policy of insisting on grassroots activism, building deep connections to rural India and trying to democratize the hierarchical Congress party itself. He was credited for Congress winning the General Elections in 2009. His keen eye for detail and ability to learn and adapt quickly makes him a leader for the future.

- **Maintains poise and dignity in response to comments and criticism:** Being constantly in the public eye and having to take a stance on all the debatable issues, his opinions and statements are always under close scrutiny of the opposition. He also has to face scathing remarks because of all the mudslinging that happens during campaigning. But Rahul Gandhi has shown tremendous calm in handling such situations. He generally comes out as someone with a sharp wit and grounded values.
- **Accessible to all strata of people:** Brand Rahul Gandhi is built upon the promise of connecting with the rural masses. His rallies across the villages of India where he met with the underprivileged, heard their problems and formed a bond have portrayed him as being accessible to all strata of the society.
- **Respectful to elders even in opposition parties:** Respect for the elders is a virtue greatly admired in the Indian culture, and Rahul Gandhi always mentions the senior leaders of opposition in his speeches with utmost respect. This facet of Brand Rahul Gandhi has endeared itself with the Indian masses.

Weakness

- **Lacks aggression of a young man with leadership potential:** Although the result of this election and the aggressive role taken upon by Rahul Gandhi will help in boosting his image, but still Rahul Gandhi is seen upon as a mama's boy, finding it difficult to come out of the shadows of Sonia Gandhi.
- **Shy of articulating position on important national and international issues:** Often Rahul Gandhi has been found shy of articulating position on issues of national and international importance. This can also be due to the fact that some of his comments on Babri Masjid Demolition, have come under scathing criticism, and the presence of experienced leaders in the party, makes it sensible to leave the decision of stance of the party to them.

Opportunities

- **General dislike among people for corrupt, wily, opportunistic, casteist, unprincipled and amoral politicians:** The mandate that came through this election was loud and clear, 'junta[1] has voted for development. There is a general discontent amongst the masses for corrupt and unprincipled leaders. Rahul Gandhi as the image of an ideal young leader has the perfect opportunity to build on his brand.
- **Nation is young and looking for a fresh alternative that can inspire confidence:** India is a young nation and with the surge of many young Turks in the field of politics, the scene is bubbling with energy and dynamism. Rahul Gandhi has the utmost benefit of age being by his side, at only 39 he displays exuberance of youth and a passion to bring about a change. He is looked upon as the messiah for development by the rural masses of Uttar Pradesh, where he has campaigned and worked at the grassroots level.

Threats

- **History of caste, religion and region based political ideologies:** Although the scenario is changing but the Indian political scene has always been mired by the presence caste, religion or region based politics. In such a scenario, Rahul Gandhi might find it hard to combat the threat posed by strong stature leaders who have an unbreakable stranglehold on the segment of voter population they are targeting. In other words, since Brand Rahul Gandhi is not being positioned for any particular strata or section of the society, and is rather a Brand intended to have a mass appeal, it may feel threatened by brands positioned to specific set of audience.

Brand Identity: Rahul Gandhi

We map the brand identity of brand Rahul Gandhi using Kapferer's Brand Identity Prism (Figure 7 and Figure 8). Using this construct we map out how Brand Rahul wants to be perceived externally vis-a-vis how it looks internally. We begin by studying the actual construct. Then, we develop this construct for brand Rahul Gandhi as shown in Fugure 8:

- First of all brand contains an external verification that the physical appearance, which is the core of the brand and its value. It sets a traditional brand management orientation about the positioning system, selecting primary brand attributes and benefits. The first step to build a brand is the defining physical factors, determining what they are and how they appear.
- The second element of a prism is personality. The traits of brand personality are drawn from inner source. It should not be mixed with the image of consumers are thinking, which is a good picture of each recipient. The brand personality is defined and measured by attributes of individual users directly to related brands. Brand personality is closely connected to self-image and the image of consumers, because consumers identify with a certain segment that reflects the brand attributes.
- The third aspect of brand identity is the culture which is the primary source of inspiration for the brand to form an identity of its own which would differentiate it from others. Most values that a brand seem to project is inherited from the culture which gives an underlying meaning to the brand concept. Even to a large extent the freedom a brand has depends on the culture as this is the most visible brand feature.
- The next aspect of brand identity (i.e. brand relationships) draws its importance in the context of human transactions and exchanges. The most important element in this aspect is the behavior the brand projects towards the consumers.
- Consumer reflection is a critical part of brand identity for any marketer. From the perspective of a brand manager consumer reflection drives the target segment for a brand. This is basically how the brand is perceived by its target audience and hence becomes a critical factor for the success of the brand.
- Consumer Mentalisation deals with the inner relationships the consumer builds between himself and the brand image. This facet has significant influence on consumer behaviour and hence is of prime importance to the brand managers.

Physique

This is the part of a brand identity which makes the first connect with the target audience. Physique goes a long way in forming the image of a brand in the minds of its audience. It's this impression which helps the other facets of the brand identity to make the positive image a lasting one. Rahul Gandhi has been touted widely as one the most eligible bachelor in India. He is a man who features in list of most well dressed men though he is mostly seen in khadi kurta pyjama. He is a charismatic character without any frills. There has been a lot of talk in media about how brand Rahul Gandhi is popular among the opposite sex

Figure 7. Kapferer's brand identity prism

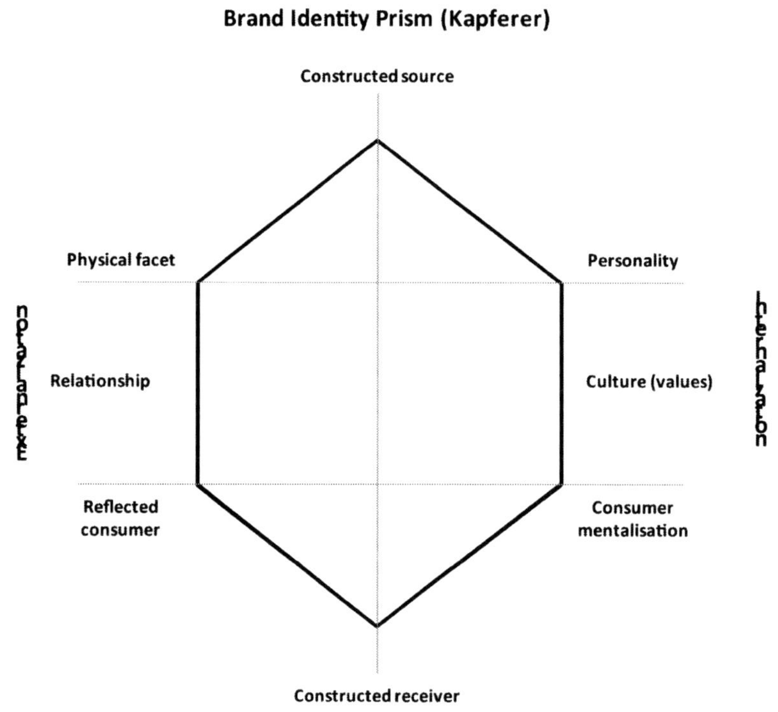

Figure 8. Brand identity of brand Rahul Gandhi using Kapferer's brand identity prism

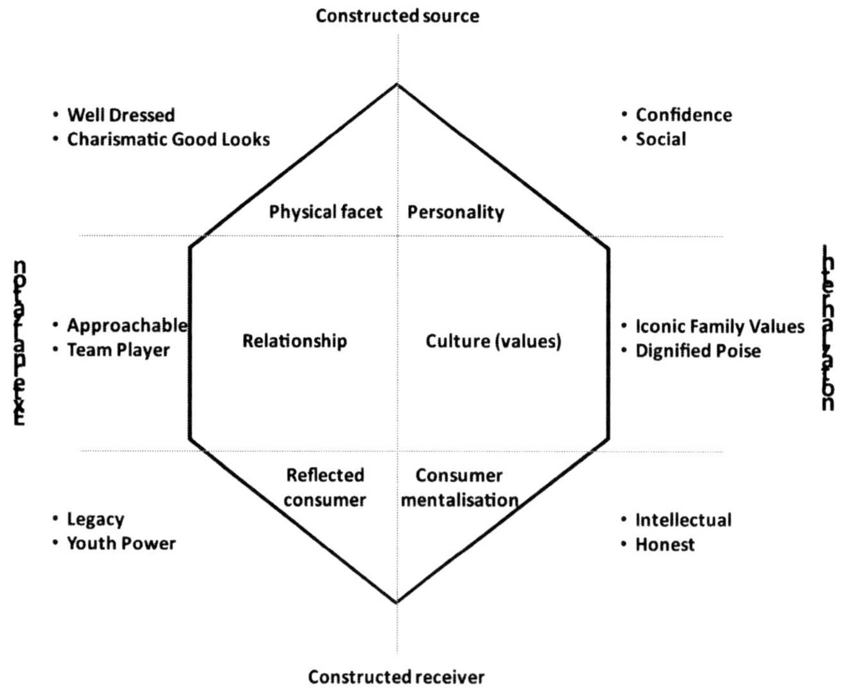

and how this popularity is due to reasons beyond his political acumen. But yet this physique could help him take the brand to the next level where even political acumen would get associated with this brand.

Relationship

This facet of brand is mainly related with human exchanges. The survey results show that Rahul Gandhi is generally perceived as a team player and approachable. This is an important criterion in how the general population conceptualizes the brand Rahul Gandhi. Being perceived as approachable adds significant value to the brand as a new age politician and more so in the context where new India tries to break free from the clutches of bureaucracy and hassles of red tape. Large part of this perception is formed through conscious effort to get involved with ground level work and widespread media focus on such efforts.

Consumer Reflection

The survey results show brand Rahul Gandhi is perceived as someone with legacy and ability to motivate and mobilize youth power. The legacy is very much something he inherits from his iconic family background which runs parallel with Indian history for the past century or so. His high involvement with youth Congress has also helped his cause in being perceived as a youth leader who can inspire and motivate the youth. Rahul Gandhi has apparently brought a wave of freshness to the otherwise ageing cluster of politicians. He has successfully connected with the youth through various nationwide drives and addressing rallies as well as student meets.

Personality

Ever since Rahul Gandhi made his entry into Indian politics he has been a symbol of confidence and poise. Rarely has he been seen in a situation of discomfort. He has handled issues with ease and has been a poster boy for the media in the last five years or so. He has shown his inclination to interact with people and is not shy of the attention and focus media and party supporters shower upon him. He remains a man with self composure under most situations and so far in his short political career has not shown any ego problems which many might have expected given the family lineage he belongs to.

Culture

Iconic family background lays the foundation for the culture aspect of Brand Rahul Gandhi. Coming from a family which is touted as the most powerful family in contemporary India gives the brand the cultural heritage needed to make a mark in politics. Its this culture which brings with it plenty of expectations from all his fellow country men that brand Rahul Gandhi can possibly bring that much needed change in otherwise corrupt and dull Indian politics. Along with such a background Rahul Gandhi brings upon a dignified poise which is very much a virtue accrued through the culture he has been brought up in. Brand culture is something which can play a pivotal role in differentiating the brand from its rivals and in the case of Rahul Gandhi it certainly does so. His culture definitely lets him stand ahead of his peers in the Indian political scenario and it is this culture which fuels media speculation about his prime ministerial candidature.

Consumer Mentalisation

This is the part where a brand connects with its target audience. In this case the target audience lies in the new age India who wants clean politics. Honesty and intellect is something which has made deep inroads in to consumer mentalisation for India in 21st century and more so for the

Figure 9. Aaker's brand personality framework

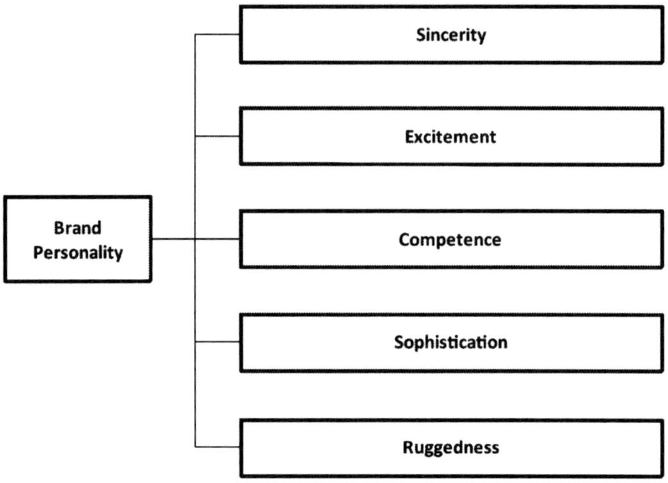

youth India whom Brand Rahul Gandhi considers the major target audience. Media and changing environment in India and by India it's not just the major cities but even the hinterland India has made this change in consumer mentalisation a reality. To succeed in such India the brand needs to exploit this consumer mentality towards brand Rahul Gandhi to actually succeed and fulfill the brand promises it seems to make.

Brand Personality: Rahul Gandhi

In this stage, we interpreted consumer understanding of brand Rahul Gandhi using parameters of Aaker's brand personality framework. We begin by understanding the framework. Then we develop the framework on the basis of primary research.

Aaker's Brand Personality: The Framework

This framework can be described as follows: The brand personality dimension of Jennifer Aaker is a framework to describe and measure the 'personality' of a brand in five core dimensions, each divided into a set of facets. It is an easy to understand model to describe the profile of a brand by using analogy of a human being. This model can be used to describe current status of a brand and describe future status (Figure 9).

Five Dimensions of Brand Personality (Aaker)

The five core dimensions and their facets are:

- Sincerity (down-to-earth, honest, wholesome, cheerful)
- Excitement (daring, spirited, imaginative, up-to-date)
- Competence (reliable, intelligent, successful)
- Sophistication (upper class, charming)
- Ruggedness (outdoorsy, tough)

Each facet is in turn measured by a set of traits. The trait measures are taken using a five-point scale (1= not at all descriptive, 5=extremely descriptive) rating the extent to which each trait describes the specific brand of interest.

The traits belonging to each of the facets are:

- Down-to-earth (down-to-earth, family-oriented, small-town)

- Honest (honest, sincere, real)
- Wholesome (wholesome, original)
- Cheerful (cheerful, sentimental, friendly)
- Daring (daring, trendy, exciting)
- Spirited (spirited, cool, young)
- Imaginative (imaginative, unique)
- Up-to-date (up-to-date, independent, contemporary)
- Reliable (reliable, hard working, secure)
- Intelligent (intelligent, technical, corporate)
- Successful (successful, leader, confident)
- Upper class (upper class, glamorous, good looking)
- Charming (charming, feminine, smooth)
- Outdoorsy (outdoorsy, masculine, Western)
- Tough (tough, rugged)

Using this framework, we developed and floated the questionnaire to 80 target audience however, only 25 responded at two levels, namely:

1. Core Personality parameter
2. Personality Facet

Under core personality parameter, as per the framework, we set out to understand to what degree brand Rahul Gandhi has core features of sincerity, excitement, competence, sophistication and ruggedness.

Table 1 shows the average scores obtained on a scale of 1-5.

From Table 1, we can interpret that brand Rahul Gandhi was found to be much more sophisticated and competent than excited or rugged. This analysis gives a combined perception of Rahul Gandhi-the politician, Rahul Gandhi-the person, Rahul Gandhi-the strategist, Rahul Gandhi-the family man and Rahul Gandhi-otherwise.

Under personality facet, as per the framework, we set out to understand to what degree brand Rahul Gandhi is down-to-earth, honest, wholesome, cheerful, daring, spirited, imaginative, up-to-date, reliable, intelligent, successful, upper class, charming, outdoorsy, and tough. Table 2 shows the average scores obtained on a scale of 1 to 5.

Table 1. Average scores

Parameter	Average Score (rounded off)
Sincerity	3.1
Excitement	2.9
Competence	3.2
Sophistication	3.7
Ruggedness	2.2

From Table 2, we can see that brand Rahul Gandhi is rated very high on the 'up-to-date' 'reliable,' 'intelligent' and 'upperclass' scale. It is interesting to note that these four personality facets result from three core parameters, namely-excitement, competence, and sophistication.

Also, the brand is rated low on 'tough' and 'down-to-earth' parameters. Brand Rahul Gandhi is thus perceived less 'macho' and 'grounded' and more of a successful and energetic leader. Also, it can be noted that the average parameter scores came out differently when individual facets were rated by respondents than when the parameters as a whole were rated by the same respondents. This gives quite an insight in terms of consumer perception and understanding of the core parameters, vis-à-vis the individual personality facets.

It can be recollected that Rahul Gandhi's strengths of being 'up-to-date,' 'spirited' and 'reliable' were used very well by the Indian National Congress during the 2009 General Elections where he was solely responsible for turning around the party's fortunes in Uttar Pradesh and many other states. One of the major reasons for this was his road-shows by which, the brand image of Rahul Gandhi as a young, dynamic and charismatic leader was created.

Table 2. Detailed average scores

Parameter	Facet	Average Score (rounded off)
Sincerity (avg:2.9)	Down-to-earth	2.4
	Honest	3.1
	Wholesome	2.9
	Cheerful	3.4
Excitement (3.2)	Daring	2.9
	Spirited	2.8
	Imaginative	3.1
	Up-to-date	4.2
Competence (2.9)	Reliable	4.2
	Intelligent	3.8
	Successful	3.5
Sophistication (3.6)	Upper class	4.0
	Charming	3.2
Ruggedness (2.4)	Outdoorsy	2.8
	Tough	1.9

COMPETITOR ANALYSIS

Brand: L. K. Advani

Brand Status

LK Advani (Figure 10) has remained as one of the most non-secular leaders of India. The brand Advani conveys a perception of an orthodox, strong, Hindu politician. However, in the last general elections, he underwent rebranding. His stance has diluted from an uncompromising orthodox Hindu leader to a moderate leader. Many regard this as a major cause of BJP's underperformance in Elections 2009.

Brand Strategies and Activities

1. **Supporter of the Youth:** Though LK Advani's age is 81, he has been developing strategies and activities that extend his brand to target the youth also. Some of the recent activities he has been involved for implementing this brand strategy is as follows:

Figure 10. LK Advani

a. **Slogan for the youth**: "Ek kaam desh ke naam" was a slogan he devised for the youth to connect with them.
b. **Campus visits**: As a part of his election campaign, he started with Advani@ Campus. This programme was designed to develop a personal connect with the youngest voters; the college students. He targeted visiting 5600 campus visits under Advani@Campus

   c. **Youth Conferences:** Advani has especially conducted many youth meetings and conferences before this year's elections. All in all he wants to create a better connect with the youth.
   d. **Trying weights in a gymnasium:** In February 2009, Advani inaugurated a gymnasium built by Ahmedabad Municipal Corporation. He picked up two 1 kg dumbbells and lifted them above his shoulders. Advani also flexed his muscles with some shoulder crunches at the gymnasium.
2. **Modernized, technology savvy leader:** This was an aspect of brand 'Advani' targeted to the E-generation/Net Savvy voters. Some active steps in this regard are as follows:
   a. **Website:** There is an official web portal www.lkadvani.in where the latest topics of BJP and LK Advani's views are posted.
   b. **Blogs and online chats:** Advani has been very active in posting articles and also indulging in online chats. This was targeted to create a sense of approachability in the net savvy citizens. Also, his viewpoints on various issues could be accessible.
   c. **Social networking on Facebook, Orkut and Youtube:** More than 200 videos of BJP were doing rounds on Youtube with an extensive advertising on social networking sites like Facebook and Orkut.
   d. **Online Newspapers in Pakistan and America:** Advani has been showcased and also links to his website been put on various Pakistani and American online newspaper websites. This has been done to keep the relatives of those net savvy people informed and interested about Advani.
3. **Visionary leader:** Advani was the face of BJP for the general elections this year. His gravity as a potential Prime Minister candidate increased as he wrote his autobiography "My Country My Life." This activity helped him increase his brand value to all the readers of the book. The book has sold more than 1,000,000 copies worldwide and the brand equity of Advani has been on the upsurge.
4. **Transformation into a moderate face from the rightwing hardliner:** LK Advani has been known for his extremist views. However, of late he has been trying to rebrand his image as a moderate leader much like his senior-pro A B Vajpayee. Some activities in this regard are as follows:
   a. His liberal comments on political issues on his blog.
   b. His comments on Jinnah on his trip to Pakistan
   c. Him conning closer to the youth
   d. The non-orthodox pleas in his speeches for the election make up
5. **Prior Image: Hindu Conformist:** Advani stormed into the national political brand wagon by leading the 'rath yatra' to demolish the Babri Masjid in 1989. The Masjid was finally demolished in 1992 and he drew his brand identity of an orthodox, strong, Hindu politician which helped him garner votes especially in Northern India. He also supported the RSS and Bajrang Dal with a solid backing. Till 2008, he was considered as the most non-secular, Hindu supporting, and conformist politician.

Brand: Narendra Modi

Brand Status

Brand Modi (Figure 11) is one of the most controversial brands in political India. On the one hand it stands for hardcore Hindutva, on the other it

Figure 11. Narendra Modi

stands for honesty and sincerity in work. It is to be seen how corporate brand of BJP uses Brand Modi on the National level. Early signs are not good, as positioning of Modi as a prime-ministerial candidate has been touted as a reason for BJP's dismal performance in recent election.

Is Modi's brand promise a tempting value propostion for the entire country? Wait and watch.

Brand Strategies and Activities

1. **Creating a favourable image post Godhara:** The first task in front of Narendra Modi is to create a favourable image in front of the masses after the Godhara kand. Following were some of the activities which were undertaken
    a. **Branding Modi as Gujarat's saviour:** Modi knew exactly what he stood for. He branded himself as Gujarat's savior who knew what was best for his state and did not hesitate to portray this very effectively. While the opposition struggled with a variety of issues and befuddled thinking, Modi's objective regarding what he meant to Gujarat was spot on.
    b. **A strong core brand image:** Moditva did not mean differently to different people. Modi stressed on a few key messages like development, good governance, zero tolerance against terrorism and industrialization. These are the values communicated by brand Modi to one and all.
2. **Creating overpowering brand personality:** Within BJP, Sangh Parivar and NDA as well Modi tried to create an overpowering brand personality whereby he was the key decision maker and also the central pivotal point of all activities
    a. **Gujarat elections:** Modi dominated Gujarat elections single handedly time and again. The sheer force and power of brand Modi was so brute and magnetic that no one could stand up to the man. Through repeated wins at Gujarat elections he created a strong position for himself in the coalition.
    b. **Communicating the right USP:** Modi communicated his USP to the state of Gujarat very well. His vision of a safe, secure, developed industrialized Gujarat (without any hint of a vote bank politics) showed himself as a person who was not ready to compromise any of his principles convictions he stood for. His USP lay in the fact that he was able to communicate his product attributes regarding Gujarati pride and all the middle class sensibilities of an average Gujarati. While the opposition failed to even communicate what it stood for. Modi was a master in communicating his brand message and succeeded in making his USP so pronounced that even areas that no one expected him to do well, gave him thumping margins.
3. **Connect with the Middle Class:** Narendra Modi never tried to break away from his image of a common man. Instead he has been strengthening his bonds with the middle class and thus is able to generate popular support

despite a lot of negative publicity after the riots of 2002.

a. **Pure, strong and assertive ideology:** Modi's ideology is too simplistic and too idealistic for any other politician of the current age. This combined with the fact that he is so firm on this ideology makes him an instant hit with the masses.

b. **Modern day role model:** Modi has been able to combine his unflinching ideology and his iron fisted actions in order to emerge as **a** modern day role model for the Gujaratis. Add to that the fact that since the days of Karsanbhai Patel no strong political leader came from Gujarat, Modi has been able to mobilize the Gujarati community in his favour present a new Gujarati role model after two decades.

4. **Creating the image of Gujarat's Saviour:** Modi always tried to portray an image whereby he projected himself as the saviour of Gujarat and its people. Due to some developmental work and due to taking credit of developments at the right time he has been able to create and manage this image effectively

a. **Gujarat Asmita:** This slogan worked wonders for Modi post 2002 when he was able to showcase his critics as critics of the state of Gujarat. Through his arrogant righteousness he was able to brandish a morality of his own when he was being severely attacked by the 'secular* political parties which helped him get the title of 'Lok Hriday Samrat.'

b. **Reform work:** Modi carried out a lot of reforms which gave him an instant connect with the public. Opening of SEZ and SIR in Gujarat further added to the image of the 'state of opportunities.'

c. **Making use of the existing facilities from centre:** Whatever support Modi got from the centre was reformed and put into the service of common Gujarati man. For example, Modi was able to rope in Japanese investments for two government projects which will result in a lot of development in Gujarat. Also, Modi used centrally sponsored popularly known 108 scheme of Emergency Medical Service to develop a network of emergency service in Gujarat. Despite all hue and cry of the Congress leaders about the UPA paternity of the 108, for a common man in Gujarat the scheme, a boon for millions in rural areas, is fathered by none other than Gujarat Chief Minister Narendra Modi.

5. **Refurbishing Brand Modi:** All the activities that were done had a central aim and that was to constantly refurbish the brand Modi to incorporate new features and make the values associated with the brand so much dynamic in nature so that they could be transmitted through any medium

a. **Roping in of the new brand manager:** Vandana Raj was roped in as a new brand manager for the brand Modi. Varna communications, her agency, designed a website for Narendra Modi and also decided which all attributes to be communicated and in what manner. For all the photographs were chosen very carefully for the campaign but all the caricatures, favourable or unfavourable were used in the campaign because they create a good connect with the audience.

b. **Unique branding exercise:** In the campaign the brand manager highlighted Modi as a person beyond the personality, and brought that person out of the personality. Modi's personality has been observed and presented holistically, showing his evolution as a person, to a leader, to a mass leader and onwards to a visionary leader. Emphasis was given on softness in communication.

c. **New age tech savvy brand promotions:** Many new promotion activities were carried on during the election campaign so that brand Modi could reach more people. They run a SMS campaign, a video campaign on YouTube and also designed a new website for Narendra Modi. *Hu khaato nathi aane khaawaane deto nathi* is one of the typical sms sent out in this campaign.

Brand: Manmohan Singh

Brand Status

Dr. Manmohan Singh (Figure 12) recently assumed responsibilities of prime minister for the second consecutive time making him the only person after Jawaharlal Nehru to do so. Dr. Singh is highly respected for his economic reforms and Indo-US nuclear deal. He is deeply appreciated for his clean image in and out of politics. He comes across as an unassuming, soft spoken and modest person which at times gives an impression of weakness. In fact he battle with this image for five years but his resolute stand on nuclear deal finally spoke for his determination and vision.

Brand Strategies and Activities

1. **Image of a non-politician:** Picked from nowhere Dr Manmohan Singh a totally non-political person was made Finance Minister by Narsimha Rao way back in 1991. Since then Dr. Singh has created for himself the image of a person who does not participate in dirty politics. After the Congress went into hibernation, he was never seen bragging about his achievements and never tried to wear the cap of a politician. This has enhanced the image of Manmohan Singh in the public domain.

Figure 12. Manmohan Singh

2. **Man with a vision for India:** Dr. Singh was made finance minister in 1991 when the Indian economy was in shambles and sinking. He along with P Chidambaram the then commerce minister fully backed by their PM not only brought in the cool breeze of liberalisation but effectively freed the Indian economy from a deep crisis. It was perhaps the beginning of new Indian economy with a tag "Brand Manmohan Singh." This legacy of economic reforms along with the nuclear deal showed the nation that here was a man with a vision for India.
3. **An Unassuming gentleman:** Dr. Singh once told an interviewer that he was "very surprised" when he was invited to become the finance minister by PV Narsimha Rao. This is the simplicity with which he conducts himself, he always keeps a very low profile and generally stays away from media spotlight.
4. **Determined, Resolute and Loyal:** As a person, Dr. Singh does not have any individual equity. He is a thoroughly non-controversial person with absolutely no personal ambition but possess personal loyalty as his core

value. This prompted Mrs. Sonia Gandhi to nominate him to the top post in 2004. For five years, Manmohan battled the popular perception that he wasn't master of himself and that he simply followed the voice of his master Sonia Gandhi. He was seen as a weak leader with no initiative of his own. But all this changed after the nuclear deal, his firm stand against the Left even at the cost of risking his premiership and his polite and humble reply to BJP's charges came across as actions of a resolute leader.

Brand: Mayawati

Brand Status

Seen as the "behenji" of the dalits across India, she is perceived to stand for burning ambition and aggressive attitude (Figure 13). Clever in reading opportunities and capitalizing on them, her brand shows a strong female autocratic leader who champions the cause of deprived classes. A woman from the bottom of the social and gender ladders position herself as the true inheritor of Ambedkar's legacy. Sometimes she is seen as the "angry woman of India."

Brand Strategies and Activities

1. **A Dalit leading a rainbow coalition of deprived castes, classes and upper caste poor across India:** She provided tickets to upper hindu castes and muslims in her election campaign in 2009. This has been a marked difference to what she had been doing till this time. This has also ted to division of votes of both Congress and BJP.
2. **Creates an iconic image so that nation can connect with her:** She has been constructing statues of her own across the state of Uttar Pradesh. This is **an** attempt to create an iconic image.

Figure 13. Mayawati

3. **Cash in on every opportunity and connect with masses and the electorate:** She has been throwing lavish parties on her birthdays and making pompous public appearance. All this are attempts at creating a brand of her own.
4. **Positioning as the strongest leader in the nation:** Doesn't hesitate to puts her own MPs and MLAs behind bars if they are found involved in crime. This is an attempt to portray strength in her leadership.
5. **Substantiating speeches with examples:** Gave away apartments in UP for low income group at 7500 rupees. This was another attempt at showing brand Mayawati is about a leader of masses.

CONCLUSION

The chapter discusses as to how politicians have built their personal brands and how successful they have been at it. More specifically, the chapter elaborates and analyses Rahul Gandhi as a brand vis-à-vis his competitors. It discusses the current status and strategies being used by various political leaders, who are strong brands in their own right along with the SWOT analysis for Rahul Gandhi to find his current position with regard to others on the Indian political scene. Further, Kapferer's identity prism and Aaker's brand personality framework were used for mapping a brand-activity match and for analyzing consumer understanding of the brand Rahul Gandhi. It resulted in a conclusion that for a Sustainable a personality brand we should evaluate the brand in terms of:

- **Brand Equity:** Measured in terms of the price the market is ready to pay for the brand
- **Brand Identity:** This is what the brand aspires to be and how it is received by the people.
- **Brand Personality:** This is people's perception about the brand, can be found by using surveys, media reports/news
- **Brand Promotion:** Evaluate the stage the brand is in using Brand Life Cycle and then act accordingly

Finally, it suggests that personality brands in Politics work well when the brand personality matches with the party's ideology, and stays strong through right activities and image building choices. There should be a sustainable synergy between the leader and the party to avoid brand equity dilution.

REFERENCES

Aaker, J. L. (1997). Dimensions of brand personality. *JMR, Journal of Marketing Research, 34*(August), 347–356. doi:10.2307/3151897

Arruda. (2007). Career advice. Retrieved from www.msn.careerbuilder.com/ custom/msn/careeradvice/ viewarticle.aspx?

Butler, P., & Collins, N. (1999). A conceptual framework for political marketing. In Newman, B. I. (Ed.), *Handbook of political marketing* (pp. 55–72). Thousand Oaks, CA: Sage Publications.

Hansen, R. S., & Hansen, K. (2007). The student experience in speed teaming: A new approach to team formation. *Journal of College Teaching and Learning, 4*(7), 69–78.

Henneberg, S. C. (2004). The views of an Advocatus Dei: Political marketing and its critics. *Journal of Public Affairs, 4*(3). doi:10.1002/pa.187

Henneberg, S. C., & O'Shaughnessy, N. J. (2002). *The idea of political marketing*. Praeger.

Hussaini. (2009). *Website*. Retrieved from http://www.political-marketing.net

Kapferer, J. N. (2008). *The new strategic brand management* (4th ed.). London, UK: Kogan Page.

Lees-Marshment, J. (2001). Marketing the British Conservatives 1997-2001. *Journal of Marketing Management, 17*(9-10), 929–941. doi:10.1362/026725701323366674

Lees-Marshment, J. (2001). The product, sales and market-oriented Party and how Labour learnt to market the product, not just the presentation. *European Journal of Marketing, 35*(9/10), 1074–1084. doi:10.1108/EUM0000000005959

Lees-Marshment, J. (2001). *Political marketing and British political parties: The party's just begun*. Manchester University Press.

Lees-Marshment, J. (2001). Let's go comprehensive: Reaching the full potential of political marketing. *Proceedings of The Political Marketing Conference*, Dublin (September).

Lees-Marshment, J. (2001). Comprehensive political marketing: What, how and why. *Proceedings of The Academy of Marketing Conference*, Cardiff University (2-4 July).

McNally, D., & Speak, K. D. (2003). *Be your own brand - A breakthrough formula for standing out from the crowd*. Berrett-Koehler Publishers.

Montoya, P. (2005). *The brand called you: The ultimate personal branding handbook to transform anyone into an indispensable brand*. Peter Montoya Pub.

Peters, T. (2007). *Personal branding blog spotlight: Tom Peters brand talent*. Retrieved from http://personalbrandingblog.wordpress.com /2007/10/17/personal-branding- spotlight-tom-peters-brand-talent/ 03

Rampersad, H. K. (2008). *Authentic personal branding*. Charlotte, NC: Information Age Publishing.

Reeves, P., & de Chernatony, L. (2003). *How voters choose political brands*. U K: Seminar Series at School of Public Policy, University of Birmingham.

Reeves, P., & DeChernatony, L. (2003). Political brand choice in Britain. In *6th Annual Political Marketing Conference, University of Middlesex, Thistle Hotel/ House of Commons*, London, UK.

Reeves, P., DeChernatony, L., & Carrigan, M. (2006). Building a political brand: Ideology or voter driven strategy. *Journal of Brand Management, 13*(6). doi:10.1057/palgrave.bm.2540283

Stockman, S. (2009, March 13). *Personality branding defined*. Retrieved from http://www.customproductions.tv/2009 /03/personality-brand-defined.html

ADDITIONAL READING

http://www.personalbrandinggroup.com

http://www.indian-elections.com /dr-manrnohan-singh.htrnl

http://www.thaindian.com/newsportal /uncategorized/pm-hopeful-advani-wooing-young-voters _l 00158012.html

http://www.ignitee.com/ newsroom/bip_advani_online.html

http://www.indiastudychannel.com /forum/24112-Rahul-Gandhi- P-M-coming-etections.aspx

www.wikipedia.org/wiki /Manmohan_Singh

http://www.brandchannel.com/ features_effect.asp?pfjd=203

http://leftthebox.com/marketing /image-versus-personality-branding

http://www. hindustantimes.com

http://el ection.rediff.com

http://www.merinews.com

http://www.dnaindia.com

http://newsx.com

http://www.thaindian.com

ENDNOTES

1 http://personalbrandingblog.com/politics

2 http://www.thepersonalbrandinggroup.com/PressReleases

Section 3
Consumers and Brands

Chapter 8
Brand Engagement and Brand Loyalty

Ronald E. Goldsmith
Florida State University, USA

ABSTRACT

Marketers value and seek brand loyalty. Consequently, they have developed a variety of strategies to encourage both behavioral (repeat purchase) and attitudinal (emotional) loyalty among customers. A recent concept has emerged related to the latter goal: brand engagement. Although marketers give a variety of definitions for brand engagement, the essential concept is an emotional attachment to a brand as though the customer has an emotional relationship with it perhaps because the brand acts as an important reflection of self-identity or is an important symbol of something meaningful to the consumer. Consumers manifest different types of engagement (with advertising, media, web sites, a company, as well as specific brands). Engagement is also conceptualized at different levels of abstraction: engagement with the marketplace, engagement with a product category, engagement with a specific brand, and brand engagement in self-concept, which refers to differences in how much consumer use brands in general to represent themselves to others. This chapter discusses these issues in some detail and presents theoretical, managerial, and theoretical implications of this concept.

INTRODUCTION

Marketing has a tradition of studying consumers and their brands. These topics include brand loyalty, brand commitment, brand equity, and relationship marketing. Brand engagement is one of the most recent manifestations of this interest. The *Webster's Seventh New Collegiate Dictionary* (1965) lists several synonyms for engagement (e.g., involved, entangled committed) and defines "engaging" as "tending to draw favorable attention." The marketing and advertising community

DOI: 10.4018/978-1-61350-171-9.ch008

uses the term engagement in a variety of ways, but they all share this core concept of engagement as a conscious emotional and cognitive reaction to marketing stimuli. The present chapter first discusses the traditional topic of brand loyalty. It then presents brand engagement from three perspectives: theoretical, managerial, and methodological. The theoretical component describes types and levels of engagement and emphasizes their antecedents and consequences. The managerial component briefly describes management interests in branding and brand loyalty and how brand engagement is related to loyalty. Finally, the methodological component briefly describes how the engagement concepts can be operationalized.

BRAND LOYALTY

Marketers have long desired loyal customers because it is easier and cheaper to sell to the loyalist than to attract a new customer, but loyalty to specific brands could only occur after brands themselves appeared. As manufacturers created branded products toward the end of the nineteenth century, consumers learned to trust certain brand names as quality guarantees, and over time, brand loyalty began to characterize the behavior of many consumers (Robinson & Etherington, 2006). The concept of customer brand loyalty as a managerial and academic concern seems to have emerged in the 1950's with the publication of Cunningham's (1956, 1961) *Harvard Business Review* articles. Once he showed empirically that loyal customers did exist and that their loyal purchasing behavior had a financial impact, customer loyalty became increasingly the goal of many marketing strategies. Not only is it less expensive to market to loyal customers; they tend to buy more of the brand; they pay higher prices for "their" brand; they see subtle differences in brands; they are more likely than non-loyalists to purchase brand extensions, to provide suggestions for improving the brand, and to spread positive word-of-mouth about the brand, including advocating for it.

Brand loyalty, however, presents marketers and consumer researchers with definitional and operational problems. Jacoby and Chestnut (1978) pointed out that at that time there were over fifty different definitions and operationalizations of brand loyalty, and that there was little agreement among them. Ehrenberg (1988) demonstrated that at least in the area of fast-moving consumer goods, most customers show multi-brand purchasing; that is, they have a repertoire of brands from which they buy, but they frequently switch among these brands (see Foxall, 1999). Often, managers and researchers think of loyalty as a pattern of consistent buying over time, but from another perspective, loyalty can be conceptualized as an emotion, attitude, or predisposition. It is common for the former (i.e., consistent buying) to be termed "behavioral loyalty" and the latter (i.e., emotion) as "attitudinal loyalty" (Dick & Basu, 1994). Clearly, customer loyalty is a wide-ranging and varied phenomenon with many useful dimensions and perspectives. Customers may buy the same brand repeatedly for its low price or out of inertia because it is the easiest thing to do, but they may have few real feelings about these brands. Customers may like several brands, but not see pronounced differences among them and so vary their purchases among this acceptable set. Some customers seek the lowest prices and are largely indifferent to branding appeals; point of sale marketing strategies or circumstances might influence their purchases of some brands. However, most consumers do develop strong feelings about some brands so that they feel they have a relationship with the brand. Loyal buyers trust the brand and feel it is relevant to their values and lifestyles. This is the realm of brand engagement, which strives to understand this aspect of brand loyalty.

To respond to this variety of consumer behaviors, marketers have developed several strategies to create and to maintain brand loyalty (e.g., Fassott, 2004; Payne & Frow, 2005; Reichheld, 1996). Prominent among these strategies are improving customer support, service, and satisfaction; formal loyalty or frequency marketing programs; adding value to brands; innovation and product improvements; co-creation with consumers; developing employee loyalty; personalizing the marketing strategy; focusing segmentation and targeting efforts on the customers most likely to become loyal; using alliances such as cause-related marketing and co-branding; developing customer relationship management (CRM) or customer experience (CEM) programs; and finally, striving to create emotional ties or relationships between the brand and its buyers.

We are concerned with this final aspect of brand loyalty. Marketers know that often, loyalty is not just the result of quality or satisfaction, but that customers sometimes feel that the brand is special in some way. Some consumers form "relationships" with brands. Schultz et al. (2009, p. 12) define brand relationships as "those bonds that bring the buyer and the seller of branded products or services together on a continuing basis." Although brand relationships may be formed on the basis of reliability or effectiveness, this concept necessarily transcends the utilitarian and cognitive aspects of consumer brand behavior to incorporate emotional reactions such as trust and even love (Tsiotsou & Goldsmith, 2011). In particular, consumers may view the brand as a reflection of their self-identity so that it plays an important role in communicating their identity to other people. Research shows that brand identity emerges among young children and that these young consumers form connections between brands and themselves (Chaplin & Roedder John, 2005). Fournier (1988) documents the nature and consequences of such brand relationships among middle-aged women consumers. Several journalistic treatments describe examples of consumers forming strong attachments to brands and using these brands to express personal and social identities (e.g., Hill & Rifkin, 1999; Lewis, 2000; Walker, 2008). Recently, however, scholars have approached this topic systematically to investigate how and why consumers form these brand relationships. This topic has been termed Brand Engagement.

BRAND ENGAGEMENT: THE THEORETICAL PERSPECTIVE

Brands are more than mere identifiers; they differentiate products that would otherwise only be commodities. Even more than that, brands are bought for emotional as well as rational reasons (Chaudhuri, 2006; Sutton & Klein, 2003); brands evoke strong feelings and have meaning for their buyers. These meanings can be important to how consumers view themselves and how they project their social images (Allen, Fournier, & Miller, 2008). Advances in understanding many consumer brand behaviors now focus on this aspect of branding.

In order to understand brand engagement, we must distinguish between *types* of engagement and *levels* of engagement. The former refers to the various ways in which the term "engagement" is used in discussions of marketplace behavior, where it has been applied to advertising engagement (Nielsen, 2009), media engagement (Nail, 2006), engagement with web sites (Calder, Malthouse, & Schaedel, 2009), or engagement with the company (Peppers & Rogers, 2008). Each of these usages refers to emotional reactions to situations and to other stimuli where the consumer forms some bond or relationship with the stimulus. Synonyms might be involvement or commitment. Our specific concern is engagement with brands themselves, but consumers invest emotional energy into several aspects of the marketplace, especially at different *levels* of generality or abstraction, of which brand engagement is only one.

Market Mavenism

At the highest level of generality we have engagement in the marketplace itself. This is the realm of *market mavenism*. First presented by Feick and Price (1987), the market maven is a consumer who is highly engaged in the marketplace in general. A body of research has accumulated describing their many distinguishing characteristics (e.g., Goldsmith & Clark, 2005). These consumers pay close attention to ads and brands, they like to shop, they think about shopping and buying, and they like to talk to others about ads, stores, products, shopping, and consuming in general. They clip and trade coupons. They are aware of and eager to buy new products, and they act as general opinion leaders. They know the best places to buy and actively recommend them to their friends. Market mavens derive favorable emotional satisfactions from their marketplace activity; they feel proud, helpful, and savvy. In short, the market maven manifests the attitudes and behaviors that characterize engagement with some stimulus. Market mavenism is the outcome of specific motivations, is characterized by positive emotions, and is related to a variety of outcomes in a consistent pattern of motivated behavior.

Enduring Product Involvement

But being engaged with the marketplace is only one way that the consumer's emotions can be focused. Consumers also become involved with specific product categories that take on special importance and meaning for them. From the utilitarian and functional perspective, product categories can be important to consumers because these products solve important problems for consumers. Consumers therefore judge these categories to be "important" and "matter" to them, but the category does not elicit emotional reactions such as delight or fun, neither is the category an important signal of the consumer's personal and social image. For example, tires or detergent are important and matter to most consumers, but most consumers have little emotional involvement with their tires or their detergents. These functional products are expected to perform their jobs reliably and completely without evoking emotional bonds or relationships for most consumers. (Marketers often want consumers to trust these brands, but the trust is based on their ability to solve a problem or to perform effectively, not tell others who the customer is.) We do not want to confuse this type of customer evaluation, which we should call *perceived product importance*, based as it is on satisfaction and perceived value, with the consumer responses of interest and enthusiasm represented by the involvement concept. The term *product involvement* should be reserved to refer to instances where the consumer finds the category interesting and exciting because of the emotional and social benefits of the product. The product is therefore important to them, but for reasons other than the functional, utilitarian, and problem solving benefits of consuming the product. Every product that consumers consider to be involving is important to them, but not every product that is important to them is also involving or engaging.

When we examine product involvement we find a large body of literature describing how and why particular product categories occupy the time, emotions, money, and energy of many consumers. Houston and Rothschild (1978) first articulated the concept of enduring product involvement and distinguished it from involvement with advertising, which occurs when audience members make connections between the ad they are viewing and aspects of their own lives (Krugman, 1965, 1966). Bloch (1986) used the synonyms "interest," "enthusiasm," and "excitement" to portray the involved consumer. Consumers are involved in product categories when these "matter" to them because they elicit strong hedonic and experiential emotions (Chaudhuri, 2006), when there are psychological linkages to them (Laaksonen, 1999), and when they act as symbols of personal and social identity (Allen et al., 2008).

Product involvement is domain specific, that is, the reference is to a product category and not to the overall marketplace, distinguishing it from the concept of market mavenism. Market mavens likely have product categories in which they are involved, but being enthusiastic about a specific category does not entail being a market maven. Enduring product involvement with a category is a strong driver of a variety of other consumer behaviors including product knowledge, innovativeness, loyalty, price insensitivity, and opinion leadership (Goldsmith, 2000; Ramirez & Goldsmith, 2009).

Specific Brand Engagement

If we drill further down in the generality/specificity ladder, we come to yet another use of the term brand engagement that is similar to those that came before but expresses a more specific concept. At this level, consumers differ in how engaged they are with individual brands, so brand engagement refers here to how a consumer feels about a *specific brand.* In March 2006, the Advertising Research Federation defined engagement as "turning on a prospect to a brand idea enhanced by the surrounding context." This definition reflects the diversity with which the marketing and advertising community thinks about engagement, but provides little guidance for operationalizing or using the concept (Nail, 2006; Spilman, 2006). The brand management literature is replete with recommendations and exhortations telling managers to encourage their consumers to become engaged with specific brands (e.g., Schultz, 2007; Uncles, 2008). Thus, although enduring product involvement is an important driver of many important consumer behaviors, managers typically focus on individual brands, so that it is this form of brand engagement that attracts the most managerial attention.

Keller (2001) makes engagement with the brand a key component of his Customer-Based Brand Equity model. Building systematically from the basic concept of brand salience, this model proposes that mangers can take specific steps to create brand equity by connecting with customers and making their brands relevant to their customers' lives. The final goal is an intense, active relationship between the brand and the customer, part of which is engagement with the brand expressed as customer eagerness to talk about the brand, learn about it, and exhibit its use to others. One can see this phenomenon clearly in the "brand prophet" phenomenon (Klaassen, 2006) or the "brand evangelist," described by McConnell and Huba (2003), who is compelled to tell others about the brand and otherwise promotes its purchase. In this sense, brand engagement (with a specific brand) leads to behavioral brand loyalty (Rozanski, Baum, & Wolfsen, 1999).

Specific Brand Engagement is independent of enduring involvement with a product category. Consumers may be more or less involved with a category, but they can be further distinguished as loyal or non-loyal toward specific brands (Coulter, Price, & Feick, 2003). For example, a consumer involved in clothing, a fashionista, for whom clothing is important, exciting, and interesting, may be indifferent to some brands of clothing and greatly attached to others that she sees to be integral elements of her self-concept. These brands she loves and buys repeatedly. A consumer who is largely indifferent to clothing (but still thinks it is an important purchase) may buy the same brands because she believes them to be high in quality, durability, or fit. Engagement at one level (product category) can be, but is not necessarily related to engagement at another level (specific brand engagement).

Brand Engagement in Self-Concept

The final and latest manifestation of the brand engagement concept parallels these descriptions of levels of engagement by proposing an individual difference variable, *brand engagement in self-concept* (BESC), which refers to individual differences in how much consumers form emotional bonds with brands. BESC is defined as a way to understand how consumers react to brands that stresses their "tendencies to include important brands as part of their self-concept" (Sprott, Czellar, & Spangenberg, 2009, p. 92). BESC portrays consumers along a continuum ranging from the low end, where consumers do not see brands as important elements of self-concept, to the high end where they identify with brands and have special bonds with them. Brand Engagement in Self-Concept is a new and different way to think about consumers' relationships with brands. Not only is it well grounded in consumer theory, for the first time it offers researchers a scale to measure the concept as an individual difference variable that permits empirical research into the antecedents and consequences of brand engagement.

Sprott et al. (2009) show that BESC is positively related to materialism. As people's materialism grows, they seek to acquire material goods to compensate for low levels of well being and psychological health (Kasser, 2002). Materialistic people often have a fragile sense of self-worth and they form poor relationships with others (whom they view as objects); thus brands and the way brands can represent self-concept may fill the gaps in their lives ordinarily filled by human relationships. Sprott et al. (2009) also found that brand engagement was positively related to stronger links between self-concept and favorite brands, better recall for names of current branded possessions, paying more attention to brands in incidental brand exposure, and willingness to wait longer for a new product introduced by the favorite brand. This last finding suggests that new products, at least those of their favorite brands, are sought by consumers high in BESC. Evidence supporting this surmise can be found in Goldsmith et al. (2010).

It can be further speculated that besides materialism, other antecedents of BESC are market mavenism and enduring product involvement. Market mavenism implies interest and enthusiasm for marketplace activities. This interest directs consumers to devote time, money, and energy into noticing and learning about brands, shopping, buying, and sharing advice and information with others. Brands are surely to be an important concern for these consumers so that they are likely to be more engaged with brands at both of the lower levels of specificity: enduring product involvement and specific brand engagement. Because market mavens are interested in what is going on in the market place, they likely are involved with specific product categories, although which ones would depend on other factors and be individual to each maven. And because they are knowledgeable about brands and are innovative buyers, they are likely to have their favorite brands, thus manifesting specific brand engagement. Finally, it is reasonable to conclude that market mavenism is positively related to BESC; mavens are more likely to use brands to form and to express self-concept than are consumers who are less interested than they are in the marketplace. The psychological glue that holds these concepts together is the positive emotions stimulated in some consumers by brands.

BRAND ENGAGEMENT: THE MANAGERIAL PERSPECTIVE

As it is used by many consultants, journalists, and managers, the term brand engagement is highly related to three other currently popular terms in marketing management: loyalty, relationship marketing, and customer relationship management. This section strives to distinguish among them and to suggest how they are related. It also seeks to delineate how managerial strategies are related to desired managerial outcomes. Engagement seems to be the common denominator connecting these diverse concepts (see Table 1).

As the discussion above suggests, loyalty to a company, store, or brand consists of an antecedent psychological state of positive attitudes and feelings linked to behavioral outcomes such as repeat buying, price insensitivity, willingness to

Table 1. Strategy, engagement, and brand loyalty

STRATEGIES	MECHANISM	OUTCOMES
CRM Loyalty Programs Relationship Marketing Advertising Promotion Co-creation Social Networks	Engagement Relationship	Attitudinal Loyalty Knowledge Repeat Buying Cross-Purchasing Price Insensitivity Innovativeness Positive Feedback Brand Advocacy Brand Equity

buy more of the brand, and to provide positive brand recommendations. These are important outcomes for marketing strategy. Marketers strive to create positive brand attitudes so as to build their brand's equity. Over the years, different streams of thought have developed which promise managers tools and techniques for reaching their desired goals. The key, they are told, is to build *relationships* with customers that go beyond the one-off sale so that customers will feel committed to the brand. The idea of companies having "relationships" with customers has a long history. Service marketers may have been the first to promote the idea that service managers should create relationships with their customers (Berry, 1983). Dwyer, Schurr, and Oh (1987) provided one of the first systematic rationales for marketers to move away from thinking of their goal as discrete transactional exchanges to developing on-going relationship with customers. Morgan and Hunt (1994) extended this paradigm to propose a theory of "relationship marketing" that has been a topic of intense theoretical and managerial concern ever since (see Buttle, 2009), but which stands as one of the basic foundations of modern marketing theory.

Customer relationship management (CRM) has developed as the key technique for creating these relationships (Fassott, 2004). Unfortunately, and much like the term "engagement" itself, CRM is understood and defined in a variety of ways, blending as it does technology to manage data with customer oriented strategy. Payne and Frow (2005) suggest that significant confusion exists among practitioners and academics as to what CRM is. Conceptualizations range from one extreme of being defined narrowly as a specific tactic involving the implementation of a specific technology to being defined in broad terms as a high-level strategic initiative. They suggest CRM be defined as "a strategic approach that is concerned with creating improved shareholder value through the development of appropriate relationships with key customers and customer segments. CRM unites the potential of relationship marketing strategies and IT to create profitable, long-term relationships with customers and other key stakeholders. CRM provides enhanced opportunities to use data and information to both understand customers and co-create value with them. This requires a cross-functional integration of processes, people, operations, and marketing capabilities that is enabled through information, technology, and applications" (p. 168). The overlap in concept and purpose between CRM and relationship marketing is self-evident.

Other proposals to promote engagement and loyalty feature similar themes. Advertising (and by extension other promotional activities such as sponsorships and cause-related marketing) are argued to "engage" customers and establish emotional responses to the brand that can lead to loyalty. Astolfi et al. (2008, p. 77) provide a succinct summary of the place of the engagement concept in advertising and marketing: "... the term engagement is a complex concept and rather elusive, it is widely recognized that advertising engagement refers to the ability of the message to go beyond the simple exposure and to trigger in the consumer mind a progression of responses towards the brand advertised leading to a shift of awareness, interest, favourability, preference, purchase and repurchase."

Another school of thought argues that the most important element in winning loyal customers is to *manage the customer experience* (Meyer & Schwager, 2007; Peppers & Rogers, 2008).

"Customer experience encompasses every aspect of a company's offering – the quality of customer care, of course, but also advertising, packaging, product and service features, ease of use, and reliability.... Customer experience is the internal and subjective response customers have to any direct or indirect contact with a company" (Meyer & Schwager, 2007, p. 118). Customer experience is the precursor of customer satisfaction because satisfaction is simply the end result of repeated customer experiences; however, satisfaction is a necessary but not sufficient requirement for engagement, and ultimately, loyalty. According to Sutton and Klein (2003):

The brand experience is simply a way to describe the sum of a customer's interactions with a brand. If a brand is the bundle of functional and emotional benefits, attributes, icons and symbols that, in total, comprises the meaning of the product or service, then the brand experience is the name for a customer's complete experience with the brand. The term brand implies a perspective from the company outwards (inside-out). The term brand experience implies a perspective from the customer to every interaction with the company (outside-in). (Sutton & Klein, 2003, p. 64.)

The goal of customer experience management is to ensure that every "touch-point" or interaction with the firm is positive so that it contributes to satisfaction. Like CRM, customer experience management uses research to understand customer interactions with the firm, but in contrast to CRM's focus on transactions, customer experience data "capture customers' subjective thoughts about a particular company" (Meyer & Schwager, 2007, p. 121).

Peppers and Rogers (1993) emphasize building customer relationships using customization principles. Frequency marketing (loyalty programs) offers a way to create customer loyalty through rewards, but unless they are structured to build a relationship, this approach may not return it real value to the company (see O'Brien & Jones, 1995). Reichheld (1996) emphasizes developing employee engagement and loyalty as the means to engage customers. Vargo and Lusch (2004) and Prahalad and Ramaswamy (2004) argue that facilitating co-creation of the product and the brand will win customer loyalty. Social networking is being touted as an effective means to establish relationships with consumers (Li & Bernoff, 2008), but there is evidence that without engagement, they are not very effective (Straczynski, 2009). Finally, consulting companies are appearing that make customer engagement their chief focus as they integrate online and offline marketing activities to engage the customer with a brand (Pekala, 2009).

Engagement (commitment) is the emotional tie that binds the customer to the brand and consequently to the company. Although relationships based on functional and utilitarian benefits certainly exist, the thrust of much of the management thought on this topic has emphasized emotional relationships between customers, brands, and firms. Thus, the desired relationship between the company and the customer or the brand and the customer is based on the emotions evoked by the brand as it acquires meaning for the customer (Allen et al., 2008). For example, consider the following recommendation: "Emotional brand loyalty is the ultimate achievement for marketers building brands. Consumers who are emotionally bonded to your brand are much more likely to stay loyal, repeat purchase or cross-purchase, happily recommend the brand to others and accept no substitutes" (Donbavand, 2007). Another example addresses the current negative economic situation, in which marketers are encouraged to "... bolster trust (by treating customers well and reinforcing their emotional connection with the brand)" (Quelch & Jocz, 2009, p. 55). Thus, engagement with the brand or company appears at the center of the model shown in Table 1. It connects the strategic initiatives taken by managers with the goals these managers seek by providing one mechanism explaining how the strategies accomplish their goals. Every strategy is intended to increase the emotional bonds customers form with brands, thereby establishing "relationships" with them, which lead to the desired goals of attitudinal loyalty followed by the panoply of loyal behaviors.

BRAND ENGAGEMENT: THE METHODOLOGICAL PERSPECTIVE

In order for both consumer researchers and marketing managers to most effectively use the concepts of brand loyalty and brand engagement, they must first delineate precisely the concepts in which they are interested. Then they must have ways to operationalize these concepts for the purpose of testing theory or developing effective strategy. Because brand loyalty has had so many different definitions and proposed operationalizations, this topic is too extensive to be discussed here, but in general, brand loyalty operationalizations have tended to group into either self-report attitudinal measures or behavioral measures (via either self-report or scanner type data).

Research into brand engagement also has ranged across a variety of empirical methods, from informal and qualitative approaches to self-report and then to physiological measures. Interest in brand engagement has stimulated a number of observers who have provided what can be termed "journalist" or anecdotal examples of consumers who are engaged with individual brands. Hill and Rifkin (1999) vividly describe the passion of groups of consumers who follow the Grateful Dead or are devoted to the Harley-Davidson brand. In these examples we can see the key themes of "loyalty," "relationships," and "emotional bonds" with brands. Lewis (2000) argues that there are "old" consumers driven by functional and practical motives, and "new" consumers who seek individuality and authenticity in the brands they buy. These new consumers manifest an "individual, involved, independent and informed approach to consumption" (p. 21). Solomon (2003) describes the "consumerspace" in which consumers define brand meanings and use them to express who they are or want to be. Finally, Walker (2008) presents many examples of individuals who either buy brands specifically for the meanings they have or who even create brands expressly to express their lifestyles and values.

More rigorous research has been undertaken by academic researchers using qualitative techniques. For example, Fournier (1998) used "phenomenological interviewing" with three adult women to investigate the extent and nature of the relationships they formed with brands of common household products. Chaplin and John (2005) used in-depth interviews and projective tests to shows that by middle childhood, young consumers develop self-brand connections. Coulter et al. (2003) employed depth interviews and participant observation with a sample of Hungarian and Romanian women to show how they became involved with cosmetics and with specific brands with which they formed relationships. Chaplin and John (2005) had children construct collages to represent what their favorite brands meant to their self-concepts.

Researchers have developed a variety of self-report scales to operationalize the various types of engagement we have described (see Table 2). At the marketplace level, Feick and Price (1987) describe the six-item Market Maven scale. Several self-report scales are intended to measure enduring product category involvement. Table 2 presents one example from Mittal and Lee (1989). Keller (2001) proposes a six-item scale to measure a consumer's engagement with a specific brand. And finally, Sprott et al. (2009) describe their eight item Brand Engagement Self-Concept Scale and present evidence for its reliability and validity.

Brand engagement has an unconscious dimension. Consumers often cannot explain exactly why they prefer certain brands to others, they just know they like them better. Understanding the uncon-

Table 2. Examples of engagement measures

Construct	Developers	Characteristics	Item Example
Market Mavenism	Feick and Price (1987)	Six items, Likert format	I like introducing new brands and products to my friends.
Product Category Involvement	Mittal and Lee (1989)	Three items, Likert format	I have a strong interest in ________.
Specific Brand Engagement	Keller (2001)	Six items, Likert format	I really like to talk about this brand with others.
Brand Engagement Self-Concept	Sprott et al. (2009)	Eight items, Likert format	I have a special bond with the brands that I like.

scious meaning of brands requires different methodological perspectives. For example, Zaltman (2003) has patented a research method to study brand engagement called the Zaltman Metaphor Elicitation Technique or ZMET. Research participants are asked to collect pictures from magazines, catalogs, and family photo albums that represent their thoughts and feelings about a product. They subsequently discuss these pictures in depth with trained interviewers. Then, a technician uses Adobe Photoshop to help the consumers build collages of their thoughts and feelings. Researchers interpret the verbal responses as metaphors and stories to gain insights into how consumers relate to products and to brands.

In addition to Zaltman's (2003) qualitative approach that probes the consumer's unconscious for insights into the meaning of products, he also pursues studies of consumers and their brands by using the latest tools of neuroscience. Positron emission tomography, a type of brain scan, can reveal areas in the brain where activity increases when consumers think about brands. This evidence can show which neurological mechanisms are activated by different marketing stimuli, such as brand names and logos, thereby suggesting the physiological processes associated with the subjective experiences of thinking and feeling about brands. Studies such as Astolfi et al. (2008) also endeavor to reveal the neural networks and cerebral processes involved during the observation of TV commercials. These findings are important because they reveal at the neurophysiological level, how consumers react to brands. For example, McClure et al. (2004) showed that brand associations that triggered emotional reactions to the Coke brand played an important role in directing test subject preference for the brand that was lacking when Pepsi was the stimulus. Foxall (2008) argues that ultimately, a comprehensive model of consumer reaction to brands will be provided by integrating the stimulus-response conditioning explanation of the Behavioural Perspective Model of consumer behavior with the findings of neuroeconomics to show how brands elicit the engagement response in consumers and how this response shapes their reactions to marketing stimuli.

Overall, it is apparent that not only has the concept of brand engagement attracted the interest of a variety of researchers, the future of this topic should see the integration of the different methodologies to yield a comprehensive picture of the antecedents, operations, and consequences of brand engagement. Advertising researchers have their own concepts of advertising engagement and methods to measure it (e.g., Nielsen, 2009). Consultants will propose and use many ways to operationalize engagement with the firm for their purposes.

CONCLUSION

The goals of this chapter are to summarize briefly the concepts of brand loyalty and brand engagement and to show how they are linked to several others concepts that are currently important to marketing management and consumer research: frequency marketing, relationship marketing, and customer relationship management. These ideas are related, but the situation is like the proverbial blind men and the elephant, where each man "saw" only part of the beast and not the whole animal. Brand managers are eager to create brand loyalty; it represents a sustainable competitive advantage for brands that have it. Loyalty in turn can be conceptualized as either a state of mind or a pattern of behavior. To create loyalty, managers are encouraged to use a variety of techniques and philosophies that include loyalty programs, customer relationship management programs, or relationships building. For these techniques to work, however, they must stimulate emotional connections among consumers generally termed "engagement," of which brand engagement properly so called is only one type. Consumers can also be engaged with the market itself, product categories, social networks and other online sites, companies, and advertising. In short, marketing managers want customers to be become engaged with their ads, their brands, their websites, and their companies so that they will be loyal buyers, buy without discounts, and spread positive word-of-mouth about the brand to other consumers.

All applications of the term "engagement" share the notion that consumers' (or employees') emotions are stimulated by the ad, the website, the brand, the job, etc. Although engagement is considered as a synonym for commitment and obligation, engagement seems to have a positive connotation, expressing excitement and joy, rather than duty or dedication. This is the intent of those who use it. They want consumers to enjoy and to be enthusiastic about the ad, the company, the product, or the brand. Thus, all uses of engagement in this context emphasize a positive emotional relationship between the consumer and the brand. As research continues, we will gain a clearer picture of how engagement is created by the brain, how it is expressed by consumers, and how it influences their behavior. From neural networks to social networks, brand engagement is fast becoming a central component of consumer models and marketing strategies alike.

To achieve Peter Drucker's maxim that the goal of a business is to create and keep a customer, firms are turning more and more to the experiential aspects of consumption. They are viewing marketplace behavior from the customer's point of view. They are beginning to understand that brands mean something to consumers and that often this meaning is created or at least co-created by consumers. Satisfaction and quality are becoming the price of admission. Firms must try to manage the overall brand experience if they are to win loyal customers. Brand engagement is a key concept in understanding these aspects of consumer behavior, and it will play a growing role in shaping the marketplace of the future.

ACKNOWLEDGMENT

This chapter was supported by a summer research grant to the author from the College of Business, Florida State University.

REFERENCES

Allen, C. T., Fournier, S., & Miller, F. (2008). Brands and their meaning makers. In Haugtvedt, C. P., Herr, P. M., & Kardes, F. R. (Eds.), *Handbook of consumer psychology* (pp. 781–821). New York, NY: Psychology Press.

Astolfi, L., Fallani, F., Serenella, S., Cincotti, F., Mattia, D., Marciani, M. G., Soranzo, R., & Babiloni, F. (2008). Brain activity related to the memorization of TV commercials. *International Journal of Bioelectromagnetism, 10*(2), 77-79-86.

Bloch, P. H. (1986). The product enthusiast: Implications for marketing strategy. *Journal of Consumer Marketing, 3*(3), 51–62. doi:10.1108/eb008170

Buttle, F. (2009). *Customer relationship management: Concepts and techniques*. Oxford, UK: Butterworth-Hinemann.

Calder, B. J., Malthouse, E. C., & Schaedel, U. (2009). An experimental study of the relationship between online engagement and advertising effectiveness. *Journal of Interactive Marketing, 23*(4), 321–331. doi:10.1016/j.intmar.2009.07.002

Chaplin, L. N., & Roedder John, D. (2005). The development of self-brand connections in children and adolescents. *The Journal of Consumer Research, 32*(1), 119–129. doi:10.1086/426622

Chaudhuri, A. (2006). *Emotion and reason in consumer behavior*. Amsterdam, The Netherlands: Butterworth-Hinemann.

Coulter, R. A., Feick, L., & Price, L. L. (2003). Rethinking the origins of involvement and brand commitment: Insights from post-Socialist Central Europe. *The Journal of Consumer Research, 30*(2), 151–169. doi:10.1086/376809

Cunningham, R. M. (1956). Brand loyalty-What, where, how much? *Harvard Business Review, 34*(1), 116–128.

Cunningham, R. M. (1961). Customer loyalty to store and brand. *Harvard Business Review, 39*(6), 127–137.

Dick, A. S., & Basu, K. (1994). Customer loyalty: Toward an integrated conceptual framework. *Journal of the Academy of Marketing Science, 22*(2), 99–113. doi:10.1177/0092070394222001

Donbavand, R. (2007, June). Brands need to get emotional. *Brand Strategy, 36*.

Dwyer, F. R., Schurr, P. H., & Oh, S. (1987). Developing buyer-seller relationships. *Journal of Marketing, 51*(2), 11–27. doi:10.2307/1251126

Ehrenberg, A. S. C. (1988). *Repeat buying: Facts, theory and applications* (2nd ed.). New York, NY & London, UK: Oxford University Press & Griffin.

Fassott, G. (2004). CRM tools and their impact on relationship quality and loyalty in e-tailing. *International Journal of Internet Marketing and Advertising, 1*(4), 331–349. doi:10.1504/IJIMA.2004.006328

Feick, L. F., & Price, L. L. (1987). The market maven: A diffuser of marketplace information. *Journal of Marketing, 51*(January), 83–97. doi:10.2307/1251146

Fournier, S. (1998). Consumers and their brands: Developing relationship theory in consumer research. *The Journal of Consumer Research, 24*(March), 343–373. doi:10.1086/209515

Foxall, G. R. (1999). The substitutability of brands. *Managerial & Decision Economics, 20*(5), 241–257. doi:10.1002/(SICI)1099-1468(199908)20:5<241::AID-MDE936>3.0.CO;2-U

Foxall, G. R. (2008). Reward, emotion and consumer choice: From neuroeconomics to neurophilosophy. *Journal of Consumer Behaviour, 7*(4/5), 368–396. doi:10.1002/cb.258

Goldsmith, R. E. (2000). Characteristics of the heavy user of fashionable clothing. *Journal of Marketing Theory & Practice, 8*(4), 21–28.

Goldsmith, R. E., Flynn, L. R., & Korzenny, F. (2010). Brand engagement and consumer innovativeness. *Proceedings of the Association of Marketing Theory and Practice*.

Hill, S., & Rifkin, G. (1999). *Radical marketing*. New York, NY: HarperBusiness.

Houston, M. J., & Rothschild, M. L. (1978). Conceptual and methodological perspectives in involvement. *Research Frontiers in Marketing: Dialogues and Directions, Conference Proceedings*, (pp. 184-187).

Jacoby, J., & Chestnut, R. (1978). *Brand loyalty: Measurement and management*. New York, NY: John Wiley.

Kasser, T. (2002). *The high price of materialism*. Cambridge, MA: The MIT Press.

Keller, K. L. (2001). *Building customer-based brand equity: A blueprint for creating strong brands*. Marketing Science Institute, (Working Paper 01-107).

Klaassen, A. (2006). This is the Avon lady... on steroids. *Advertising Age*, *77*(36), 1–39.

Krugman, H. E. (1965). The impact of television advertising: Learning without involvement. *Public Opinion Quarterly*, *29*(3), 349–356. doi:10.1086/267335

Krugman, H. E. (1966). The measurement of advertising involvement. *Public Opinion Quarterly*, *30*(4), 583–596. doi:10.1086/267457

Laaksonen, P. (1999). Involvement. In Earl, P. E., & Kemp, S. (Eds.), *The Elgar companion to consumer research and economic psychology* (pp. 341–347). Cheltenham, UK: Edward Elgar Publishing.

Lewis, D., & Bridger, D. (2000). *The soul of the new consumer*. London, UK: Nicholas Brealey Publishing.

Li, C., & Bernoff, J. (2008). *Groundswell: Winning in a world transformed by social technologies*. Boston, MA: Harvard Business Press.

McClure, S. M., Li, J., Tomlin, D., Cypert, K. S., Montague, L. M., & Montague, P. R. (2004). Neural correlates of behavioral preference for culturally familiar drinks. *Neuron*, *44*(2), 379–387. doi:10.1016/j.neuron.2004.09.019

McConnell, B., & Huba, J. (2003). *Creating customer evangelists: How loyal customers become a volunteer sales force*. Chicago, IL: Dearborn Trade Pub.

Meyer, C., & Schwager, A. (2007). Understanding customer experience. *Harvard Business Review*, *85*(February), 117–126.

Mittal, B., & Lee, M.-S. (1989). A causal model of consumer involvement. *Journal of Economic Psychology*, *10*, 363–389. doi:10.1016/0167-4870(89)90030-5

Nail, J. (2006). *The 4 types of engagement*. Retrieved from www.imediaconnection.com.

Nielsen. (2009). *Nielsen global online consumer survey: Trust, value and engagement in advertising*. Retrieved from http://blog.nielsen.com/nielsenwire /wp-content/uploads/2009/07 / trustinadvertising0709.pdf

O'Brien, L., & Jones, C. (1995). Do rewards really create loyalty? *Harvard Business Review*, *73*(3), 75–82.

Pekala, N. (2009, June 26). The age of the 24/7 consumer creates emergence of customer engagement agencies. *Marketing Matters Newsletter*.

Peppers, D., & Rogers, M. (1993). *The one-to-one future: Building relationships one customer at a time*. New York, NY: Currency Doubleday.

Peppers, D., & Rogers, M. (2008). *Building equity through the customer experience*. White Paper.

Prahalad, C. K., & Ramaswamy, V. (2004). Co-creation experiences: The next practice in value creation. *Journal of Interactive Marketing*, *18*(3), 5–14. doi:10.1002/dir.20015

Quelch, J. A., & Jocz, K. E. (2009). How to market in a downturn. *Harvard Business Review*, *87*(4), 52–62.

Ramirez, E., & Goldsmith, R. E. (2009). Some antecedents of price sensitivity. *Journal of Marketing Theory and Practice*, *17*(3), 199–213. doi:10.2753/MTP1069-6679170301

Reichheld, F. F. (1996). *The loyalty effect*. Boston, MA: Harvard Business School Press.

Robinson, S., & Etherington, L. (2006). *Customer loyalty*. Houndmills, UK: Palgrave Macmillan.

Rozanski, H. D., Baum, A. G., & Wolfsen, B. T. (1999). Brand zealots: Realizing the full value of emotional brand loyalty. *strategy+business, 17*, 51-62.

Schultz, D. E. (2007). Focus on brand changes rules of engagement. *Marketing News*, *41*(13), 7–8.

Schultz, D. E., Barnes, B. E., Schultz, H. F., & Azzaro, M. (2009). *Building customer-brand relationships*. Armonk, NY: M. E. Sharpe, Inc.

Solomon, M. R. (2003). *Conquering consumer-space: Marketing strategies for a branded world*. New York: AMACOM.

Spilman, M. (2006). *Cracking the engagement code*. Retrieved from www.imediaconnection.com

Sprott, D., Czellar, S., & Spangenberg, E. (2009). The importance of a general measure of brand engagement on market behavior: Development and validation of a scale. *JMR, Journal of Marketing Research*, *46*(1), 92–104. doi:10.1509/jmkr.46.1.92

Straczynski, S. (2009, September 3). *Social network branding fails to sway female purchasing*. Retrieved from progressivegrocer.com

Sutton, D., & Klein, T. (2003). *Enterprise marketing management*. Hoboken, NJ: John Wiley & Sons.

Tsiotsou, R., & Goldsmith, R. E. (2011). Exploring the formation process of brand love: a comparison between goods and services. Presentation 2011 Academy of Marketing Science World Marketing Congress, Reims, France July 19-July 23.Uncles, M. (2008). Know thy changing consumer. *Journal of Brand Management*, *15*, 227–231.

Vargo, S. L., & Lusch, R. F. (2004). Evolving to a new dominant logic for marketing. *Journal of Marketing*, *68*(1), 1–17. doi:10.1509/jmkg.68.1.1.24036

Walker, R. (2008). *Buying in*. New York, NY: Random House.

Zaltman, G. (2003). *How customers think*. Cambridge, MA: Harvard Business School Press.

KEY TERMS AND DEFINITIONS

Brand Commitment: Similar to brand engagement and often used synonymously. Commitment implies that the brand is the first choice of the consumer and that the consumer will pay more or put forth extra effort to get the brand.

Brand Engagement: Emotional attachment to a brand; strong feelings (usually positive) about a brand; viewing a brand as more than a means to an end, but means something to the consumer.

Brand Engagement in Self-Concept: An individual difference variable by which consumers differ in the extent to which they see and use brands to create and to project their self-concepts; "I am what I buy."

Brand Loyalty: Brand loyalty as tow aspects: (1) attitudinal loyalty or the positive emotion that the brand is the right one for the customer; it is the one the customer wants to buy; and (2) behavioral loyalty, a consistent pattern of purchasing the brand.

Cause-Related Marketing: When a brand partners or allies with a not-for-profit organization, donating a portion of sales to them.

Customer Relationship Management (CRM): Using technology to collect information about customers and using this information to develop relationships with customers, managing these relationships for their long-term value.

Involvement: Feelings of interest, enthusiasm, and excitement; a positive emotional response to a stimulus. Consumers often become involved in favored product categories.

Market Mavenism: Some consumers are involved in the marketplace itself, deriving pleasure from viewing advertisements, shopping, buying, and talking with others about their experiences. Market mavens accumulate knowledge and expertise in the market and eagerly share their opinion with others.

Relationship Marketing: Used in a variety of ways with no universally agreed upon definition. All descriptions imply an active strategy to win customer loyalty by performing actions that go beyond the provision of the product (good or service) in an effort to get the customer to bond with the brand. Strategies include sponsorships, cause-related marketing, personalization, loyalty programs, and efforts to increase the value of the brand by adding extra benefits.

Chapter 9
The Brand Stakeholder Approach:
Broad and Narrow-Based Views to Managing Consumer-Centric Brands

Jonathan A. J. Wilson
University of Greenwich, UK

ABSTRACT

With the emergence of schools of thought which examine brands and branding according to relationships, brand communities, and popular culture, consumers are becoming more significant in shaping the brand agenda. Furthermore, the evolutionary growth and mutations spawned by Web 2.0 draw non-brand users, social networks, and anti-branding movements towards engagement and the possession of greater social capital. When gifting stakeholders with a larger share of voice, consumption definitions become judged less by tangible transactions; and more by figurative, intangible, and co-dependent communication drivers. In addition, with the increase in interactivity afforded by media channels, two-way communication, and the inclusion of more parties; a normalisation and levelling of information also occurs. Therefore, this chapter presents stakeholders as occupying grouped, interconnected, and dynamic states, which are subject to time-specific communication, influence, and self defined legitimacy. Following this, the creation of brands becomes a collaborative process with brands seeking to engage consumers in new and innovative ways in order to gain authenticity.

DOI: 10.4018/978-1-61350-171-9.ch009

INTRODUCTION

Following such hard rules of classification based upon economic factors, there has been a movement towards expanding brand definitions to also regard 'selling' in a more figurative manner. In doing so more intangible and psychological pricing constructs are accommodated—which are reflective of the application of marketing and brand theory to other supporting business disciplines; not to mention the premium attached to associated emotional components. Therefore in retrospectively applying current brand definitions to creations and instances throughout history, it can be argued that brands and branding, despite their relatively recent study, in fact stretch right back much further to ancient civilisations.

The analogy often conveyed within branding literature is that of a cowboy branding his cattle; which is perhaps a reflection of majority of branding literature hailing from the US. However pre-dating this, clans, tribes, armies, artists, societies, leaders and nations, amongst others, have also clearly demonstrated desires to 'brand' themselves. Their intention appears to be as a means of identification and for future strategic gains – economically, emotionally, societally, and politically. Within these constructs, the common denominator lies in defining boundaries and terms of engagement. In doing so, identities according to easily communicated membership and ownership are central. This chapter houses and addresses these issues through stakeholder analysis, and is structured in the following way:

- Stakeholder Analysis: origins and approach
- Refining stakeholder theory for Brand Stakeholder analysis
- Broad view: Brand Stakeholders from a macro/mezzo-perspective
- Narrow view: Brand Stakeholders from a micro-perspective
- Case examples in practice
- Moving forward and managing the branding process for stakeholder gains

BACKGROUND

Where business literature has previously commented on these phenomena surrounding stakeholder relations, seldom have they been described as being part of branding. Rather, for example Bernays (1928, 1955) talks of 'ideas' and describes his processes as a method of *Engineering Consent;* a term that has later been adapted by Herman and Chomsky (1988), becoming *Manufacturing Consent.* The following section examines branding from the perspective of mapping communications relationships between stakeholders and their frames of reference. The argument put forward is that with branding's demonstrable efficacy and in search of further understanding in the field; academics and practitioners have been drawn towards new means by which brands and branding can be understood.

Brand Stakeholders: Homo Economicus vs. Homo Sociologicus

As branding has initially been defined as being a creation positioned within an economic construct, it follows that their stakeholders would in turn engage for economic gains. The American Marketing Association (1960) defines a brand as being:

"A name, term, sign, symbol, or design, or combination of them which is intended to identify the goods or services of one seller or group of sellers and to differentiate them from those of competitors."

More recently, Brand Channel (2009) defines brands as:

"[A] mixture of attributes, tangible and intangible, symbolised in a trademark, which, if managed properly, creates value and influence."

Within the Brand Channel definition, brand components have been made more ambiguous and a brand must be able to demonstrate a legally defensible position. In addition, the focus shifts towards the idea of value. In doing so, as sellers are not explicitly mentioned, there is an inference that value is subject to parties outside of marketing functions and organisations. Furthermore, brands appear to gain their status through a perceived ability to influence.

Collectively these support the argument that as branding has been able to demonstrate exponential economic gains; brands rather than merely tools; in fact afford status and premium price-tags. Secondly, as branding is also able to exist outside of hard business functions, they have become societal phenomena. From this, the assumption is that stakeholders have predetermined goals: which they seek to attain for the least cost. Furthermore it suggests that these goals are achieved through drivers rooted in individualism. Such a standpoint frames a brand stakeholder as being Homo economicus; a term which has been used within the field of economics for over a century, Persky (1995), Zabieglik (2002). A challenge to the concept of Homo economicus, has come from anthropological economists Mauss (1924), Polanyi (1944), Sahlins (1972) and Godelier (1999); through empirical cross-cultural comparisons. Their main point of concern is that a Homo economicus perspective fails to take into account kinship-based reciprocity. This therefore turns production into fictitious commodities, through a disembedding process, Polanyi (1944). In support of these concerns, through an extension Durkheim's (1895) discussion on *Social facts*, Dahrendorf (1958) postulates the counter term Homo sociologicus. In this, the assertion is that the pursuit of fulfilling social obligations holds a greater pull than selfish interests. With these in mind, brands and their stakeholders appear to fulfil greater obligations than merely monolithic unilateral transactions. Instead, they occupy a position in society which may drive economic gains; but secondarily also provides social capital, which binds individuals and ascribes meaning to their existence.

Brand theory reflects such tensions, when trying to position stakeholders according to their role, influence, motivations and gains. From a corporate perspective, the idea of Homo sociologicus is apparent in the formalisation of Corporate Altruism, and Corporate and Social Responsibility (CSR) functions. Branding is used in many of these cases as a means by which activities can be linked back to the organisation—using Public Relations frameworks. In doing so organisations are operating under an idea of reciprocity and delayed gratification. Branding plays a supporting role to integrated Marketing Communications in these activities. However through adopting this role there is also a reciprocal value enjoyed by the brand; which helps to build its efficacy. Furthermore, with management theory suggesting that employees should be viewed as being internal customers; the idea that a brand is an external function and marketing tool appears outdated.

Through technological advancements and shifts in behavioural patterns; marketing and economic theory have had to respond to changes in consumption. Peer-to-peer file shares and downloads have caused the music industry to continually revaluate their position and ability to gain revenue. Reed (2008) reports how major label music recording artists REM, Radiohead and The Charlatans have elected to give away their new album releases for free. This would appear to be an extreme course of action which places the idea of reciprocity at the forefront, and sacrifices the pursuit of economic gains. Through this, stronger kinship and emotional ties will be forged—culminating in products and services being championed by more the intangible aspects of brands, and the inclusion of more stakeholders; due to their importance. The success of this approach centres on creating a strong brand, with a transferable brand equity, which can be deployed to all business functions and product/service offerings. This paradigm shift has also seen the creation of new consumer-centric channels; where economic barriers have been removed and consumers have sought to market themselves. Consumer-to-Consumer (C2C) online reverse auctions; social networking; weblogs; and user-generated content upload websites have placed branding further into the hands of consumers. Following the points raised, this chapter attempts to classify and group these various stakeholders; according to their brand roles and perspectives.

STAKEHOLDER ANALYSIS: ORIGINS AND APPROACH

This section takes presents an overview of stakeholder analysis, which also focuses attention on the role of external stakeholders. This is in line with more consumer-centric brand approaches and following the increase in two-way media communication channels—which are both creating new stakeholders, and broadening the field of study.

Freeman (1984) defines a stakeholder as being *"any group or individual who can affect or is affected by the achievement of an organisation's objectives,"* (p.46).

It is worth noting that brands with duplicitous transient and transcendent attributes push stakeholder analysis towards more figurative, tacit and implicit states, demanding the inclusion of additional parties—due to their influence. Furthermore, brands require analysis that reflects this departure from purely economic value drivers.

What Defines a Stakeholder?

Following Freeman's (1984) definition, Mitchell, Agle and Wood (1997) (Figure 1) state that stakeholders can be identified as being,

"[P]rimary or secondary stakeholders; as owners and nonowners of the firm; as owners of capital or owners of less tangible assets; as actors or those acted upon; as those existing in a voluntary or an involuntary relationship with the firm; as rights-holders, contractors, or moral claimants; as resource providers to or dependents of the firm; as risk-takers or influencers; and as legal principals to whom agent-managers bear a fiduciary duty" (pp.853-854).

Within the extensive list of identifying factors provided by Mitchell, Agle and Wood (1997), appears a construct which seeks to classify parties according to a scale of:

1. Ownership of associated assets
2. Participatory positive/neutral/negative relationships
3. Propensity to influence positively/negatively
4. Reciprocal duty, trust and confidence.

Other perspectives suggest:

- Stakeholders are usually regarded as targets rather than partners (Gregory, 2007), as traditional approaches focus on the needs of the owner and the effects on their brand.
- External stakeholders become more crucial in relational and community-based approaches (Heding, et al, 2009).
- Each stakeholder group should be communicated to in different ways, as a reflection of their differing needs (Roper and Davies, 2007).

Figure 1. Stakeholder typology

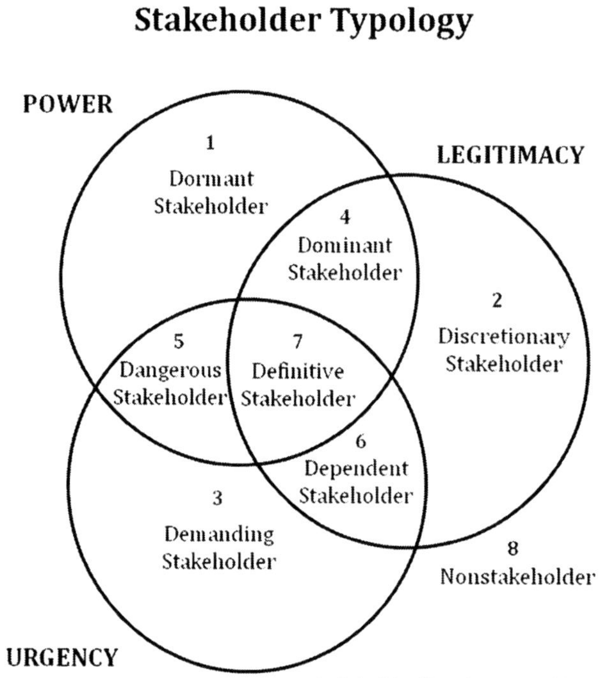

"Stakeholder Typology: One, Two, or Three Attributes Present", Mitchell, Agle and Wood (1997), p.874

Broad vs. Narrow View of Stakeholder Analysis

Broad: "*companies can indeed be vitally affected by, or they can vitally affect almost anyone*" (Mitchell, et al, 1997, p.857)

Narrow: focussing on those whom an organisation is dependent upon "*for its continued survival*" (Freeman and Reed 1983, p.91)

Windsor (1992) highlights that broad or narrow views of stakeholders' universe effects the way in which they are defined and subsequently classified. The Freeman (1984) definition takes a broad view, suggests that "companies can indeed be vitally affected by, or they can vitally affect almost anyone" (Mitchell, Agle and Wood 1997, p.857) whilst that expressed by Freeman and Reed (1983) in parallel is narrower, focussing on those whom an organisation is dependent on "for its continued survival" (p.91).

Clarkson (1995) suggests that "corporations manage relationships with stakeholder groups rather than society as a whole" (p.92) and that stakeholders' interests may be towards past, present, or future corporate activities (p.106). He also asserts that the term "*stakeholder* is not synonymous with *shareholder*" (p.112). Following this, Clarkson (1995) classifies stakeholders into *primary* and *secondary* groups. Primary stakeholders are defined as being those "without whose continuing participation the corporation cannot survive as a going concern" (Clarkson 1995, p.106). Clarkson (1995) states that they "typically are comprised of shareholders and investors, employees, customers, and suppliers, together with what is defined as the public stakeholder group" (p.106). Secondary stakeholders according to Clarkson (1995)

"[A]re defined as those who influence or affect, or are influenced by, the corporation, but they are not engaged in transactions with the corporation and are not essential for its survival... They have the capacity to mobilize public opinion in favor of, or in opposition to, a corporation's performance" (p.107).

Stakeholder Analysis' Relationship with Brand Architecture and Positioning

Beyond the physical market positioning and architecture of brands, their spatial relationship in the mind of consumers is of significance; according to ownership and alignment with consumers' value systems (Ries and Trout, 1982; Marsden, 2002). As an extension of associative network mapping of the human memory (Galton, 1880; Freud, 1924; Deese, 1965; Anderson and Bower, 1973) and also drawing from Zipf (1965) and Dawkins (1976), Marsden (2002) ascribes the science of culture and creativity to a process of positioning *memetics* (genes of meaning). Within this process, brands aim to offer a transparent paper trail of heritage antecedents; which both attract and guide consumers on a path of assimilation. From this, a brand's essence housed within a cultural context and sustained by stakeholders, maintains its strategic value (Holt, 2002, 2004, 2005; de Chernatony, 2001). Brands rely on stakeholders to their ascribe meaning and value. However it can also be argued that brands are the glue that binds stakeholders together—and therefore a relationship of symbiosis and reciprocity exists.

REFINING STAKEHOLDER THEORY FOR BRAND STAKEHOLDERS

Within the *Cultural Approach*, as one of the seven schools of thought that have been identified by Heding, Knudtzen and Bjerre (2009) when analysing brands, a macro level focus is adopted. "...consumers' identity projects are analysed at a (macro) collective level. The relational approach is concerned with the understanding of individual identity projects as important contributors to brand meaning," (Heding, Knudtzen and Bjerre 2009, p.210). Moving forward, the cultural approach is a by product of a phenomenon where,

"The brand is subjected to social and cultural changes completely outside the brand manager's control... this means that the marketer is not the only author behind the brand meanings," (Heding, Knudtzen and Bjerre 2009, p.211).

A cornerstone of the cultural approach lies in the assertion that a brand is a perceived as a cultural artefact. Holt (2002) asserts that in the cultural approach,

"A 'bottom-up' interpretation of data is applied; the informants are not expected to express idiosyncratic meanings, but rather to be acting as mouthpieces of the surrounding culture" (p.73).

From this Holt (2002) adopts a methodological approach which uses "microlevel data—people's stories about their consumption—to investigate macrolevel constructs," (p.73). In keeping with this school of thought, Garsten and Hasselström (2004) state that "*Market man* is forged out of the interplay between different technologies" (p.213)—namely that of production, sign systems, of power, and of the self. Therefore as technology has a stakeholder levelling effect, which encourages inclusion and interaction between more parties; stakeholder definitions will become more communication based.

Research undertaken by Fiedler and Kirchgeorg (2007) supports the view that stakeholder groups can be identified and "the attributes differ substantially among customers, employees, shareholders and journalists" (p.183). This correlates with Jones (2005) view, where he seeks to arrange internal and external stakeholder groups around a brand centred "daisy wheel" (p.18); which is also termed as a hub-and-spoke model by other sources. In contrast, Bhattacharya and Korschun (2008) assert that

"Much of the current thinking in stakeholder theory is still tied to the classic hub-and-spoke model, in which stakeholders are distinct and mutually exclusive. However there is a growing consensus that a firm's constituents are actually embedded in interconnected networks of relationships through which the actions of the firm reverberate with both direct and indirect consequences," (Bhattacharya and Korschun 2008, p.113). Therefore they suggest that "one urgent need involves frameworks that identify key stakeholders and describe their motivations for collaborating with the firm," (p.116).

As mentioned, Mitchell, Agle and Wood (1997) classify stakeholders according to their *power, legitimacy and urgency,* grouping them accordingly (Figure 1). From their literature search they cite that legitimacy is rooted in either some form of contractual relationship, or desirability. However, the brand communication stakeholder interplay, in turn yields the idea that legitimacy will become problematic—as it is in fact self-governed, self defined and difficult to regulate. From this desirability may not be experienced by all associated parties, nor might formal contractual relationships exist. An example of this occurs when observing the prominence of the self-elected anti-branding and no-Logo movements that have been able to exert their influence. Furthermore when examining the issue of power it might help to think of the analogy of rugby players—where a large slow heavy player, or a small fast light player, may both be able to generate the same amount of impact in a contact situation; but their power is used in different ways and has a different effect. In the same way the power of a stakeholder will differ and will be effectual in specific situations.

Wolfe and Putler (2002) mention that stakeholder analysis tends to rank groups primarily according to role; which they feel is not a problem when stakeholders have a similar priority. However difficulties with this perspective occur in situations "in which self-interest is not the primary motivator of individuals' priorities" (p.64). For these reasons Wolfe and Putler (2002) draw from customer segmentation literature and propose an approach which accommodates "heterogeneous priorities within role-based stakeholder groups" (p.64). In a similar thread Miles, Munilla and Darroch (2006) observe that there are increasing examples "of firms that manage to demonstrate a pluralistic mindset" with regards an "ability to provide superior returns to shareholders whilst maintaining a strong CSR profile" (Miles, Munilla and Darroch 2006, p.203). This seems to suggest that roles can and will shift, and interest groups may oscillate between homogeneity and heterogeneity.

Gregory (2007) states that "stakeholders are usually regarded as targets rather than partners," in the development of corporate brands; and that literature seldom provides guidance on how their involvement can be facilitated (p.59). This is perhaps reflective of traditional approaches which focus on the needs of the owner and the effects on their brand. However if stakeholder brand analysis is to reflect the emerging schools of brand thought—such as the consumer, personality, relational, or community based-approaches, as identified by Heding, Knudtzen and Bjerre (2009), external stakeholders become more crucial. Mossberg and Getz (2006) state that some stakeholders (by which they mean non-Owners) demand, "active participation in the branding process whilst others are not interested in being involved." Similarly, Roper and Davies (2007) suggest that each stakeholder group should also be communicated to in different ways, as a reflection of their differing needs.

Chevron (1998) asserts that "the concept of a 'brand' and that of a 'product' are diametrically opposed in many ways." (Chevron, 1998, p. 261). In support of Chevron's (1998) and Collins' (2001) findings, Wilson and Liu (2009) argue "that a brand is created with the aim of transcending the tangible boundaries faced by a product," (p.47). They cite Klein's (2000) observation of the Nike *swoosh* being one of the most requested tattoos in the USA as being not only evidence of this, but in addition proof that consumers feel free to adapt or separate the brand from the product in some way; and extend their level communication and consumption of the brand. Wilson and Liu (2009) assert that the permanence of a tattoo goes towards "explicitly demonstrating that the brand is of more significance and desirability than the product... In addition, it appears that brands can develop sublime characteristics, which outlive their associated products," (Wilson and Liu 2009, p.47).

These emerging trends appear to be observing stakeholder groups according to their brand communications and brand message consumption; as opposed to just their more tangible stakes. Furthermore, Bourdieu (1977) discusses the concept of symbolic capital and its accumulation which manifest in prestige, status and reputation. Following this Pitt et al (2006) suggest that organisations and individuals that give more away, contribute to community, or provide more services "are held in higher regard and reputation" (p.124).

From this it can be taken that branding attempts to do just this—embedding itself within more and more communities. In doing so brands draw in more stakeholders, ultimately sacrificing power from the hands of the brand owner, knowingly or not—but as a necessary evil to ensure its success. Brands require the oxygen of communication to survive and therefore depend on their stakeholders to breathe life into them. It therefore follows that the more stakeholders that exist and discuss a brand's existence—warts and all, the positive and negative; the longer their life and potentially the more health they will enjoy. Following these discussions, this chapter presents two approaches to brand stakeholder analysis: a *Broad-based Macro View* and a *Narrow-based Micro* view.

BROAD VIEW: BRAND STAKEHOLDERS FROM A MACRO/MEZZO-PERSPECTIVE

Having reviewed the theoretical relationship between brands and their various stakeholders, the following section now attempts to position stakeholders according to their involvement. In the interests of attempting to take a broad-based view of involvement, or *stake,* parties will be mapped according to their level of interest, demonstrated through communication. From this stakeholders are investigated, according to ownership, and non-ownership of the brand. In doing so, the focus is shifted towards values rooted in opinion. The strategic value to brand management is that participation and inter-connected *who/what/how/where/when/why* opinions are communicated—converging towards the brand. In-keeping with Mitchell, Agle and Wood (1997), a coefficient of time is also introduced, which preserves dynamism in relationships and stakes.

Figure 2 and Table 1 summarize the key concepts in this approach.

Stakeholders are positioned according to:

1. Ownership/nonOwnership/temporary Ownership, *Donership*
2. Usage/nonUsage
3. Communication
4. Stake: qualified according to: bargaining power/interest/impact.

Each of these states is seen to have a positive, negative or neutral effect on the brand in question.

The dotted line represents a notion of contractual obligations: which are actual, in a physical format; or implied and psychological. For example, when looking at the media, advertising channel partners are bound by formal written agreements;

Figure 2. Brand stakeholder model through communication mapping

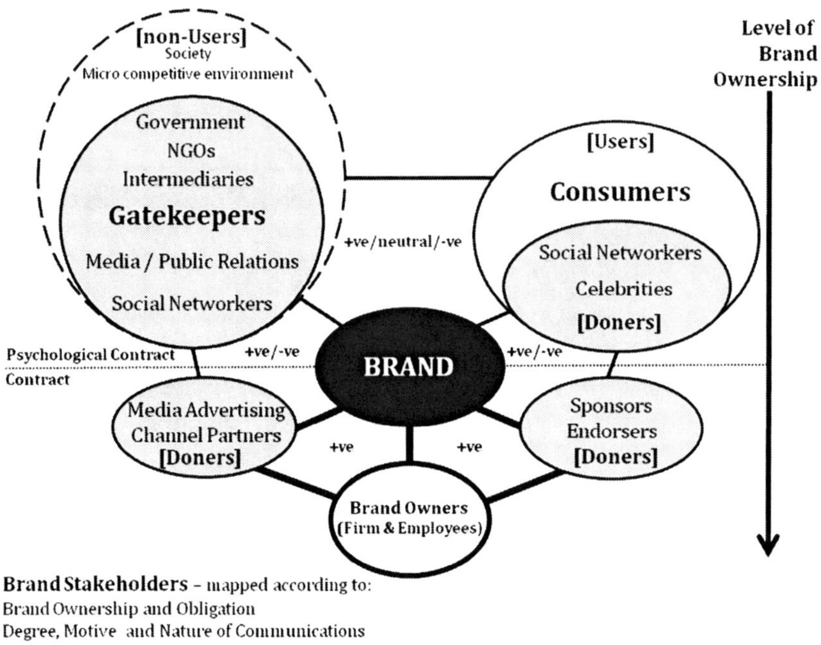

whilst journalists who act as public relations gatekeepers, have no obligation to support or champion a brand. From this it can also be seen that those who share a psychological contract pose a greater potential threat to brands, due to a lack of control over their communications and ability to influence brand meanings and perceptions.

An additional form of classification is used to differentiate between the *Owner* and *nonOwner*, in order to reflect situation-specific ownership; which has been termed '*Doner*' (temporary ownership). Mitchell, Agle and Wood (1997) assert that stakeholder dynamism affects salience with managers through: variable Stakeholder attributes; socially constructed stakeholder attributes, rather than objective reality; a presence, or lack of consciousness, and wilful exercise (p.88). In response to Clarkson (1995) the suggestion is that primary and secondary status should be aligned with ownership of the brand, due to the increased number of stakeholders, homogenous sub-groups, their significance and the levelling effect of technology. External parties to an organisation and brand therefore all are classified as being secondary. A further distinction has been made in which certain stakeholders are viewed as being key—due to their influence or importance in the brand communication process.

The value of this approach, is that it gives brand managers a strategic framework through which they can plan the best way to attract further support and engagement from stakeholders, in order to preserve brand salience. Due to the nature of this proposed framework, promotions and marketing communications are of more significance to a brand than the actual product and service offering, as indicated by Klein (2000), Holt, (2002), Wilson and Liu (2009).

Table 1. Brand stakeholders key: ownership and obligation; degree, motive, and direction of communications

Who	Main attributes	Stake	Power / Bargain	Legitimacy/ Interest	Urgency /Impact	Main Direction of Communication	Stakeholder Evaluation
Owner (Internal)	**Commercial brand accountability & interest in others' consumption/ stake**	**Key/Primary**	**High-Low***(subject to role & externals)*	**High-Med** *(subject to role & externals)*	**High-Low** *(subject to role & externals)*	**To other Owners, non-Owners & Doners**	**Level of influence, Duties, Involvement, Accountability, Share of Voice**
non-Owner (External)	**an interest in consumption - without commercial gains**	**Secondary/ Key**	**Low-High**	**Low-High**	**Low-High**	**To Owners & non-Owners**	**Level of influence, Duties, Involvement, Share of Voice, Opinion, Involvement, Emotional attachment/ disassociation**
User Key Consumer (e.g..Celebrity, Social Networker)	Awareness & active brand opinion - driving consumption	Secondary/ Key	Med-High	Med-High	Med-High Consistent	To Users and non-Users	Brand loyalty/satisfaction/importance, level of consumption, level of emotional attachment/ involvement, Opinion, ability/volume/type of communication
Active non-User Gatekeeper (e.g. Media, NGO, Government, Social Networkers)	Awareness & active brand opinion - but no consumption	Secondary/ Key	Med-High	High/Low	High Temporal	To decision-making Owners, Doners, Users & non-Users	+ve/-ve opinion, priority, level of influence, nature of communication, share of voice, willingness to engage with owner
User Consumer	Awareness & active brand opinion - driving consumption	Secondary	Low-Med	Med	Med Consistent	To Users & non-decision making Owners	Brand loyalty/satisfaction/importance, level of consumption, level of emotional attachment/ involvement, Opinion
Passive non-User (e.g. Gen. Public, Brands, Firms, Intermediaries)	Awareness & passive brand opinion - but no consumption	Secondary	Low	Low	Low Temporal	To Users & non-Users	Top of mind awareness, +ve/-ve opinion, level of influence, interest, pull to recommend
Doner (External)	**drawn towards an interest in others' consumption**	**Key/Secondary**	**Med-High**	**High-Low**	**High**	**To Owners & non-Owners**	**Opinion, Influence, Involvement, Emotional attachment**

continued on following page

Table 1. Continued

Who	Main attributes	Stake	Power / Bargain	Legitimacy/ Interest	Urgency /Impact	Main Direction of Communication	Stakeholder Evaluation
Key Consumer (Celebrities, Social Networkers)	User-initiated brand opinion, driving consumption	Key/Secondary	High-Med	High-Med	High-Med Consistent	To Users, non-Users, Owners & Doners	Brand loyalty, level of influence, share of voice, willingness to engage with owner, ability/volume/type of communication
Media (Paid for promotion)	Owner-initiated brand opinion, driving consumption	Key/Secondary	Med-High	Med-High	High Temporal	To non-Owners & decision-making Owners	Level of influence, share of voice, priority, frequency/reach, level of involvement
Endorser (Individuals/Firms, binding contract)	Owner-initiated brand opinion, driving consumption	Key/Secondary	Med	High	High Temporal	To non-Owners, decision-making Owners	Level of influence, loyalty, share of voice, priority, frequency/reach, level of involvement, adherence to Owner's terms
Channel Partner	Collaborative, driving consumption	Key/Secondary	Low-High	High	High Persistent	To Owners & non-Owners	Level of involvement, level of influence, reach, loyalty, pull to recommend

Notes:

A broad view of stakeholders is taken - at a macro/mezzo level, drawing from the cultural approach to branding, along with Freeman's (1984) definition, and the attributes listed by Mitchell et al (1997). This presents stakeholder roles as *interconnected* and *dynamic* states, which are subject to time specific communication, influence and self defined legitimacy. Here, intangible and figurative aspects of branding are taken into consideration, which also suggest that:

- Roles can and will shift
- Interest groups may oscillate between homogeneity and heterogeneity
- Individuals occupy *states* which are subject to variance; and are a culmination of collective interactions

NARROW VIEW: BRAND STAKEHOLDERS FROM A MICRO-PERSPECTIVE

Brand Cognition

Abbott, Shackleton and Holland (2007) conclude that Brand Product Concepts are being driven towards recognition, which is viewed through the lens of the consumer. In doing so the suggestion is that the cognitive and communication patterns of external stakeholders have a significant effect on brands, brand communities and external parties; requiring analysis. Pinker (1997) explores how inferred relationships and definitions can be identified and explained—by using Categorisation Theory, which encompasses 'Classical Theory'. When observing interdependent communication occurrences, which hinge on perceived meaning and definitions, and are subject to motives and frame of reference; a broad base of interpretation becomes crucial.

For example whether a hoover is in fact a *Hoover*, or a vacuum cleaner is less critical to external stakeholders. Rather, their perceptions and activities are key. In addition, *a posterior concepts* such as brand knowledge and acculturation are experience driven (Fodor 1998, Mason and Bequette 1998, Simon 1996). Aaker (1991), de Chernatony & McDonald (2003), Czellar (2003), Franzen and Bowman (2001), Keller (1993), Lindstrom (2005) state that brands are best understood from a consumer perspective. Following this, as consumers interact and are subject to the influence of non-Consumers outside of their brand community, their understanding should also be examined with respect to those 'others' that they choose to engage with; and hence will have a bearing on their stake.

Diamond et al (2009) talk of the *brand gestalt* which best explains brand power though "a combination of elements, and the reciprocal influences among them" In this, they assert that powerful brands may be **not** those

"[W]ith the greatest number of positive associations or those with the most compelling myths" or "the largest and most interactive communities or those with the largest and most interactive communities or those that provide spectacular retail environments with the most opportunities for emplaced coercion. They may be instead be brands whose components evidence the greatest degree of synergy and whose constituent parts best complement and enhance one another" (Diamond et al 2009, p.131).

With this in mind, stakeholder theory is more closely aligned with such advertising models as the Shannon and Weaver (1949) communication model; as Polonsky and Hyman (2007) assert that it "explicitly integrates the actions of many stakeholders," (p.6). In Shannon and Weaver's (1949) model, stakeholders' presence is representative as being proactive, reactive, positive, neutral, negative and latent.

Virgin Store in a Shopping Mall, Jeddah, Saudi Arabia

Virgin has adapted its logo, which usually appears in English, for an Arabic-speaking audience; to increase its brand resonance with the host population (Figure 3). The Arabic phonetically reads 'Virgin'. It still maintains its design characteristics, preserving a strong identity, whilst ensuring that non-Arabic speakers can still recognise and decode it. Furthermore, by having their brand on the outside of the shopping mall, which also houses other shops and brands, Virgin enriches its brand identity and personality—through experiential laddering.

Brand-Centric Communities

Historically, brands have used a 'top-down', 'board level' approach when disseminating brand personas and 'big ideas'. Now more brands are adopting 'bottom up', 'employee level' approaches (Liu and Yang, 2009). And so here, by using dialogue and quick responsive 'little ideas' overall brand perception, relations, and value become collaborative process (Phillimore and Wilson, 2010).

With the above evidence in mind, the move by brands to a more employee dictated customer-relationship models [as an adaptation of McAlexander *et al*'s (2002) Customer-Centric Model of Brand Community, will push the marketer out of the immediate community into a 'puppeteer' like role [as an extension of the *Pinocchio effect* analogy experienced by brands; as observed by Wilson and Liu, (2009)].

Figure 3. Virgin Jeddah

Loyalty and Intimacy: Setting the Brand Agenda

Gupta *et al* (2004) assert that a 1% increase in customer retention can increase a company's profit potential by 3-7% (cited in Slater *et al*, 2009). From 2000 to 2006, new loyalty scheme subscriptions in the United States increased 35% to 1.5 billion (Ferguson & Hlavinka, 2007). Meyer-Waarden (2007) and Benavent (2006) contend that firms must now incorporate loyalty programs as necessary marketing costs, built into wider marketing strategies—where loyalty plans are a pre-requisite for market entry (Ferguson & Hlavinka, 2007). However, as consumer adoption to these programs is so high, counter observations also suggest that no beneficial competitive advantage can be leveraged (Magi, 2003 cited in Liu & Yang, 2009). In response to both positions, brands seek to connect with advocates beyond simply price, promotions and loyalty schemes. Steve Ballou (2006) argues that:

"The old [customer relationship management] agenda as a bandage should now be replaced with the new agenda of customer intimacy, that is, to make customers feel good whenever they make contact with your company. Every interaction isn't a moment to be avoided or cut short, but an opportunity for further intimacy with the customer...." (Steve Ballou, IBM Institute for Business Value, IBM Global Services 2006, p741)

Fournier *et al* (1998) point to the inability of some firms/brands in achieving high levels of customer loyalty—due to a reluctance or failure to create strong emotional bonds with their customers. Also, such engagement

"[M]ay be used as a proxy measure of the strength of a company's customer relationships based on the extent to which customers have formed both emotional and rational bonds with a brand" (McEwen, 2004, p 487).

Alcohol-Free Beer Aimed at Children in Japan

Japanese society exhibits strong traits of collectivism, which encourages group participation, amongst friends, family and co-workers. An example of this lies in social drinking—which is valued as a central point to relaxation, celebration and bonding. Within Japanese culture, responsibility and obligation are cornerstones; which are communicated through observation and participation. This socialisation starts at an early age and for these reasons parents encourage their children to drink in an inclusive and supportive environment. Here, alcohol-free beer is a welcome product offering, which is attached to strong emotional constructs and should in turn encourage loyalty (Figure 4). However, it is apparent that such an approach may have completely the opposite effect in a different culture, like the US. It is most likely there that it would be perceived as being exploitative—potentially encouraging under-age drinking and associated alcohol-related health and crime issues. Therefore, brand loyalty, messages and perceptions are heavily subject to the sociocultural context that they exist in.

Figure 4. Japanese beer

Mapping Brand Communities

Muniz and O'Guinn (2001) place the brand at the focal point of the community, in an almost matriarchal role—defining communities' commonalities from derivations of sociological theory (Gusfield, 1978; Marshall, 1994). McAlexander *et al* (2002) argue that in addition to the factors cited by Muniz & O'Guinn, committed consumers are placed at the focal point of communities. This customer-centric model implies a shift in perspective—explaining the relative autonomy and interactions of individual elements. In this setting the brand, product, and marketer do not assume the singular role of brand community facilitator; but instead are shown to be active community members creating experiences which circumnavigate around a focal consumer. Ouwersloot and Schroder (2008) suggest that there are two forms of brand community: one where the brand is implicitly involved within the community (and often the founder and orchestrator); and one where the brand is explicitly uninvolved.

Practitioners question the typical methods by which brand messages are communicated 'down' the company chain and 'out of the doors' to consumers, in an *'age of deference'*. Senior-level complacency is often cited as one of the reasons why many companies have been slow to react to the changing demands of the industry and their component brands. An example of this can be seen through media channels' reluctance or inability to accommodate and integrate fully new digital platforms. Web 2.0, peripherals, consoles and media players are cited as creating both revenue stream losses and gains. Elio Leoni-Sceti, Chief Executive of EMI argues that:

"As an industry we lost touch with consumer behaviour. Because we didn't understand it, we didn't have the right product at the place and time where they intend to buy it" (Elio Leoni-Sceti, CEO of EMI Music, cited in The Times, 2009)

Advertising agencies, marketers and the media are citing this new era of 'through the doors' information gathering by consumers as the *'age of reference'*—where all employees carry the burden of directing the brand. Employees on the ground floor have direct access to the mindset of the consumer, in daily rhyme and verse. This is reflected in the suggestion of an emerging additional quadrant; as an adaptation of McAlexander *et al*'s (2002) approach. Here, the increasing importance of employees within the community is reflected—which has the reciprocal effect of pushing marketers to the periphery of the brand community. This is due to the fact that marketers are not directly involved in consumer relationships. Rather, they coordinate efforts, relationships and friendships (Figure 5)

In the Figure 5 daisy wheel network, communication hinges upon referential bottom-up information exchanges, placing focal consumers at the heart of all activities. Such an approach is in-keeping with CRM and brand-centric strategies. In addition it is also reflective of the ambitions of emerging technologies and phenomena—such as social television and multimedia platforms. Within this network, a sub-group represented here as a diamond exists—where the brand remains central. In doing so the focal consumer is drawn into the role of a brand surrogate. In the model two types of relationship-driven consumer appear: one which is more influenced by society, whilst the other taking their cue from employees and ambassadors of the brand.

The Effects of Online and Mobile Communication

Since the time of Clarkson's (1995) writing the might of the media, internet and mobile media have risen in their ascendency. The legacy of news and views which remain assessable online, not to mention the accessibility afforded by the internet, have extended the status of *gatekeeper* to more parties; other than have been traditionally held by journalists and senior decision makers. Consumers, bloggers and social networkers are able to shape the agenda—which then suggests that secondary stakeholders according to Clarkson's (1995) groupings, may in fact also be worthy of primary classification; in that an organisation needs to also garner their support; for fear of demise. Further to this, corporations should in the information age consider society as a whole, rather than just current stakeholder groups; due to the information legacy which remains accessible.

Maio (2003) states that "The shift in power from corporation to stakeholder has come with a thud, accelerated by e-commerce and internet activism," (p.246). Search website www.news-sift.com, classifies articles according to their source, and positive/neutral/negative sentiments. Meanwhile Twitter monitoring sites (such as http://twendz.waggeneredstrom.com and www.tweetfeel.com) also offer the same facilities based upon the words used in tweets. With the increased importance of search, the nature of the participation of external stakeholders will increase in importance. Reprise Media (2004), discuss findings of SEMPO's (The State of Search Engine Marketing) 2004 report. They cite that "61% percent of firms surveyed revealed branding to be their primary online objective, ranking it over product sales, lead generation, or driving traffic—although those objectives were also considered key" (Reprise Media 2004).

Further to this, Payne, Ballantyne and Christopher (2005) state that "relationship-based approaches to marketing offer a reformist stakeholder agenda with an emphasis on stakeholder collaboration beyond the immediacy of market transactions" (p.856). Johnson (2007) discusses the idea of Stakeholder Relationship Management (SRM) as a "means to manage, monitor and measure communications and stakeholder relationships." However Payne, Ballantyne and Christopher (2005) conclude that their experience of working "with stakeholder models suggests that exchange relationships with many relevant stakeholders

Figure 5. Referential brand community network

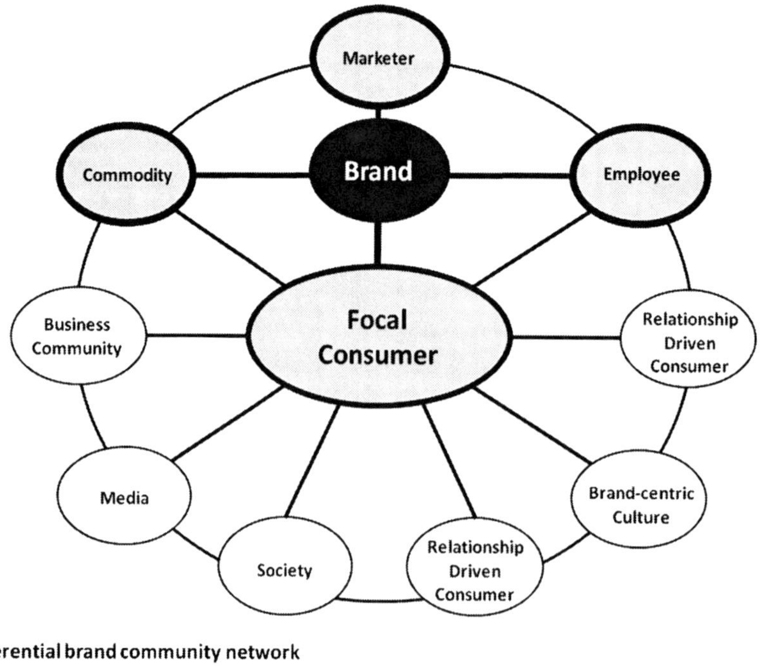

are inadequately recognised by and planned for by organisations"; and "may not previously have been entirely understood"—due to "systemic (or cumulative) effects of interdependencies" (Payne, Ballantyne and Christopher 2005, p.866).

CASE EXAMPLE IN PRACTICE: CONSCIOUS OBJECTORS GATHER STEAM

Richardson (2002) reports of a situation where Frank Whitestone, a disgruntled broadband customer of NTL (website: ntlworld.com), created NTHellworld.com. This site gained a search listing directly below that of NTL's and became a platform for fellow customers and employees to share their less than positive views. NTL were able to purchase the site from Frank and offered him a job, which he duly accepted. Following this, NTL rebuilt the site reframing the vitriolic content as being more humorous and tongue-in-cheek; making it an additional arm to their less than popular customer support. Eventually NTL migrated the site to a new domain that they purchased, which was NThelpworld.com. In this example it is apparent that the interplay between stakeholders is indicative of attributes which shift and also the rising significance of the non-Owner. Furthermore, Frank demonstrates a stakeholder journey which is reflective of him having moved states from non-Owner to Owner.

Rigopoulou et al (2007) examine the effects of crisis management on brand equity. Following the mention of negative communication, which may translate in some way towards creating negative stakeholders; it is felt that the field of PR and more specifically crisis management are of significance and possess different attributes. For these reasons media stakeholders should be split to differentiate gatekeepers from paid for advertising. Within gatekeepers also exist those parties that are not media owners, but have access to these channels; for example YouTube and Weblogs. Holt (2002) asserts that whilst there are tensions between iconic brands and the anti-brand movements, which appear at first glance to suggest contradictory and opposing standpoints; they may in fact upon further analysis be logically connected. This qualifies their inclusion in stakeholder analysis and their presence can be quantified according to positive, neutral, or negative communication.

MOVING FORWARD AND LOOKING TO THE FUTURE

In what has been termed by Krotoski (2010) as *The Great Levelling* of the digital revolution, access to knowledge capital and social networking has the ability to empower and drive cosmopolitanism. Johnson (2007) also charts a change in mindset amongst corporations when engaging with consumers: "Today's media is evolving beyond monetizing audiences and more towards fostering dialogue and community—and monetizing these interactions directly or indirectly." Therefore, through the lens of diffusion of innovations, the increasing acceptance of cultural branding represents a convergence continuum, which is comparable to that observed by Dailey, Demo and Spillman (2005) who present a 5 Cs model of convergence, when studying the collaborative practices of media newsrooms—namely: (a) cross-promotion, (b) cloning, (c) cooperation, (d) content sharing, and (e) full convergence (pp.152-153).

The Hip-Hop Generation

It is perhaps for these reasons that contemporary culture has afforded itself as a powerful tool for advertising, marketing and brand managers; because it acts as a conduit for entry into the psyche of consumer-centric communities, which have previously been thought to exhibit heterogeneous traits. Wilson and Liu (2009) cite Timberland's successes (Lelyveld, 2001) and Tommy Hilfiger (Dye, 2000) as an observation of this phenomenon. Both appealed to and then responding to an avid Hip-Hop audience; whom they had not initially attempted to target. In further support, Holt (2002) lists the domain of Hip-Hop as being within the "arts and fashion communities, ethnic subcultures, professional communities and consumption communities" (Holt, 2002, p.84). Whilst it might appear that these inroads are not unique to Hip-Hop, in that other music genres, such as Electronica, Punk, Grunge and Indie have become the soundtracks to generations and an integral means by which individuals can ascribe meaning to their identities (Zaltman and Puccinelli, 2001; Hesmondhalgh, 2008); what Hip-Hop has been able to do is become the bedfellow of marketers—through giving centre stage to brands. Also, it can be argued that this trend has encouraged brand consumerism in other sub-cultures. However, a further differentiator is that Hip-Hop lyrics contain numerous references to brands, often accompanied by descriptions, similes and metaphors; which reciprocally enrich the personality of both the brand and the Hip-Hopper (Bryant, 2008). Furthermore, for an MTV generation which is used to seeing brands blurred out in Hip-Hop music videos, along with weapons, this has become a badge of honour to the artist; encouraging them to increase their affiliations with brands, as a means of celebrating authenticity, edginess and rebellion.

From this, brand strategies benefit from low media-cost exposure, which attracts attention, encourages inquisitiveness and is accompanied by a narrative, akin to an extended esoteric infomercial. Viewers have been observed playing a guessing game with peers as to which brand appeared on the screen, which reinforces brand notoriety, recall and hyper-brand sensitivity. Traditionally such blurring of logos would have been viewed as hampering promotional activities, but now this has become a gritty and offensive anti-branding strategy; which adds to a brand's personality, allure and edginess. An extension of this phenomenon can be seen in the thirst for authentic reality television and online user generated content, which some marketers covertly attempt to replicate.

Hip-Hop Culture and its Synergy with Branding and Stakeholders

The following model captures the essence of Hip-Hop creation—in sequential, dynamic, reciprocal and interconnected elements. Also, in-keeping with the spirit of Hip-Hop and branding, the acronym represents their creative mastery and magic (Figure 6).

Within this approach, the *abracadabra* model shares a commonality with the Shannon and Weaver (1949) communication model, in that it is reflective of an *encoding-decoding-feedback* sequence of events. As an extension, due to the emergence of creative reciprocity, through consumer-brand-centric models, user generated content, social networking and a concept of legitimacy through shared ownership; the presence of the media is diffused throughout.

Hip-Hop's competitive element ensures that engagement and inclusion nourish its existence. Therefore, as in the cultural stakeholder approach to branding, discussed in this chapter, ownership and obligation become collective and collaborative processes, diffused throughout the brand's life cycle. Now that Hip-hop culture has reached the domain of mainstream consumption, it proves to be a fertile ground for many marketers, drawing from Hip-hop orientated language, music, fashion, symbolism and ethea (Gibbons, 2007; Brace-Govan and de Burgh-Woodman, 2008; Cox Edmondson, 2008). Notably, Reebok have sponsored rappers as endorsers of their sportswear; HSBC have incorporated Hip-hop terms such as 'bling' in their advertising copy; MacDonald's have paid lyricists to incorporate references to 'Big Mac' into their chart songs; and artists such as Banksy have been able to reframe their once frowned upon artistic graffiti criminal practices, towards being seen more as objects of desire. In

Figure 6. Abracadabra approach to creativity

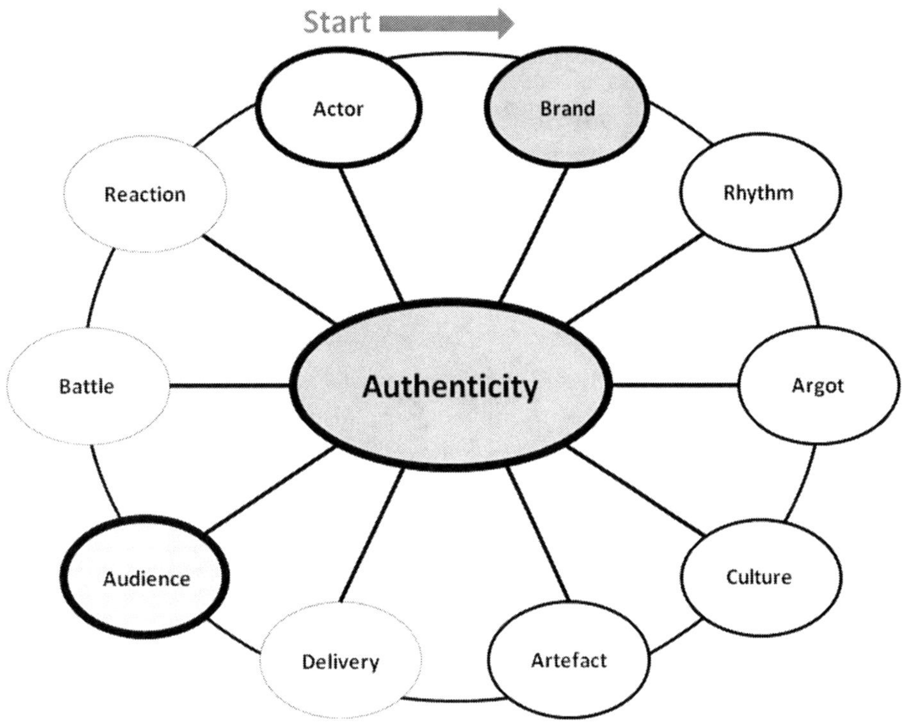

Key:
Creation
Actor: avatar-esque created identity and personality of the creator
Brand: product concept of the creation: co-branded/ingredient brand with Actor and manifest in a distinct personality and identity. Actors will seek to cite and profile themselves within the product offering. The rise in reality generated content and celebrities is seen to drive this explicit phenomenon.
Rhythm: signature style: visual/kinaesthetic/audio attributes which are embedded into all creations
Argot: encoded slang which restricts membership and creates sub-cultures. This helps to preserve and create unique cultural elements
Culture: created hybridised sub-cultures which drive collective individualism
Artefact: final creation, blending elements - which pay homage and reference to existing entities; whilst creating innovation through: adaptation, sampling, nostalgia and retro

Marketing: Push/Pull/Profile
Delivery: deconstruction/diffusion innovation/convergence: supported by esoteric story-telling, which flips meanings, brings new perspectives and shows multiple perspectives. How the artefact is presented
Audience: those intended for communication and offering
Battle: a signal of competitive intent, demonstrating skills, value, legitimacy
Reaction: resulting from battling, reciprocating, interacting and sharing creations

Destination
Authenticity: achieved through the culmination the previous elements

tandem, observations and literature indicate that brands are not only shorthand for a gamut of product attributes, but also part of a collaborative negotiation process which serves to support the identities and personalities of individuals. Collectively, branding and Hip-Hop have been successful in weaving themselves into rich tapestries of cultural and societal norms; and building bridges between global communities—providing social capital.

"Desi" Snacks: Delhi, India

Desi is Hindi word, which when translated means 'native' or 'traditional' to the Indian Sub-Continent. What is interesting in this case is that a non-traditionally Indian style snack is communicating to their target audience, that it is for them, and it has all of the characteristics they would look for, from a truly authentic snack (Figure 7). This is likely to be interpreted as meaning that it is spicier than usual 'Western' offerings and therefore seasoned for an Indian palate. The brand messages are aimed at an audience, who have adapted Indian culture, demonstrating strong elements of cultural hybridization. The language used fuses Hip-Hop inspired terms such as *beats* and rather than using Hindi script, phonetically indicates the tomato flavour as *tamatar.* Furthermore, in the US and the UK the word *Desi* has also crept into the vocabulary of those not from the Indian Diaspora. Comparably, they too use the term to communicate authenticity, in order to gain assurances that an Indian product offering hasn't been adapted for a Western palate. Following this trend, UK public service broadcaster the BBC uses the term *Desi* on their music iPlayer website, with a dedicated section named as such—which denotes Indian and Asian Underground fusion music. From these observations, it appears that the product has the potential to attract a much larger global audience of not only those with heritage from the Indian sub-continent, but also consumers who crave what they perceive as authentic food, which balances accessibility and resonance—through its brand messages.

CONCLUSION

By drawing from the cultural approach to branding, along with Freeman's (1984) definition, and the attributes listed by Mitchell, Agle and Wood (1997), a broad view of stakeholders at a macro level is presented; positioning them according to:

1. Ownership/nonOwnership/temporary Ownership (*Donership*)
2. Usage/nonUsage
3. Communication
4. Stake: qualified according to bargaining power, interest and impact.

In doing so, brand stakeholder analysis is able to more successfully accommodate the No Logo/anti-branding movements, social networkers and bloggers—under what have been termed by Holt (2002) as being *citizen artist brands*. In branding,

Figure 7. Desi Delhi snacks

due to the significant nature of communication and meanings, and the values and opinions held by stakeholders; it is possible that one stakeholder may in fact oscillate between more than one of these fields, depending on the situation—as opposed to being a static model which seeks to group stakeholders in one field. Stakeholder thinking here is aligned with communications models observed in transactional analysis—which refer to individuals occupying *states* which are subject to variance; and are a culmination of collective interactions. An area which is notably absent from much stakeholder analysis is also that of the role of the non-user. The suggestion is that in brand communication, through moving away from an analysis based primarily on consumption and ownership, their significance is also in fact crucial. As brand health, messages and values are subject to cognitive, affective and conative patterns; there is a danger that existing stakeholder analysis places too much weight on judgements which observe only behaviour. Therefore through only evaluating behaviour, and that of the most visible; deep-structured responses may be misread and future predictions limited.

This chapter also reflects upon avenues of enquiry into how marketing communications and brand strategies can be managed, when faced with increasingly referential community-centric consumers, as active participants. It remains difficult for brands to replicate all of the provisions required, when initiating and participating in meaningful friendships. However at the very least, there do exist 'brand friendships' and 'brand communities', which attempt to fulfil some social promises. To this end, McAlexander *et al*'s (2002) customer-centric model of brand community requires adaptation—which is reflective of the views of practitioners, when considering a new 'age of reference'. Here, the dissemination of communications, logistics and operations become a collective and collaborative responsibility. A by-product of this process is that whilst marketers still manage 'upstream' and 'downstream' information flows, they in turn move them out of immediate communications channels (within brand communities)—placing marketers behind the brand, commodity and employees.

REFERENCES

Aaker, D. A. (1991). *Managing brand equity: Capitalizing on the value of a brand name*. New York, NY: Free Press.

Abbott, M., Shackleton, J. P., & Holland, R. (2007). *Brand as category: An analysis of categorisation and branded product concepts*. IASDR 07 Conference, International Association of Societies of Design Research, The Hong Kong Polytechnic University, 12th-15th November, 2007.

Anderson, J. R., & Bower, G. H. (1973). *Human associative memory*. Washington, DC: Winston & Sons.

Benavent, C. (2006). The impact of loyalty schemes on repeat purchase behaviour. *Journal of Marketing Management*, *22*, 61–88. doi:10.1362/026725706776022308

Bernays, E. (1928). *Propaganda*. New York, NY: Liveright.

Bernays, E. (1955). *The engineering of consent*. Norman, OK: University of Oklahoma Press.

Bhattacharya, C. B., & Korschun, D. (2008). Stakeholder marketing: Beyond the four Ps and the customer. *Journal of Public Policy & Marketing*, *27*(1), 113–116. doi:10.1509/jppm.27.1.113

Bourdieu, P. (1977). *Outline of a theory of practice*. Cambridge, UK: Cambridge University Press.

Brace-Govan, J., & de Burgh-Woodman, H. (2008). Sneakers and street culture: A postcolonial analysis of marginalized cultural consumption. *Consumption Markets & Culture*, *11*(2), 93–112. doi:10.1080/10253860802033639

Brand Channel. (2009). *Online branding, glossary section*. Retrieved September 29, 2009, from http://www.brandchannel.com/ education_glossary.asp

Bryant, Y. (2008). Relationship between exposure to rap music videos and attitudes towards relationship among African American youth. *The Journal of Black Psychology, 34*(3), 356–380. doi:10.1177/0095798408314141

Chevron, J. R. (1998). The Delphi process: A strategic branding methodology. *Journal of Consumer Marketing, 15*(3), 254–264. doi:10.1108/07363769810219125

Clarkson, M. B. E. (1995). A stakeholder framework for analysing and evaluating corporate social performance. *Academy of Management Review, 20*(1), 92–117.

Collins, D. (2001). The branding of management knowledge: Rethinking management fads. *Journal of Organizational Change Management, 16*(2), 186–204. doi:10.1108/09534810310468152

Cox Edmondson, V. (2008). A preliminary review of competitive reactions in the hip-hop music industry – Black American entrepreneurs in a new industry. *Management Research News, 33*(9), 637–649. doi:10.1108/01409170810898536

Czellar, S. (2003). Consumer attitude toward brand extensions: an integrative model and research propositions. *International Journal of Research in Marketing, 20*, 97. doi:10.1016/S0167-8116(02)00124-6

Dahrendorf, R. (1958). Homo sociologicus: On the history, significance, and limits of the category of social role. In Dahrendorf, R. (Ed.), *Essays in the theory of society*. London, UK: Routledge and Kegan Paul.

Dailey, L., Demo, L., & Spillman, M. (2005). The convergence continuum: A model for studying collaboration between media newsrooms. *Atlantic Journal of Communication, 13*(3), 150–168. doi:10.1207/s15456889ajc1303_2

Dawkins, R. (1976). *The selfish gene*. Buckingham, UK: Open University Press.

de Chernatony, L. (2001). A model for strategically building brands. *Brand Management, 9*(1), 32–44. doi:10.1057/palgrave.bm.2540050

de Chernatony, L., & McDonald, M. (2003). *Creating powerful brands* (3rd ed.). Elsevier Butterworth Heinemann.

Deese, J. (1965). *The structure of associations in language and thought*. Baltimore, MD: John Hopkins Press.

Diamond, N. (2009). American Girl and the brand gestalt: Closing the loop on sociocultural branding research. *Journal of Marketing, 73*, 118–134. doi:10.1509/jmkg.73.3.118

Durkheim, E. (1895). *Les règles de la méthode sociologique, 18*. Paris, France: Presses Universitaires de France.

Ferguson, R., & Hlavinka, K. (2007). *Quo Vadis: Sizing up the U.S. loyalty marketing industry.*

Fiedler, L., & Kirchgeorg, M. (2007). The role concept in corporate branding and stakeholder management reconsidered: Are stakeholder groups really different? *Corporate Reputation Review, 10*(3), 177–188. doi:10.1057/palgrave.crr.1550050

Fodor, J. A. (1998). *Concepts: Where cognitive sciences went wrong*. UK: Oxford University Press.

Franzen, G., & Bouwman, M. (2001). *The mental world of brands – Mind, memory and brand success*. NTC Publications.

Freeman, R. E. (1984). *Strategic management: A stakeholder approach*. Boston, MA: Pitman.

Freeman, R. E., & Reed, D. L. (1983). Stockholders and stakeholders: A new perspective on corporate governance. *California Management Review*, *25*(3), 93–94.

Freud, S. (1924). *Collected papers*. London, UK: Hogarth.

Galton, F. (1880). Psychometric experiments. *Brain*, *2*, 149–162. doi:10.1093/brain/2.2.149

Garsten, C., & Hasselström, A. (2004). Homo mercans and the fashioning of markets. In Garsten, C., & de Montoya, M. L. (Eds.), *Market matters: Exploring cultural processes in the global marketplace*. New York, NY: Palgrave Macmillan.

Gibbons, W. C. (2007). A librarian's guide to hip-hop culture. *Collection Building*, *26*(7), 119–126. doi:10.1108/01604950710831924

Godelier, M. (1999). *The enigma of the gift*. Chicago, IL: University Of Chicago Press.

Gregory, A. (2007). Involving stakeholders in developing corporate brands: The communication dimension. *Journal of Marketing Management*, *23*(1-2), 59–73. doi:10.1362/026725707X178558

Heding, T., Knudtzen, C. F., & Bjerre, M. (2009). *Brand management – Research, theory and practice*. New York, NY: Routledge. doi:10.4324/9780203996171

Herman, E. S., & Chomsky, N. (1988). *Manufacturing consent: The political economy of the mass media*. New York, NY: Pantheon Books.

Hesmondhalgh, D. (2008). Towards a critical understanding of music, emotion and self-identity. *Consumption Markets & Culture*, *11*(4), 329–343. doi:10.1080/10253860802391334

Holt, D. B. (2002). Why do brands cause trouble? A dialectical theory of consumer culture and branding. *The Journal of Consumer Research*, *29*(June), 70–90. doi:10.1086/339922

Holt, D. B. (2004). *How brands become icons: The principles of cultural branding*. Harvard Business School Press.

Holt, D. B. (2005). How societies desire brands: Using cultural theory to explain brand symbolism. In Mick, D., & Ratneshwar, S. (Eds.), *Inside consumption*. Routledge.

IBM Global Services. (2006). CRM: The myth vs. The new agenda. Executive Brief. In C. K. Yim, et al. (Eds.), Strengthening customer loyalty through intimacy and passion: Roles of customer-firm affection and customer staff relationships in services. *Journal of Marketing Research, 45*, 741-756.

Johnson, C. (2007, August 15). *Managing brand in the shifting media landscape*. Retrieved from http://www.odwyerpr.com/members /0815johnson_oped.html

Jones, R. (2005). Finding Sources of brand value: Developing a stakeholder model of brand equity. *Brand Management*, *13*(1), 10–32. doi:10.1057/palgrave.bm.2540243

Keller, K. L. (1993). Conceptualizing, measuring and managing consumer-based brand equity. *Journal of Marketing*, *57*(1). doi:10.2307/1252054

Klein, N. (2000). *No logo*. London, UK: Flamingo.

Krotoski, A. (2010, February 2). The virtual revolution: The great levelling? *BBC News Online*. Retrieved May 31, 2010, from http://www.bbc.co.uk/worldservice /documentaries/2010/02/100128 _the_virtual_revolution_part_one.shtml

Lindstrom, M. (2005). *Brand sense: How to build powerful through touch, taste, smell, sight and sound. London, UK & Sterling*. VA: Kogan Page.

Liu, Y., & Yang, R. (2009). Competing loyalty programs: Impact of market saturation, market share, and category expandability. [American Marketing Association.]. *Journal of Marketing*, *73*, 93–108. doi:10.1509/jmkg.73.1.93

Maio, E. (2003). Managing brand in the new stakeholder environment. *Journal of Business Ethics*, *44*(2-3), 235–246. doi:10.1023/A:1023364119516

Marsden, P. (2002). Brand positioning: Meme's the word. *Marketing Intelligence & Planning*, *20*(5), 307–312. doi:10.1108/02634500210441558

Mason, K., & Bequette, J. (1998). Product experience and consumer product attribute inference accuracy. *Journal of Consumer Marketing*, *15*(4), 343. doi:10.1108/07363769810225984

Mauss, M. (1924). *The gift - The form and reason for exchange in archaic societies*. London, UK: Routledge.

McAlexander, J. H. (2002). Building brand community. *Journal of Marketing*, *66*, 38–54. doi:10.1509/jmkg.66.1.38.18451

McEwen, W. (2004, November 11). Why satisfaction isn't satisfying. *Gallup Management Journal*. Retrieved February 17, 2009, from http://gmj.gallup.com/content/14023/why-satisfaction-Isnt-Satisfying.aspx

Meyer-Waarden, L. (2007). The effects of loyalty programs on customer life time duration and share of wallet. *Journal of Retailing*, *83*, 223–236. doi:10.1016/j.jretai.2007.01.002

Miles, M. P., Munilla, L. S., & Darroch, J. (2006). The role of strategic conversations with stakeholders in the formation of corporate social responsibility strategy. *Journal of Business Ethics*, *69*, 195–205. doi:10.1007/s10551-006-9085-6

Mitchell, R. K., Agle, B. R., & Wood, D. J. (1997). Toward a theory of stakeholder identification and salience: Defining the principle of who and what really counts. *Academy of Management Review*, *22*(4), 853–886.

Mossberg, L., & Getz, D. (2006). Stakeholder influences on the ownership and management of festival brands. *Scandinavian Journal of Hospitality and Tourism*, *6*(4), 308–326. doi:10.1080/15022250601003273

Muniz, A. M., & O'Guinn, T. C. (2001). Brand community. *The Journal of Consumer Research*, *27*, 412–427. doi:10.1086/319618

Ouwersloot, H., & Schroder, G. O. (2008). Who's who in brand communities and why? *European Journal of Marketing*, *42*(5-6), 571–585. doi:10.1108/03090560810862516

Payne, A., Ballantyne, D., & Christopher, M. (2005). A stakeholder approach to relationship marketing strategy: The development and use of the six markets model. *European Journal of Marketing*, *39*(7-8), 855–871. doi:10.1108/03090560510601806

Persky, J. (1995). Retrospectives: The ethology of Homo economicus. *The Journal of Economic Perspectives*, *9*(2), 221–231.

Phillimore, M., & Wilson, J. A. J. (2010). *Social media newsrooms: Exploring identity through user generated comment.* Euprera Spring Symposium, 25th-27th February 2010, University College Arteveldehogeschool, Ghent, Belgium.

Pinker, S. (1997). *How the mind works*. Penguin.

Pitt, L. F., Watson, R. T., Berthon, P., & Zinkhan, D. W. G. (2006). The penguin's window: Corporate brands from an open-source perspective. *Journal of the Academy of Marketing Science*, *34*(2), 115–127. doi:10.1177/0092070305284972

Polanyi, K. (1944). *The great transformation*. New York, NY: Rinehart.

Polonsky, M. J., & Hyman, M. R. (2007). A multiple stakeholder perspective on responsibility in advertising. *Journal of Advertising*, *36*(2), 5–13. doi:10.2753/JOA0091-3367360200

Reed, J. (2008, March 25). REM launch new album on the web. *BBC Radio 1*. Retrieved September 29, 2009, from http://news.bbc.co.uk/newsbeat /hi/technology/newsid_7312000 /7312288.stm

Reprise Media. (2004, December 16). *SEMPO talks brand, generic terms score big and Sullivan on search*. Retrieved June 24, 2009, from http://www.searchviews.com/index.php / archives/2004/12/sempo-talks-brand -generic-terms-score-big-and-sullivan-on-search.php

Richardson, T. (2002, April 12). NTHellworld. com founder takes job with NTL. *The Register.* Retrieved from http://www.theregister.co.uk

Ries, A., & Trout, J. (1982). *Positioning: The battle for your mind*. New York, NY: Warner Books.

Rigopoulou, I., Siomkos, G., Kehagias, J., & Vassilikopoulou, A. (2007). *Brand equity elements and crisis management.* Academy of Marketing Conference, 2007, 4-6 July, Kingston University, Surrey – UK.

Roper, S., & Davies, G. (2007). The corporate brand: Dealing with multiple stakeholders. *Journal of Marketing Management*, *23*(1-2), 75–90. doi:10.1362/026725707X178567

Sahlins, M. (1972). The original affluent society. In Sahlins, M. (Ed.), *Stone age economics* (pp. 1–39). New York, NY: Aldine.

Shannon, C., & Weaver, W. (1949). *Mathematical theory of communication*. Urbana, IL: University of Illinois Press.

Simon, H. A. (1996). *Sciences of the artificial* (3rd ed.). Cambridge, MA: MIT Press.

Slater, S. F. (2009). Know your customers. *Marketing Management*, *18*(1), 36–44.

The Times. (2009, March 8). EMI has a new spin on record market. *The Times Online*. Retrieved October 12, 2009, from http://business.timesonline.co.uk/tol /business/industry_sectors/media / article5864044.ece

Wilson, J. A. J., & Liu, J. (2009). The Pinocchio effect – When managing the brand creation process, across cultures. *TMC Academic Journal*, *4*(1), 45–58.

Windsor, D. (1992). Stakeholder management in multinational enterprises. In S. N. Brenner and S. A. Waddock (Eds.), *Proceedings of the Third Annual Meeting of the International Association for Business and Society* (pp. 121-128). Leuven, Belgium.

Wolfe, R. A., & Putler, D. S. (2002). How tight are the ties that bind stakeholder groups? *Organization Science*, *13*(1), 64–80. doi:10.1287/ orsc.13.1.64.544

Zabieglik, S. (2002). The origins of the term Homo economicus. In *Economics and values*, (pp. 123-130). Gdansk.

Zaltman, G., & Puccinelli, N. (2001). *Strategic use of music in marketing, a selective review*. (Harvard Business School Note, 9- 501-056).

Zipf, G. K. (1965). *Psychology of languages*. Cambridge, MA: MIT Press.

KEY TERMS AND DEFINITIONS

Brand Architecture: The physical and experiential positioning of a brand within a strategic portfolio.

Brand Community: Relationships which ascribe their existence and meaning by converging around focal consumers and through a brand.

Brand Culture Approach: The school of thought which views brands from a macro-perspective—as artefacts outside of the full control of brand manager and mouthpieces of surrounding culture and society.

Brand Stakeholder: A *collective individual* who holds an explicit view of a brand, which is dynamic, situation specific and expressed implicitly through communication.

Broad View: analysing all of those individuals that can be affected by, or can affect an organisation or brand.

Collective Individualism: The concept of holding onto a strong sense of personal identity, behaviour and opinion—whilst maintaining and seeking inclusion within a wider community.

Homo Economicus: Stakeholders who have individualistic economic predetermined goals—which they seek to attain for the least cost.

Homo Sociologicus: Stakeholders with primary motivates and objectives which are achieved through a sense of societal obligation and kinship-based reciprocity.

Macro/Mezzo Perspective: A frame of reference and influence outside of the immediate competitive brand relationship environment.

Memetics: A Darwinian-inspired approach which examines the *genes of meaning* that map out the essence of a brand. From them, a brand's identity and personality can be determined.

Micro Perspective: The competitive market environment which a brand community exists in

Narrow View: Focusing on those individuals on whom an organisation or brand are dependent on.

Sampling (in a Hip-Hop Context): A systematic and qualitative process of selecting elements or pieces from source material, with the purpose of fusing them with other elements in order to create something new. This could be from songs, literature, dance, or pieces of artwork. Hip-Hop dancers have adapted ballet and gymnastics, whilst musicians have taken sections from pieces of classical music, Shakespeare, or even created melodies from sirens.

Chapter 10
Brand Obsessed Society:
Branding Yoga Guru Baba Ramdev in India

Chinmaya Kulshrestha
Management Development Institute (MDI), India

Avinash Kapoor
Management Development Institute (MDI), India

ABSTRACT

He is a Yoga Guru, spiritual beacon, Nano-Bio Ayurveda expert, brand ambassador of Indian States, brand ambassador of the UNO mission, political influencer, animation series character, media czar; Baba Ramdev is overall a huge brand! The purpose of this chapter is to explore the value propositions and the sustainable key differentiators to analyze the brand status and brand strategy of spiritual beacon Baba Ramdev. The chapter concludes that there is a strong synergy between image and identity of brand Baba Ramdev resulting in strong personality that offers him a competitive advantage to get across to the consumers.

INTRODUCTION

Baba Ramdev is a renowned Yoga and Ayurveda guru. He is well versed in Sanskrit Grammar, Ayurveda, and Vedic Philosophy. His practical approach to Yoga has won him millions of followers throughout India. Yoga and Pranayam were once considered as something exotic. Swamiji has given a new birth to Yoga by bringing it to public and benefiting people with it. He has helped Yoga become popular among the common man. He is responsible for a revolution in Yoga and health. His vision of an India claiming back its once coveted leadership position through Yoga has found resonance with millions. In addition, this yoga Guru, Spiritual beacon, Nano-Bio Ayurveda expert is brand ambassador of states, Brand ambassador of the UNO mission political influencer, animation series character, media czar: Baba Ramdev! Overall, a Huge Brand!

DOI: 10.4018/978-1-61350-171-9.ch010

India has a tradition of mystical gurus, albeit Swami Ramdev represents a new phenomenon: the television yoga evangelist. Almost all his congregations have been drawn through his shows. The television guru is also available in other continents including Africa, Australia, Europe, and America. The huge power, respect, and awe that Brand Ramdev commands can be judged by the fact that his yoga shows "Swami Ramdev's yoga" on Aastha television channel are shown across 170 countries and have a viewership of 20 million people. After taking over Aastha channel, Swami Ramdev is now all set to launch two channels exclusively for bhajans and Vedas.

Further, at 5 a.m. beneath the Shivalik hills in northern India, Swami Ramdev sits cross-legged swaddled in saffron robes commanding the rapt attention of 500 devotees of his brand of yoga. The crowd consists of people suffering from chronic conditions for which traditional medicine offers comfort. Each "patient" pays 7,000 to 40,000 Indian rupees, to be among the first to spend a week at the swami's village of 300 bungalows offering spiritual retreat. In sum, Swami Ramdev's vouches that pranayama, the ancient Indian art of breath control, can cure an incomprehensible range of diseases. "Asthma, arthritis, sickle-cell anemia, kidney problems, thyroid disease, hepatitis, slipped discs and it will unblock any fallopian tubes," he tells his audience in the yoga village, who line up to have their blood tested and receive herbal remedies.

Baba's Brand Strategy

Baba Ramdev also addresses the value Propositions like Product, Leadership, Operational Excellence and Customer Relationship. He has developed a unique blend of Ayurveda and Vedic philosophy to cater to create value for his customers. This brand has mass customized itself to satisfy all and thus have made a distinct place for itself. In an era when the marketers are faced with the challenge of getting their message heard by consumers who are hard to find and even harder to influence, this brand has worked wonders and all because of its all-inclusive image.

Unique Selling Proposition/ Unique Yogic Proposition

The factors that differentiate Swami Ramdev are his emphasis on teaching and making available the practice of Pranayama for the masses. This is different from other yoga teachers who place more emphasis on yoga postures along with his 500 hospitals in the country that are said to register 30,000 patients per day. He has constantly utilized his target segment as partners in innovation, marketing, and growth of his organization. Similarly, he also studies his programs during his yoga camps where his staff collects on-the-ground data from participants before, during, and after the camp. Given the vast attendance in each of his nearly weekly camps, the volume of data that is collected and analyzed is large. He takes this feedback and periodically revises his programs, based on the results of constant research. The way his yoga camps have evolved, it is clear that he has succeeded in simplifying the efforts required to gain maximum benefits from his exercises, with enough room for flexibility and ease of involvement for the average follower.

Swami Ramdev has built some powerful partnerships with various well-known TV channels to broadcast his yoga camps worldwide. During the camps, he routinely asks participants to get up and share their 'pranayama success stories'. Inspirational accounts ranging from control of diabetes, blood pressure to healthier cholesterol readings and curing joint pains and skin aliments have proven to be invaluable marketing assets for him. Moreover, best of all, they come at no cost!

Swami Ramdev has not done any charity. He has skillfully veiled what could have been straightforward 'pay-per-service' such as the Art of Living programmes. He charges for attending his camps but through price discrimination. Those that can pay more are able to get better seats the front. It appears that Ramdev's dynamic revenue management is an adaptation of the pricing model used by airlines worldwide.

Target Audience

His target audience is the common person. He has revived Yoga and established it once again in the minds of people. Yoga is becoming very popular among all strata of the society be it common person or prominent personality, many people are openly advocating that their health issues got resolved by doing the same. In addition, these methods as propagated by Ramdev are not under any patent or control and are free for all to follow and lead to suppression of ailments like hypertension, diabetes, heart problem, arthritis, thyroid, etc.

Engaging the Target Audience

Baba Ramdev knows how to engage and captivate the audience. He is an effective communicator who does not give sermons but talk as if to become a part of the common people. He is an interactive speaker who motivates the crowd to follow the guidelines of Yoga to become healthy, share the personal experiences of people who have benefited from it, joke and laugh with people, sometimes quote ancient scriptures and great Indian leaders, and sometimes speak up against some socio-political issues, thereby connecting with the audience at an emotional level. Also, he has effectively used the reach of the media and utilized its benefits by tying up with various media channels, which actually stream live the sessions being conducted by him in various locations so that millions of viewers are able to tune in and follow mostly in early morning or evening hours.

Furthermore, he offers various sets of fixed exercises that take care of a plethora of basic health problems. People with different symptoms are advised not to follow particular steps that are meant for other health issues. He also offers various ayurvedic solutions in form of medicines supposed to help in different illness and health issues promoted through the Patanjali Yogpeeth.

Apart from these physical offerings, he also provides motivation, and upliftment of self-esteem for the millions of people following his school of thought that believes in a greater vision of taking India and humanity to greater heights.

Thus, Baba Ramdev has been successful in creating a unique combination of products offerings unlike any other at a global platform. He has been able to present yoga and ayurveda in a spiritual light, thus reintroducing the ancient shastras in an extremely novel way. This uniqueness and novelty makes Baba Ramdev a one-of-its-kind brand with few direct competitors that can challenge it in all its aspects (i.e. Spirituality, Fitness, and Medicine). Therefore, all of the above coupled with the challenges in analyzing a personality and brand as rich and multifarious as this has motivated us to take up this as branding problem.

The purpose of this chapter is to discuss and identify the competitors of the brand and study the competitive environment for the brand Ramdev to identify the strengths, weaknesses, opportunities, and threats for the Brand Ramdev. Finally, the chapter analyses the Ramdev's brand Personality and the consumer perception of Ramdev.

LITERATURE REVIEW

Successful branding requires a strategic perspective (de Chernatony, 1998) wherein strong brand concepts are communicated and presented to target segments in such a manner that it results in favorable brand images reflecting the brand's identity (Gardner and Levy 1955, Reynolds and Gutman 1984, Kapferer 1997). However, if identity is based on competences and capabilities then the brand identity should be considered as the representative of the resource-based view. Although branding is widely accepted as a marketing issue it has until now not been dealt with within the scope of the marketing paradigm. Thus, Adding branding to the highest level in the marketing theory hierarchy (marketing as concept/paradigm, strategy, and tactics), has important implications for marketing practice and leads to a research agenda with more emphasis on the relation between (changes in) brand identity and customer perceptions and needs (Alsem, & Kostelijk, 2008). Similarly, a credible and compelling brand extension is driven by a deep brand identity, an identity with associations that are profound and multi-layered. Like a hero who headlines a blockbuster movie, a brand must captivate its audience's imagination. And like hit sequels that feed on the desire to know more about the hero, successful brand extensions satisfy their targets' appetites for more information and innovation"(Yohn D.,2008). Thus, with a vision of creating a "Disease Free Society: Medicines Free World" Brand Ram dev has successfully delivered the brand extension from yoga and Pranayam in to ayurvedic medicinal preparations.

Further, "Cultural value is identified as an influential factor on brand image and is widely accepted as one of the crucial concepts in understanding consumer consumption value, which determines choices of consuming everyday products and services. Most firms endeavoring to establish and maintain consistent global brand images, however, adopt a standardized brand image strategy that usually does not consider individual target markets characteristics, including the concepts of cultural value and consumption value"(Park & Rabolt, 2009).

In addition, "Brand Image is a key component of Customer-Based Brand Equity (CBBE), and refers to the associations a consumer holds in memory. Such associations are often directional; one should distinguish between brand-to-attribute and attribute-to-brand associations. Information on these associations arises from two ways of collecting data, respectively: brand-by-brand evaluations of all attributes and attribute-by-attributes evaluations of all brands" (Torres, & Bijmolt2009).

The survey sample responded that Baba Ramdev's brand image is also based on consumer's memory regarding Yoga, Pranayam, Patanjali, and God like Preacher and helping others. Other factors associated with brand image of Ramdev are Persuasiveness, Freedom, Libertarian, and Hard Working. In sum, all these brand elements have built the Brand Image for Baba Ramdev.

Consumer Perception

Consumer Perception is a generic response to the brand about its strengths, weakness, opportunity and threat. Consumer Perception is primarily the belief of the consumers' on a particular product or a particular brand.

Based on the above factors the authors have deduced the consumers' perception for Swami Ramdev as mentioned below;

1. **Core Benefit:** Healthy Life
2. **Generic Product:** Pranayam, Other Yoga Aasans, Green Leafy Vegetables
3. **Expected Product:** Consumers believe that through these natural mechanisms apart from the exercises prescribed for loosing weight, removing heart blockages, there should be facility for gaining weight, removing other incurable diseases like Cancer, AIDS etc.
4. **Augmented Product:** Apart from yoga sessions conducted by Ramdev himself, which means that a city is covered, only once or twice in an year, there should be yoga camps conducted by other members of the community so that people should follow a proper mechanism of exercise. There have been reports that due to bleak knowledge about which exercises are to be performed there have harmful effects on practitioners.
5. **Potential Product:** Ramdev is not using his powers to mint money or commercialize his knowledge. Nevertheless, various other elements involved with the prodigy are into pooling of money from followers. This

can hamper the brand Ramdev indirectly. Therefore, a proper administration should be setup to curb these practices.

Brand Personality

"The idea of Self-Branding just won't go away. Among the books released over the past year: Me, Inc.; You, Inc.; Brand You; and one that casts branding as 120 ways to promote yourself. Quietly doing a good job is cast as, well, pathetic. Infact, in the present age of Google, MySpace, YouTube, and blogging, everyone is a brand. Marketers brand you, Politicians brand you, your colleagues brand you, and so does your boss. Numerous big names say, self-branding will increasingly become the mantra of every ambitious individual" (Diane, 2007).

Similarly, Brand Ramdev has managed an excellent attempt at self-branding. The simple, unassuming, merry, Yogi who has a declared mission to rid India and the world of all disease through promotion of Pranayam and Yoga, has done a fabulous job at Self-Branding. Brand Ramdev has witnessed exponential growth in recent times. The huge patronage and consequently branding by politicians, media barons, and the general milieu alike has definitely added a lot of 'sheen and sustainability' to the brand!

Media and advertising creative that have promoted both Brand Ramdev and Patanjali Yog Peeth have managed to connect with people across the social spectrum. Aastha Channel that carries TV Programs of Baba Ramdev's Yoga Camps from different parts of India, and the world has a presence in around 170 countries. Perhaps, the reason of the superb success of their Branding efforts lies in their extensive reach. Even though there are few direct promotion and marketing efforts, but videos etcetera that are made and posted on several fan blog posts, connect with audiences the world over because they are made by devotees and hence mirror their sentiments effectively to other devotees.

In addition the following are the dimensions of the brand personality (Aaker, 1997)

1. Sincerity
    a. Down-to-Earth
        i. Down to Earth
        ii. Family Oriented
    b. Honest
        i. Honest
        ii. Sincere
        iii. Real
    c. Wholesome
        i. Wholesome
        ii. Original
    d. Cheerful
        i. Friendly
2. Excitement
    a. Daring
        i. Daring
    b. Spirited
        i. Spirited
        ii. Cool
    c. Imaginative
        i. imaginative
        ii. Unique
    d. Up-to-Date
        i. Up-to-Date
        ii. Independent
        iii. Contemporary
3. Competence
    a. Reliable
        i. Reliable
        ii. Secure
    b. Intelligent
        i. Intelligent
    c. Successful
        i. Successful
        ii. Confident
4. Sophistication
    a. Upper-Class
        i. Upper-Class
        ii. Glamorous
    b. Charming
        i. Charming
        ii. Smooth

5. Ruggedness
    a. Outdoorsy
        i. Outdoorsy
    b. Tough
        i. Tough

The above personality dimensions have been utilized to study Brand Ramdev as per the identity established.

Brand Identity

According to Kapferer (2003), brand identity could be defined by answering the following questions:

- What is the aim and individual vision of a brand?
- What makes a brand distinguished?
- How satisfaction could be achieved?
- What is the brand's equity?
- What are brand competence, validity and legitimacy?
- What are the features of its recognition? Elements of brand identity:

Further, we discuss the various parameters associated with identity using Kapferer identity Prism (Figure 1).

Physical Appearance

This is the core of brand and its value added. This determines a traditional brand management due to orientation to "know how," classical positioning, selecting a principal good or brand features and the benefit. The first step building up a brand is the definition of physical factors, identifying what it is, what it does and how does it look like. Physical appearance is closely connected with a brand prototype, revealing the quality of a brand.

Brand Personality

With a help of communication brand character is being developed and this is a way by which any brand "talks" about its goods and services and indicates a particular human person. The trait of personality within the prism of identity is inner source. It should not be mixes up with the image of consumer's reflection which is an ideal portrait of every recipient. Brand personality is described and measured using those features of consumer personality that are directly related to brands. Since 1996 the research was directed towards studies of brand personality (Kapferer, 2003). D. Grundey (2002) claims that the success of brand expression percentage in the market depends on the choice of every element of personality and its

Figure 1. Kapferer brand identity prism

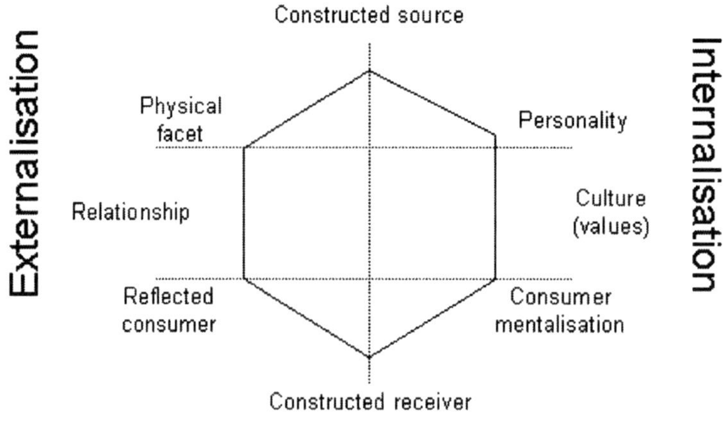

reconciliation. Brand personality is closely connected with self-image and image of a consumer because the identification of consumers' with a particular segment reflects brand features.

Brand Culture

Brands possess that culture in which they originated. Brand is a representative of its culture, including communication. From this perspective culture entails a lot of values that provide brand with inspiration. Cultural features a correlated with external principles of brand management (a good and communication) Culture is in the core of brand. The aspect of culture enables to discover differences between other competing brands. The attention is focused on brand personality; however, eventually only those brands become leaders that possess not only personality but culture. Brand culture is based on the culture, values and aims of an enterprise.

Brand Relationship

Brand includes relationship as brands frequently take the most important place in the process of human transactions and exchange. This is extremely reflected in the sphere of services and retail companies. This feature emphasizes the way of behaviour which is identified with brand most of all. A lot of actions such as the fact how brands influence and provide services in connection to their consumers determine this feature. According to Kapferer (2003), brand is a voice that consumers should hear because brands survive in the market because of communication. D. Grundey (2002) singles out the following ways of communication:

- Advertising and other support elements;
- Direct consumer's communication while purchasing a good.

Customer Reflection

Brand is a customer reflection. Consumers can easily define what goods of a particular brand are produced for a particular type of consumers (for example, this automobile was developed only for show stars). Brand communication and goods aim at reflecting a consumer, for whom those goods are addressed. Consumer reflection is often confused with the target market (Kapferer, 2003). The target market determines potential consumers though consumer reflection does not define target market. A consumer has to be reflected in a way, which would show how he or she could image themselves consuming a particular good. The representatives of the target market should be presented differently from what they are but what they would like to be. Consumers use goods of certain brands seeking to create their own identity. Brands should control their consumer reflection. A constant repetition stating that this brand was developed for a certain target group weakens brand image.

Consumer Self-Image

Brand is closely related to the understanding of consumer self-image that is the features with which consumers identify themselves and the very same features they would like to be reflected by the chosen good and its brand. Consumer self-image is important in the explanation of consumer behaviour as consumers purchase goods, corresponding to their self-image. The conception of consumer self-image includes an amount of individual ideas, thoughts and feelings about him in relationship with other objects within socially defined boundaries (Onkvisitir Shaw, 1994). This is the understanding of an individual about his ability, semblance and characteristics on personality.

ISSUES

In view of the above discussion the purpose is to establish as to whether the Image of the Brand Ramdev is perceived as equivalent to the Identity of the brand Ramdev. And for this, the authors conducted a survey on 80 people. The respondents were carefully chosen such that they had an idea of Brand Ramdev and had actually watched him teach yoga on television or in reality. The age group of the respondents varied from 25 to 60 years. The respondents were given a set of questions and were asked to answer them with a purpose to understanding the consumer perception of the brand and then to analyze if it actually fits the brand personality of Ramdev.

CONCLUSION

We started with discussing the rationale for selecting Swami Ramdev as the subject of our study. It was of significant interest to us to note that 'Baba Ramdev' is not just an exceptional Spiritual leader, but also a Nano-Bio Aurveda expert, Brand Ambassador of states, Brand ambassador of the UNO mission on poverty, a scholar of the Vedas and languages, a major political influence, an animation series character, and a media czar. This confirmed our suspicions that Baba Ramdev is all this and so much more. 'Baba Ramdev' is a Huge Brand!

We then went on to elaborate on the Brand Status and Brand Strategy. The chapter answers the questions of what is the value proposition, and what are the key differentiators of the brand. The Growth strategy that Baba Ramdev has adopted is that of partnerships with his audience as well as the media. Swami Ramdev exploits the most powerful means of promotion, the 'word-of-mouth'. During the camps, he routinely asks participants to get up and share their 'Pranayama success stories'. Inspirational accounts ranging from control of diabetes, blood pressure to healthier cholesterol readings and curing joint pains and skin aliments have proven to be invaluable marketing assets for him. Moreover, best of all, they come at no cost!

Besides Yoga and Pranayam sessions, Baba Ramdev has a rich and diverse portfolio of offerings like Ayurvedic medications, and counseling sessions. The Patanjali Yog Peeth is often instrumental in dispensing such medicines.

The chapter presents an elaborate literature review on important issues like Brand Personality, Brand Identity, Brand Image, and Consumer Preferences.

Finally, the results obtained from the survey analysis suggest that the brand image is Sophisticated (trendy, reliable, successful, leader, confident, glamorous, good looking, feminine, and smooth), Down to earth (family oriented, small town, wholesome, spirited), Cheerful (friendly, unique, outdoorsy), Intelligent, Honest (real and imaginative), Sentimental, Upper-class (cool and upper-class), Sincere (honest, original, hard working). The findings on Brand attributes like Sincerity, Competence, Ruggedness, Excitement, and Sophistication are illustrated through pie-charts and Rotated Component Matrix Table (See Appendix A).

Also, the results of our survey were put to scrutiny based upon the Kapferer's Brand Identity Prism. Analyzing the match between the brand personality obtained from the literature review and the results of the survey, we observed that 6 out of the 9 traits of the facets of brand identity and image are the same (See Appendix A) and thus we observe that the image of the brand Ramdev is perceived as equivalent to the identity of the brand Ramdev. The similarity among the brand image and identity suggests that the creation of personality is a joint venture between the brand management and the consumer. The positive perception suggests strong brand personality. Hence personality is a vital guide for those seeking to get the brand across to the consumer.

REFERENCES

Aaker, J. L. (1997). Dimensions of brand personality. *JMR, Journal of Marketing Research*, *34*(August), 347–356. doi:10.2307/3151897

Alsem, K. J., & Kostelijk, E. (2008). Identity based marketing: A new balanced marketing paradigm. *European Journal of Marketing*, *42*(9/10), 907–914. doi:10.1108/03090560810891064

Azoulay, A., & Kapferer, J.-N. (2003). Do brand personality scales really measure brand personality? *Journal of Brand Management*, *11*(2), 143–155. doi:10.1057/palgrave.bm.2540162

Brady, D. (2007). Creating brand you. *Business Week*, *4047*, 72-73.

de Chernatony, L. (1998). Developing an effective brand strategy. In Egan, C., & Thomas, M. (Eds.), *The CIM handbook of strategic marketing*. Oxford, UK: Butterworth Heinemann. doi:10.1016/B978-0-7506-2613-2.50012-6

de Chernatony, L. (1998). *Brand management*. Aldershot, UK: Ashgate Publishing Limited.

Gardner, B. B., & Levy, S. J. (1955, March-April). The product and the brand. *Harvard Business Review*, 33–39.

Grundey, D. (2002). *Partnership marketing: Present and future reviews compilation: Marketing methods and theories*. The 4th International Conference Marketing Methods and Theories, (pp. 153-161). ISBN 9986-19-516-0

Kapferer, J.-N. (1997). *Strategic brand management*. Great Britain: Kogan Page.

Kapferer, J.-N. (2008). *The new strategic brand management* (4th ed.). London: Kogan Page.

Onkvisit, S., & Shaw, J. J. (1994). Standardization versus localization: The need for the compromising perspective. In Hassan, S. S., & Blackwell, R. D. (Eds.), *Global marketing: Perspectives and cases*. Forth Worth, TX: Dryden Press.

Park, H., & Rabolt, N. (2009). Cultural value, consumption value, and global brand image: A cross-national study. *Psychology and Marketing*, *26*(8), 714. doi:10.1002/mar.20296

Reynolds, T. J., & Gutman, J. (1984). Advertising is image management. *Journal of Advertising Research*, *24*, 27–37.

Torres, A., & Bijmolt, T. (2009). Assessing brand image through communalities and asymmetries in brand-to-attribute and attribute-to-brand associations. *European Journal of Operational Research*, *195*(2), 628. doi:10.1016/j.ejor.2008.02.020

Yohn, D. (2008). The brand ultimatum. [The American Marketing Association.]. *Marketing Management*, *17*(4), 34–38.

ADDITIONAL READING

http://entertainment.oneindia.in/ bollywood/news/2008/shilpa-dvd-india-launch-240308.html

http://en.wikipedia.org/wiki/ Swami_Ramdev

http://greathumancapital.wordpress.eom /category/management-guru/page/2/

http://indianrationalists.blogspot.com/ 2008/07/tv-swamy-ramdev and-his-cures.html

http://kamyabology.com/ramdev/

http://www.businessworld.in/index.php/Lessons-from-Swami-Ramdev.html

http://www.clnaindiaxom/world/report_ramdev-s-yoga-brand-launched-in-america_1107155

http://www.expressindia.com/news/ fullstory.php?newsid=64934

http://www.indianmba.com/Faculty_Column/FC343/fc343.html

http://www.indianmba.com/Faculty_Column/FC851/fc851.html

http://www.managementparadise.com/forums/articles/5945-lessons-swami-ramdev.html

http://www.merinews.com/ catFull.jsp?articleID=146623

http://www.pluggd.in/indian-startups/marketing-lessons-for-indian-entrepreneurs -from-the-spiritual-world-898/

http://www.thehindubusinessline.com/2006/03/31/stories/2006033101272000.htm

Interview transcripts on www.news4u.co.in

APPENDIX A

Following charts (Figures 2 to 6 and Table 1) are indicative of the average responses for the dimensions of the Aaker' model of brand personality.

Figure 2.

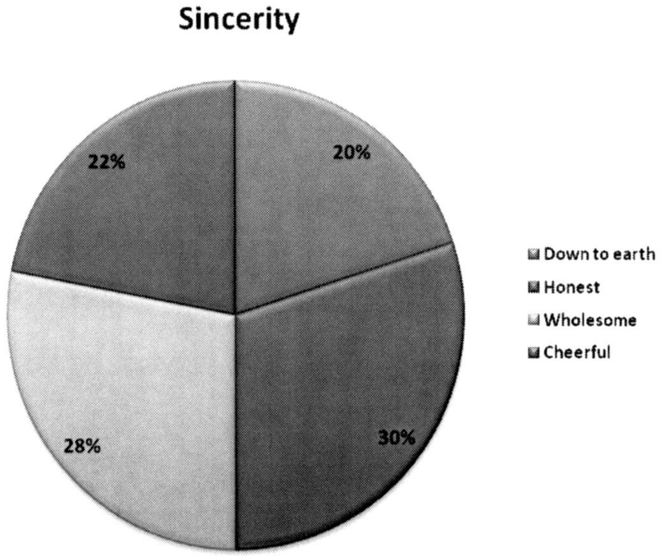

Figure 3.

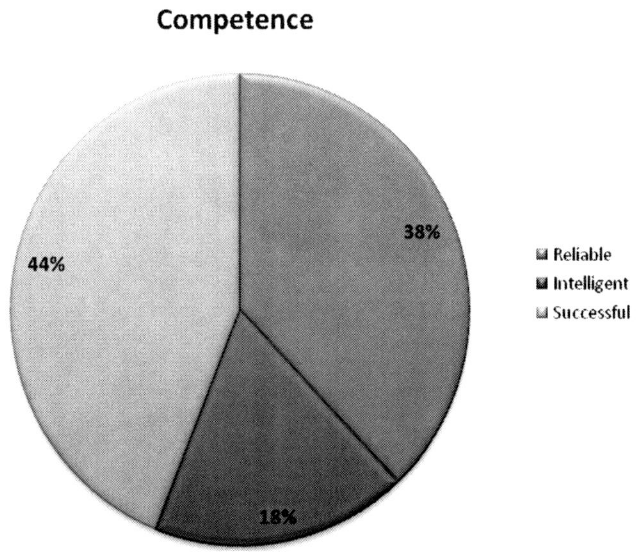

Figure 4.

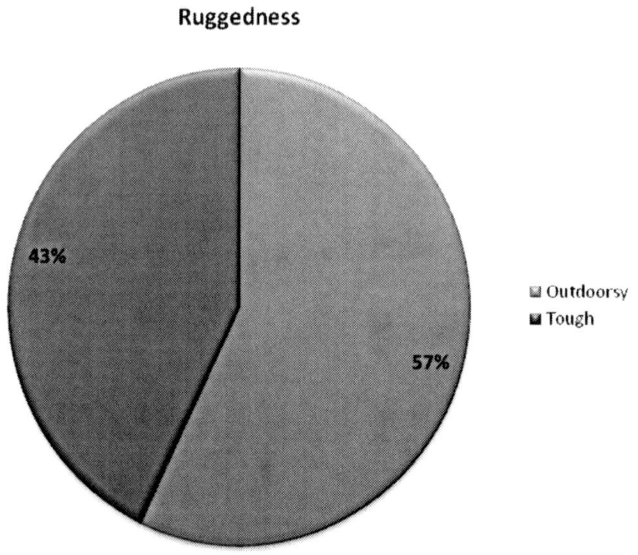

Figure 5.

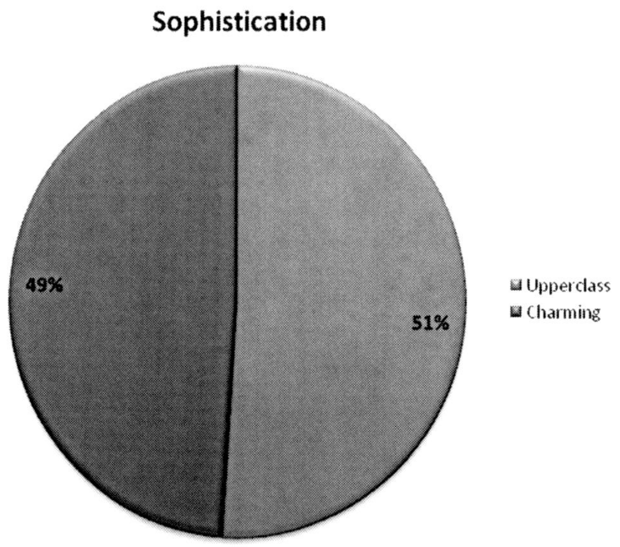

Table 1. Rotated component matrix[a]

	Component							
	1	2	3	4	5	6	7	8
VAR00002	-.181	-.601	-.360	-.395	-.454	-.082	-.111	.165
VAR00003	-.156	-.836	-.082	.052	-.112	.110	-.118	.047
VAR00004	.180	-.250	.094	-.409	-.101	-.097	.297	.653
VAR00006	-.111	.083	.174	.073	.897	.109	-.033	-.049
VAR00007	.086	.612	-.240	-.298	.377	.203	-.165	-.025
VAR00008	.265	.022	-.098	.000	.065	.154	-.204	.796
VAR00010	.102	-.147	.036	-.092	-.045	.865	.144	.200
VAROOO11	.116	.347	-.660	.054	.126	-.282	-.307	.145
VAR00013	.824	.048	-.100	-.141	-.259	.041	.035	-.040
VAR00015	-.060	.803	.006	.007	-.274	-.187	.087	-.169
VAR00016	.117	-.009	-.135	-.019	-.113	.229	.873	-.065
VAR00018	.270	.026	.120	.084	-.713	.420	.141	-.197
VAR00019	.028	-.016	.868	-.039	.069	-.015	-.001	.032
VAR00021	-.227	.410	-.168	-.373	-.245	-.535	.263	.078
VAR00023	-.704	.183	-.297	-.444	.035	.033	.098	-.073
VAR00024	-.151	-.346	.467	.384	-.059	.135	.029	.614
VAR00026	-.093	-.125	-.154	.848	.080	-.012	-.132	-.146
VAR00028	-.035	-.511	.206	.141	.558	.321	.250	-.196
VAR00029	-.796	.002	.289	-.147	.131	.202	-.064	-.123
VAR00030	-.683	-.112	.052	-.030	.065	.487	-.369	-.096
VAR00031	-.882	.124	.079	.221	.083	-.053	-.050	-.220
VAR00032	.320	.273	.281	.000	.157	-.310	.707	.034
VAR00033	.897	.138	.112	.110	.075	.240	.061	.045
VAR00034	.899	.095	.017	.127	.074	.233	.080	.103
VAR00035	.260	.023	-.108	.857	-.025	-.007	.143	.097
VAR00036	.723	.299	-.107	.000	-.167	-.280	.348	-.230
VARO0O37	.691	.090	.222	.120	.182	.488	-.046	.053
VAR00038	-.062	.272	.792	-.226	.218	.035	-.186	.085

Extraction Method: Principal Component Analysis.
Rotation Method: Varimax with Kaiser Normalization.
a. Rotation converged in 10 iterations.

Based on the results of the survey, the following dimensions of brand personality have been established:

1. Sincerity
    a. Down-to-Earth
        i. Family oriented
        ii. Small town
    b. Honest
        i. Honest
        ii. Real
    c. Wholesome
        i. Wholesome
        ii. Original
    d. Cheerful
        i. Sentimental
        ii. Friendly
2. Excitement
    a. Daring
        i. Trendy
    b. Spirited
        i. Spirited
        ii. Cool
    c. Imaginative
        i. Imaginative
        ii. Unique
    d. Not Up-to-Date
3. Competence
    a. Reliable
        i. Reliable
        ii. Hard working
    b. Intelligent
        i. Intelligent
    c. Successful
        i. Successful
        ii. Leader
        iii. Confident
4. Sophistication
    a. Upper-Class
        i. Upper-Class
        ii. Glamorous
        iii. Good looking
    b. Charming
        i. Charming
        ii. Feminine
        iii. Smooth
5. Ruggedness
    a. Not Outdoorsy
    b. Not Tough

These results help us establish a relationship between the identity and image of the brand personality (Figure 6).

Figure 6. Kapferer's identity prism

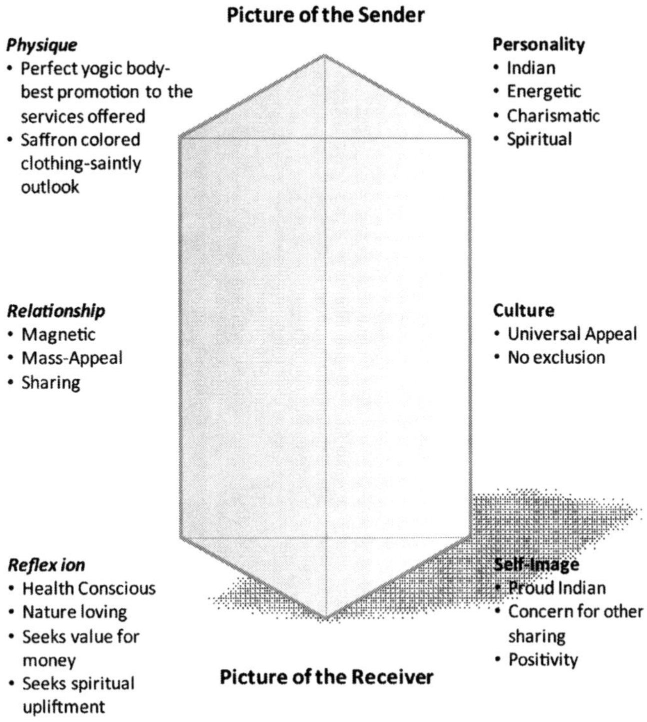

Section 4
Digital and Virtual World

Chapter 11
GeoFree BrandComms: Building and Sustaining Virtual Brand Communities

P. Raj Devasagayam
Siena College, USA

Dana A. VanDen Heuvel
Pheedo, Inc., USA

ABSTRACT

Marketing literature has established the strategic importance of building communities centered around strong brands—brand communities. Our research adds to the current understanding of brand communities by extending the notion of brand community being non-geographically bound. While prior research acknowledges this characteristic of brand community, it fails to, firstly, illustrate the strategic importance of such freedom, and secondly, provide directions for an operational, tactical, or strategic tool to truly build and sustain non-geographically bound brand communities. We refer to such communities as geographically free brand communities (GeoFree BrandComms). This research presents the conceptual underpinnings and characteristics of GeoFree BrandComms. Further, the use of Weblogs (Blogs) and related technologies such as video blogs, podcasts, and RSS as strategic tools in building GeoFreeBrandComms is explored. We then proceed to posit the applications of GeoFree BrandComms in Web-based marketing strategies that find their basis in strong brands and loyal customers.

INTRODUCTION

This year the Facebook community will welcome its 500 millionth member, far outnumbering the entire population of the United States! It's size in sheer numbers is third only to China and India! One quarter of Web browsers pay a visit to Facebook and make a revisit to the site almost a daily ritual. Members on this site interact with others, search out lost acquaintances, comment on the lives of others and look for similar communications from others! This is a strong community with active

DOI: 10.4018/978-1-61350-171-9.ch011

participation. In fact, the community is strong enough to make the mighty Mark Zuckerberg (founder of Facebook) to alter the very nature of the site. In the past three years there has been more than one occasion on which the Facebook community has made corporate managers at Facebook to rescind and retract corporate policy decisions pertaining to membership privacy. As one reads through this research, it will become evident that Facebook is face to face with a well entrenched community of brand fanatics that have virtually hijacked the object of their affection. With this vignette in mind, one can easily see the wisdom of managing one's brand in a fashion such that the control of the brand is retained yet the followers of the brand feel involved and important. We suggest ways to conceive, sustain, and grow such a community in the virtual world with the strategic imperatives of brand equity being preserved and protected. In order to comprehend our thesis on this issue, the reader must first understand the socio-anthropological foundations of a community.

A community is an organized network of member entities and the interrelationships. Communities tend to be identified on the basis of commonality or identification among their members, whether a neighborhood, an occupation, a leisure pursuit, or devotion to a brand. Through communities, people share essential resources that may be cognitive, emotional, or material in nature. Recently researchers have drawn our attention to communities built around (and often sustained by) strong brands—brand communities (McAlexander, Schouten, and Koenig, 2002).

Brand communities are communities whose primary bases of identification are either brands or consumption activities, that is, whose meaningfulness is negotiated through the symbolism of the marketplace. In an ongoing effort to retain customer loyalty and build a strategy based on lifelong partnerships, brand communities offer a way to enmesh the customer in a network of relationships with the brand and fellow customers as opposed to the traditional one-to-one relation between brand and customer. It is presumed that such an approach would strengthen the bonds with the customer in a much superior fashion, thus building and strengthening strategic brand loyalty.

Muniz and O'Guinn (2001, p.412) posit: "*A brand community is a specialized, non-geographically bound community, based on a structured set of social relations among admirers of a brand.*"

Brand Community is conceptualized as being "specialized" because at its center is a branded good or service. McAlexander, Schouten, and Koenig (2002) further envisioned a brand community from a customer point of view as a fabric of relationships in which they are situated in relationship to the brand, to the firm and to other customers of the brand.

Our research adds to the current understanding of brand communities by exploring the notion of brand community being "non-geographically bound." While prior research acknowledges this characteristic of brand community it fails to, firstly, illustrate the strategic importance of such freedom. And, secondly, provide directions for an operational, tactical, or strategic tool to truly build and sustain non-geographically bound brand communities. We refer to such communities as geographically free brand communities–GeoFree BrandComms.

We propose that GeoFree BrandComms present relatively inexpensive strategic tools to build brand loyalty and brand equity. We examine the characteristics of such GeoFree BrandComms, and compare and contrast them to the more traditional brand communities (Jeep Jamborees, Harley-Davidson Owners' Groups [HOGS]). We then proceed to illustrate the use of one such on-line tool—Web Based Logs (Blogs) -- as a possible strategic tool to build GeoFree BrandComms in the virtual world.

Brand Communities vs. GeoFree BrandComms

Brand communities have been seen as being fundamental contributors to a brand's larger social construction. Customers value their relationships with their favorite brands and with firms that build and foster those brands. Being a member of a brand community leads to shared experiences with the brand, the firm, and fellow customers. As time progresses the brand community begins to draw its lifeblood from relationships with fellow community members rather than the brand itself.

Companies like Chrysler, Harley Davidson, and the Green Bay Packers have shown a remarkable sensitivity to the existence of brand communities and have actively sought their development leading to an amazing level of brand loyalty from their customers. Events like Jeep Jamborees, Camp Jeep, HOG (Harley Davidson Owners' Group), Packer's Stock Holders Meetings, and the Packer Experience, bring together people who often share no connection other than an interest in a brand and its consumption. Eventually, the fellow members of the community become as important (if not more important) to the product experience as the brand itself.

All such "geographically bound" brand communities offer opportunities for context-rich interaction and communication within a limited geographical location. Offsite communication is either initiated or fostered by the firm that owns the brand (membership newsletters, email notifications, and e-updates, for instance) or is rendered nonexistent. While gathered in a central geographic location, participants build community and are able to interact in a fashion that strengthens relationships. However, upon returning from such momentous events, a sense of loneliness follows. Communication is often faceless and moderated by the owner of the brand. All company-initiated communication is usually limited to mass media. Participants share extraordinary consumption experiences with each other through the company media. Relational ties often die down or at least ease up until the next big community gathering is planned.

All of this holds true for a physical event that fosters community. We suggest that the virtual world of the Internet might be able to sustain, supplement, and perhaps even strengthen the relationships developed in a geographically bound brand community. Consider the use of the Internet in virtual community gatherings and events for members that await the next geographically bound sponsored event. Further, consider the strategic value of continued communication to keep members informed about each other and their product experiences. The Internet could provide opportunities for members to communicate one-on-one with each other, affording them the freedom to do so directly—without the intervention of the brand owner. Studies have shown that relationship between customers that form communities around a brand are indeed the foundations of strong relationships between the brand and the customer (see McAlexander, Schouten, and Koenig, 2002, for an extensive reference list). We reiterate: brand communities find their identity through shared experiences and consumption of the brand, therefore, increased opportunities to share consumption experiences will lead to a stronger brand community. The Internet presents the marketer and the customers with a multitude of such opportunities.

Sufficient evidence exists to suggest that brand building and brand communities are evident and thriving on the Internet. (DM News, July 7, 2003). Brand communities on the Web (e.g., ivillage.com and webmd.com) offer strategic advantages as compared to geographically bound brand communities. Geographical gathering is no longer an issue to establish relationships. The process of socialization is based on non-contemporaneous and non-personal communication. Preexisting tools of community building in the cyberspace offer low cost alternatives to building brand communities that have largely remained unnoticed by marketers. Opportunities to build communities via the Internet have largely been viewed as the responsibility of the consumers. The brand has not been made a participant in forging a triad of commitment in the relationship.

This paper suggests one possible tool: Web Based Logs (Weblogs, or Blogs) as a possible strategic device in establishing GeoFree Brand-Comms. The phenomenon has implications for both building new brand communities and sustaining pre-existing brand communities. For those companies with little or no (geographically bound) brand community Blogs may be used to build an inexpensive virtual brand community. While companies that already enjoy a traditional geographically bound brand communities Blogs could aid in sustaining a secondary, supportive, and more on-going GeoFree BrandComm. Such communities would then not be solely driven by short term and expensive community events.

Growing Importance of Blogs

The Wall Street Journal (Sept. 30, 2003; pD2) describes the phenomenon of Weblog as "...one of the fastest growing activities on the Web." Weblogs are online diaries or journals, typically written in a personal nature, that are then available to anyone in the world via the Internet. In fact, the word "Blog" has gained credence as a legitimate word in the virtual lexicon (Webopedia, 2003).

Blogging refers to publishing a regularly updated Weblog of links and entries. More specifically, blogs are identified as having frequently modified pages in which all entries are dated and listed in reverse chronological order. Blogging has now taken on several additional formats, including mobile blogs, video blogs, photo blogs and audio blogs, also known as podcasts. Mobile blogs, commonly referred to as a Mo-blog are blogs where an author with a smart wireless phone can take pictures and record sounds to their Blog while they are nowhere near a computer. The popularity of camera phones and the freedom afforded to update a blog while on road has further spurred consumer interest in blogging (The Sacramento Bee, 9/2/03). Video blogs, or vlogs as they are commonly known, allow their authors to upload video clips not only to their personal or corporate blogs, but also to sites like YouTube.com and Google Video. The potentially viral nature of video content, coupled with the power of social media can turn brands or even individuals into celebrities almost overnight, as evidenced in the summer of 2006 by the rapid circulation of a series of videos featuring Diet Coke and Mentos which were originally created by Fritz Grobe and Stephen Voltz of Eepybird.com. Podcasting, or a method of distributing multimedia files, such as audio programs, over the Internet using RSS or other syndication formats, for playback, is another variation on the theme of blogging,

The importance of Blogs in the overall business strategies of corporations and the critical mass they may have attained in formulation of marketing strategies might best be illustrated by a series of converging factors:

1. The growth of the blogosphere (aggregate of all of the publicly available weblogs) over the past several years. According to research by the firm Technorati, the size of the blogosphere has been doubling every year over the past three years.
2. The volume of articles, news stories and popular media mentions of blogging over the past few years. A search for the term "blogging" in Google turns up over 234 Million results in 2006, and in 2010 - 44,500,000 hits!
3. The growing number of Fortune 500 companies that have implemented blogs as part of their communication structure. As of April of 2006, 29, or 5.8% of the Fortune 500 were blogging, by December 2009 this number had gone up to 79 (15.8%) accord-

ing to research conducted for the Fortune 500 Business Blogging Wiki (http://www.socialtext.net/bizblogs/index.cgi). This is a three-fold increase!

4. A series of books on blogging by noted blogging authorities extolling the benefits of corporate blogging for a variety of purposes.
5. Since 2002, over 133,000,000 blogs have been indexed by Technorati. In their "State of the Blogosphere" report of 2009, Technorati (http://technorati.com/state-of-the-blogosphere/) respondents report:
    - Two-thirds are male, roughly 60% are in the age group 18-44. They are highly educated, about three out of four have college degrees and about 40% have graduate degrees. These demographics of bloggers are among those coveted by most companies as being very lucrative customer segments.
    - Bloggers are often wealthy, one in three has an annual household income of $75K+ and one in four has an annual household income of $100K+
    - Around half of bloggers are working on at least their second blog, and 68% have been blogging for two years or more, eight out of ten have been blogging for at least a year
    - Seventy percent of bloggers are talking about brands on their blog organically, 46% of respondents post about the brands they love (or hate). 38% post brand or product reviews.
    - Part-Timers, and Self-Employed bloggers are talking about brands at a much higher rate (80%), with one in three posting reviews at least once a week.
    - 52% syndicate their blog posts to their Twitter Account, and 41% do so while also posting tweets that are not associated with their blogs.
    - 26% of bloggers who also use Twitter say that the service has eaten into the time they spend updating their traditional blogs – though 65% say it has had no effect.

In an August 2003 survey, Forester Research indicates that only 2% of their respondents visited a blog once a week or more. In fact, 79% of the respondents reported not having *heard* of a blog (Forrester, 2003). While Blogging was gaining popularity, there seemed to be sufficient room to grow and expand markets despite the competitive frenzy. A similar study by comScore Media Metix in May of 2006 shows just how far blogs have come as tools for mainstream marketing and media. Visitation to blogs grew by 56-percent from May of 2005 to May of 2006, to 58.7 million visitors. By 2010, three out of four (approximately 77%) internet visitors were participating in (reading or writing) a blog.

Over the summer long-time blogging hold-out, Dell Computer, launched a blog called "Direct2Dell" to give customers an "accessible alternative to more formal, one-way channels of communication," according to the Dell site. According to many industry observers, Dell's foray into blogging was largely founded on their desire to revive their brand community and improve their overall declining brand image.

Blogs, different from other online community tools such as message boards, threaded discussion and chat, are vehicles of inclusion and accepted meaning rather than being underground or highly differential. Blogs exhibit inherent social characteristics through blog comments, blogrolls or citations, links to other bloggers' content. These characteristics make them ideal candidates to accommodate an open and non-threatening community. While it is true that some bloggers seek to espouse contrarian emotion and action, one finds that the majority of bloggers are seeking a voice in greater community and positing an agreeable slant on an ideology that their circle of readers readily identifies with. Moreover, after examining the existing corporate blogs, currently on the Internet, they, as with most corporate communication vehicles, tend to error on the conservative side when it comes to viewpoints on their industry, products and solutions and largely avoid social issues and other such matters, which could espouse dissent, distrust or ridicule. Blogs could support a GeoFree BrandComm, either as a stand-alone entity and the sole gather place for the community or as a support mechanism for existing brand communities, as they are tools of personal publishing and person-to-person dialogue. Through the authors' posts and readers' comments, brand communities can unite virtually any time, and from any place. Marketing managers could easily enjoy the benefits of such brand themes and subject streams being associated with shared experiences of their brand—a very non-intrusive mode of eavesdropping on the "voice of the customer," if you will.

Characteristics of GeoFree BrandComm

Like any other community, we expect a GeoFree BrandComm to be marked by shared experiences, rituals, mores, traditions, and a sense of moral responsibility. In the case of a GeoFree BrandComms, each of these qualities will, however, find expression within a commercial context on the Internet.

Consciousness of Belonging

The most important element of any community is consciousness of belonging -- members sharing a "we-ness." Members in a GeoFree BrandComm could feel an important connection to the brand, but more importantly, feel a stronger connection toward one another. The consciousness of belonging found in GeoFree BrandComms transcends geographic boundaries. It may also be characterized by a belief in the legitimacy of cause and oppositional brand loyalty. The members would almost be compelled with a deep moral obligation to rally around their favorite brand due to a felt sense of legitimacy of the focus of their community. In the same manner, competing brands would be seen as threats to community and therefore there would be a unity of opposition to competing brands. In arenas such as sports, one often witnesses legitimacy in membership through shared opposition to a competing team.

Blogs are uniquely effective in fostering a "we-ness" among brand followers, as they allow for expressions of both, legitimacy of cause and oppositional brand loyalty. For instance, in the case of a sports team fan base, Blogs could serve as a medium for venting frustrations on a team's performance or for voicing opposition to rivals. Moreover, Blogs are emerging as integral support mechanisms for geographically bound (local/parochial) efforts such as "Smart Mob" gatherings (Rheingold, 2002) through such technologies as Geourl.org or Blogmapper.com, which provide tools that create "geoblogs" in the virtual world that are organized by geography, rather than date. (The Economist, 2003). Geographical proximity might allow for physical events to bind the GeoFree BrandComm further in its sense of belonging.

Existing corporate blogs, such as the blogs hosted by Dell Computers, Google and 37Signals, a web-based Internet tools company, all exhibit characteristics which expose the deep sense of "we-ness" that the brand followers feel. In the context of the GeoFree BrandComm blog, this "we-ness" is manifested in the following forms

1. Comments left on the blog by readers, pundits, brand aficionados, brand opponents and other bloggers. Comments may be positive, and supportive of the brand, or negative.
2. Links from other bloggers who fall into the aforementioned categories of blog readers and comment contributors. These links are manifested on the blog in the form of a Trackback, which is the recognition by the blog software that an outside source has ref-

erenced it, and in turn offers a reciprocal link back to the inbound content, fostering and "automatic connection" from the corporate blog to another blogger.

Legitimacy of Membership

Legitimacy is a process whereby members of the community differentiate between true members of the community and those who are not, or who occupy a more marginal space. In the context of brands this is demonstrated by "really knowing" the brand as opposed to using the brand for the "wrong reasons." The wrong reasons are typically revealed by failing to fully appreciate the culture, history, rituals, traditions, and symbols established by the brand community.

GeoFree BrandComms are generally open social organizations in that they do not deny membership, but like most communities, they would have status hierarchies. Ostensibly, anyone who is devoted to the brand can be a member of the community, regardless of ownership. However, the devotion to the brand must be sincere and for the right reasons. Legitimacy is however not a necessary condition in all brand communities.

The worldwide reach and open nature of the Blogs prevents it from discriminating between legitimate and illegitimate members of the brand community. However, just as consumers may self-select into or out of geographical brand communities, they might choose to regularly read, or never revisit a particular blog. The legitimate brand consumer can be easily discerned from a colleague of lesser status based on comments left about a post in the brand's or ones personal Blog. One could always gain legitimacy of membership in GeoFree BrandComm over time, by expressing their belief in the legitimacy of cause or expressing oppositional brand loyalty toward competing brands.

Rituals and Traditions

Rituals and traditions are easy ways for a community to propagate and perpetuate its membership. Rituals and traditions also aid in transmitting the mores of the community within and beyond the community. In case of GeoFree BrandComms, such rituals and traditions would be expected to center on experiences associated with brand consumption. In effect, such rituals and traditions would shape the culture of the GeoFree BrandComm.

Some of the rituals and traditions could include celebrating the history of the brand and sharing brand stories. HOGS and Cheeseheads take pride in the history of their brands. The very mention of Lambeau Field or Vince Lombardi makes the Packer fan repeat stories of the "Snow Bowl."

The preservation of what the brand is and stands for is important to the GeoFree BrandComm. Members often feel that they have a better understanding of the brand than the brand owner does. They can be, and frequently are, critical of aspects of the brand and/or its management to the extent that the brand's very ownership may be contested.

We find that Blogs provide a feasible venue to manifest such rituals and traditions in GeoFree BrandComms. The ritualistic nature of authors posting and readers commenting gives Blogs that give and take feel that espouses ownership and sentiment toward the brand or shared consumption experience being discussed. Bloggers provide ways to amplify the voice of the brand message and such communication is much more likely to reach the target consumer than a standard marketing message from a corporate marketing department. On a Blog, the copy is written by customers that have experienced the product and offers a very noise-free communication medium between an unsolicited testimonial and its reader. In addition, Blogs allow for a chronologically ordered discussion on the merits of the brand's attributes by its most ardent supporters. The Blog serves to extend the experience of the physical rituals of attending a game or participating in an event by allowing brand aficionados to share discussions for weeks after an event, laying a firm foundation for the GeoFree BrandComm.

Obligation to the Community

A community bears an implied responsibility for its members to share responsibilities as an obligation to the collective members-at-large and to individual members as well. This sense of moral responsibility is what produces collective action and contributes to group cohesion. The goal now becomes to add to the ranks by strengthening existing community and making new member of the GeoFree BrandComm feel welcome.

There is a sense of common purpose, obligation, interest and social responsibility within the Blogosphere that centers on the idea of the Internet as the great equalizer, and great mobilizer. Blogs serve the GeoFree BrandComms by allowing everyone to have a voice in the community. In addition, the Blog authors typically seek to fulfill the obligation of providing an insightful and rewarding reader experience on their weblog. Bloggers are intent on being part of the broader conversation, which is manifested through the obligation to write quality entries that are likely to resonate with the greater community. "Being part of that broader conversation is what gives Blogs unique, fascinating appeal," writes Sullivan (2002). Moreover, the blogger's obligation to the community only strengthens as the GeoFree BrandComm grows in membership and tenure—expecting continued freshness, honesty, and candor.

Social Anonymity

Interactions within a GeoFree BrandComm may be rich in social context or nearly devoid of it (Fischer, Bristor, and Gainer 1996). GeoFree BrandComm members may have a great deal of information about one another, including such data as age, gender, attractiveness, and personal history, or they may know nothing of one another (Granitz and Ward 1996). At times, community members might be uncomfortable about providing too much information to fellow members. The weekend road warriors on Harley Davidsons are often fake tattoo wearing corporate hotshots that enjoy the open road and the psychological stimulus it provides in the garb of pseudoanonymity. Blogs offer an opportunity to participate in the GeoFree BrandComms to the degree of disclosure one would find most comfortable. Bloggers may choose to use pseudonymous "handles" to preserve their privacy. At times, it is this anonymity that enriches the candor of shared consumption experiences generating a renewed sense of community in the GeoFree BrandComm.

Strategic Implications of GeoFree BrandComms

Marketing Implications

Customers who are highly integrated in the GeoFree BrandComms would also be emotionally invested in the success of the brand and the welfare of the brand owner. As community members, marketers also contribute to the process of community building by supporting the context (e.g., Blogs) in which owner interaction occurs. Marketers may also take an active role in establishing the shared rituals, traditions, and meanings that foster consciousness of kind. Promotional materials that depict the product in use may help establish shared aspirations and support viral marketing efforts as they make their way through the Blogs of the brand aficionados.

The benefits to a firm of cultivating GeoFree BrandComms are many and diverse. GeoFree BrandComms could carry out important functions on behalf of the brand, such as sharing information, perpetuating the history and culture of the brand, and providing customer care and assistance. GeoFree BrandComms provide a social structure and communication conduit to the relationship between marketer and consumer. Further, customers integrated into the greater GeoFree BrandComm constitute a strong market for licensed products and brand extensions.

GeoFree BrandComm integrated customers could serve as brand missionaries, carrying the marketing message into other communities, which may involve blogging extensively on the brand communications from the company. GeoFree BrandComm members are expected to be more forgiving than nonmembers are of product failures or lapses of service quality. In addition, such tolerance could manifest itself in bloggers writing on not only the negative experience, but also the follow through and turn around exhibited by the company.

GeoFree BrandComm members are expected to be less apt to switching brands, even when confronted with superior performance by competing products. After having communicated about the benefits of a particular brand, they are likely held accountable by the greater community. GeoFree BrandComms are intrinsically motivated to provide feedback to corporate ears, which, through the power weblogs and the Internet, is an exceptionally easy thing to receive for today's technology savvy marketing managers.

A brand that evokes a powerful sense of brand community would generally have greater value to a marketer than a brand supported with a weak sense of community. However, a strong GeoFree BrandComm can be a threat to a marketer, should the community reject marketing efforts or product change, and then use efficient communications channels to disseminate the rejection. Recognizing the power of this community, attempts should normally be made to appease and perpetuate the GeoFree BrandComm by maintaining links with the brand's past.

GeoFree BrandComm members who purchase a product often do so with the support of other users, which leads to the possibility of brand-focused interpersonal bonds. To the extent that the brand owner facilitates such interactions, the customer base is likely to reciprocate with increased appreciation for the company and a sense of being an important part of a larger set of social phenomena. The key here is for the brand owner to become an *integral* part (a full member) of the GeoFree BrandComm, not a guest of the community that visits periodically.

Part of the reason for the establishing a strong GeoFree BrandComm of customer-centered relationships may be their role as exit barriers. Customers value the relationships available to them as a result of the efforts of the brand owner. GeoFree BrandComm ties become exit barriers as owners realize that valued interpersonal relationships would be altered or lost if they were to defect to another brand. Positive relationships with brand owners and bonding with brand itself also contributes to a GeoFree BrandComm based exit barrier. The same elements that lend longevity to successful interpersonal and community relationships in the physical realm, such as reciprocity investment, commitment, interdependence, and integration in social networks exist in the GeoFree BrandComm.

For the more insular marketer, a more connected and empowered GeoFree BrandComm can be a real problem. For instance, brand communities, particularly those operating within computer-mediated environments, could pose enormous rumor control problems. Competitors could easily snoop on one's GeoFree BrandComm and their internal communication. Insurgents with the potential of misappropriating or subverting community values and interest could sabotage GeoFree BrandComms. In short, GeoFree BrandComms that are managed poorly could derail a marketing strategy.

Branding Implications

The GeoFree BrandComms serve an important signaling function, both positive and negative. The concept of GeoFree BrandComm indicates that brands are shared objects, which are socially constructed, and that consumers are involved in that creation. GeoFree BrandComms have important implications for brand equity. Just as brand quality perceptions can be affected by alliances with other brands, brand quality might be inferred from the character of the GeoFree BrandComm associated with the brand. Marketing researchers conceptualize brand equity as having four components: perceived quality, brand loyalty, brand awareness, and brand associations. GeoFree BrandComms affect all four of these components and are consistent with the trend toward broadening definitions of consumer brand loyalty in general. A strong GeoFree BrandComm can lead to a socially embedded loyalty and brand commitment.

Member Implications

The implications of GeoFree BrandComms presenting an efficient form of consumer feedback loop are obvious. By virtue of their accessibility through the Internet, GeoFree BrandComms provide members with a louder and clearer means of having their voice heard. GeoFree BrandComms represent an important resource for members seeking information on a brand. The information might be provided by the brand owner or a fellow participant in the shared consumption experience. GeoFree BrandComms based on Blogs are, by their very nature, archival knowledge repositories that can serve as a surrogate to storytelling in the physical context when a new consumer enters the GeoFree BrandComm circle. GeoFree BrandComm members can more easily turn to one another in an established collective for information on the brand.

GeoFree BrandComm interaction may generally provide wider social benefits to its members. For instance, the process of brand socialization between more and less experienced owners is symbiotic in nature. New owners benefit from the expertise and social approval of veterans. At the same time, veterans benefit from the status accorded them in their assumed leadership roles. Moreover, the GeoFree BrandComm as a whole benefits from exchanges of knowledge that cements relationships through exchanges of value, further enhancing customer satisfaction with the brand.

CONCLUSION

The traditional customer-brand community relationship has been forged over time, usually at the behest and strategic initiatives of the brand marketer. Even as the brand community models have evolved to a more customer-centric view in recent years the two-way communication essential in building lasting relationships has been strangely one-sided in its origin. The volume of a brand marketer's communication has continued at a proverbial near deafening roar, with nary a whimper from the brand consumer.

The tide in brand community marketing has turned as of late, largely due to the advent of the Internet. Brand aficionados now have the ability to connect outside the context of brand owner sponsored communiqué and events in a kind of dynamic ad hoc alliance that simply was not feasible before the Internet. The once feared, online brand 'chatter', consisting of posts, flames, and rants on Internet bulletin boards, is evolving into a conversation where brand owners and brand aficionados are becoming more transparent to each other. In effect, bilateral communication is now available to build a foundation for lasting customer-brand relationships. In fact, there is empirical evidence to extend the notion of brand communities further—brand cults (Acosta and Devasagayam 2010). In a recently published article in the Marketing Management Journal, these author's make a case for a brand community evolving into a cult like following of the brand. There are additional studies in journals that explore the notion of creating brand communities within an organization (Devasagayam, Aurand, Judson, and

Buff 2010) and one that looks at various modes of participation and membership in a brand community (Thurston, Buff, and Devasagayam 2009). All these studies relate to geographically bound brand communities, their extensions to GeoFree BrandComms is the next logical step in building this knowledge and presents a unique research opportunity for marketing scholars and students.

Most of the marketing world is either unaware or unappreciative of the potential of Internet based community building opportunities that would help serve their customers better. This research has attempted to draw marketers' attention to the fact that the optimization of the true brand community, via the Internet, can be greatly assisted by one such medium—weblogs—in creating and sustaining GeoFree BrandComms. Further, we explore how GeoFree BrandComms may foster a system of 'feedback' between brand consumer, and brand creator, allowing each to read the emotions of the other while expanding the affinity of the brand and growing the brand community.

ACKNOWLEDGMENT

This chapter is based on prior research published by authors Devasagayam, Raj and Dana VanDen-Heuvel (2008), "Building Brand Communities on the Internet: GeoFree BrandComm," *DIAS Technology Review: The International Journal for Business and IT, Vol. 4, Number 2, pp. 10-16.*

REFERENCES

Acosta, P., & Devasagayam, R. (2010). Brand cult: Extending the notion of brand community. *Marketing Management Journal, 20*(1), 165–176.

Devasagayam, R., Aurand, T., Judson, K., & Buff, C. (2010). Building brand community membership within organizations: A viable internal branding alternative? *Journal of Product and Brand Management, 19*(3), 210–217. doi:10.1108/10610421011046184

Devasagayam, R., & Van Den Heuvel, D. (2008). Building brand communities on the Internet: GeoFree BrandComm. *DIAS Technology Review: The International Journal for Business and IT, 4*(2), 10–16.

Fischer, E., Bristor, J., & Gainer, B. (1996). Creating or escaping community? An exploratory study of internet consumers' behaviors. In Corfman, K. P., & Lynch, J. (Eds.), *Advances in consumer research* (*Vol. 23*, pp. 178–182). Provo, UT: ACR.

Forrester Research. (2003). Forrester's consumer technographics Q2 2003 North American study and Forrester's consumer technographics 2003 retail and media online study.

Granitz, N. A., & Ward, J. C. (1996). Virtual community: A sociocognitive analysis. In Corfman, K. P., & Lynch, J. (Eds.), *Advances in consumer research* (*Vol. 23*, pp. 161–166). Provo, UT: ACR.

McAlexander, J. H., Schouten, J. W., & Koening, H. W. (2002). Building brand community. *Journal of Marketing, 66*(1). Chicago.

McIntosh, N. (2003, February 18). Google buys blogger web service. *The Guardian*. Retrieved from http://www.guardian.co.uk/business/story/0,3604,897610,00.html

Muniz, A.M., Jr., & O'Guinn, T. C. (2001). Brand community. *Journal of Consumer Research, 27*(4). Gainesville.

PaidContent.org. (2003, September 25). *Bourland.* Retrieved from http://www.paidcontent.org/ stories/bourland.html

Rheingold, H. (2002). *Smart mobs: The next social revolution*. Cambridge, MA: Perseus Books Group.

Sullivan, A. (2002, October 13). An honest blogger will never make a quick buck. *Sunday London Times*.

The Economist. (2003, March 13). The revenge of geography. *The Economist Magazine*.

Thurston, P., Buff, C. L., & Devasagayam, P. R. (2009). Participation preferences and brand community integration: An empirical investigation. *Review of Business Research, 9*(2), 34–44.

Webopedia. (2003, October 1). *What is a blog?* Retrieved from http://www.webopedia.com/TERM/B/blog.html

Zimmerman, D. (2003, July 7). Mix DM, branding online? Just do it. *DM News,* (p. 20).

Chapter 12
Enhanced Social Presence Through eBranding the Consumer in Virtual Communities

Robert Pennington
Fo Guang University, Taiwan

ABSTRACT

Brands have evolved from representations of property rights through representations of product attributes to representations of consumer attributes. As components of cultural discourse, brands have become an important mode of consumer communication, identifying and distinguishing consumers as social objects within consumer market culture.

Virtual communities have evolved from telephonic verbal communication to highly interactive electronic media, which provide the rich audio-visual sensory detail that gives consumers a sense of being in an environment.

As a fundamentally cultural phenomenon, marketing communication reflects shared patterns of consumer thoughts, feelings, emotions, and behaviors. Virtual communities are particularly suited for communication in consumer culture because they afford consumers authentic cultural presence. Culture depends on communication. Communication depends symbols. Symbols constitute electronic environments.

eBranding affords consumers the necessary tools to represent themselves by communicating their roles and relationships in virtual consumer culture environments for transfer to actual consumer culture environments. Consumption in actual environments results in brand viability and marketing success.

DOI: 10.4018/978-1-61350-171-9.ch012

INTRODUCTION

This chapter discusses brands as critical design elements in virtual communities. All human behavior communicates, including brand consumption, which is so important to consumer culture that any electronic environment without brands will seem unrelated to any actual environment. The increasing use of electronic technology in marketing communication requires that marketers understand the culture of consumption and the function of brands as consumer communication. This understanding will enable marketers to create effective electronic environment designs for product and brand trial, and to integrate electronic environments with other marketing communication.

This chapter is about the evolution of brands and virtual communities, projecting that evolution into future trends. The chapter begins by discussing the evolution of brands from representations of property rights to representations of consumer properties. The next section discusses the evolution of virtual communities. The following sections discuss culture generally, the system of meanings in consumer culture, culture in virtual communities, communicating culture through products and brands, and branding consumption. The final section discusses future trends, a continuing evolution in which marketers design virtual communities that include brands to give consumers a sense of being in those communities.

Evolution of Brands

Brands are signs, components of system of symbolic representations that largely constitutes culture. The origin of brands is cloudy. Centuries ago in traditional Indian marketplaces, some merchants already used tokens to distinguish their products from competitors' commodities. Brands have also been statements of property (i.e. the right to possess, use, enjoy and dispose of an object). Brands were necessary to distinguish objects that were difficult to distinguish by their own inherent properties, attributes or characteristics. Brands further developed into statements of the outcome of product use when the attributes that cause the outcome were difficult to distinguish. That is, brands evolved to represent the expected outcome of human interaction with products.

Originally, brands most often occurred in the context of the products to which they were attached. By association, products primarily represented objects and secondarily the outcome on the environment of interacting with the product. Contemporary brands, however, most often occur within the context of marketing communication. That is, brands most often occur within the context of the system of symbolic representations. Therefore, consumers interpret brands based upon the context of communication more than upon product use or relationship with the producer.

Even the products have become components of the system of representations. During the rapid industrial expansion after World War II, relatively high wages permitted workers to acquire greater amounts of the products that the sizzling economy was producing. Advertising and promotion encouraged increasing acquisition by setting goals and standards for the developing consumer culture. Product possession represented the achievement of those goals and standards. Marketing communication had set the rules for achievement. High wages provided an accessible route through those rules. Industrial consumer culture transformed products into consumer representations. Brands provided incremental distinctions within the representational system.

Brands are not always depicted attached to products in marketing communication. Even when marketing communication does depict a product with which a brand is associated, the depiction is not the product itself (Mick, 1986). The depiction itself is a cultural representation with its own cultural meaning derived from cultural context. Within marketing communication, brands acquire meaning by association with other culturally meaningful symbolic elements. Indeed, marketing communication is critical to managing brand meaning. To the extent that brand meaning is connected to the product at all, brand meaning derives from the cultural meaning of the product or its symbolic representation.

McCracken (1990) has explained how marketing communication transfers cultural meaning to products, which then transfer meaning to consumers who use them. In fact, the product is a peripheral element in meaning transfer, important chiefly because consumers generally cannot acquire the brand without acquiring the product. Acquiring the product is one of the cultural rules for brand acquisition. The success of counterfeits demonstrates the greater importance of brands in relation to products.

Because brands derive significance from a context detached from any product, consumers can consume a brand without consuming the product that increasingly serves merely as a vehicle for the brand. Contemporary marketing communication identifies the target segment using symbolic elements that represent the target's attributes. By association in the context of marketing communication, brands represent the attributes of their target consumers. In consuming brands, the outcome that consumers expect is that by interacting with brands, the represented attributes will accrue to them.

Brands generally do not represent products; they represent consumers. This chapter discusses brands as consumer assignations in the context of online interaction. This perspective does not apply to all brands in all situations. In some cases, brands represent the products or objects to which they are attached. Indeed, this use of brands is important to e-commerce. In other cases, brands represent relationships that exist between consumers and products, consumers and producers, and consumers and resellers. This chapter, however, examines brands as representing consumers' cultural, social, psychological and philosophical relationships. In other words, the focus in on brands as they represent consumers, their relationships with other consumers, with themselves and with the rest of the world.

All brands represent a relationship between consumers and an environment. However, brands differ on which environment, which aspect of that environment and which consumers they relate. In online environments, consumers cannot physically inspect and evaluate the products or services offered. Branded products and services afford consumers assurance of certain specific attributes and standards of quality. This is a return to the early period of branding in the actual marketplace in which consumers looked for brands for assurance (Editors 1988). With the possibility of counterfeit products and services, however, a branded web site affords further assurance. The policies of Amazon.com and eBay have made them into recognized brands that represent a secure relationship, as did tokens in traditional Indian marketplaces centuries ago.

Such brands assure that physical interaction with a product or service will result in a desired modification of the physical environment. However, these brands do not represent the modification of the physical environment. Rather, they represent assurance. To succeed in a competitive environment, any competitor must meet consumers' non-compensatory decision-making criteria. Assurance becomes a standard that all brands must meet. When all brands represent the same level of assurance, a parity situation exists in which consumers assume assurance.

Ironically then, when all competing brands represent assurance, none of them especially represents assurance within the framework of consumers' decision-making criteria because the market itself represents assurance. Each brand carries equal assignation of assurance in relation to competing brands. Effectively, each brand is synonymous with every other competing brand. Further, competing brands will likely match any successful product or performance change any other brand introduces. Therefore, brands lose their capacity to represent distinctions in product features or performance (i.e. they become discursively worthless).

Consumers, however, will still use brands discursively to represent identities and distinctions. The new distinctions will be consumer-created. Although consumers may report product or performance distinctions where none exist, the actual distinctions they create are among consumers themselves. Consumers distinguish, compare and identify themselves, projecting those distinctions, comparisons and identities onto the brands they choose in a reverse meaning transfer. Consumers brand themselves and each other in creating virtual communities (McWilliam 2000). The challenge for brand managers in the parity environment, then, is to represent distinctions among consumers. Those distinctions are based not only on cultural categories (Pennington 2006), but also upon culturally accepted and prescribed methods for dealing with experience and for modifying environments.

The following sections discuss relationships among consumers and how brands represent those relationships in virtual communities. The discussion treats online behavior as occurring in a cultural environment, with recognizable and detectable patterns of behavior. It builds upon previous work on marketing in virtual reality, presence in virtual environments and methodology for distinguishing idiosyncratic behavior from shared patterns. Further, it builds upon previous work on brands as a non-verbal language in consumer culture and the semiotics of brands in consumer discourse. This chapter explains how brands provide the forms, patterns and symbols with which consumers deal with the electronic environment. The result is an e-culture in which brands represent consumers and their interrelationships.

Virtual Communities

Although Lynd's (1939) definition of culture referred to inhabitants of a geographical area, communication theorists of the early twentieth century had already argued that electronic communication could create communities independent of geographic contiguity (Susman, 1984). Electronic media began the progression toward virtual communities by breaking the geographic boundaries altogether. Although people could still share characteristics with others in their geographic communities, electronic media illuminated, fostered and developed shared characteristics with others in distant communities. Culture was no longer bound by geography. The new pseudo-environment was one of cultural and social location. Behavior in response to the pseudo-environment of social and cultural location, however, continued to occur in the actual world of the geographic environment.

A characteristic of industrialism is the use of technology not only to adapt to and modify environments, but also to create environments that could not have occurred naturally. The beginning stage of industrial technology created new tangible, physical environments. Media technology marked the creation of primitive intangible pseudo-environments. Further development of technology created more sophisticated pseudo-environments, virtual environments. In virtual communities, people can group themselves by choice more easily than they can in geographic environments; they can choose their virtual neighbors.

Presence, the sense of being in an environment unmediated by technology (Gibson, 1977), depends up the range and detail of sensory inputs the environment provides and on the ability to effect change in the environment in real time. Vividness and interactivity, respectively the range and detail of sensory inputs and the ability to effect changes, provide a greater sense of presence in the cultural and social environments. Further, they allow human behavior in the actual world to have consequences in the pseudo-environment. The result is that consumers in the actual world respond to a pseudo-environment with behavior in the actual world that has consequences in the pseudo-environment.

Virtual communities comprise the inhabitants of e-locations created through technology. Consumers' sense of presence in e-communities depends, in part, on the vividness of the online experience. The concept of vividness refers to the range and detail of sensory inputs that technology provides. But vividness also refers to the sense of social location, which depends upon the range and detail of social inputs. Cultural discourse through the system of symbolic representations provides those social inputs. All societies define, identify and distinguish social concepts through the representational system. However, actual communities can attach representations to actual social objects (i.e. people). Any representational system is useless unless its representations function in the absence of what they represent. In virtual communities, that quality is imperative because actual social objects cannot occur in virtual communities. Only their representations can occur.

In virtual communities, just as in actual communities, consumers organize and deal with their experience by creating and choosing sets of forms, patterns and symbols. They create a culture that makes experience meaningful. As social concepts within the online culture, consumers choose forms, patterns and symbols to place themselves in relation to other concepts of the online culture. These forms, patterns and symbols constitute the social dimension of online cultural representations. (Representations of a background environmental context are another dimension.) These representations may coincide with cultural representations from an actual social environment. But such a coincidence is not imperative because in any environment, actual or virtual, the choice of representations is arbitrary. Their meanings derive from consistency of use (Pinker, 1994). Any new representation in a virtual community, just as in an actual community, must establish a history of use consistency to acquire meaning.

The vividness of the virtual community depends not only on the technology but on the cultural significance of the content as well. Technology must provide range and detail of a meaningful cultural environment to evoke a sense of cultural presence. The virtual community must include a range of representations sufficient to accommodate the discursive needs of members. In actual communities, material goods constitute a code through which members define themselves (Baudrillard, 1988). Members utilize goods as symbolic representations. The online environment is composed only of signs, not actual goods. For the online environment to be culturally meaningful in the actual environment, the signs must conform to the material cultural code of the target. Because they are culturally meaningful, the range of representations of material goods in the online environment must be as expansive as the range of actual material goods in the actual environment.

Studies of virtual communities (VCs) treat VCs as purely abstract (i.e. intangible, unavailable for physical sensation). Although VCs form through the mediation of tangible electronic devices, Bagozzi & Dhloakia (2006) assert that VCs themselves are available for sensation only as verbal text. The significance of meaning of verbal text may be shared through social or cultural convention. But except in the reader's imagination, verbal text lacks both the range and depth of sensory inputs and the interactivity necessary for a sense of presence. Indeed, as discussed in the literature, VCs call attention to the mediating role of technology that users must fail to acknowledge for a sense of presence to occur. Except for the visual evidence of verbal text, then, VCs are not only impersonal but also intangible in the human sense that the technology that connects members also separates them. From this perspective, the only tangible attribute of VCs is the technology that mediates them. Or as Marx (1967) observed, relationships increasingly occur between objects rather than between people.

Memmi (2006) discusses virtual communities as a progression of the movement away from *Gemeinschaft*, the traditional community based on location, and toward *Gesellschaft*, modern communities based on association (Tönnies, 1963). However, the association-based character of virtual communities reflects technological limits that are disappearing rapidly. Increasingly, technology affords development of communities based on virtual locations, which implies a potential for a movement toward *e-Gemeinschaft*. Pentina, Prybutok & Zhang (2008) have noted the similarities between real-life and virtual communities. Even before the emergence of contemporary high-speed, high-resolution multi-media capable technology, Rheingold (1993) observed that people in virtual communities relate to each other very much as they do in actual communities. Hagel & Armstrong (1997) noted the congruence in the characteristics of actual and virtual relationships. Ngyuyen, Torlina, Peszynski and Corbitt (2006) observed that social relationships in virtual communities reflect off-line relationships.

VCs draw members for a variety of reasons. Citing uses and gratification theory and social psychology literature, Pentina et al (2008) list several motivations, including social integration, achieving goals, economic exchange and status enhancement. They point out that members with stronger social motivation to join also identify themselves with the VC more strongly. Further, people join VCs to fulfill communication needs (c.f. Gupta & Kim, 2007; Memmi, 2006). Recognizing the necessity of communication, Bagozzi and Dholakia (2006) define VCs as mediated social spaces in the digital environment that allow social collectives to form and be sustained primarily through continuing communication processes.

All human behavior communicates (Watzlawick, Bavelas & Jackson, 1967). Further, all products of human behavior communicate. Verbal text is only one category of artifact. Any evidence of human interaction with the environment is an artifact that communicates. Technology is a component of the environment. Evidence of interaction with technology communicates. In VCs, the purpose of interaction with technology is to create artifacts that not only communicate but also create a new environment. Users feel present in virtual environments when they cease to be aware of the mediating role of technology. A sense of presence in a VC depends upon the interactivity and vividness of the VC. Vividness demands a richness of detail in communication. The greater the range of communication forms, the greater the likelihood of a sense of presence in the VC. According to Chen, Wu & Chung (2008), social presence enhances intimacy and shortens psychological distance, easing uncertainty from the lack of physical contact. Therefore, the capacity for detailed communication is essential for forming and sustaining satisfying VCs.

Yet Memmi (2006) suggests that vividness be a criterion for excluding telephony from consideration as a VC. He also suggests that telephony be excluded from consideration as a VC because the technology is long established. If the purpose in studying VCs is to study recent technology only, then telephony can be excluded. However, newer technology and techniques integrate actual voice communication, such as voice-over-Internet protocol (VOIP), with other forms of audio-visual communication. Projecting new design considerations for VC development must include telephony. Most important, voice communication, whether actual or synthetic, contributes to a sense of presence by making more inputs available for sensation.

According to Preece (2000), a VC is a community of people with common interest of shared purpose, whose interactions are governed by policies in the form of tacit assumptions, rituals, protocols, rules and laws, and who use computer systems to support and mediate social interaction and to facilitate a sense of togetherness. In essence, Preece has defined a culture sustained through the use of computer systems. This is an e-consumer e-culture in which both products and brands communicate cultural information. That is, products and brands are the social hieroglyphics that Marx (1967) described.

VC studies have derived categories based on analysis of participants needs: shared interest, relationship building, transaction and fantasy (Hagel & Armstrong, 1997; Talukder & Yeow, 2007). But these categories are not mutually exclusive. This chapter concerns marketing communication within VCs. Therefore, the principle category of concern would seem to be transaction. However, relationship is, in fact, the dominant concern. In the absence of face-to-face interaction, Pentina et al (2008) found that the affective component of social identification is the strongest determinant of action based on information from the group. Social identification is what Song & Kim (2005) define as knowledge of belonging to certain group that has some emotional value. For marketing communication, meeting relationship-building needs is an effective route to meeting transaction needs.

Yet studies often exclude relationships from their research designs. For example, Daugherty, Li & Biocca (2001) and Li, Daugherty & Biocca (2002) conducted product-trial studies in which they applied consumer experience in virtual reality to product use in actual reality. But as Ritson & Elliot (1999) pointed out, marketing-study methodology often excludes by design the context within which a product is used that gives the product meaning. In the studies cited above, the product was a camcorder, which is most often used within a social context. Therefore, a study of product use in virtual reality that excludes any social context ignores product meaning. In other words, a valid virtual product trial must occur within the context of a VC.

A complete sense of virtual community depends upon the completeness of features and attributes available for sensation. A sense of presence depends upon vividness, which comprises not only the range of senses the environment stimulates, but also the amount of detail available for sensation (Pennington 2006). An environment that conspicuously lacks expected detail fails to elicit an empirical sensation of reality (Pennington 2001). An environment that fails to offer visual and auditory sensation of social objects is unlikely to elicit social presence for a sustainable sense of community.

Cultural Environment

Culture is not an isolated independent variable with occasional limited effects, as most marketing research treats it. Culture is a paradigm, a worldview, a unifying theory of interrelated concepts comprising all social experience. Early social science literature considered culture to be "all the things that a group of people inhabiting a geographical area do, the ways they do things and the ways they think and feel about things, their material tools and their values and symbols" (Lynd 1939). The relation between geography and culture stems from traditional communication forms that required physical proximity. With contemporary communication technology, culture is geographically boundless.

We can only observe culture through its manifestations (i.e. the system of symbolic representations). Through that system, we can identify culture operationally by observing patterns that not only account for but also shape individual behavior within groups. Culture is the shared, learned patterns of thoughts, feelings, appetites and behaviors, based upon a climate of values, for organizing or adapting to the natural and social environments (Pennington 2001a). We recognize culture through the artifacts of those patterns that coincide with those of a group. Thoughts, feelings and appetites may be cultural, but until an individual manifests them through overt actions, they cannot constitute the communicative discourse that identifies the individual with and within a culture. Overt actions distinguish her from other individuals and cultures. Culture provides the forms for overt actions in the system of symbolic representations.

Through the system, culture creates an imaginary environment. People live within natural, actual environments. But they learn to interpret and interact with those environments mostly through culture. Culture defines not only what is in the environment, but also what can be in the environment. In other words, culture defines the concepts. Further, culture defines the interrelationships among concepts. Everything within shared human experience has cultural definition. Therefore, everything within shared human experience is representative of a cultural definition. Members of a culture interpret their environments according to cultural definitions. They interact not with the components of an actual environment, but with representations of cultural definitions.

Interactions with actual environments are culturally prescribed and occur through the system of representations. But they do occur in an actual environment, although filtered by cultural definition and interpretation. Culture members are incapable of acknowledging the mediating role of culture. They have a cultural sense of being in the environment. But they also actually are in the environment. This strong role of cultural representations facilitates the sense of presence in virtual environments. Reproducing the representational system online elicits interpretations congruent with off-line representations, giving culture members a sense of being in the environment (i.e. presence). However, the other side of the coin is absence; culture members fail to acknowledge that technology has removed them psychologically and emotionally from the actual environment. This failure to acknowledge absence facilitates the transfer of brand consumption patterns between virtual and actual environments.

Perhaps without realizing that they were doing so, marketers have studied culture for many years. The study of consumer behavior is a study of culture, as is the study of values and lifestyles, psychographics and other common research areas. These areas are not outside of culture, but rather integral components of culture. Although we can inquire legitimately into the effects of culture on behavior, we can inquire just as legitimately into the effects of behavior on culture. The patterns we observe in the artifacts of human behavior or that we elicit through research are evidence of cultures and subcultures. The greater the commonality of occurrence, the more confident we are that we have found evidence of a culture. The distinguishing commonalities within larger patterns are evidence of subcultures.

In marketing, when we observe commonalties in behavior, we call the groupings segments rather than cultures. But even common demographic groupings reflect cultural concepts and definitions. We study categories of age, sex, income, education, taste etc. because they are culturally significant. Each category attribute stands in a distinct cultural relation to other attributes of the same category. Each attribute has some distinguishing pattern of thought, emotion or behavior made tangible through an associated representation, a culturally designated and recognizable object, symbol or object as symbol. These objects and symbols allow community members to identify, compare and distinguish their roles in relation to others. In consumer culture, the objects and symbols are products and brands.

Consumer Meaning

In consumer culture, "consumer" is a paradigmatic class of all those whose marketplace activities that go beyond the satisfaction of material needs and wants. Consumption is a discursive process of identity and distinction that entails interrelationships. The use of physical objects may be necessary for interacting with the physical environment to achieve physical outcomes. But in consumer culture, the objects and outcomes carry value that is secondary to what the objects and outcomes represent culturally, which is relationships with the environment. Consumers communicate relationships through marketplace activity and marketplace signs, which are the consumer culture system of symbolic representations. Because all human activity communicates (Watzlavick, Bavels &Jackson, 1967), those who are not consumers (i.e. those who merely utilize objects) also communicate through marketplace activity. But for consumers, communication plays a major role in that activity. As a paradigmatic class, consumers are distinct from those who are not consumers. As a paradigm example, each consumer is identical to each other. But within the class, further classifications permit consumers to compare and distinguish themselves.

All consumers are not alike, as any beginning marketing student knows intuitively. Some distinctions have tangible foundations. To say that a consumer is female is one such distinction that implies not all consumers are female. Physical attributes determine whether a consumer is female, but those attributes may often elude observation. Consumption allows identity with or distinction from that attribute, which is discrete and has a binary opposite: male. Consumer culture provides representations for either attribute that replace the natural physical attributes and facilitate communication through consistency of use.

Some distinctions have less tangible foundations. To say that a consumer is feminine is such a distinction within the paradigmatic class, which implies that not all consumers are feminine. This distinction also has a binary opposite: masculine. But feminine is not a discrete attribute; one consumer can be more or less feminine than another. And a consumer can be male and feminine or female and masculine. Although tangible and observable, the distinctions between feminine and masculine, and the degrees of those qualities, are not physical characteristics. Behavior patterns prescribed by a cultural code define femininity and masculinity. Further, although feminine and masculine are binary opposites, they are only the poles for a range of positions of a continuous variable. Consumer culture provides a range of representations adequate to consumers' needs for positions along the scale. As consumer need for distinction increases, consumer culture, through marketing, provides a finer scale of incremental distinctions by increasing the number distinguishing representations, mostly brands.

Within consumer culture, categories of consumers actualize their attributes through a specified code. Consumption objects are components of that code (Douglas & Isherwood, 1996). Without the objects that the code specifies, a consumer is a cultural commodity with no identity. In fact, without the specified objects, the consumer is not even a consumer, but merely an indistinguishable human being. To consumers using the code, people outside the code are no more distinguishable than kernels of corn. All non-consumers look alike, quaint and perhaps interesting, but irrelevant.

Within the code however, consumers face a continuing process of identifying, comparing and distinguishing themselves. As the market becomes saturated with a paradigm class of consumption objects, the object class itself loses the capacity to distinguish among consumers. In the use of such objects, consumers once again become cultural commodities. When all consumers have automobiles, for example, they cease to be consumers because consumption specifies a relationship, which supposes the possibility of distinction. When an object class loses the capacity to distinguish, the code then requires an additional object class to communicate distinction. However, because object acquisition and storage has a practical limit, the code of consumer culture has created a symbolic distinction within paradigm classes (i.e. brands).

Communicating E-Culture

The core of culture is communication (Hall, 1969). Culture provides consumers with a system of symbolic representations, an inventory of meaningful objects and signs with which to communicate and recognize concepts and relationships. Because culture is learned and shared, dissemination depends upon access to communication. To disseminate culture, formal institutions and organizations tend to utilize formal mechanisms such as schools, churches and other formal meetings. Products and signs acquire and retain meaning through explicit definitions and expressions.

Although consumption is not a formal institution, it is a significant form of cultural communication. Within consumer culture, consumption is an act of encoding, decoding and deciphering that requires mastery of the consumption code (Bourdieu, 1984). This cultural code specifies the use and display of artifacts as cultural representations (Douglas & Isherwoood, 1996). Through shared experience, consumers learn to use products for artifactual communication (Mick, 1986). Consumption is the process of consumers communicating their cultural identities (Levy, 1986). The communication takes place not only between consumers and producers but also between consumers and others, even reflexively between consumer and self (Nöth, 1988; Williamson, 1978).

Because consumer culture is informal, its communication mechanisms are also informal. Artifacts acquire meaning (i.e. representational value) through implicit definition and expression. Consumers acquire competence in cultural meanings through repetition of informal contact similar to language acquisition outside of formal education. All culture is text in the sense that all shared human behaviors represent something. They at least represent sharing itself. As in verbal language, collocation and context give meaning to representations. As cultural representations, consumers themselves acquire meaning through collocation and context.

Before the advent of mass communication, the dissemination of culture tended to be limited to those within a geographic area in which people had regular interpersonal contact. Oral tradition tended to insure cultural stability. Early recorded communication tended to be time-based; the same message was available to many generations of receivers with little change in content. Spatial and temporal limits on communication determined cultural boundaries. Mass communication laid the foundation for virtual communities by expanding the boundaries of communities and decreasing the importance of oral communication in disseminating culture. Culture defined media and their relationships to other cultural concepts. Media disseminated the culture that gave rise to them and within which they operated (Pennington, 2000b).

In the early 1920s, Lippman (1965) noted the insertion of a pseudo-environment between man and his actual environment. Media technology created the pseudo-environment by presenting another mode in the system of symbolic representations, a mode that expanded the inventory of representations. Because humans responded to the pseudo-environment as a representation of the actual environment, the consequences occurred in the actual environment. Media then disseminated representations of those actual-world consequences within the context of the pseudo-environment to which humans responded further with actual-world consequences. This was the beginning of not only the sense of being in an actual environment through technological representations, but also the lack of a sense of absence from the actual environment. The situation was ideal for the emergence of consumer culture and marketing. Mass media disseminated pseudo-environment culture in which consumption of specific products, and increasingly brands, were the appropriate behaviors for dealing with pseudo-environment experiences.

Branding Consumption

Most human behavior involves interaction with either a physical or social object. Every interaction modifies the physical or social environment in some way. Gibson (1977) used the term "affordance" to mean the result of interaction with an object, that is, the modification of the environment. Every affordance is a potential brand. A company web site is a cultural tool that affords consumers the ability to acquire other cultural tools. The result of interacting with the web site includes information, in the sense of uncertainty reduction, and acquisition. The company name brands the specific triadic relationship that binds the consumer, the object (the web site) and the interaction result.

As morphemes in consumer-culture system of representations, brands convey meaning. And as in other forms of communication, brands as morphemes can convey more than one meaning, depending on collocation and context. In the acquisition process, brands often mean the relationship between the consumer and the branded product. They can also signify the relationship between the consumer and the producer. The fundamental qualities of such relationships are trust and assurance that interaction between the consumer and the branded object will afford the desired modification of the actual physical environment.

However, a general assertion that all brands signify a relationship between a consumer and a company may overstate the importance of that relationship. In the consumption process, a brand signifies another relationship. Once a consumer has acquired the brand, it belongs to the consumer, not to the marketer (Schultz & Barnes, 1995). The consumer owns the right to possess, use and enjoy the brand. It is the consumer's property. From that point at least, the brand stands for a triadic relationship that does not include the marketer. Often, the triadic relationship includes a resulting modification of a social environment.

Holt (2004) asserts that consumers participate in cultural myths through brand consumption. In fact, however, brands represent metaphors for qualities that consumer culture values. The culture treats the attributes attached to consumers as if they were independent of consumers. Through brand consumption, consumers attach qualities to themselves, signifying their roles in relation to other roles. Consumers do not so much form an emotional bond with the brand as with the role that the brand represents. The consumer no more forms an emotional bond with the brand than a plumber forms an emotional bond with the word "plumber," no matter how much he or she may enjoy that occupation.

Semiotics distinguishes among three types of signs. An icon shares a physical resemblance with what it represents. An index has a strong association with what it represents through co-occurrence. A symbol is purely arbitrary in what it represents. What brands represent is intangible, abstract. Therefore, physical resemblance between the brand and what it represents is not possible. A sign that becomes the concrete form of an abstract concept becomes the symbol of that concept. For example, good aesthetic taste has no tangible form. But Starkist, through the persona of Charlie the Tuna, utilized indexes and symbols of good taste to make a point about tunas that taste good as opposed to tuna with good taste. In the process, they imbued the brand with both meanings of good taste. In this case, the brand represented both the product and the consumer. The brand became a symbol of a product that tasted good to consumers with good taste.

The word "plumber" has an intensive meaning, which represents the qualities or characteristics that an object, in this case a social object, must have for the word to apply accurately. The word applies to a social and cultural role. The word also has an extensive meaning, which is all of the objects to which the word accurately applies within a culture (i.e. all those who play the specific role). Similarly, a brand has an intensive meaning, which is the qualities or characteristics of the cultural role it represents. A brand also has an extensive definition, which is the set of all consumers who play the cultural role that the brand represents and, therefore, who meet the requirements for brand acquisition.

Even in modern economic systems with great division of labor, culture expects multiple roles. A plumber may also be a parent, baseball player, golfer, photographer, conservationist, and more. Each word represents a different cultural category with various attributes, qualities, characteristics or specific roles. A single individual may fit into all of those categories, each with its own attribute of role, such as centerfielder or duffer. Consumer culture expects individual consumers to communicate their fit into multiple categories, each with specific respective attributes, through multiple brand consumption.

Marketing communication serves as a lexicon of brand meaning (McCracken, 1986). However, for the consumer code to have any meaning outside of the purely lexical, it must have some relation to actual experience (Pennington 2002). This is fundamentally important to marketers because to continue providing consumers with cultural meanings, marketers require revenue generated by consumer spending. Although consumption as culture is merely symbolic, the viability of the culture requires the actual-world consequence of purchase.

Marketing communication composes a pseudo-environment. Attitude change based upon marketing communication is a response to the pseudo-environment. The results of that attitude change can have consequences in the actual environment. Brands consumed in the actual environment effect attitude change by communicating about the actual consumer rather than about an endorser selected by a marketer. The relationship between brand and actual consumer can establish, ratify, reinforce or modify attitude toward the brand that is a response to the pseudo-environment.

Meaning established in the pseudo-environment enables consumers to recognize relationships in the actual environment. Consumers refer to marketing communication for trust and assurance that a brand signifies actual, specific social and cultural qualities. Integrity is an antecedent of trust, which is a precursor to transactions (Mayer, Davis & Schoorman, 1995; McKnight, Choudhury & Kacmar, 2002). Brands that establish integrity of meaning are likely to realize transactions in the actual world. Therefore, integrated communication is essential to the management of brand meaning.

Through technology, consumers can enter the pseudo-environment to form virtual communities (VCs). They bring their cultures with them, contributing to the system of representations in the online environment. Their contributions increase the social presence within the VCs by increasing the social vividness of the environment (i.e. they increase the range of social inputs available for perception). Further, consumer inputs increase the interaction possibilities for other VC members not only in number but also in type (i.e. emotional and psychological). Expanding participation in VCs requires an expanding range of representations for cultural discourse. The text of words alone is inadequate. As in actual environments, consumers in VCs utilize objects and brands as representations. Brands are especially well suited for consumer representation because the only value that have in any environment is purely representational. Further, brands constitute a substantial part of the off-line representational system in consumer culture. Brand use within VCs, therefore, contributes to the sense of social presence and detracts from the sense of absence.

Products can convey virtually any cultural meaning (McCracken, 1986). But brands have even greater capacity to convey meaning because, as symbols, that is their only capacity. Consistency of use establishes meaning (Pinker, 1994). Holt (2004) asserts that myth brands must violate that principle periodically. But he has actually misinterpreted the market change. Brands signify cultural roles rather than entire myths. Consistency of signification requires periodic adjustments in the cultural symbols associated with that role. Just as the Morton Salt girl, Betty Crocker and Aunt Jemima have undergone periodic symbolic modifications to retain their value as specific cultural representations, consumers undergo periodic symbolic modifications to their cultural representations. To maintain consistency of use within a cultural role, a brand must match the symbolic changes culture associates with that role.

FUTURE TRENDS

Lippman (1965) referred to all mediated environments as pseudo-environments. This included all marketing communication. But he did not foresee how technology would advance in the ninety years after he wrote. Technology affords consumers the opportunity to expand their environments into virtual environments and virtual communities. Further, Lippman's was an outsider's perspective. From the outsider's view, no actual environment exists in media. Although that is technically correct, when technology provides sufficient vividness and interactivity, consumers on some level do not acknowledge the mediation of technology. They experience presence, the sense of being in the environment. From the insider's view then, that environment does exist. At the same time, with no sense of absence, the actual environment does not exist. Philosophically however, we can argue that people only observe appearances, not actual objects (Kant, 1977). Culture merely defines what those appearances represent.

Lippman (1965) also observed people's tendency to interpret others according to stereotypes. But people interpret all experiences according to cultural stereotypes. And just as people tend to interpret others based upon a small number of observable attributes, they tend to interpret all experiences based upon a similarly small number of attributes. In the online environment, this means that many sensory inputs may be absent, yet consumers will still interpret the experience as actual. The stereotypical attributes of sight, sound and interactivity in VCs evoke interpretations assigned by culture in actual environments.

Culture provides the shared framework or schema for interpreting experience. Any experience comprises current sensory inputs perceived and interpreted according to previous experiences and interpretations, which are not components of the actual environment. Consumers respond to their interpretations of an actual environment, not to the actual environment itself. In a virtual community environment, consumers similarly respond to their interpretations of the environment, not to the signs or other stimuli that compose the environment. Therefore, whether the environment is actual or pseudo is irrelevant because to the consumer, the interpretation is always actual; it can never be pseudo.

As discussed previously, technology affords consumers a sense of presence, the failure on some level to acknowledge technological mediation. With a sense of presence, the consumer is in the environment. The range and depth of sensory inputs combined with real time responses to physical inputs elicit interpretations similar to those associated with previous actual experiences having similar inputs. Eventually, the signs that stand for actual experiences not only displace but also become actual experiences.

Consumers can have a sense of being in virtual community through their ability to interact with the online physical environment. However, presence is incomplete without interaction with the social and cultural environment. As in the actual world, consumers must communicate about themselves in the online world. They must be able to interpret others through the observable meaningful attributes that culture defines. They must have the capacity to communicate their cultural identities.

Just as actual environments do, virtual communities afford consumers the capacity to use consumption objects to communicate. Consumer interaction with virtual consumption objects can have virtual consequences. For the purpose of actual-world marketing, those consequences must be parallel to the consequences of interaction with actual objects in the actual world. Driving an online automobile, for example must have similar consequences online as driving an actual automobile.

However, the social and cultural consequences must be similar as well, if not identical.

Identical social and cultural consequences are possible, although identical physical consequences are not, because the virtual community is only a physical approximation created by technology. A consumer may have a strong sense of presence in driving an automobile online, but physically, that consumer remains in the same location. However, social and cultural consequences result from communication, which depends on signs. Technology utilizes culturally meaningful signs to compose the online environment. The response to the online environment is by nature a cultural response.

The virtual community can be a practice environment through which consumers can observe symbolic behaviors for social and cultural consequences. Further, consumers can test their own symbolic behaviors in order to observe social and cultural consequences. Current technology affords consumers the opportunity to engage in symbolic behaviors that approximate actual behaviors. Technology affords consumers the capacity to select culturally meaningful physical attributes of a desired online appearance. More important, however, technology affords consumers the opportunity to associate themselves with culturally meaningful signs and observe responses in a risk-free environment.

Virtual communities offer marketers a richer opportunity to collect data on consumer choices and respond rapidly in modifying the environment. As I have discussed previously (Pennington, 2001a), marketers can collect data on consumer choices and probabilities of occurrence based upon previous consumer choices and consumer attributes. An important consequence is that online environments afford marketers the possibility of more timely upgrades to the symbolism surrounding the cultural roles that brands signify.

As opposed to traditional media, interactive electronic media afford marketers greater control over brand meaning with greater input from consumers. Brands acquire meaning from the contexts within which they occur (Pennington, 2004a). With traditional media, marketers can control the cultural signs in message presented, but they have limited control over the context within which the message occurs. Marketers can select media, vehicles and even time, but they cannot select the surrounding content. Rather, they select based upon previous or proposed content. But content rarely matches perfectly the message of marketing communication. Interactive electronic media afford marketers complete control over content with the opportunity to create a sense of presence.

A list of universal cultural concepts available for branding has already been compiled. Osgood, May & Miron (1975) have listed concepts common to dozens of cultures. They have also provided a list of modifiers to distinguish further the relationships among concepts across cultures. Within any culture, all concepts have distinguishing properties or attributes that allow identification and distinction according to the cultural code. Within consumer culture, brands are cultural markers critical to identifying and distinguishing cultural concepts in both actual environments and virtual communities. Further, brands afford unlimited expansion of distinguishing increments within the code.

I have discussed previously an approach to computer-assisted design (CAD) for consumer-generated virtual communities (Pennington, 2001). The vividness and interactivity available in those virtual realities evoke the sense of presence (Pennington, 2004). Both articles discuss giving tangible form to virtual communities (i.e. taking virtual communities out of the realm of imagination and making them available for sensation). Previously, making social objects available for sensation has been a challenge. Increasingly, electronic games offer a solution to that challenge by using avatars to represent players. The technique extends easily to consumer avatars.

Avatars are the tangible features users give themselves to make themselves available for sensation by others in the time and space of online environments. Song & Kim (2005) define avatars as a graphical representation of a user in virtual environment. Observers do not sense the actual person as object. But through cultural definition, observers in the actual world do not sense actual objects. Rather, they observe only the appearances of cultural representations in time and space. Just as consumers in actual environments, avatars in virtual environments convey information to identify and distinguish themselves through conspicuous consumption of brands.

Without any observation distinction, each avatar would be just a commodity. But without observable distinctions, consumers are just commodities. Within consumer culture, behaviors and products associated with those behaviors can distinguish. But within a pattern of behaviors and products, brands are the cultural tool for further distinction. This is true not only for actual consumers but also for their avatars in virtual communities.

Consumers do not always compete with each other in the process of distinction, comparison and identity. To say that a consumer is masculine makes no sense unless culture recognizes the possibility of being not masculine. But consumers do not have to compete to determine who is masculine. All consumers who exhibit behaviors culturally associated with masculinity can be masculine. Of course, consumer can and do compete to determine who is more or less masculine, feminine, youthful, honest, attractive, intelligent or any other quality that culture designates as variable and valuable. In part, the competition determines not only which consumers possess more or less of a quality, but also the observable behaviors and artifacts that signify the varying degrees of a quality.

Brands are a key component of the cultural signification process. As such, brands do not always compete with each other. To say that one brand of deodorant is masculine makes no sense unless another brand can be not masculine (i.e. feminine or neutral). However, to the extent that culture recognizes degrees of masculinity, one brand can signify a greater or lesser degree of masculinity than other brands. For example, one brand can be "the best a man can get." In order to establish such significance, marketing communication must associate a brand with observable behaviors and artifacts culturally designated as corresponding to the degree of a quality.

Often, other brands are among the culturally designated artifacts. Indeed, one can expect to find other brands among the artifacts because consumers rarely use a single brand in a symbolic vacuum. The virtual community that includes only a single brand lacks the cultural vividness necessary for a sense of presence. Multiple brands are part of the consumer code. Just as no two consumers are identical, no two brands are identical. Each brand modifies consumer identity. In combination, brands interact to refine consumer identity. Therefore, e-branding consumers requires carefully analyzed cultural meanings of brand combinations rather than single brand placement in virtual communities.

REFERENCES

Bagozzi, R. P., & Dholakia, U. M. (2006). Intentional social action in virtual communities. *Journal of Interactive Marketing, 16*(2), 2–21. doi:10.1002/dir.10006

Baudrillard, J. (1988). *Selected writings. Translated by Mark Poster*. Stanford, CA: Stanford University Press.

Bourdieu, P. (1984). *Distinction: A social critique of the judgment of taste* (Nice, R., Trans.). Cambridge, MA: Harvard University Press.

Chen, Y.-H., Wu, J.-J., & Chung, Y.-S. (2008). Cultural impact on trust: A comparison of virtual communities in China, Hong Kong and Taiwan. *Journal of Global Information Technology Management, 11*(1), 28–48.

Daugherty, T. M., Li, H., & Biocca, F. (2001). Consumer learning and 3D ecommerce: The effects of sequential exposure of a virtual experience relative to indirect and direct product experience on product knowledge, brand attitude and purchase intention. In F. Biocca, (Ed.), *Proceedings of the Experiential E-Commerce Conference* (CD-ROM). East Lansing, MI: Michigan State University.

Douglas, M., & Isherwood, B. (1996). *The world of goods: Toward an anthropology of consumption*. New York, NY: Routledge.

Editors of Advertising Age. (1988). *Proctor & Gamble: The house that ivory built*. Lincolnwood, IL: NTC Business Books.

Fournier, S. (1998). Consumers and their brands: Developing relationship theory in consumer research. *The Journal of Consumer Research, 24*(March), 343–373. doi:10.1086/209515

Gibson, J. J. (1977). The theory of affordances. In Shaw, R., & Bransford, J. (Eds.), *Perceiving, acting and knowing: Toward an ecological psychology* (pp. 67–82). Hillsdale, NJ: Lawrence Erlbaum Associates.

Gupta, S., & Kim, H. W. (2007). Developing the commitment to virtual community: The balanced effects of cognition and affect. *Information Resources Management Journal, 20*(1), 28–45. doi:10.4018/irmj.2007010103

Hall, E. T. (1969). *The hidden dimension*. Garden City, NY: Anchor Books.

Hirschman, E. C., & Thompson, C. J. (1997). Why media matter: Toward a richer understanding of consumers' relationships with advertising and mass media. *Journal of Advertising, 26*(1), 43–60.

Holt, D. B. (2004). *How brands become icons*. Boston, MA: Harvard Business School Press.

Huang, W.-Y., Schrank, H., & Dubinsky, A. J. (2004). Effect of brand name on consumers' risk perceptions of online shopping. *Journal of Consumer Behaviour, 4*(1), 40–50. doi:10.1002/cb.156

Kant, I. (1977). *Prolegomena to any future metaphysics. (P. Carus, Trans., J. W. Ellington, Rev.)*. Indianapolis, IN: Hackett Publishing Company, Inc.

Levy, S. J. (1986). Meanings in advertising stimuli. In Olson, J., & Sentis, K. (Eds.), *Advertising and consumer psychology* (*Vol. 3*, pp. 214–226). New York, NY: Praeger Publishers.

Li, H., Daugherty, T., & Biocca, F. (2002). Impact of 3-D advertising on product knowledge, brand attitude, and purchase intention: The mediating role of presence. *Journal of Advertising, 31*(3), 43–57.

Lippman, W. (1965). *Public opinion*. New York, NY: The Free Press.

Lynd, R. S. (1939). *Knowledge for what? The place of the social sciences in American culture*. Princeton, NJ: Princeton University Press.

Marx, K. (1967). Commodities. In *Capital: A critique of political economy, vol 1. The process of capitalist production*. (S. Moore & E. Aveling, Trans.). New York, NY: The International Publishers Co.

Mayer, R. C., Davis, J. H., & Schoorman, F. D. (1995). An integrative model of organizational trust. *Academy of Management Review, 20*(3), 709–734.

McCracken, G. (1986). Culture and consumption: A theoretical account of the structure and movement of the cultural meaning of consumer goods. *The Journal of Consumer Research, 13*(June), 71–84. doi:10.1086/209048

McCracken, G. (1990). Culture and consumer behavior: An anthropological perspective. *Journal of the Market Research Society. Market Research Society, 32*(1), 3–11.

McKnight, D. H., Choudhury, V., & Kacmar, C. (2002). Developing and validating trust measures for e-commerce: An integrative typology. *Information Systems Research, 13*(3), 334–359. doi:10.1287/isre.13.3.334.81

McWilliam, G. (2000). Building strong brands through online communities. *Sloan Management Review, 41*(3), 43–54.

Memmi, D. (2006). The nature of virtual communities. *AI & Society, 20*(3), 288–300. doi:10.1007/s00146-005-0020-7

Mick, D. G. (1986). Consumer research and semiotics: Exploring the morphology of signs, symbols and significance. *The Journal of Consumer Research, 13*(September), 196–213. doi:10.1086/209060

Ngyuyen, L., Torlina, L., Peszynski, K., & Corbitt, B. (2006). Power relationships in virtual communities: An ethnographic study. *Electronic Commerce Research, 6*, 21–37. doi:10.1007/s10660-006-5986-9

Nöth, W. (1988). The language of commodities: Groundwork for a semiotics of consumer goods. *International Journal of Research in Marketing, 4*(3), 173–186. doi:10.1016/S0167-8116(88)80003-X

Osgood, C., Suci, G., & Tannenbaum, P. (1957). *The measurement of meaning*. Urbana, IL: University of Illinois Press.

Osgood, C. E., May, W. H., & Miron, M. S. (1975). *Cross-cultural universals of affective meaning*. Urbana, IL: University of Illinois Press.

Pennington, R. (2000a). Brands as the language of consumer culture. *Journal of Global Competitiveness, 8*(1), 318–329.

Pennington, R. (2000b). *The theory is the press: A view of the press as developer of informal theory*. Association for Education in Journalism and Mass Communication Annual Convention (Communication Theory and Methodology Division). Phoenix.

Pennington, R. (2001a). Signs of marketing in virtual reality. *Journal of Interactive Advertising, 2*(1). Retrieved from http://jiad.org/vol2/no1/pennington.

Pennington, R. (2001b). The conceptual definition of culture in advertising, marketing and consumer research literature. In M. Roberts & R. L. King (Eds.), *Proceedings of the 2001 Special Asia-Pacific Conference of the American Academy of Advertising* (pp. 34-40). Gainesville, FL: The University of Florida.

Pennington, R. (2004a). Brands, culture and semiotics (revisited) in creative strategy development. In Ribeiro Cardoso, P., & Nora Gaio, S. (Eds.), *Publicidade e Comunicação Empresarial: Perspectivas e Contributos* (p. 29043). Porto, Portugal: Edições Universidade Fernando Pessoa.

Pennington, R. (2004b). Revising a psycholinguistic application of information theory for the consumer psychology of brands. In Williams, J. D., Lee, W.-N., & Haugtvedt, C. P. (Eds.), *Diversity in advertising* (pp. 201–214). Hilldale, NJ: Lawrence Erlbaum Associates, Inc.

Pennington, R. (2005). Affording cultural and social presence in e-marketing. In Gao, Y. (Ed.), *Web systems design and online consumer behavior* (pp. 305–318). Hershey, PA: The Idea Group Inc.

Pennington, R. (2006). A cultural framework for studying youth, brands and lifestyles. In Ribeiro Cardoso, P., Nora Gaio, S., & Pérez Seoane, J. (Eds.), *Jovens, Marcas e Estilos de Vida* (pp. 15–24). Porto, Portugal: Edições Universidade Fernando Pessoa.

Pentina, I., Prybutok, V. R., & Zhang, X. (2008). The role of virtual communities as shopping reference groups. *Journal of Electronic Commerce Research, 9*(2), 114–136.

Pinker, S. (1994). *The language instinct*. New York, NY: William Morrow and Company, Inc.

Porra, J., & Parks, M. S. (2006). Sustainable virtual communities: Suggestions from the colonial model. *Information Systems and eBusiness Management, 4*(4), 309-341.

Preece, J. (2000). *Online communities: Designing usability, supporting sociability*. New York, NY: John Wiley & Sons.

Rheingold, H. (1993). *The virtual community: Homesteading on the electronic frontier*. New York, NY: Harper Collins.

Ritson, M., & Elliott, R. (1999). The social uses of advertising: An ethnographic study of adolescent advertising audiences. *The Journal of Consumer Research, 26*(December), 260–277. doi:10.1086/209562

Schultz, D. E., & Barnes, B. E. (1995). *Strategic advertising campaigns* (4th ed.). Lincolnwood, IL: NTC Business Books.

Song, J., & Kim, Y. J. (2005). Social influence process in the acceptance of a virtual community service. *Information Systems Frontiers, 8*, 241–252. doi:10.1007/s10796-006-8782-0

Susman, W. I. (1985). *Culture as history: The transformation of American society in the twentieth century*. New York, NY: Pantheon Books.

Talukder, M., & Yeow, P. H. P. (2007). A comparative study of virtual communities in Bangladesh and the USA. *Journal of Computer Information Systems, 47*(4), 82–90.

Tönnies, F. (1957). *Gemeinschaft and Gesellschaft. (C. P. Loomis* (Trans, A., Ed.). East Lansing, MI: Michigan State University Press.

Watzlawick, P., Bavelas, J. B., & Jackson, D. D. (1967). *Pragmatics of human communication*. New York, NY: W. W. Norton & Company.

Williamson, J. (1978). *Decoding advertisements: Ideology and meaning in advertising*. London, UK: Marion Boyars.

Chapter 13
E-Branding and Institutional Web Sites:
The "Visiting Card" of the Municipalities of Rome and Paris

Annamaria Silvana de Rosa
Sapienza University di Rome, Italy

Elena Bocci
Sapienza University di Rome, Italy

Massimiliano Picone
Sapienza University di Rome, Italy

ABSTRACT

The research presented in this chapter is at the intersection of two large research programs designed and directed by de Rosa, both inspired by the Social Representations Theory: the first is aimed at mapping and comparing both representational and experiential imagery dimensions of tourists and citizens interacting with European historical capitals; the second explores the contribution of new internet based communicational systems to psychosocial research under different forms and through different channels, with a focus on communication applied to the field of tourism. In particular, this chapter presents the analysis of the municipal web sites of two historical capitals, Rome and Paris, considered as the Visiting Cards these two cities offer citizens and tourists.

In order to study the contents of both institutional web sites (www.comune.roma.it and www.paris.fr), a multi-method approach has been applied and in particular: the use of a grid designed by de Rosa & Picone, Nielsen's usability test, and the Atlas/ti program for a qualitative analysis of both web sites in two versions downloaded simultaneously.

The use of the three tools has enabled the identification and comparison of the elements that characterize the web sites of the Municipalities of Rome (analyzed lengthwise in time, comparing the versions

DOI: 10.4018/978-1-61350-171-9.ch013

downloaded in June 2003 and April 2004, with a replication of the usability test in November 2004) and of Paris (downloaded the first of April 2004 the same day of the Roman web site, with which it was compared). The analyses have allowed to highlight aspects related to contents, structure, and several technical elements important from a user's point of view (graphics, interactivity and usability in particular), emphasizing strengths and weaknesses.

Other than the descriptive value and the possible function of guiding web professionals and institutional communication managers of the city, the results presented in this chapter have a historical value (given the volatility and dynamicity of web sites, like many other Internet environments) with respect to the evolution towards web 2.0 scenarios, assuming a particular interest for further comparative analysis with 2010 web sites, currently under investigation.

INTRODUCTION

Being on the web is more and more equivalent to existing. This is true for single individuals, organizations and institutions. Institutional web sites of cities are like *visiting cards* for both citizens and tourists.

Manuel Castells has dedicated an entire volume of his "Network Society" trilogy to the theme of identity on the web (Castells 1996, 2000), offering an interesting contribution to the debate on the pervasive need to be visible on the web – at times polarized on "apocalyptic" (cfr. InteraliaInteraliaInter-alia: Slouka, 1995; Maldonado, 1997; Wolton, 1999; Calegari, 2000) and "integrated" (cfr. InteraliaInteraliaInter-alia: Turkle, 1995; Levy, 1997; Mitchell, 1999; Castells, 2001) viewpoints.

In the '90's the debate became more lively among experts belonging to different disciplines on topics related to new "virtual" identities of individuals, institutions and online organizations, and the spreading of social internet habits. Contemporaneously de Rosa together with collaborators of the Chair of Psychology of Communication and New Media (Faculty of Psychology2 – La Sapienza University of Rome) gave way to a series of longitudinal empirical researches aimed at monitoring the developments of Social Representations of internet and the metaphors associated to them (navigation, ocean, global village, place, marketplace etc.). The main focus of the studies was relative to the evolution of social practices and more specific fields (i.e. tourism) in which changes tied to e-commerce and web-marketing have radically redefined the relationship between possible customers that buy travel packages, tour operators and travel agencies.

The present contribution satisfies the interests of research on communication via internet applied to tourism (de Rosa & Bocci, 2001a, 2001b, 2002, 2005; de Rosa. Bocci & Saurini, 2006) and a wider research program, led by de Rosa, on citizens and European and non-European first-visitors to nine historical capitals (Helsinki, Lisbon, London, Madrid, Paris, Rome, Wien and recently also Warsaw and Brussels) This program is contextualized in the framework of previous empirical studies on Social Representations of Rome in first-visitors of six different nationalities (de Rosa, 1995; de Rosa, 2006; de Rosa, Bonaiuto, Calogero, & Antonelli, 1992a, 1992b, 1992c; de Rosa, Calogero, & Antonelli, 1992; de Rosa, Antonelli, & Calogero, 1995; de Rosa & d'Ambrosio, 2009, 2010) and meets the interest of the "Environmental Psychology" and "Social Representations of urban places" research areas (Ardone, de Rosa, & Bonnes, 1987; Ardone, de Rosa, Bonnes, & Secchiaroli, 1987; Bonnes, de Rosa, Ardone, & Bagnasco, 1990; Bonnes, Bonaiuto, Ercolani, & de Rosa, 1991a, 1991b; Nenci, de Rosa, Testa, & Carrus, 2003).

The main goal of the wider research program is the comparison between the imagination (before the visit) and experience (after the visit) of places and the Social Representations of the entire capital city and of its historical center in particular, guided by a series of hypotheses regarding the stability and transformation of the Social Representations and their dimensional elements. The multi-method research design guiding the wider research program is inspired by the Social Representations Theory (Farr & Moscovici, 1984, 1989; de Rosa, 1990, 1993, 1994, 2002, 2006; Jodelet, 1989; Moscovici, 1961, 1989; Moscovici & Duveen, 2000) integrated with other constructs derived from Environmental Psychology, like the social memory of urban places Ardone, de Rosa & Bonnes, 1987; de Rosa, 1997; Jodelet, 1982; Hass, 2004; Hass & Jodelet, 2000). The relationship between different constructs is investigated, assuming that they are mediated by various communication systems such as anticipatory experience.

During the analysis of these communication systems we assumed that a crucial role could be played by Cities' Institutional web sites, considering them as official "*visiting cards*" that Municipalities present to citizens and tourists. The analysis of results will inform us if this hypothesis was (at the time of the first data collection) and is still well-founded (inspiring new and further still ongoing data collections) and applicable both to citizens and tourists, if it highlights the prospective potential areas of development of the web sites in time and tracks and gives direction to content enrichment, technical aspects, also in relation to potential targets (citizens/tourists).

In particular, this article is aimed at analyzing the Institutional web sites of the Municipalities of Paris (www.paris.fr) and Rome, both downloaded with *Teleport pro 1.29 version* the 1st of April 2004 (important historical data, as an anchorage for further comparative analysis, since web sites evolve continuously and past versions are hard to retrieve) according to a multi-method perspective and multi-step level analysis.

These web sites have been studied by highlighting different but complementary perspectives (Stockinger, 2002):

1. in relation to the socio-economic context of reference: sector of activity, functions, targets, relationships with the "mother" Institution;
2. as a form of virtual organization (complex system characterized by web pages interacting with each other);
3. as a technological object that needs special technology in order to be produced, managed and used;
4. as a semiotic object, characterized by contents, expressive modes and forms of interactions between different components and users.

So globally, three levels of analysis have been used: structural (internal organization, contents, functions), interactionist (relationship with other web objects, relationship with other users) and socio-paradigmatic (accessibility and usability).

The evaluation of web the sites was performed by means of:

1. a grid for web site assessment devised by de Rosa & Picone in 2003 within the frame of activities carried out by the Chair of Psychology of Communication and New Media;
2. a usability test (Nielsen, 1994);
3. the Atlas/ti program for qualitative analysis of both web sites

USABILITY OF A WEB SITE

The idea of "usability" emerges in the 1960s within the domain of studies on cognitive ergonomics centered on human-machine interactions: the attention of researchers focused on the way a user constructs a mental model of the product he/she is using, developing certain functionalities. The scope of studies on usability is to align the designer's model of the software with the user's model (Boscarol, 2003).

These researches have brought to the definition of guidelines that are applied as support to the design of interfaces which are the elements users interact with.

Up to the 1970s, the main users of IT products were designers themselves, or experts of the specific field. This means that the design model overlapped with user model.

In the '80s and '90s, with the pervasive diffusion of IT technologies in different work and domestic domains, a final fracture occurred between final user and designer; consequently it became necessary to identify strategies that could make the use of software easier for non experts. An epochal change was provoked by Macintosh, the first *user-friendly* computer characterized by the metaphor of a desk and the intuitive movement of objects.

The birth of Internet and the proliferation of web sites has shifted the problem of usability to a new domain and new problems have emerged: since a software is usually used after purchase, a web site is first used and, only if this first approach is satisfactory, a transaction will follow and maybe, profit too. The consequence is that, relatively to web sites, the theme of usability is an element strongly connected to economics, image and communication of brand identity.

Combining literature on this topic, Nielsen's studies (1994) and the rules expressed by the *ergonomic requirements for office work with visual display terminals (VDTs) – Dialogue principles* ISO 9241-10 standards, 9 heuristic principles have been defined:

1. **Visibility of the system status:** it is very important to keep users informed of the status of their actions. For example, one of the most common actions that can be executed on a web site is to follow the links (mouse sensitive website zones – both text or images- that allow us to shift from one page to the other). A suggestion is to change the color of the active link (in the moment it is clicked on) to inform the user that the action is being executed (the standard is to pass from the blue color of the non visited link to red color of an active link). It is also suggested to distinguish visited links from the other two statuses (non visited link and active link), to remind the user of the links he/she already visited, among those listed on the page.
2. **Match between system and the real world:** it is always worth knowing and using final users' language for the concepts they are familiar with, either textual or graphical elements. This solution assures on one hand a better visitors' comprehension and memorization of contents and on the other avoids that users, interested in the available information, exit the web site without considering it, because mislead by the use of a wrong terminology and/or images that he/she doesn't recognize (or has a hard time associating to the information he/she is looking for).
3. **User control and freedom:** normally, it is a good practice to give users control over the web site's information, allowing them to easily access topics they are interested in and browse around them according to their needs. For this reason, it is important to mark links adequately, in a non ambiguous manner (avoiding false expectations) and positioning them where the user is expecting

to find them. This allows a first-time visitor to easily understand if there are contents that satisfy his/her needs and eventually to explore them.

4. **Consistency:** it is important to mark every page with the same textual or graphical elements that reassure the user that he/she is moving inside the same web site. For example if passing from one page to the other users encounter different graphical styles, they are forced to analyze all the objects to check if they are still within the same web site, in which section, or if they exited by mistake. Consistency helps users search and use information.
5. **Error prevention:** it is important to avoid situations in which users could make mistakes and end up in the wrong place; in any case, the possibility of exiting and returning to the previous status must be guaranteed. It is furthermore important to put a link on every page allowing to return to the home page and to the main sections of the web site: the user can then go back to more familiar sections if he/she doesn't enter the page he/she is expecting to.
6. **Recognition rather than recall:** simple and schematic layouts are recommended, to facilitate the identification and examination of information on the pages
7. **Flexibility and efficiency of use:** users should have the chance to follow different paths while browsing a web site, according to his/her experience of the Web and/or knowledge of the same. For non expert users visiting the site for the first time, it is useful to design a hierarchical access to contents (that makes the progressive deepening of topics explicit); on the contrary, for expert users short-cuts from the home page are recommended, in order to directly access sections of the site closer to their needs. Also in this case, it is important to signal them adequately, so they can be noticed.
8. **Aesthetic and minimalist design:** if graphical elements inserted in the pages (browsing elements, images or photos) are too colorful, complex and/or too big related to texts, there is the risk of putting informational contents in the background: users will then be too engaged in identifying the meaning of images and looking for coherence with the other elements of the site, instead of analyzing the informational contents of pages. Furthermore, big and complex images are too heavy in terms of Kb in Internet, uselessly increasing time for download. It is then suggested to choose graphical solutions that highlight meanings in the text, few simple colors (overall a web page shouldn't have more than 6 colors) with subjects users are familiar with.
9. **Help users recognize, diagnose, and recover from errors:** it is always useful to try and find which errors could be made by end users on the web site. If, for example, we set up a page with which users can send their personal data, a confirmation page should then appear, informing them if data has been sent successfully.

The ISO 9241 standard defines usability as:

the extent to which a product can be used by specified users to achieve a specified goals with effectiveness, efficiency and satisfaction in a specified context of use.

This complex concept can be represented with three perpendicular axes intersecting, a graphical expression of the three measurable attributes (Figure 1).

Analyzing the three concepts separately, it is possible to define:

- ***Effectiveness*** as: "*the accuracy and completeness with which specified users can achieve specified goals in particular en-*

vironments" and can be measured by counting how many times, with respect to the number of trials, *specified users have achieved specified goals in particular environments*.

- ***Efficiency*** is defined as: *"the resources spent in relation to the accuracy and completeness of goals achieved"* and can be measured by counting resources spent to reach defined goals.
- ***Satisfaction***, finally, is defined as: *"the comfort and acceptability of the work system to its users and other people affected by its use"* and can be measured in different ways, for example through questionnaires aimed at surveying users' reactions to the system.

DESIGN OF A GRID TO EVALUATE WEB SITES

Reviewing the literature (Nielsen, 1994; Stockinger, 2002) and publications for experts of the IT sector, available through online thematic web sites (like www.usable.it; www.manuali.it), indications have emerged for the construction of a grid to evaluate web sites. This grid allows to highlight both technical features (i.e. graphical aspects and applied technologies, clearly those available at the time of the research), and elements that can facilitate or, on the contrary, complicate the usability of the web site (i.e. different levels of video resolution, compatibility with different browsers, consistency and flexibility characteristics).

Figure 1. Graphical expression of the concept of usability

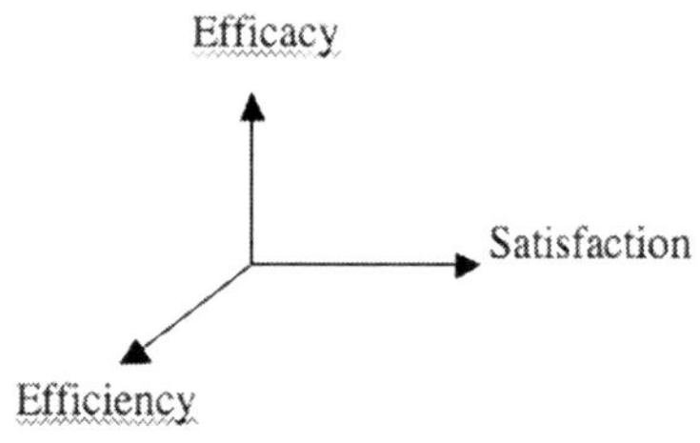

The different elements of web site pages are: graphical elements (static or dynamic), utilities (i.e. archives, calendars, post-cards, sms...), elements that influence accessibility and usability, interactive components (with users/ other sections of the web site and the web) e-branding (organizational charts, banners...), contents (news, bulletins, information...). Filling out the grid basically means mapping the presence/absence of these elements. The evaluation of web sites can differentiate according to users' characteristics and the goals of the evaluation; the grid contains questions that map the evaluator's characteristics (socio-demographic and perceived level of expertise in Internet use) in order to trace these variables.

Main Results of the Application of the Grid to the Web Sites of the Municipalities of Paris and Rome

In this research, to evaluate the most important elements of the web sites of the Municipalities of Rome and Paris (downloaded simultaneously the 1st of April 2004), de Rosa & Picone's web evaluation grid was used (applied in a pilot study in 2003 in collaboration with Sara Saurini & Ilaria Botti[1]). The use of this grid allows to highlight different aspects of a web site: graphics, technology, contents, interactivity, usability characteristics.

Graphics, Multimedia and Technical Features: Municipality of Paris Web Site

The web site, visualized with Internet Explorer 6 and Netscape 7.1 (the updated versions available at the time of the research), has 10 sections on the home page, white background and blue links, while every section has different colors for headers and titles (Figure 2).

In the different pages we find many tables with headers but with no legends. The logo of this site is in the upper left hand corner. It is a static logo made of text and color: the name of the site *paris.fr* is inside an orange rectangle and beneath it the writing: *Maire de Paris* closed in a blue rectangle.

Between these two texts we find a small image that changes according to the section we are in and the home page is the only one containing the images of all the different logos (Figure 3).

So we will find these symbols for each of the sub-sections:

- a *"house":* when we are on the *home page*
- a *"handshake:"* when we are in the *solidarité* (solidarity) section;
- an *"eye":* for the *cultural* section;
- a *"briefcase":* for the *education* section;
- a *"jogger":* for the *sports* section;

Figure 2. Paris' web site map

Figure 3. Logos of sub-sections

- a *"man and a bus"* for the *déplacements* (transports) section;
- *a* "hill with a tree and a building*": for the* environment *section;*
- a "*city": for urbanisme* (urbanism)*;*
- *an* "office door": for économie *(economy)*
- a "*group of people*" for *citoyenneté* (citizenship and associative life).

From the Paris city map it is possible to access every *arrondissement* (municipal administrative district) by clicking on the zone of interest (Figure 4).

Graphics, Multimedia and Technical Features: Municipality of Rome Web Site

Differently from Paris's web site, the Roman site doesn't always recall the same colors: as a matter of fact, even if the background is always white, in various sub sections colors vary and may be complementary or in contrast: the home page is mainly orange, blue and red, while in the subsections *municipi* (municipal administrative district) *and companies, thematic areas, on-line services,*

Figure 4. Arrondissements of Paris

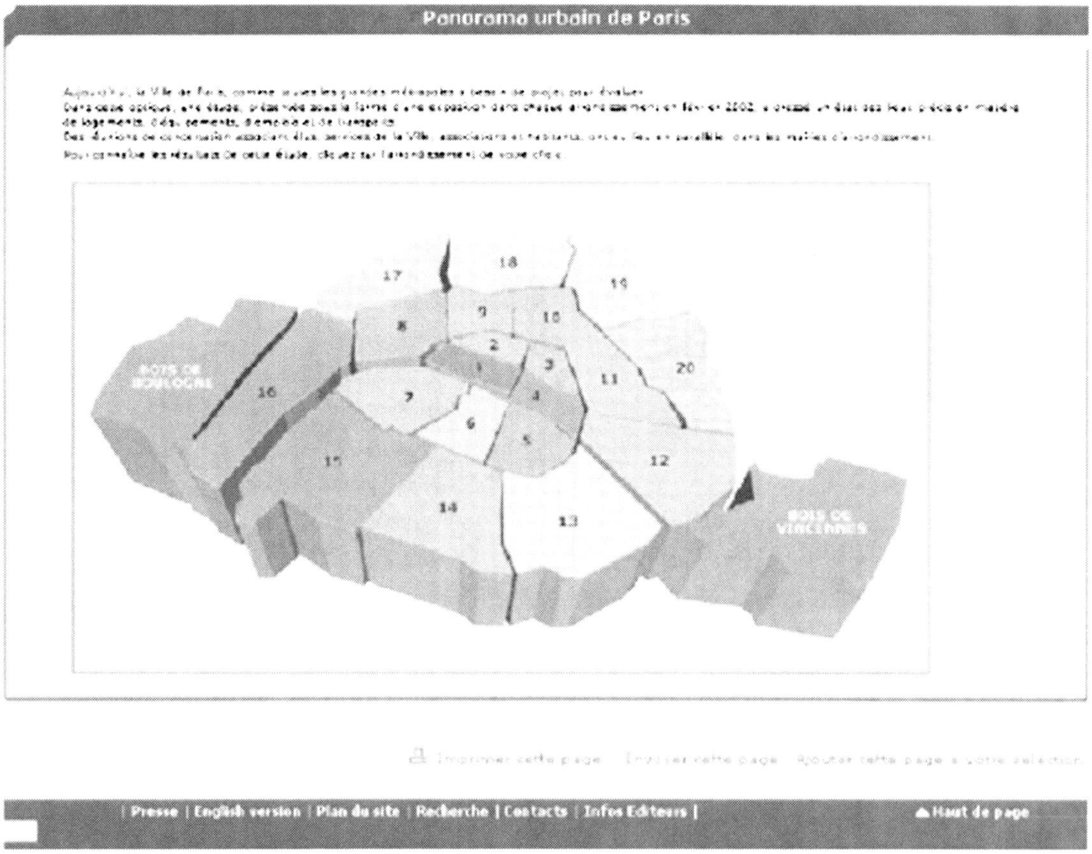

citizen's network, projects are a combination of red and blue, two contrasting colors that prevail in the entire web site.

Even in this case the logo is in the upper left hand side, but while on main pages there is a complete version of the logo (Figure 5), made of images, text and pictures (institutional SPQR shield, the text comune.roma.it, and in the background we find an architectural evolution that represents Rome yesterday and today (Colosseum and Auditorium and the paving of P.zza del Campidoglio), in other web pages we only find the SPQR symbol in different positions.

The choice of the logo is connected to the thematic area of the sub section, for example, the *library* section uses an open book, while the mobility and transport section uses a public transport vehicle.

Differently from the web site of the Municipality of Paris, the level of multimedia is sophisticated: animated gifs, 3D graphics, flash animations and videos with audio. For example, by clicking on the *radioromacomune* link (on the right side of the home page) it is possible to listen to the news of the past 30 days, or, entering the bulletin section (libraries) videos are also available. HTML language is used for still pages and ASP for dynamic pages.

There are few territory maps and it is difficult to find them inside the web site. A non-expert user not familiar with the structure of the city of Rome is not aided by the web-site.

Summing up, we can state that while multimedia and technologies used for this web site have not changed in a year, in both versions we find a high level of multimedia and the same program language to construct web pages, whereas graphics have slightly changed.

In the pilot study, performed on the version downloaded in June 2003, the static logo used was composed of the text commune.roma.it, of the SPQR shield and of the picture of the Colosseum; in the present study (using the version downloaded the 1st of April 2004), apart the elements already listed, the logo also includes a picture of the Auditorium and the paving of P.zza del Campidoglio.

Even the colors have slightly changed; while the 2003 version of the web site mainly contained complementary colors (yellow-red, cyan blue-red, green-magenta) and contrasting colors (blue-red, green-red, yellow-magenta, cyan blue-magenta), in the analysis conducted in April 2004 the homepage is characterized by the use of orange, light blue and red, whereas other sections of the site mainly show a combination of red and blue.

Utilities

Municipality of Paris Web Site

The web site of the Municipality of Paris does not contain screen savers, wallpapers, online postcards, online help, web telephony or e-commerce areas, there are no utilities related to short messages on traffic, news and services, nor information about the number of visitors or archives of on-line directories, bibliographies and virtual libraries, but agendas of events are published.

On the contrary, there is a large amount of information on employment: the *solidarité* (soli-

Figure 5. Municipality of Rome logo

darity) section allows users to enter the *emploi* (employment) link, in which we find addresses to which CVs can be sent, information on public employment and internships.

Municipality of Rome Web Site

This section of the grid dedicated to utilities does not highlight differences with the previous pilot study. Here also among the utilities, in particular in the section *comunica*, it is possible to receive short messages on one's mobile phone relatively to:

- traffic updates
- news
- services
- cultural events in Rome

It is possible to consult on-line magazines, that are visible with Acrobate reader (PDF file).

Statistics on how many people have visited the web site cannot be found on the Home Page but on secondary pages, as in the case of web pages dedicated to *libraries and Department VII.*

Book archives can be found in the libraries section, along with the addresses of Roman libraries etc.

On the *Training and Employment* link, accessible from the *thematic areas* section, information on every kind of job and employee contract are available, together with links to external job opportunity web sites (i.e. www.romalavoro.net thematic areas/ training on the job/ jobs: Employment Department web site*).*

We also find the agenda of main events: municipio V (local town hall) /departments / municipio and company.

Usability

Municipality of Paris Web Site

Generally, the web site presents a fixed structure and, as a matter of fact, while visiting it only few parts change. This kind of coherence allows rapid movements from one page to the other because the images remain the same. (The uniformity that characterizes the Municipality of Paris web site allows the user to easily understand if he\she is in the site itself).

The structure of the home page is typical of modern portals (obviously in line with the technology available at the time of the research): the logo is in the upper left hand side, followed by pictures of the city of Paris, a drop menu positioned horizontally, information positioned centrally and technical data at the bottom (Figure 6).

On the right side of the home page we find links to internal search engines and links to external web sites that contain useful information on the city of Paris, both for citizens and tourists.

The structure of the home page is not replicated in every web page; as a matter of fact constant links related to logo, drop menu and information at the bottom disappear; furthermore, every time we access the current news section (the link is present in every sub section of the web site), on the left hand side the menu of the specific section opens.

It is possible to access the site map at every moment. It is rather coherent, even if the menu does not maintain the same order of the drop menu.

This site is also available in English, but in a simplified version: if we are on any web page and click *version anglais* we are automatically sent back to the site map (and on the page we were on before) that has a different structure from the French version. The English version only has four sections focused on tourism, lifestyle, education opportunities and government.

When the document is too large vertical scroll bars appear, but at the beginning of each page we find a list of all the paragraphs it contains to help the reader, so by clicking on the link we quickly find ourselves on the section of the page we are interested in.

We have opened the Municipality of Paris web site with different browsers (Safari, Netscape, Explorer…) and operating systems to verify if it

Figure 6. Home page web site of the Municipality of Paris: www.paris.fr

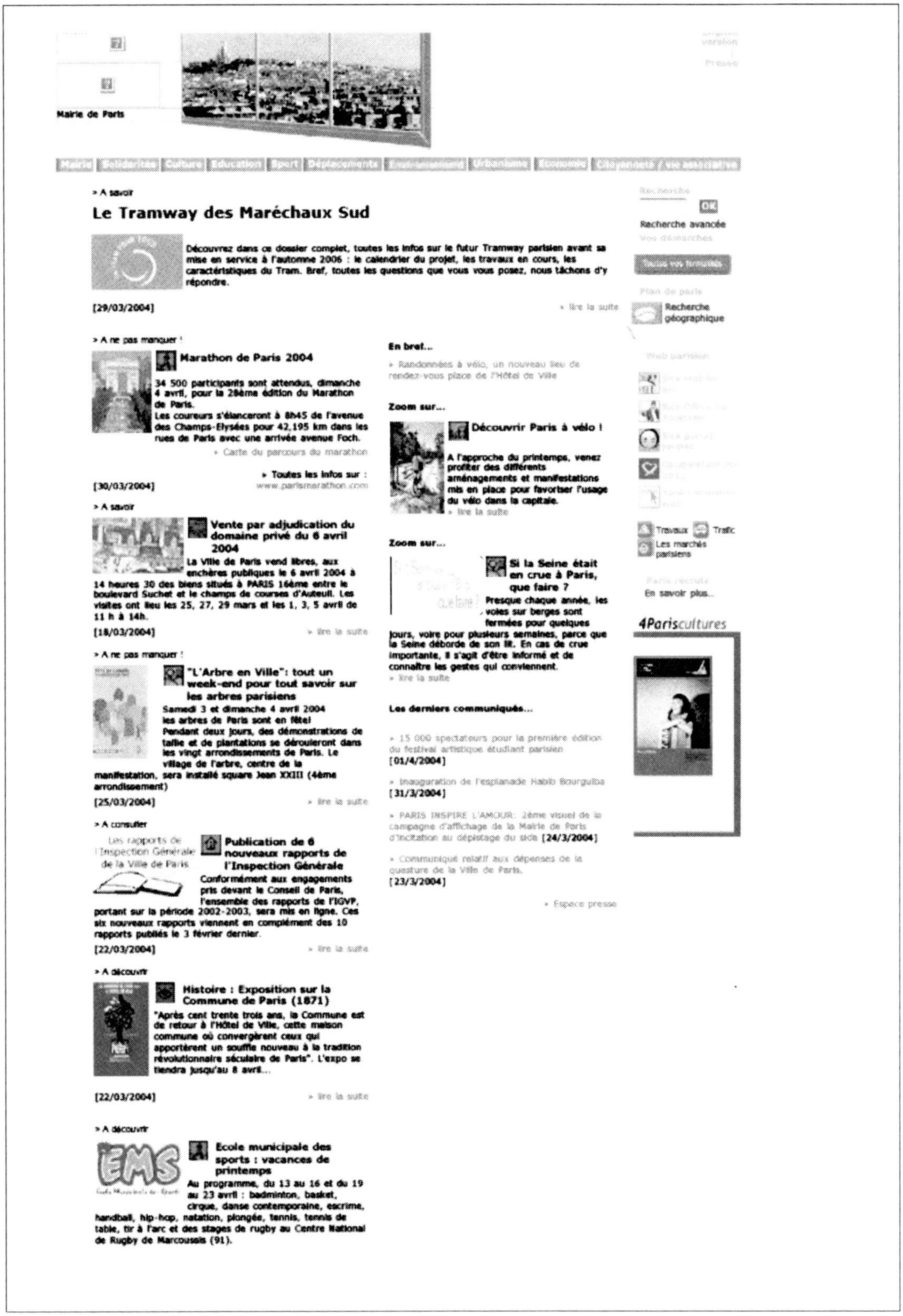

was designed to be compatible with both systems. There generally is a certain stability while using the different browsers, but errors are more frequent with Netscape: for example, when we are in the site map some subsections remain out of the table and are not accessible.

When we access a thematic area the color and the header of the pages are not complete. Furthermore, the blu links often overlap words of the previous lines creating reading difficulties, in the page *accueil économie /tissu économique paris* graphics are not centered and are at the bottom, or in *environnement / Parcs et jardins / liste jardins / bois boulogne* if we click on a picture to zoom it the dimensions do not change.

Furthermore, in some pages a horizontal scroll bar appears (i.e.: *accueil déplacements / dossiersville / un tram pour tous)* and it is not easy to visualize the whole file because it is necessary to move the cursor from left to right and vice versa.

In this site elements that could facilitate navigation have been found, for example combo box or jumps in navigation and *bread crumbs* (that allow the user to go backwards by tracing, if he desires, his own steps).

The constant presence of the drop menu on every section of the site, other than the home page, makes navigation flexible, allowing to explore pages according to the needs of the user and not according to a rigid order predetermined by the webmaster.

Municipality of Rome Web Site

The web site is built according to w3c standards (HTML 4.01 recommendations and level 2 CSS) to guarantee maximum accessibility and usability of the information for all kinds of users and without distinctions of platforms or browsers.

The Municipality of Rome web site still maintains the previous year's structure: logo at the top, information at the center of the page, menu on the left, and links (Figure 7). Standards used on the home page are not found on the rest of the site and the result is a non-stable structure that gives pages little homogeneity, therefore the visitor does not understand if he is still inside the site. This non-homogeneity is due to a graphical update limited to the home page.

The main navigation is planned to be carried out through the menu on the left, articulated in six sections:

Municipi and Companies, on-line services, Projects, thematic areas, Useful Links and Other Sections (Table 1).

To access the links contained in the sections, it is necessary to click on every one of them except for "thematic Areas," a section that automatically expands.

This site is available in two languages, Italian and English, both accessible from the home page; however in the *municipio II* section a richer multi-language version is available in French and Spanish.

As for the Municipality of Paris web site, the English version has fewer pages and gives limited information on:

- the main events of the city: fun, exhibitions, theatre and cinema
- tourism
- available transport
- information related to school, family etc.

The button *Search on this site* is a search engine only present on the main pages and allows to search in internal pages.

The expression *Other Sections* is not intuitive for the user because it is not clear what will happen by clicking on it. This section allows to directly access the link *search engine* with which it is pos-

Figure 7. Home page web site of the Municipality of Rome: www.comue.roma.it

Table 1. Sections of the Municipality of Rome web site

Municipality and Companies - City Council - District Council - Departments - Extra-Department offices - Local Town Halls - Companies	Thematic Areas - Environment - Registry Office, Citizens and equal Opportunities - Children - Housing - Communication and Simplification - City, Municipality and Opening Hours - Culture, Sports and Tourism - Economy, Business, Development and Taxes - Training and Employment - Youth, Education and Civilian Duties - Mobility and Transport - Personnel - Multi-ethnic Rome - Safety, Emergency Service and Out of Service - Social and Health - City Statistics and Analysis - Planning, Suburbs and Public Works
Online Services - Public Job Advertisements - Library/Newstand - Tax Computation (ICI) - Online Deliberations - Frequently Asked Questions (FAQ) - Elections - Municipality Offices Opening Hours - City Council Agenda - Price Observatory - Payment of School Fees - Online Taxes - Useful Files - Single Front Office for Production Activities - Street Plan of Rome - Towed Vehicles	Useful Links - Useful Links - Teletext - Netiquette - Intranet
Projects - Marco Aurelio - European Projects - Leonardo Project - Online Science - International House for Women - Global Junior Challenge - RomaPreview - Schools online - PEOPLE Project - Major Cities - TeleCities	Other Sections - Search ENgines - Contact Offices - 060606 - RomaSMS - Sp@rnews - RadioRomaComune - The Event - InComune - Internet editorial office - English version

sible to make an advanced search by intersecting the following voices that:

- contain all the following words;
- contain the following phrase;
- contain any of the following words;
- do not contain the following words.

Furthermore it is possible to choose the section in which one wishes to look for the object:

- all statistical documents;
- Main News;
- News;
- F.A.Q.;

- District Council measures;
- on-line deliberations

Links to external search engines are also available on this site. They allow access to Public Administration offices by inserting the information (even if partially) and by clicking on the button. For example, if we insert the word "work" we find a link to the "Ministry of Labor" and the "National Council of Economy and Labor"

The expression *Accessible site* is also not clear; this link is in the upper left hand side and allows the visualization of the site only in a textual mode.

The site was designed to be visualized at a dimension of 800 x 600 pixel or superior, the most common video setting for the creation of a web page, with which lateral horizontal scroll bars are never visible. Whereas, the quantity of information present on the site makes it impossible to eliminate the vertical scroll bars. Differently from the Municipality of Paris web site, very long texts are not broken down into small paragraphs and this is not very appreciable because people prefer going to a new paragraph and having the impression of a forward movement: clicking to continue to read gives the idea of progression (Burns, 2002). As for the previous research there are no elements that aid navigation regarding: facilities, personalization of interface (language, character dimension, graphical object positioning), the *undo* and *redo* buttons, *home* and *back,* but accelerators have been found, for example *combo box* present in the advanced search.

Even if the site has been designed according to the concept of modern portals, with the logo in the upper left hand side, main menu on the right (since left elements are always more important than right elements), contents are not in order and a graphic coherency is missing: form, order and position of objects change from one page to another and this gap in the structural backbone does not help the visitor to explore and navigate.

Interactivity

Municipality of Paris Web Site

By inserting the word "intranet" in the internal search engine, various thematic areas accessible by different categories of users have emerged: municipality, job search help etc. This site has a high hypertext complexity, with links both to other sites on different topics (i.e. culture: www.culture.fr, or education: wwww.crous-paris.fr) and to internal pages. Among the first we can cite links directly available on the right hand menu of the home page. In any case all links, both internal and external, are easy to find because differently from the rest of the text, they are blue. Other tools that facilitate communication with users and among users, like forums or chats, are not identifiable inside or outside the home page, nor in other parts of the site. The home page offers the opportunity for users to subscribe to a newsletter.

Municipality of Rome Web Site

By inserting the word "intranet" in the search engine, many internal sections appear, usable only through special passwords, like for example the "MARCO AURELIO" project, and special learning software packages produced as an experiment, together with the documents of the "Jubilee 2000" event, by consultancies that deployed classroom training.

From the *Useful Links* section it is possible to find links to Intranet Services of the Municipality of Rome without accessing the Marco Aurelio Portal.

In the site we find different links that send us back to internal sections and external sites (example: www.televideo.rai.it, www.inferentia.it*)*. To allow an easy identification of internal and external links present within the web site, two colors have been used (red and blue).

Vice versa, in the previous version (2003) of the Municipality of Rome web site these two colors had never been used with the same criteria: inside the *online Services* section, for example, external links were red, whereas inside the section *Municipi*, external links were blue.

Now instead, a significant improvement in coherency is apparent. The use of red and blue is consistent as red is used for internal sites and blue for external links.

No sections dedicated to forums or chats have been found, but F.A.Q. are available in an internal area of the *on line Services* section present on the home page.

As for the previous research, visitors have the opportunity to contact different professionals of the Municipality of Rome, through a special section that can be found both on the top right hand side of header of the home page *Write to Offices* and the *Comun.ica* area.

From this research it also emerged that main pages do not give the possibility to periodically receive special information, but if we enter in *Municipio* V, it is possible to subscribe to a newsletter to receive news via e-mail, appointments and press releases from the Social Affairs Department.

A Glance at Contents

Municipality of Paris Web Site

In the present research, as for the pilot study carried out a year before on the Municipality of Rome institutional web site, the contents downloaded the 1st of April 2004 have been evaluated by using two parameters: "level of update of information measured in terms of frequency of update in defined periods of time (daily, weekly, monthly)" and "level of reliability," intended as clearness and certainty of sources. The information inserted on the home page is almost all referred to news: new tram line, the Paris marathon, public offering for book purchase, Paris by bike etc. As already said, the Municipality of Paris web site is articulated in 10 sections, each of which contains *actualité* links referred to current events discussed in that section. With reference to the "contents" addressed in the grid of analysis, we find information sections that are separated in three areas:

- **"transport":** inside the *déplacement* section it is possible to find information on all kind of transport available in Paris: collective transport, subways, trains, "batobus," special transport for the disabled;
- **"tourism":** from the *économie* section it is possible to access general information related to tourism, for further information the web site directs the user towards a specific address www.paris-touristoffice.com;
- **"sports":** an entire section is dedicated to this topic and it is possible to have information not only on which sports can be practiced in Paris but also which are the gyms present in each *arrondissement*;
- **"culture":** an entire section is dedicated to this topic. In addition to the information about Paris' cultural heritage, it provides information about: municipal museums and all those that can be found in different *arrondissements*, theatres, libraries and cinemas, as well as an updated agenda of the city's cultural events (exhibitions, cinemas, theatres, ballets and scientific events). Furthermore, for each of these themes more in-depth information is available by clicking on the external links published on the Municipality of Paris web site (www.paris-bibliotheques.org, www.theatredelaville-paris.com, www.ensemble-orchestral-paris.com, www.chatelet-theatre.com, www.maisondelapoesie-moliere.com, www.espci.fr/espla);
- **"education":** it includes more than one topic. It is very focused on information regarding student lifestyle, scholastic system

and teaching cycles (elementary school, high school, superior education, apprenticeship and orientation). Information on single *arrondissements* is also accessible: schools' addresses can be found thanks to combo box. In this section we also find information on health and prevention for children in school age.

- **"health":** we find this topic in the *solidarité* section in which, apart providing information about health, more specific sites are suggested to provide the users with more detailed information;
- **"economy":** an entire section is dedicated to this topic in which the economic structure of Paris is discussed: industries, services, tourism, apprenticeship, entrepreneurship etc.

Municipality of Rome Web Site

The home page contains a large section dedicated to news (clearly sensitive to the time period of the date of download: 1st of April 2004) with a central zone of the page dedicated to news on the Municipality of Rome: 4th World Forum of the cities against poverty, four new Municipal board members, traffic block for odd numbered license plates etc.

At the bottom, at the center of the home page, we find news from the Campidoglio (City Hall), also accessible from the first menu at the top right hand side of the screen. One of the main characteristics of these contributions is the total absence of references to the sources of information.

Every *municipio* is an independent entity and independently manages news. Consequently, significant differences emerge between the information published on each page: some do not have spaces for news (i.e. *Municipio* V), others publish news and bulletins for citizens highlighting them in clickable columns at the margin of the page (i.e. *Municipio* IV); amongst the most complete sections we find Municipio XI, in which we find a large area containing information and news from the municipality, from which we can access the Municipal Newspaper that can be read on-line thanks to an archive of previous editions; all sources are reliable and news is always up to date.

The grid of analysis for web sites contains, in the section on information, different categories of contents that in the Municipality of Rome refer to specific thematic areas, listed in the menu on the left hand, and to departments.

These content categories are the same that have been already identified in the previous pilot study:

- **"transport":** allows to access up to date and complete pages managed by *Mobility Policies* of *municipio* VII; furthermore, an external link allows to access the *city traffic* service offered by the regional RAI Televideo www.televideo.rai.it/televideo/pub/index.jsp;
- **"culture, sports and tourism":** by accessing these thematic areas it is possible to obtain complete, up to date and reliable information on culture and sports. Information on tourism is scarce and the visitor is directed to three external sites -*Romaturismo (*www.turismoroma.i*t)*; *Azienda per la promozione turistica* (www.aptprovroma.it*)*; *Stazioni, orari treni e tariffe* (www.ferroviedellostato.it)-. The culture section contains information from the cultural department and has a rich list of culturally interesting places (historical archives, LibraryNewstand – book search in Roman libraries). Updated and reliable information on sports can be found in the pages of the Sport Office: a clear presentation of the institution, sections dedicated to news, laws, sports organizations, contacts;
- **"economy":** it is possible to find information on this topic in the related thematic area, which present external

(*RomaEconomia* site www.romaeconomia.it) and internal pages on commerce, crafts, heritage, local development, revenue and taxes Department section;

- **"social and health":** this area is characterized by the presence of updated content related to different users (families, elders, disabled, immigrants) directly managed by the Social Policies and Health Department; furthermore, external links offer information on pharmacies (www.comune.roma.it/Muoversi_nel_Municipio/Vivi_il_centro/Farmacie/) and social-health services present in the *Municipio*;
- **"youth and education":** this section represents a valid resource to access updated information on schools, through external links to on-line schools and external ones such as those to *useful schemes on superior education, university and other information* and the site of *Educational and School Policies*. News on extra-scholastic activities, news on different topics such as music, employment and city events, are present on the external site *Informagiovani.* (www.comune.roma.it/Sezioni_del_portale/Per_Conoscenza/) The pages of the Municipality of Rome dedicate a lot of space to the problem of drug addiction on the *Municipal Agency for drug addiction* web site (www.drogachefare.it/agenzia.html.).

USABILITY TEST

The purpose of evaluating of the usability of a web site is to obtain information on users' needs, on their understanding of the system and on the aspects they appreciate or dislike. The tools available for the evaluation of technical features (i.e. the one designed by UsableNet) and the standards of production of good interfaces (i.e. Comolli, 2000) cannot substitute trials with real users. Typically, these methods are applied in different moments of the design process and can be used as formalized guidelines. In the usability test, users test the system by performing simple tasks under observation.

The observer tracks:

- time need to execute the tasks;
- error rate;
- percentage of tasks finished successfully;
- frequency of alternative navigation paths used to perform specific tasks;
- number of backtracks while executing a task;

Nielsen (1994) highlights that a test with 5 users allows to map 85% of usability problems.

The usability tests of the Municipalities of Paris and Rome websites (www.paris.fr, www.comunediroma.it) involved 5 French subjects for the Municipality of Paris and 5 Italian subjects for the Municipality of Rome, each of which were asked to perform the following 4 tasks:

1. identify the members of the municipality council
2. send an e-mail to the web master
3. find a map that presents the structure of the cities of Paris and Rome;
4. visit the section dedicated to employment search/offering

It is clear that it would be interesting to extend this kind of research by involving non-residents of different nationalities and focusing on tasks that are most important for a newly defined research population: for example non-national citizens or tourists that consult the web site of the municipality they intend to visit, considering them as official information channels, supposedly more reliable than commercial ones.

Table 2 shows the bi-lingual (French and Italian) form used to collect information on the Municipalities of Paris and Rome:

As shown in Table 3, among the four tasks that the subjects must perform, the third (related to *finding a map of the structure of the city – arrondissements* in the case of Paris and *Municipi* in the case of Rome) has required a higher average execution time compared to other tasks, both for French (average time = 3 min.) and Italians (average time = 5 min., a result that does not differ much from the previous pilot study). Furthermore, while French users did not show an explicit uneasiness towards this task, Italians judged it as more problematic.

In both cases, most errors were related to the "path" chosen by users (total of errors made by French = 11, total of errors made by Italians = 19). In the case of the French subjects, 3 managed to see the map of Paris by going through the path: *home page / plan de paris* e *urbanisme / panorama de Paris.* Only 2 Italians managed to perform the task through the path: *città (city), municipi, orari (time table)/ decentramento amministrativo (administrative decentralization)/ municipi.*

Identify the members of the Municipal Council and *Visit the section dedicated to job search/offers* have been, *for both* web sites, the tasks that required less execution time (for the first task average execution time was 1'2" for Italians and 1'6' for the French; for the second task both populations registered an average of 1'6")

The task *identification of Municipal Council members* was successfully completed by all French and Italian users with respectively 4 and 2 errors and the last task was completed successfully by 4 subjects out of 5 with 3 errors made by the French and only 1 made by Italians.

To identify municipal council members, users went through the following paths:

- **French site:** *maire (mayor) / exécutif municipal (municipal executive) / liste des adjoints* (list of *City Council members)*
- **Italian site:** *comune (municipality) agenzie (agencies), aziende (companies), / giunta comunale (city Council)/ composizione della giunta (composition of the city Council).*

Whereas, relatively to the section dedicated to job search/offers, paths were shorter:

- **French site:** *solidarité (solidarity) / emploi (employment)*
- **Italian site:** *aree tematiche (topics) / formazione lavoro (job training).*

Send an e-mail to the webmaster required the same time for French (average time 2 minutes) and Italian (average time 2,2 minutes) users and execution was successful for 4 subjects in the first group and 3 in the second. The paths followed by users were:

- **French site:** (*contact / un message pour la Maire de Paris (a message for the mayor of Paris),* or by using the internal search engine and inserting the word webmaster;
- **Italian site:** by using the search button and writing the word *webmaster*, using *on line services / Internet editor*, *write to offices* or simply selecting the *central editor* link at the bottom of the home page.

After performing all four tasks, users have been asked to give an overall judgment of the usability of the web site on a value scale from 1 to 5 (1 = negative judgment, 5 = completely positive judgment). None of the Italian subjects has given a completely negative or positive judgment: 60% chose value 3, 20% value 4 and 20% value 2. Among the French, one user made a completely positive judgment and the others gave an overall positive judgment, appreciating accessibility (80% value 4 and 20% value 5).

The usability test applied to the www.paris.fr and www.comune.roma.it web sites has produced similar results with respect to different tasks, but with differences between groups on the same

Table 2. Usability test data collection form

Tâche/ Compito (task)	*Temps/ Tempo (Time)*	*N° erreurs N° Errori (N° Errors)*	*Succès du travail / Successo nell'esecuzione (Success Rate)*	*N° de backtrack N° di backtrack (N° of backtracks)*	*Parcours choisi/ Percorso scelto (Chosen Path)*
Trouver la composition Du conseil municipal / Individuare la composizione della giunta comunale *(Identify the members of the municipal council)*					
Envoyer un email au web master / Mandare un'e-mail al web master *(Send an e-mail to the web master)*					
Trouver le plan de la ville/ Individuare una mappa che presenti la struttura della città *(Find the map of the city)*					
Consulter la section du site concernant les demandes/offres d'emploi / Visionare la sezione del sito dedicato alle domande/offerte di lavoro *(See the section dedicated to employment search/offering)*					

Table 3. Usability test results for French and Italian subjects relatively to the Municipalities of Rome and Paris web sites

Tasks assigned to evaluate the Municipalities of Rome and Paris web site	**Average time in minutes**		**Number of errors**		**Execution success rate (yes=1; no =0 for each subject)**		**Number of backtracks**	
	French	**Italians**	**French**	**Italians**	**French**	**Italians**	**French**	**Italians**
Identify the members of the municipal council	1,6'	1,2'	4	2	5	5	4	3
Send an e-mail to the webmaster	2'	2,2'	5	3	4	3	8	8
Find the city map	3'	5'	11	18	3	2	11	19
Find the section dedicated to job search/offer	1,6'	1,6'	3	1	4	4	5	3

task, that could reflect the differences of the two web sites illustrated earlier. *Find the city map* was difficult for both groups, compared to other tasks, but even more for Italians (that took more time, made more mistakes and used more backtracks).

The major difficulties encountered by Italians are probably due to the fact that the map is not directly accessible from the home page, but through the *Municipality and Companies* link that contains primarily text information on the Municipal Council, Departments, *Municipi*, Companies. As a matter of fact, to visualize the map of Rome's *municipi* a different and not easily deducible path must be followed from the thematic area *city, municipio and hours / administrative decentralization.*

Almost all French subjects have dedicated more time to other tasks (but less compared to Italians), to click on the links: *déplacements* and *urbanisme* and the drop menu compared to other tasks – even if the Paris city map could be accessed directly from the home page, *home page / recherche géographique.* Furthermore, both groups easily found information on the *municipal council members* and *job search/offer* pages.

To evaluate the *stability of these results in different conditions* of use of the web site (allowing navigation in small groups, without constraining interactions among individuals and with the computer, with a methodology currently defined as *Think Aloud Protocol*[2]), we replicated the *Usability Test for the Municipality of Rome web site on 7 groups of Italian subjects in November 2004, asking them to perform the same tasks.* In Table 4 summarized average results are shown for all 7 groups.

In this group setting, the only task performed successfully by the whole group in less time (average time = 1'11") and with no errors is *find the section on job research/offering;* whereas in this study (as in the two previous ones) the most difficult task (only 3 groups successfully performed the task), making the highest number of mistakes (5) and spending an average time of 6 minutes, was again the *search of the structure of the city of Rome.*

In this case also, at the end of the tasks we gave the groups a value scale that allows to give a brief judgment of the site. The site has generally been evaluated as accessible and the average evaluation of the 7 groups was 3.

By comparing results obtained by the three researches performed in sequence: June 2003, April 2004 (same usability conditions of the pilot study) and November 2004 (use in small groups) performed on the Municipality of Rome web site, we can conclude that the judgments related to the Municipality of Rome do not differ from 3 (average accessibility) in a year, in both usability conditions (individual and small group). Instead, on the basis of the results that emerged in 2004, the Municipality of Paris web site was judged more positively by French subjects (values between 4 and 5 that indicate a good accessibility of the site).

Qualitative Analysis by the Means of Atlas/ti

The use of the Atlas/ti software requires a series of preliminary steps:

- site download with Teleport pro version 1.29 (available in 2004);
- copy of the sites on CD;
- visualization of contents;
- opening of files and visualization of contents;
- opening of Atlas/ti
- introduction of text (htm, html) files in Atlas/ti and exclusion of image files (i.e. those with extensions gif, jpg, png, swf).

The Download of the Municipalities Web Sites by Means of Teleport Pro Version 1.29

The path used to download the Municipality web sites of Paris and Rome, www.comune.roma.it and

Table 4. Results of the repeated Usability Test on 7 groups of Italian subjects relatively to the Municipality of Rome web site

Municipality of Rome web site	Average Time	Errors	Success/Failure	Backtracks
Identify members of Municipal Council	2' 01"	1	7/0	1
Send an e-mail to the webmaster	2' 29"	2	6/1	2
Find a map of the city	6'	5	3/4	6
Find the section on job search/offers	1' 11"	0	7/0	1

www.paris.fr, with Teleport pro version 1.29 has been: *file/new project wizard / create a browsable copy of a web site on my hard drive/introduce name of site to download/project proprieties everything.*

Teleport pro is a highly sensitive program that allows to download every single page of a web site, along with images, texts, sounds, videos and other elements.

The main characteristic of this program is to maintain the functionalities of a web site so, browsing through the downloaded pages:

- we get the impression of visiting an on-line site because every section can be visited with internal links
- pages maintain their dynamicity and, according to the level defined in the download phase, it is possible to download external sites signaled by the web site.

Therefore, the program allows downloading of every page whatever its size. According to the path one desires to follow, Teleport pro allows two different download modalities:

- reconstructs the structure (partial or complete) of the site on the computer that executes the download
- complete: entire web site
- partial: choice of elements to download (i.e. only text)
- reconstructs the structure of the site positioning downloaded files in a single folder

This second approach, used to download the Municipalities of Rome and Paris web sites, follows two main criteria:

a. download is performed according to the type of file (i.e. gif, jpg, html)
b. maintains an alphabetical order of each file

According to these criteria files are downloaded in the following order:

still or dynamic images in alphabetical order:
- animated and static gif images
- jpg images
- png images

text files in alphabetical order
- htm
- html (objects of interest in the 'Atlas/ti analysis)
- asp

style sheet:
- css

javascript:
- js

dynamic images (flash):
swf

Main Steps of Analysis by Means of Atlas/ti

The pages of both web sites (www.paris.fr end www.comune.roma.it) downloaded contemporarily with *Teleport pro version 1.29,* have been qualitatively analyzed with Atlas/ti. This tool facilitates the interpretation of research material, allowing a parallel work on different texts.

We have worked on 1735 text files for the Municipality of Paris web site, and 2462 for the Roman web site, all downloaded the 1st of April 2004.

Two hermeneutic units, namely work units (see Figure 8), were created: one for the Municipality of Rome and the other for the Municipality of Paris. With the drag and drop function all the text files of both web sites have been dragged inside the first box.

Primary Documents (PDs)

In the Primary Documents (PDs) box the name of each inserted file appeared, preceded by the code P1 (automatically assigned by the program) for the first file, P2 for the second file and P3 for the third and so on, up to Pn of introduced files.

To improve the readability, it is possible to rename every single dragged file by executing the following procedure:

- click on the file with the mouse's right hand button;
- chose *rename*;
- insert the new title and confirm.

To eliminate a file:

- click on a note pad put on the left hand side of the box for PDs;
- select the file we want to eliminate;
- click on the eraser in the upper right hand side.

Codes and Quotations

Codes are a series of instructions that allow to visualize a web page from a browser. Codes allow the identification of the most important parts of every text, namely *quotations*.

Inserted codes have been extracted from the 2003 pilot study and translated in French and are inserted in the third box by following the path: *codes / create free code.* The name of the code is then typed in and we click on confirm. It is possible to eliminate a code by selecting it and clicking on the eraser in the upper left hand side. The code that will appear in this box will have a value equal to 0 because quotations have not yet been calculated.

The quotations corresponding to each code, namely the statistics of how many times an instruction or code is repeated on web pages, can be obtained with the path: *codes / coding / autocoding,* or by opening the note pad on the left of the code box, clicking on the rectangular symbol in the upper right hand side, typing the name of the code and then clicking on confirm.

As soon as the program will have found all the quotations corresponding to a *code,* the total number of codes will automatically be introduced inside the parenthesis that follow the code.

After creating an hermeneutic unit, these pages have been set among primary documents (PDs) by using a drag and drop technique (dragging each file inside the documents' section). This mode has allowed to visualize the content of pages as text, without losing the html program language,

Figure 8. Hermeneutic unit of the del Atlas/ti program

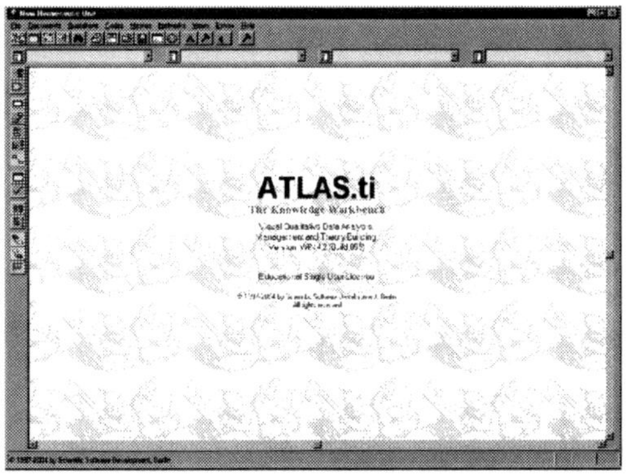

Table 5. Dimensions and codes used for the application of Atlas-ti software

Dimensions to be mapped	Codes used for the Municipality of Paris web site	Codes used for the Municipality of Rome web site	English Translation of the Codes
Page content	*description | contenu*	*Descrizione | contenuto*	*Description |content*
User	*public |publique | usage | usager* | utilisateur*[3]|*citoyen* | touriste* |jeunes | âgés | âgé | personnes âgées*	*Pubblico | utenza | utenti | cittadin* | turist* | giovani | anziani | anziano*	*public | users | citizen* | tourist* | young people | elderly*
Information	*information* | new* | actualité | communiqué* | événement* |*	*informazion* | new* | attualità | comunicat*| avveniment* evento eventi |*	*information*| news* | statements* | event*|*
Communication	*forum | chat | mail | faq | téléphone | appelle | écris |*	*Forum | chat | mail | faq | telefono | chiama | scrivi |*	*Forum | chat | mail | faq | phone | call | write |*
Presentation of Institution	*slogan | organigramme | adjoint | conseil | thématiques | gadget*	*slogan | organigramma | giunta | consiglio | tematiche | gadget*	*slogan | organization chart | committee | Council |main themes | gadget*
Presence and type of link	*link| href| mailto*	*link| href| mailto*	*link| href| mailto*
Presence and description of images	*img | alt | plan* |* carte routière | *film | vidéo*	*img | alt | map*|cartin* | film | video*	*img | alt | map*|cartin* | film | video*
Services	*service* | help | aide | recherche | traduction*| calendrier* | agenda* | carte postale | sms | plan*|statistiques| bibliographie**	*Serviz* | aiuto | cerca | traduzion* | calendar* | agend* | cartolin* | sms | mapp* | statistiche | bibliografi**	*service* | help | search | translation* | calendar* | agend* | postcard* | sms | map* | statistics | bibliograph**
Colors	*Color*	*Color*	*Color*
Key words	*Keyword**	*Keyword**	*Keyword**
Descriptive Information	*head*	*head*	*head*
Page Title	*title*	*title*	*title*
Thematic Areas			
Transport	*mobilité | transport* | tram | voiture* | automobile*|train* | métro**	*mobilità | trasport* | tram | auto | automobil* autovettur* |tren* | metro* |*	*mobility | transport | tram | car cars | train trains | Underground*|*
Tourism	*touriste* | hôtel | visite*| réservation* | dormir | manger | étranger* | multiethnique*| ethnique* | tourisme | itinéraire* |*	*Turist* | albergo | visit* | prenotazion* | dormire | mangiare | stranier* | multietnic* | etnic* | turismo | itinerari*|*	*Tourist | hotel | visit | booking* reservation* | sleep | eat | foreign* | multiethnic* | ethnic* | tourism | routes, itineraries|*
Sports	*sport* | sportif | compétition*	*sport* | sportiv* | competizione*	*sport sports | sportsman* | competition*
Economy	*économi* | marché* | impôt*	*economi* | mercat* | tributi |*	*economy economies | market* | taxes |*
Health	*social | santé | santé*| handicapé* | handicap |*	*sociale | salute | sanit* | disabil* | handicap |*	*social | health | health | disabled handicapped | handicap |*
Culture	*culture* | événement* | exposition | musique* |musical| concert* | livre* | exposition | littérature | éducation | théâtre* |*	*cultura* | evento | eventi | mostre | mostra | music* | concert* | libr* | esposizion* | letteratura | istruzione | teatr* |*	*culture* | event* | exhibition* | music* | concert* | book books library libraries | exposure* | literature | education | theater* |*
Space for the Youth	*formation | jeunes | jeunesse | jeune homme*| jeune femme*|enfants | jeu| jeux | jouer |*	*Formazione | giovani | gioventù | ragazz* | bambini | gioco | giochi | giocare*	*training | young people | youth | boy* girl* | children | play game**
Employment	*travail* | occupation | emploi | formation*	*Lavor* | occupazione | impiego | formazione*	*work works | employment | job | training*

continued on following page

Table 5. Continued

Dimensions to be mapped	Codes used for the Municipality of Paris web site	Codes used for the Municipality of Rome web site	English Translation of the Codes
European Contacts			
Paris	*Circonscription* | arrondissements | Paris*		
Europe	Nation*| union européenne |	*Nazioni | unione europea |*	Nations | European Union |
Rome		*Circoscrizion* | quartier* | Roma*	*district* | neighborhoods | Rome*

so as to maintain the potential of the hypertext of a web page.

In this research, the same codes of the pilot study have been used, with the aim of highlighting the most important parts of each text (Table 5).

The different components of the main menu (Primary documents, quotations and codes) have different buttons to create different outputs that allow the user to visualize specific sections of the hermeneutic unit content. In particular, outputs have been created by using the following buttons:

- *document / output / quotations*: to identify all the quotations created for the selected document;
- *quotation / output / all quotation*: to visualize all the quotations present in the hermeneutic unit;
- *codes / output / quotations for selected code*: to obtain all the quotations related to a previously selected code;
- *file / output / all object*: allows to have the list of all the objects in creation date order;
- *codes / output / codes- Primary documents / Table:* allows to visualize *with a cross-table* the frequencies related to used codes (per line) for each primary document (in a column). This table can later be exported in SPSS.

Description of Quotations of the Municipalities of Rome and Paris Web Sites Found in the Hermeneutic Units

The material in the hermeneutic unit can be initially described by visualizing the cross-table (*codes / output / codes-primary documents-table*) of all the frequencies of the used codes for each Primary Document. By analyzing the marginal totals for each line of this output, the occurrences of the used codes can be summed (tot. 42829) for the 1735 PDs of the Municipality of Paris web site. These values correspond to the sections of the text identified with Atlas/ti (Table 6).

On the Municipality of Paris web site a clear dominance of quotations of the code *titre de page* (tot. freq. 19076) emerges.

Next follows *Informations descriptives* (tot freq. 9499). The site dedicates a large amount of space to information on city events (tot. freq. 319) and transport to go from one area to another of Paris (*transport* tot freq 319) and on initiatives for youth (*espace jeune* tot. freq. 250).

Among the 2462 PDs found for the Municipality of Rome, a total of 33988 frequencies have been found as corresponding to used codes (Table 7).

For the Municipality of Rome web site there is a clear prevalence of frequencies relative to the dimensions *color* (freq. 13596), *page title* (freq. 8489) and *descriptive information* (freq. 3892).

As for the Municipality of Paris web site, there is a great deal of information regarding the city of Rome, such as available transport (freq. 903) or job offers (freq. 920).

Observing the previous output, but referring to marginal totals of columns, it is possible to select primary documents that present the highest number of quotations. In Table 8, PDs are indicated with the serial number of insertion in the hermeneutic unit; in the following tables, the PDs have been renamed referring to the obtainable output with the command button *document / output / lists*.

The PDs with the highest number of quotations, selected according to *dimensions*, are those related to the thematic areas of "urbanization" (inside which we find *housing project* - freq. 163 and *local map* - freq. 65) and *markets in Paris* (freq. 110); then follows information on *elected politicians* (freq. 100) and a series of sections dedicated to *sports* that regard sports events with a strong collective impact (as the 2004 *marathon* with freq. 97; and *sports initiatives* with freq. 70).

For the Municipality of Rome website the PDs that present most frequencies are those related to thematic areas such as *culture* (inside which we find different sections, *bibliopag* freq. 473, *libraries* freq. *160),* the *municipi* section, in which historical information is found (*centoanni* freq. 705), services (*offices* freq. 258, *disability desks* freq. 239, *municipal police* freq. 149), art (*galleries* freq. 102) and an area dedicated to the youth (*youth and education* freq. 281) (Table 9). Instead the Municipality of Paris site has many frequencies for *environment* (*land charter* freq. 241, *agenda 21* freq. 112) and information on mobility (*blue label* freq. 272 and *parking, transport, permits, pollution, limited traffic zones* freq. 115*)*. We also find an area dedicated to children (inside this area we find *Projects for childhood and adolescents in Rome* freq. 173, *front desk for families* freq. 143, *events and initiatives* freq. 101), whereas the frequencies related to the thematic areas *department* contain information on *education policies* among which *bids* (freq. 171) and circular administrative information (freq. 105).

Moving our attention from marginal totals to values inside the table, the same output allows us to identify PDs with the most number of quotations that have been categorized according to codes (Table 10 and Table 11).

Important information that characterize the Municipality of Paris web site, mainly on policies and services for citizens, emerge from Table 10: city events, press releases, elected politicians, public housing, 2004 sports calendar, custody of children and solidarity initiatives for elders over 65.

The results presented in Table 11 confirm the prevalence of information on culture and educa-

Table 6. Frequency of codes in the Municipality of Paris web site

Dimensions	Frequency of codes
Titre de la page – *Page Title*	19076
Informations descriptives- *Descriptive information*	9499
Couleurs - *Colors*	8415
Présence et typologie de lien-*Presence and type of link*	2204
Mots clés – *Keywords*	1546
Information	848
Présence et description de l'image- *Presence and description of images*	345
Transport - *Transport*	319
Espace jeunes - *Space for the Youth*	250
Santé –*Health*	141
Culture	51
Travail - *Employment*	51
Services	34
Tourisme -*Tourism*	33
Présentation de l'institution –*presentation of institution*	7
Communication -*Communication*	4
Destinataire- *User*	4
Europe	2
Totale	**42829**

Table 7. Frequency of codes in the Municipality of Rome web site

Dimensions	Frequency of codes
Colors	13596
Page Titles	8489
Descriptive Information	3892
Page Content	3068
Presence and type of link	2041
Work	920
Transport	903
Communication	264
Health	139
Keywords	126
Presence and description of images	123
Culture	110
Services	89
Tourism	70
Paris	45
Economy	42
Space for Youth	29
Information	10
Presentation of Institution	7
Users	2
Europe	2
Sports	1
Total	**33988**

tion for the Roman site: historical events, libraries and youth education. Furthermore, information on services offered to citizens, for example the presence of offices dedicated to public relations and front desks for the disabled are present.

CONCLUSION: HEURISTIC VALUE AND RESEARCH PROSPECTIVE

To conclude, three tools (web sites analysis grid, Usability Test, Atlas/ti software) have been used to identify and compare elements that characterize the web sites of the Municipalities of Paris and Rome, downloaded the 1st of April 2004 with *Teleport Pro version 1.29*, and to highlight aspects related to contents, structure, technical features, usability, strengths and weaknesses.

The application of the grid of analysis has directed users' navigation of the site so as to capture the main elements, with an as much as possible objective perspective (thanks to explicit parameters to be observed).

Through the use of this grid strengths and weaknesses of both web sites have been identified and are summarized in Table 12:

The usability test on a sample of French users for the Municipality of Paris web site and Italian users for the Municipality of Rome web site has allowed to identify navigation difficulties for both web sites, that integrate the observations obtained from the grid of analysis. The most difficult task – both in terms of time spent (3 minutes for the Municipality of Paris web site and 5 for the Municipality of Rome) and errors committed (11 for the Municipality of Paris web site and 18 for the Municipality of Rome web site) – has been the task that required users to identify a city map of Paris (for French users) and Rome (for Italian users). This result is coherent with pilot study results and has been confirmed further also in the test for small groups. Differently, the task performed in less time and with fewer mistakes for both sites has been *identification of the municipal council members* that was completed by all subjects; whereas in small groups the easiest task relatively to the Roman site was, after 7 months, *find the section on job search/offers*.

Even if the users of both web sites have had the same difficulties relatively to the 4 tasks they were asked to perform, these difficulties were different for both groups relatively to the parameters of the usability test. Furthermore Italians and French did not equally evaluate the usability of the web sites they visited. As a matter of fact, the global evaluation French users made of the Municipality of Paris web site on a scale from 1 to 5 was approximately 4-5, indicating a good level of ac-

Table 8. Municipality of Paris web site: Primary documents with the most number of quotations

Primary Documents	Primary Documents	N° Quotations
1055 info pratique (Accueil Urbanisme> Logement social) *practical info (Home planning> social Housing*	Urbanismo casa popolare *Urbanism tenement*	163
1096 liste marcheé asp (Accueil Les marchés parisiens) *list steps asp (Home markets Paris)*	mercati parigini *Parisian markets*	110
331 conseillers 1 (Accueil La Maire > Vos Élus) *consultant 1 (mayor Home>Your elected*	politici eletti *elected officials*	100
151 calendrier 2004 (Accueil Sport > Haut niveau) *calendar 2004 (Home Sport>Top level)*	sport ad alto livello *high-level sport*	99
349 courses 2004 1 (Accueil Sport > Actualités) *2004 race 1 (Home Sport> News)*	attualità sullo sport *news on sport*	97
124 baromètre (Accueil Environnement > Propreté) *barometer (Home Environment> Clean)*	ambiente pulizia *environmental cleaning*	81
528 default-235.asp.htm (Accueil Actualités > Paris > Journal 06) *default-235.asp.htm (Home news > Paris > Journal 06)*	novità *news*	80
717 default_parc_floral.ASP.htm (accueil environnement > Parcs et jardins > liste jardins >parc floral) *default_parc_floral.ASP.htm (Home environment > Parks and gardens > garden list>floral park)*	ambiente parco floreale *environment flower park*	70
780 ems.ASP.htm (accueil sport > animations sportives) *ems.ASP.htm (home sport > sporting activities)*	animazione sportiva *sports entertainment*	70
508 default-217.asp.htm (accueil Education > Guide loisirs) *508 default-217.asp.htm (home Education > leisure guide)*	educazione guida hobby *hobby education guide*	68
427 default-143.asp.htm (Accueil Environnement > Parcs et jardins > liste jardins > parc André Citroen) *427 default-143.asp.htm (Home Environment> Paks and Gardens > garden list> André Citroen Park)*	ambiente parco André Citroen *Environment park André Citroen*	67
400 default-119.asp.htm Accueil Urbanisme > Plan local d'urbanisme) *400 default-119.asp.htm Home Planning > Local Plan Planning)*	urbano mappa locale *Urban local map*	65
315 conseil_parisien-1.asp.htm (Accueil Education > Vie étudiante > Citoyenneté > Conseil Parisien) *conseil_parisien-1.asp.htm (Home Education > life student > Citizenship > Council Parisien)*	educazione consigli parigino *Education Councils Paris*	64
564 default-269.asp.htm (Accueil solidarités > enfance > Pmi) *564 default-269.asp.htm (solidarity Home > children > Pmi)*	solidarietà Pmi *Solidarity SMEs*	64
626 default-8.asp.htm (accueil environnement > actualités > crue seine) 626 default-8.asp.htm (Home Environment > News> raw seine)	ambiente senna in piena *Environment Seine in flood*	64

cessibility of the web site, whereas Italian users gave a lower judgment positioned on a value of 3, indicating an average accessibility.

The qualitative analysis performed with Atlas-Ti of the elements that compose the 1735 documents of the Municipality of Paris web site and the 2462 elements of the Municipality of Rome web site, inserted in the corresponding hermeneutic units, have confirmed some evaluations and differences already registered by means of the grid of analysis designed by de Rosa & Picone for contents. The site of the Municipality of Paris privileges political information and services for citizens (city events, namely press releases and declarations, elected politicians, public housing, 2004 sports events calendar, custody of children and solidarity initiatives for the elderly); whereas the Municipality of Rome privileges information

Table 9. Municipality of Rome web site: Primary documents with the most number of frequencies

Primary Documents	Contents	N° Quotations
219 centoanni – *one hundred years*	Municipio IV -	705
125 bibliopag – *biblio p.*	servizi on line/biblioteche, indirizzi *-on line services/libraries, addresses*	473
774 giovani e istruzione – *youth and education*	aree tematiche/giovani, istruzione e servizio civile *-themes, youth, education and civil service*	281
861 bollino blu - *Italy antiair pollution certificate*	Comune e azienda/dipartimento VII/ politiche della mobilità *-City and company/department VII/ mobility policies*	272
267 uffici *-offices*	municipio XVII-	258
840 carta dei suoli – *soil map*	comune e azienda/dipartimento/dipartimento politiche ambientali e agricole *-Town Council company/Department/ Environmental and agricoltural policy*	241
341 sportello handicap – *disability desk*	municipio XII –	239
917 Progetto per l'infanzia e l'adolescenza a Roma *-project for children and adoleescents in Rome*	Aree tematiche/bambini/vetrina informativa *-Thematic areas/children/showcase information*	173
143 bandi di gara *-notices*	dipartimento XI politiche educative scolastiche *-Department XI education policies school*	171
127 biblioteche *-libraries*	servizi on line/biblioteche, indirizzi *-online services/libraries, addresses*	160
796 polizia municipale - *municipal police*	comune e azienda/municipio XX *-City and company/Municipio XX*	149
792 sportello per la Famiglia *-family desk*	aree tematiche bambini *-areas children*	143
872 sosta, trasporti,permessi, inquinamento circolazione. Ztl *-areas, tranport, permits, pollution movement, restricted area*	comune e azienda/dipartimento VII/ politiche della mobilità *-City and company/Department VII/ mobility policies*	115
844 agenda 21 locale di Roma *-local agenda 21 in Rome*	Aree tematiche/ambiente/agenda *-Themes/environment/agenda*	112
149 info amministrative-circolari – *administrative info-circular letters*	dipartimento XI politiche educative scolastiche *-department XI educational policy school*	105
766 gallerie *-galleries*	municipio XX	102
963 eventi e iniziative *–events and initiatives*	Aree tematiche/bambini/ eventi e iniziative *-Thematic areas/children/events and initiatives.*	101

Table 10. Municipality of Paris web site pages in which sections of texts defined by dimensions have been identified

Dimensions	PDs	Quot (freq)	%
Destinataire *(Users)*	tips for young people (Home Citizenship)	3	0,0023%
Information	green areas in Paris (Environement)	17	0,0395%
	Social Action addresses (Solidarity)	17	0,0395%
	deliberation projects (mayor)	15	0,0349%
Communication	filming in Paris (Home culture)	2	0,0047%
Présentation de l'institution *(Presentation of institution)*	municipal council (mayor)	2	0,0047%
Présence et typologie de liens *(Presence and type of links)*	museums (Culture)	26	0,0605%
	collections in museums (Culture)	27	0,0628%
	assistance to the elderly (Solidarity)	8	0,0186%
	(Solidarity)	10	0,0233%
Présence et description de l'image *(Presence and description of images)*	United cities and governments: world organization (Home)	2	0,0047%
	Budget e local taxes (mayor)	2	0,0047%
Services	professional insertion (Economy)	4	0,0093%
Couleurs *(Colors)*	press releases and declarations of 2001 (mayor)	190	0,4%
	Public Gousing (Urbanisme)	111	0,3%
	Elected politicians (mayor)	81	0,2%
	Race calendars (Sport)	75	0,2%
	Children Custody (Homel)	62	0,1%
	Inter-municipal charter 2004	58	0,1%
	Improve the habitat for elders over 65 yrs. of age (Solidarity)	50	0,1%
Mots clés *(Key words)*	(Solidarity)	10	0,0233%
Informations descriptives *(Descriptive information)*	municipal events calendar (Maire)	11	0,0256%
Titre de page *(Page title)*	judicial archives (Culture)	34	0,0791%
	2004 calendar (Sport)	37	0,0861%
	budget e local taxes (Economy)	37	0,0861%
Transport *(Transport)*	Request for public housing (Urbanisme)	20	0,0465%
	markets in Paris (mayor)	54	0,1256%
Tourisme *(Tourism)*	tourist's office and congresses in Paris (Economy)	4	0,0093%
Santé *(Health)*	municipal council (mayor)	11	0,0256%
	social help for infants (Mayor)	11	0,0256%
Culture	cultural activities (Home culture)	3	0,0070%
Espace jeunes *(Space for the youth)*	events calandar (Home Citizenship)	12	0,0279%
	markets in Paris	14	0,0326%
Travail *(Employment)*	Training (Economy)	2	0,0047%
	work and training (Economy)	2	0,0047%
Paris	tramway	4	0,0093%
	tramway route	4	0,0093%
Europe	scholarships for foreign researchers (Education)	2	0,0047%

focused on culture and education (historical events, libraries and education for young people, but also information on services for citizens such as public relations and front desks for the disabled.

Considering what has been observed, it is possible to draw some conclusions by referring to Nielsen's (1994) heuristic principles described in paragraph 2.

The version of the Municipality of Paris web site we studied distinguishes itself for the consistency of its structure which, by keeping textual and graphical elements stable, allows the user to easily recognize he/she is moving inside the same site or has entered another site. Furthermore, links to the home page present on every web page prevents errors, allowing the user to return to more familiar zones if he/she should have difficulties.

The Municipality of Rome web site is characterized by a high level of hypertext, with contents integrated with information coming from external web sites. The main pages stand out for their design and minimalist aesthetics, with a dominance of text and few images and animations: this doesn't overload the site in terms of KB. The site is not easily navigable in every section: in fact the sections dedicated to *municipi* is characterized by the presence of individual textual and graphical elements; the structure of the menu, the order in which relevant information is presented, the overall design of the page change and the user often has the impression of having exited the Municipality of Rome web site. This clearly does not respect the fundamental principles such as *consistency, recognition, flexibility of use*, forcing the user to re-elaborate important information and use more time to find required information, making more errors to reach them. Further difficulties with navigation are relative to the absence of links to previous pages or home page (principle of *error prevention*) and scarce visibility of the *state of the system and completed actions.* Notwithstanding the absence of a non fixed structure which causes little conformity among pages, there is consistency in the use of links; in fact, to highlight external links the color blue has been used, whereas internal links are red in order to facilitate their identification.

Both sites respect the *control and freedom* principle: this allows the user to quickly understand if topics of his/her interest are present even during a first visit.

Generally, we can state that to make both sites under investigation easy to use for any user target, some peculiar characteristics must be integrated between them: only in this manner we would obtain a web site characterized by a high consistency and flexibility, with a clear visibility of the state of the system, allowing the user to have control and freedom over the informational content of the web site.

In particular, among the main characteristics of the Municipality of Paris web site we recall:

- *logo kept in its integral version*: this element acts as a symbol of recognition of the site, it does not have to be present only on the home page but also in other sections and subsections of the web site, allowing users to easily recognize the site it refers to;
- *fixed structure*: the advantage of such a structure is that by changing only small parts of text uniformity is guaranteed between pages allowing the visitor to easily understand if he/she is still inside the site and to rapidly move from one page to the other since images remain the same.
- *easy access to the site map*: it is important to guarantee easy access to the site map in every moment, because it illustrates the site as if it were a street map. Links from page to page are visualized and the user can see how the site flows.

Instead the Municipality of Rome web site has the characteristic of being consistent with the colors that identify links: as a matter of fact, in this site it is not only easy to identify the presence

Table 11. Municipality of Rome web site pages in which sections of texts defined by dimensions have been identified

Dimensions	PDs	Quot (freq)	%
Contenuto della pagina *(Page content)*	house, heritage, constructions	15	0,04
	public relations offices	15	0,04
Destinatari *(Users)*	Leonardo da Vinci Program	2	0,006
Informazioni *(Information)*	events agenda	2	0,01
	news	2	0,01
Comunicazione *(Communication)*	curiosity (on civic museum o zoology)	18	0,05
Presentazione dell'istituzione *(Presentation of institution)*	on-line forms	2	0,006
Presenza e tipologia di link *(Presence and type ok link)*	services to citizens	16	0,05
	library	40	0,12
	culture council	20	0,06
Presenza e descrizione di immagini *(Presence and description of images)*	2004 program (library)	18	0,1
	Services	10	0,03
Servizi *(Services)*	on-line deliberation	11	0,03
	news	4	0,012
Colori *(Colors)*	One hundred year	693	2
	Biblio p.	424	1
	Cultture lybraries	348	1
	instructions for youth	269	0,8
	Offices	247	0,7
	public relations offices	230	0,7
	ground charter	208	0,6
Keywords	bids	2	0,006
	offices and services	2	0,006
informazioni descrittive *(Descriptive information)*	bibliotecheweb	12	0,035
Economia *(Economy)*	Giordano bruno library	2	0,006
	public relations offices	2	0,006
Titoli di pagina *(Page title)*	culture council	55	0,16
	culture, sports, tourism	35	0,10
Trasporto *(Transport)*	ground charter	28	0,08
	green areas	19	0,06
Turismo *(Tourism)*	self-certifications	4	0,012
	news archive	2	0,006
	news	2	0,006
Sport	public hygene	1	0,00

continued on following page

Table 11. Continued

Dimensions	PDs	Quot (freq)	%
Sanità *(Health)*	green areas	5	0,015
	self certifications	5	0,015
	restructuring of center for the elderly	4	0,012
Cultura *(Culture)*	Agenda	41	0,12
	Tickets	4	0,01
spazio giovani *(Space for the Youth)*	library	3	0,009
Lavoro *(Employment)*	norms	62	0,2
	municipi	56	0,2
	front desk for the disabled	53	0,2
	municipal police	46	0,1
Parigi	neighborhood laboratory (Eur)	5	0,015
	number of libraries	4	0,012

Table 12. Main characteristics of the Municipalities of Rome and Paris identified by means of the grid of analysis elaborated by de Rosa and Picone

Municipalities of Rome and Paris web sites both downloaded the 1st of April 2004	Strengths	Weaknesses
Municipality of Paris web site:www.paris.fr	- The logo is always the same in every page of the site - Fixed Structure - Site map is always available - multi-language version - Presence of combo box, jumps in navigation and bread crumbs - Flexible navigation - Long texts are split in paragraphs - Hypertext complexity	- No multimedia - Few utilities such as screensavers, wallpapers, short messages, on-line post cards, web telephony etc.. - No forums or chats, no FAQs - Little consistency of colors when indicating internal or external sites
Municipality of Rome web site:www.comune.roma.it	- High level of multimedia: animations, videos, audio - Utilities: short messages, on line newspapers, virtual library, on line addresses, Job Offers - Consistent colors for external and internal links - Multi-language Versions - Combo Box - Hypertext complexity - FAQ	- Logo is not always present in its complete version - Site map is hard to find - No fixed structure - Long texts are not split into paragraphs - No facilities, no *undo* and *redo* buttons - No forums or chat

of a link, but different colors are used for external (blue) or internal (red) links.

Finally, an important element that both sites have attained to is the *position, as elements positioned on the left are considered more important than those on the right (Burns, 2002).*

In the Municipalities of Rome and Paris websites, the logo and menu are in the upper left hand side.

Making a longitudinal comparison of results obtained from three analyses performed on the Municipality of Rome web site starting with a pilot study, no significant differences emerge:

- Graphics, multimedia level and technologies remained the same, but colors change from the 2003 version (which alternated complementary colors with contrasting colors) to the 2004 version (dominant colors are red and blue).
- Utilities remained the same.
- Usability of the site has not changed: a non fixed structure causes difficulties in finding searched information. Furthermore the low graphical and language consistency of several sections (i.e. some of different departments) confuses the user. Contents are not always displayed in a rational manner, making access to the site difficult for all users. For example, a non-expert user of the territorial-administrative structure of the city of Rome will hardly be able to find a valid support in the municipal web site; as a matter of fact, the division in *municipi* is not visible on the home page, and one must follow a complicated path *(city, municipi/hours/administrative decentralization/municipi)*. However, while in the 2003 version of the web site of the Municipality of Rome a static image could be found, characterized by the simple indication of *municipi,* in the 2004 version other than information on *municipi,* it is possible to enter each of them.
- Relatively to the interactivity of the web site, what improves is the level of consistency of colors used to mark external and internal sites. In every part of the site a high coherence is maintained. On the contrary, in the previous research a low level of consistency was noticed, in some sections blue indicated external links and in others internal links, and the same for the color red.

The results presented in this chapter can be considered a model, a tool for guiding different web professionals (webmasters, content developers, web designers etc.) and institutional communication managers of the city, based on the results offered by users and on a systematic analysis of contents, structure and technical-graphical modes of the analyzed sites.

Furthermore they have a value as historical parameter with respect to the evolution that followed the new scenarios of cross-media communication. In fact, given the volatile nature of web sites, due to the continuous evolution of technologies and contents, the results based on web sites downloaded in 2004 assume a particular interest for further currently ongoing comparative analysis.

Even if institutional communication—in countries like Italy and France—is still far from fully integrating "social networks" in public administration "official web sites," one should ask if, how, and to what extent the great social and aggregating impact of web 2.0 technological developments push Institutional web sites to direct towards different forms of interactivity, virtual sociality and interface between public administration and citizens. For this reason the grid of analyses we designed in 2003 has been updated in 2010 according to the evolution both of technologies and their social use.

Due to space limits we will only comment a single feature (multi-language accessibility of the web site) - in continuity with the elements already explored and discussed in this chapter – directly deducible from the comparison between the home pages of the Municipalities of Rome and Paris downloaded on May 13 2010 (see Figure 9 and Figure 10) relatively to the implicitly privileged target according to the communication strategy used:

Figure 9. Image from the home page of www.paris.fr (retrieved on May 13, 2010)

Figure 10. Image from the home page of www.comune.roma.it (retrieved on May 13, 2010)

- in the home page of the Municipality of Rome web site there is no possibility of a multi-language access to the web site and this is limited to the section dedicated to tourism, even if it is now enriched with new linguistic versions: English, French German, Spanish and Chinese. This communication strategy for the site in general (and not only for the section on tourism) reveals an orientation towards a target of mainly Italian citizens, even if Rome is a cosmopolitan city that hosts many and large foreign communities and immigrants from every part of the world. Furthermore, even access for tourists is not facilitated by the presence of multi-lingual channels in the section for tourism starting from the home page.
- On the contrary, in the upper right hand side of the Home Page of the Municipality of Paris web site a multi-language access

to the site is available, even if limited to English and Spanish versions.

This is a short example that shows the importance of the communicational choices an e-branding strategies also on behalf of "institutional" web sites, other than commercial ones and offers interesting research material.

This research can be used as a prototype for further research aimed at comparing Municipal web sites of European Historical Capitals, but also for analyzing and comparing "official" web sites of capitals, cities and small urban centers in other cultural contexts and continents (such as America, Asia, Australia) characterized by a different development and impact of the Internet on "institutional" communication and its use on behalf of citizens.

Key questions that web professionals and heads of institutional communication departments of "cities" could ask themselves on the basis of studies and research of this kind, are:

a. if cities could talk and present themselves to citizens, tourists, potential visitors, would they say the same things their official web sites say, and in which manner? Would they like to have the same "Visiting card" their administrators have designed?
b. on the other hand, would citizens, tourists, potential visitors, according to their culture, social status, and age and relatively to their needs and expectations like to find the same contents of those "officially" communicated and in the same way?

Asking these kind of questions and trying to give non impressive answers, but based on systematic studies, could help to find effective solutions, with a strong impact also in terms of web-marketing of the city. Cities, and in particular historical capitals, with their places, monuments, museums, restaurants, churches, schools, universities, urban services, architecture, parks and urban green areas, shops and shopping centers, centers, suburbs, in continuous evolution in time and space are of crucial importance for e-branding strategies of both sections on tourism and for citizens.

REFERENCES

Ardone, R. G., de Rosa, A. S., & Bonnes, M. (1987). Aspetti soggettivi nella valutazione della qualità del proprio ambiente residenziale. In Mayer, V., & Meran, R. (Eds.), *Il Laboratorio e la città* (*Vol. II*, pp. 143–148). Milano, Italy: Guerini & Associati.

Ardone, R. G., de Rosa, A. S., Bonnes, M., & Secchiaroli, G. (1987). Dimensioni valutative del proprio quartiere di residenza, per uno studio di congruenza ambientale. In Bianchi, E., Perussia, F., & Rossi, M. F. (Eds.), *Immagine soggettiva e ambiente. Problemi, applicazioni e strategie di ricerca* (pp. 207–218). Milano, Italy: Unicopli.

Bonnes, M., Bonaiuto, M., Ercolani, A. P., & de Rosa, A. S. (1991a). Residential Satisfaction in the big city: a transactional contextual study. In Bonnes, M. (Ed.), *UNESCO programme on man and the biosphere, MAB Project 11 urban ecology applied to the city of Rome* (pp. 127–148).

Bonnes, M., Bonaiuto, M., Ercolani, A. P., & de Rosa, A. S. (1991b). Soddisfazione residenziale nell'ambiente urbano: Un approccio contestuale-dinamico. *Rassegna di Psicologia, 3*, 49-81. ISSN: 1125-5196 E141492

Bonnes, M., de Rosa, A. S., Ardone, R. G., & Bagnasco, C. (1990). Perceived quality of residential environment and urban green area. *Braun-Blanquetia, 3,* 54-62. ISSN: 0393-5434 E185631

Boscarol, M. (2000, November 11). *Che cos'è l'usabilità dei siti web*. Retrieved May 23, 2010, from http://www.usabile.it/ 012000.htm#ixzz0oHO360Jk

Boscarol, M. (2001, May 17). *I decaloghi dell'usabilità.* Retrieved May 23, 2010, from http://www.usabile.it/articoli.htm

Boscarol, M. (2003). *Ecologia dei siti web. Come e perché usabilità, accessibilità e fogli di stile stanno cambiando il modo di realizzare i siti internet.* Milano, Italy: Hops Libri.

Boscarol, M. (2003, September 25). *Quando il tempo di caricamento è troppo lento? Tempi di risposta e aspettative dell'utente.* Retrieved May 23, 2010, from http://www.usabile.it/articoli.htm

Burns, J. (2002). *Web design. Navigare, creare, gestire la rete.* Milano, Italy: Jackson Libri.

Buti Bandini, L., Cosenza, G., & Massarutto, L. (2002). *Ergonomia del web. Gli utenti, la rete, i contenuti, i siti e le pagine.* Milano, Italy: Il Sole 24 Ore Ed.

Calegari, R. (2000). Aspetti psico-sociali della rivoluzione comunicazionale. *Congresso Divisione Psicologia Sociale.* Associazione Italiana di Psicologia, (Parma, 25-27 Settembre 2000).

Cantoni, L., Di Blase, N., & Bolchini, D. (2003). *Comunicazione, qualità, usabilità.* Milano, Italy: Apogeo.

Castells, M. (1996, 2000). *The rise of the network society.* Oxford, UK: Blackwell.

Castells, M. (2001). *Internet galaxy.* Oxford, UK: Oxford University Press.

Comolli, F., & Condello, C. (2000). *Note sulla creazione di siti web.* Retrieved May 23, 2010, from http://www.manuali.it

de Rosa, A. S. (1990). Per un approccio multimetodo allo studio delle Rappresentazioni Sociali. *Rassegna di Psicologia, 3,* 101–152.

de Rosa, A. S. (1993). Social representations and attitudes: Problems of coherences between the theoretical definition and procedure of research. *Papers on Social Representations, 3*(2), 178–192.

de Rosa, A. S. (1994). From theory to meta-theory in S.R.: The lines of argument of a theoretical-methodological debate. *Social Science Information, 33*(2), 273-304. ISSN: 0539-0184

de Rosa, A. S. (1995). Psicologia del turismo: Per una psicologia sociale dell'ambiente applicata. In Zani, B. (Ed.), *Le dimensioni della psicologia sociale* (pp. 153–186). Bologna, Italy: Il Mulino.

de Rosa, A. S. (1997). Turisti di sei nazionalità per la prima volta nella città eterna: Place identity e rappresentazioni sociali di Roma e del suo centro storico. In A. Nenci (Ed.), *Conoscere e rappresentare la città* (pp. 149-214). Padova, Italy: ed. Cedam. ISBN: 8813200935

de Rosa, A. S. (2002). Le besoin d'une théorie de la méthode. In Garnier, C. (Ed.), *Les formes de la pensée sociale* (pp. 151–187). Paris, France: P.U.F.

de Rosa, A. S. (2006). "¿Por qué es importante?" Notas inspiradas en una Mirada reflexiva a la teoria de las representaciones sociales. In Valencia Abundiz, S. (Ed.), *Representaciones sociales. Alteridad, epistemologia y movimientos sociales* (pp. 79–173). Guadalajara, Mexico: Universidad de Guadalajara.

de Rosa, A. S. (2006). Paris – Rome: Contexts transformations, dynamics images and identity continuity of the twin capitals in people and media. *Proceedings 8th International Conference on Social Representations: Media and Society. Key Lecture Thematic Area: Social Representations, National and Supranational Identity in the Media and Society* (p. 437). (Roma, 28th August – 1st September 2006).

de Rosa, A. S. (2012in press). Place-identity and Social Representations of historical capital cities: Rome through the eyes of first-visitors from six nationalities. In de Rosa, A. S. (Ed.), *Social Representations in the "social arena": the theory in contexts faced with "social demand".* New York, London: Routledge.

de Rosa, A. S., Antonelli, T., & Calogero, A. (1995). Roma immaginata e Roma vissuta nelle rappresentazioni sociali di turisti di sei nazionalità. In V. Cinanni, R. Virdi & G. Fumai (Eds.), *Ambiente, Salute, Cultura* (pp. 137-155). Roma, Italy: Kappa ed. ISBN: 8878901733

de Rosa, A. S., Ardone, R. G., & Bonnes, M. (1987). Rappresentazione dell'ambiente urbano e 'place-identity'. In V. Mayer & R. Meran (a cura di), *Il Laboratorio e la città.* Milano, Italy: Guerini & Associati. (vol. I, pp. 519-527). ISBN: 8878020494

de Rosa, A. S., & Bocci, E. (2001a). Sul potere persuasivo della comunicazione via Internet: E-commerce e turismo. In Olivetti Belardinelli, M. (Ed.), *Orientamenti della ricerca in Italia sullo sviluppo e l'adattamento psicosociale. Valentini Day 12 Gennaio 2001* (pp. 378–387). Roma, Italy: Edizioni Kappa.

de Rosa, A. S., & Bocci, E. (2001b). E-commerce e turismo: Comprare pacchetti di viaggio su Internet o in Agenzia? In L. Greco (Ed.), *Accessibilità e turismo: problemi e metodologie di analisi* (pp. 85-106). Collana di Pubblicazioni – Ricerche Università di Siena /n° 1-2001.

de Rosa, A. S., & Bocci, E. (2002). E-branding strategies and development of the e-commerce and tourism: The case of Italian tour operators. *International Business & Economics Research Journal, 1*(10), 11-24. ISSN: 1535-0754 E187253

de Rosa, A. S., & Bocci, E. (2005). Rappresentazioni Sociali e turismo: Canali tradizionali e nuovi media a confronto nella ricerca di pacchetti di viaggio. In Sangiorgi, G. (Ed.), *Turista e turismi. Contributi psicologici allo sviluppo del settore* (pp. 173–190). Cagliari, Italy: Cuec.

de Rosa, A. S., Bocci, E., & Saurini, S. (2006). Risk perception as a motivational barrier for online purchasing. In Zappalà, S., & Gray, C. (Eds.), *Impact of e-commerce on consumers and small firms* (pp. 235–248). London, UK: Ashgate.

de Rosa, A. S., Bonaiuto, M., Calogero, A., & Antonelli, T. (1992a). Imaginary and experential levels in social representations of Rome in people coming from six countries: Empirical approach to the place-identity theory. *Joint Meeting of European Association of Experimental Social Psychology and the Society for Experimental Social Psychology,* (Belgium, Leuven, 15-18 July 1992).

de Rosa, A. S., Bonaiuto, M., Calogero, A., & Antonelli, T. (1992b). Place-identity and social representations of Rome in people coming from six countries. *Joint Meeting of Association pour la Recherche Interculturelle* (*IV International Congress*) and *IACCP* (*XI International Congress*), (Belgium, University of Liège, 15- 18 July 1992).

de Rosa, A. S., Bonaiuto, M., Calogero, A., & Antonelli, T. (1992c). *Social representations of Rome and its historic centre in people coming from six countries: Place-identity and social identity.* 1st International Conference on Social Representations, (Ravello, 3-5 Ottobre 1992).

de Rosa, A. S., Calogero, T., & Antonelli, T. (1992). Rome through the eyes of tourists from six nationalities. *Proceedings of the International Conference of IACCP,* (Liege, July 1992).

de Rosa, A. S., & D'Ambrosio, M. L. (2009). *Universi semantici tra luoghi immaginati e luoghi esperiti: first visitor italiani in sei capitali europee.* V Congresso ARIPT Psicologia, ambiente e salute per un turismo di qualità, (Viterbo-Tarquinia, 15-17 Ottobre 2009).

de Rosa, A. S., & D'Ambrosio, M. L. (2010). *First-visitors in European Capitals: Imagined and experienced places before and after their first visit.* Paper presented at Symposium Social Representations of Urban Places: Images, Memory and Identity organised by Annamaria de Rosa. 10th International Conference on Social Representations: Representations, Knowledge Transmission and Social Transformations, (Tunis, Tunisia 05th - 8th July 2010).

de Rosa, A. S., Nenci, A., & Testa, G. (1995). L'esperienza del quartiere di residenza nelle rappresentazioni degli abitanti: il caso di tre quartieri di Roma. In V. Cinanni, R. Virdi & G. Fumai (Eds.), *Ambiente, salute, cultura* (pp. 156-171). Roma, Italy: Kappa ed. ISBN: 8878901733

de Rosa, A. S., & Picone, M. (2007). The European Ph.D. on social representations and communication: Integrating virtual and physical mobility via the European Ph.D. Web-auditorium. In A. Boonen, & W. Van Petegem (Eds.) *European networking and learning for the future*. Antwerp, Belgium: Garant. (pp. 147-159). ISBN: 978-90-441- 2256-5

Ericsson, K., & Simon, H. (1987). Verbal reports on thinking. In C. Faerch & G. Kasper (Eds.), *Introspection in second language research.* Clevedon, Avon: Multilingual Matters. (pp. 24–54).

Ericsson, K., & Simon, H. (1993). *Protocol analysis: Verbal reports as data* (2nd ed.). Boston, MA: MIT Press.

Farr, R. M., & Moscovici, S. (Eds.). (1984). *Social representations*. Cambridge, UK: Cambridge University Press.

Farr, R. M., & Moscovici, S. (Eds.). (1989). *Rappresentazioni sociali. Problemi e prospettive*. Bologna, Italy: Il Mulino.

Formenti, C. (2000). *Incantati dalla rete*. Milano, Italy: Raffaello Cortina Editore.

Hannu, K., & Pallab, P. (2000). A comparison of concurrent and retrospective verbal protocol analysis. *The American Journal of Psychology, 113*(3), 387–404. doi:10.2307/1423365

Hass, V. (2004). Les cartes cognitives: un outil pour étudier la ville sous ses dimensions socio-historique et affectives. *Bulletin de Psychologie, 474*, 621–633.

Hass, V., & Jodelet, D. (2000). La mémoire, ses aspects sociaux et collectifs. In Roussiau, N. (Ed.), *Psychologie sociale* (pp. 121–134). Rennes, France: P. U. de Rennes.

ISO. (2010). *ISO 9241-10: Ergonomic requirements for office work with visual display terminals (VDTs) – Dialog principles.* Retrieved May 23, 2010, from http://web.tiscali.it/userware

Jodelet, D. (1982). Les représentations socio-spatiales de la ville. In Derycke, P. H. (Ed.), *Conception de l'espace, recherche pluridisciplinaire de l'Université Paris X.* Nanterre.

Jodelet, D. (Ed.). (1989). *Les representations sociales*. Paris, France: Presses Universitaires de France.

Lévy, P. (1996). *L'intelligenza collettiva. Per una antropologia del cyberspazio*. Milano, Italy: Feltrinelli.

Lévy, P. (1997). *Il Virtuale*. Milano, Italy: Raffaello Cortina Editore.

Lévy, P. (2000). *WorldPhilosophie*. Paris, France: Éditions Odile Jacob.

Lévy, P. (2002). *Cyberdémocratie*. Paris, France: Éditions Odile Jacob.

Lewis, C., & Rieman, J. (1993, 1994). *Task-centered user interface design: A practical introduction*. Retrieved May 29, 2010, from http://grouplab.cpsc.ucalgary.ca/ saul/hci_topics/tcsd-book/ chap-1_v-1.html

Lewis, C. H. (1982). *Using the thinking aloud method in cognitive interface design*. (Technical Report IBM RC-9265).

Limone, D. A., Preite, G., & Mancarella, M. (2008). *Turismatica. Un nuovo paradigma della società dell'informazione*. Trento, Italy: Uniservice.

Maldonado, T. (1997). *Critica della ragione informatica*. Milano, Italy: Feltrinelli.

Mantovani, G. (2000). *Ergonomia*. Bologna, Italy: Il Mulino.

Mc Luhan, M. (1989). *The global village*. Oxford, UK: Oxford University Press.

Mitchell, W. J. (1999). *E-topia: Urban life, Jim - But not as we know it*. Cambridge, MA: MIT Press.

Moscovici, S. (1961). *La psychanalyse son image et son public. Etude sur la répresentation sociale de la psychanalyse*. Paris, France: Presses Universitaires de France.

Moscovici, S. (1989). Des représentations collectives aux représentations sociales: éléments pour une histoire. In Jodelet, D. (Ed.), *Les représentations sociales* (pp. 62–86). Paris, France: Presses Universitaires de France.

Moscovici, S., & Duveen, G. (Eds.). (2000). *Social representations. Explorations in social psychology*. Cambridge, UK: Polity Press.

Nenci, A. M., de Rosa, A. S., Testa, G., & Carrus, G. (2003). Social and architectural legibility of the city. In Moser, G., Pol, E., Bernard, Y., Bonnes, M., Corraliza, J. A., & Giuliani, M. V. (Eds.), *People, places and sustainability* (pp. 25–37). Gottingen, Germany: Hogrefe & Huber Publishers.

Nielsen, J. (1994). Heuristics for users interface design. In Nielsen, J., & Mack, R. L. (Eds.), *Usability inspection methods*. New York, NY: John Wiley & Sons.

Nielsen, J. (2000). *Web usability*. Milano, Italy: Edizioni Apogeo.

Nielsen, J., & Loranger, H. (2006). *Web usability 2.0. L'usabilità che conta*. Milano, Italy: Edizioni Apogeo.

Nielsen, J., & Tahir, M. (2002). *Homepage usability*. Milano, Italy: Edizioni Apogeo.

Picone, M. (2006). Interview. In M. Armemi (Ed.), *Communicating physics*. (pp.173-174). Roma, Italy: 2adigroma Editore.

Proshansky, H. M., Fabian, K., & Kaminoff, R. (1983). Place-identity: Physical world socialization of the self. *Journal of Environmental Psychology*, *3*, 57–83. doi:10.1016/S0272-4944(83)80021-8

Sentinelli, M. (2003). *Usabilità dei nuovi media*. Roma, Italy: Carocci Editore.

Slouka, M. (1995). *War of the worlds: Cyberspace and the high-tech assault on reality*. New York, NY: Basic Books.

Stokinger, P. (2002). *La description-évaluation de sites web*. Séminaire dans la cadre du DESS Webmestre Editorial à l'UFR Sciences humaines et Arts de l'Université de Poitiers.

Turkle, S. (1985). *Il secondo io*. Milano, Italy: Frassinelli.

Turkle, S. (1995). *Life on the screen. Identity in the age of the Internet*. New York, NY: Simon & Schuster.

Turkle, S. (1996). Virtuality and its discontents: Searching for community in cyberspace. *The American Prospect*, *7*, 24.

Visciola, M. (2000). *Usabilità dei Siti Web*. Milano, Italy: Edizioni Apogeo.

Wolton, D. (1999). *Internet et après. Une tbéorie critique des nottveaux medias*. Paris, France: Flammarion.

ENDNOTES

1 We thank dr. Sara Saurini and dr. Ilaria Botti for their assistance in the research programme.

2 The *think-aloud method* was introduced in the usability field by Clayton Lewis (1982) while he was at IBM, and is explained in *Task-Centered User Interface Design: A Practical Introduction* by C. Lewis and J. Rieman. The method was further refined by Ericsson and Simon (1987, 1993) and more recently by Hannu and Pallab (2000), who have proposed to divide the *think-aloud protocol* in two different experimental procedures: the first focused on the concurrent thinking aloud protocol, collected during the decision task; the second focused on the retrospective thinking aloud protocol gathered after the decision task. Think aloud protocols involve participants thinking aloud as they are performing a set of specified tasks. Users are asked to say whatever they are looking at, thinking, doing, and feeling, as they go about their task. This enables observers to see first-hand the process of task completion (rather than only its final product). Observers at such a test are asked to objectively take notes of everything that users say, without attempting to interpret their actions and words. The purpose of this method is to make explicit what is implicitly present in subjects who are able to perform a specific task.

3 The * designates the words without an ending in order to regroup the word's various forms (singular/plural, feminine/masculine etc.) into one single category.

Compilation of References

Aaker, D. A. (1996). *Building strong brands*. New York, NY: Free Press.

Aaker, J. L. (1997). Dimensions of brand personality. *JMR, Journal of Marketing Research*, *34*(August), 347–356. doi:10.2307/3151897

Aaker, D. A. (1991). *Managing brand equity: Capitalizing on the value of a brand name*. New York, NY: Free Press.

Aaker, J. L. (1997). Dimensions of brand personality. *JMR, Journal of Marketing Research*, *34*(August), 347–356. doi:10.2307/3151897

Abbott, M., Shackleton, J. P., & Holland, R. (2007). *Brand as category: An analysis of categorisation and branded product concepts*. IASDR 07 Conference, International Association of Societies of Design Research, The Hong Kong Polytechnic University, 12th-15th November, 2007.

Ackerman, L. D. (2000). *Identity is destiny: Leadership and the roots of value creation* (p. 8). San Francisco, CA: Berrett-Koehler Publishers, Inc.

Acosta, P., & Devasagayam, R. (2010). Brand cult: Extending the notion of brand community. *Marketing Management Journal*, *20*(1), 165–176.

Adams, M. A., Marshall, S. J., Dillon, L., Caparosa, S., Ramirez, E., Phillips, J., & Norman, G. J. (2009). A theory-based framework for evaluating exergames as persuasive technology. In the *Proceedings of the 4th International Conference on Persuasive Technology*. Association for Computing Machinery.

Adkins, S. S. (2009). *Innovation in educational technology: The virtualization of K-12 and higher education*. Webinar. Elluminate Series.

Ahmed, Z. U., Johnson, J. P., Ling, C. P., Fong, T. W., & Hui, A. K. (2002). Country-of-origin and brand effects on consumers' evaluations of cruise lines. *International Marketing Review*, *19*(2/3), 279–302. doi:10.1108/02651330210430703

Ailawadi, K. L., Baker, W. E., Sciglimpaglia, D., & Saghafi, M. (2010). Branding of post-purchase ancillary products and services: An application in the mobile communications industry. *European Journal of Marketing*, *44*(5), 547–566. doi:10.1108/03090561011032261

Alden, D. L., Steenkamp, J.-B. E. M., & Batra, R. (2006). Consumer attitudes toward marketplace globalization: Structure, antecedents and consequences. *International Journal of Research in Marketing*, *23*(3), 227–239. doi:10.1016/j.ijresmar.2006.01.010

Ali-Sulaiti, K. I., & Baker, M. J. (1998). Country of origin effects: A literature review. *Marketing Intelligence & Planning*, *16*(3), 150–199. doi:10.1108/02634509810217309

Allen, C. T., Fournier, S., & Miller, F. (2008). Brands and their meaning makers. In Haugtvedt, C. P., Herr, P. M., & Kardes, F. R. (Eds.), *Handbook of consumer psychology* (pp. 781–821). New York, NY: Psychology Press.

Alsem, K. J., & Kostelijk, E. (2008). Identity based marketing: A new balanced marketing paradigm. *European Journal of Marketing*, *42*(9/10), 907–914. doi:10.1108/03090560810891064

Al-Sulaiti, K. I., & Baker, M. J. (1998). Country of origin effects: A literature review. *Marketing Intelligence & Planning*, *16*(3), 150–199. doi:10.1108/02634509810217309

American Banker/Gallup. (2004). What Americans think about overseas outsourcing. *Consumer Survey*. Retrieved June 1, 2009, from http://www.americanbanker.com/

American Marketing Association. (2009). Resource library: Definitions. Retrieved July 2, 2009, from http://www.marketingpower.com/ _layouts/Dictionary.aspx?dLetter=B

Anderson, E. W., & Sullivan, M. W. (1993). The antecedents and consequences of customer satisfaction for firms. *Marketing Science*, *12*(2), 125–143. doi:10.1287/mksc.12.2.125

Anderson, R. I. (2000). Making an e-business conceptualization and design process more user-centered. *Interaction*, *7*(4), 27–30. doi:10.1145/345190.345235

Anderson, J. R., & Bower, G. H. (1973). *Human associative memory*. Washington, DC: Winston & Sons.

Ardone, R. G., de Rosa, A. S., Bonnes, M., & Secchiaroli, G. (1987). Dimensioni valutative del proprio quartiere di residenza, per uno studio di congruenza ambientale. In Bianchi, E., Perussia, F., & Rossi, M. F. (Eds.), *Immagine soggettiva e ambiente. Problemi, applicazioni e strategie di ricerca* (pp. 207–218). Milano, Italy: Unicopli.

Ardone, R. G., de Rosa, A. S., & Bonnes, M. (1987). Aspetti soggettivi nella valutazione della qualità del proprio ambiente residenziale. In Mayer, V., & Meran, R. (Eds.), *Il Laboratorio e la città* (*Vol. II*, pp. 143–148). Milano, Italy: Guerini & Associati.

Arora, R., & Stoner, C. (1996). The effect of perceived service quality and name familiarity on the service selection decision. *Journal of Services Marketing*, *10*(1), 22. doi:10.1108/08876049610106699

Arruda. (2007). Career advice. Retrieved from www.msn.careerbuilder.com/ custom/msn/careeradvice/ viewarticle.aspx?

Astolfi, L., Fallani, F., Serenella, S., Cincotti, F., Mattia, D., Marciani, M. G., Soranzo, R., & Babiloni, F. (2008). Brain activity related to the memorization of TV commercials. *International Journal of Bioelectromagnetism*, *10*(2), 77-79-86.

Azoulay, A., & Kapferer, J.-N. (2003). Do brand personality scales really measure brand personality? *Journal of Brand Management*, *11*(2), 143–155. doi:10.1057/palgrave.bm.2540162

Bagozzi, R. P., & Dholakia, U. M. (2006). Intentional social action in virtual communities. *Journal of Interactive Marketing*, *16*(2), 2–21. doi:10.1002/dir.10006

Baker, D. B. (2006). Privacy and security in public health: Maintaining the delicate balance between personal privacy and population safety. In the *Proceedings of the 22nd Annual Computer Security Applications Conference* (pp. 3–22). IEEE.

Baldini, M. (2003). *Popper e Benetton: Epistemologia per gli imprenditori e gli economisti*. Roma, Italy: Armando.

Barker, S., & Härtel, C. E. J. (2004). Intercultural service encounters: An exploratory study of customer experiences. *Cross Cultural Management*, *11*(1), 3–14. doi:10.1108/13527600410797710

Barthes, R. (1964). Eléments de sémiologie. *Communications*.

Barthes, R. (1964). Rhétorique de l'image. *Communications*.

Baudrillard, J. (1988). *Selected writings. Translated by Mark Poster*. Stanford, CA: Stanford University Press.

Bearden, W. O., & Teel, J. E. (1983). Selected determinants of consumer satisfaction and complaint reports. *The Journal of Consumer Research*, *20*(1), 21–28.

Benavent, C. (2006). The impact of loyalty schemes on repeat purchase behaviour. *Journal of Marketing Management*, *22*, 61–88. doi:10.1362/026725706776022308

Bernays, E. (1928). *Propaganda*. New York, NY: Liveright.

Bernays, E. (1955). *The engineering of consent*. Norman, OK: University of Oklahoma Press.

Berry, L. L. (2000). Cultivating service brand equity. *Journal of the Academy of Marketing Science*, *28*(1), 128–137. doi:10.1177/0092070300281012

Bharadwaj, N., & Roggeveen, A. L. (2008). The impact of offshored and outsourced call service centers on customer appraisals. *Marketing Letters*, *19*(1), 13–23. doi:10.1007/s11002-007-9025-y

Bhattacharya, C. B., & Korschun, D. (2008). Stakeholder marketing: Beyond the four Ps and the customer. *Journal of Public Policy & Marketing*, *27*(1), 113–116. doi:10.1509/jppm.27.1.113

Blackmore, D., DeSouza, R., Young, A., Goodness, E., & Silliman, R. (2005). *Forecast: IT outsourcing, worldwide, 2002-2008*. Gartner.

Blain, C., Levy, S. E., & Ritchie, J. R. B. (2005). Destination branding: Insights and practices from destination management organizations. *Journal of Travel Research*, *43*(4), 328–338. doi:10.1177/0047287505274646

Bloch, P. H. (1986). The product enthusiast: Implications for marketing strategy. *Journal of Consumer Marketing*, *3*(3), 51–62. doi:10.1108/eb008170

Bolchini, D., Garzotto, F., & Paolini, P. (2007). *Branding and communication goals for content-intensive interactive applications*. 15th IEEE International Requirements Engineering Conference (pp. 173–182). IEEE.

Bonnes, M., Bonaiuto, M., Ercolani, A. P., & de Rosa, A. S. (1991a). Residential Satisfaction in the big city: a transactional contextual study. In Bonnes, M. (Ed.), *UNESCO programme on man and the biosphere, MAB Project 11 urban ecology applied to the city of Rome* (pp. 127–148).

Bonnes, M., Bonaiuto, M., Ercolani, A. P., & de Rosa, A. S. (1991b). Soddisfazione residenziale nell'ambiente urbano: Un approccio contestuale-dinamico. *Rassegna di Psicologia, 3*, 49-81. ISSN: 1125-5196 E141492

Bonnes, M., de Rosa, A. S., Ardone, R. G., & Bagnasco, C. (1990). Perceived quality of residential environment and urban green area. *Braun-Blanquetia, 3,* 54-62. ISSN: 0393-5434 E185631

Boscarol, M. (2003). *Ecologia dei siti web. Come e perché usabilità, accessibilità e fogli di stile stanno cambiando il modo di realizzare i siti internet*. Milano, Italy: Hops Libri.

Boscarol, M. (2000, November 11). *Che cos'è l'usabilità dei siti web*. Retrieved May 23, 2010, from http://www.usabile.it/ 012000.htm#ixzz0oHO360Jk

Boscarol, M. (2001, May 17). *I decaloghi dell'usabilità*. Retrieved May 23, 2010, from http://www.usabile.it/articoli.htm

Boscarol, M. (2003, September 25). *Quando il tempo di caricamento è troppo lento? Tempi di risposta e aspettative dell'utente*. Retrieved May 23, 2010, from http://www.usabile.it/articoli.htm

Bourdieu, P. (1977). *Outline of a theory of practice*. Cambridge, UK: Cambridge University Press.

Bourdieu, P. (1984). *Distinction: A social critique of the judgment of taste* (Nice, R., Trans.). Cambridge, MA: Harvard University Press.

Brace-Govan, J., & de Burgh-Woodman, H. (2008). Sneakers and street culture: A postcolonial analysis of marginalized cultural consumption. *Consumption Markets & Culture*, *11*(2), 93–112. doi:10.1080/10253860802033639

Brady, D. (2007). Creating brand you. *Business Week, 4047*, 72-73.

Brand, R. R., & Cronin, J. J. (1997). Consumer-specific determinants of the size of retail choice sets: an empirical comparison of physical goods and service providers. *Journal of Services Marketing*, *11*(1), 19–38. doi:10.1108/08876049710158349

Brand Channel. (2009). *Online branding, glossary section*. Retrieved September 29, 2009, from http://www.brandchannel.com/ education_glossary.asp

Briggs, B. (2005). Offshore outsourcing poses risks. *Health Data Management*, *13*(2), 68–78.

British Petroleum. (n.d.). *Homepage*. Retrieved from www.bp.com/US

Brown, S. P., & Chin, W. W. (2004). Satisfying and retaining customers through independent service representatives. *Decision Sciences*, *35*(3), 527–550. doi:10.1111/j.0011-7315.2004.02534.x

Brunetti, G. (2004). *Benetton: da United Colors a edizione holding*. Torino, Italy: Utet.

Bryant, Y. (2008). Relationship between exposure to rap music videos and attitudes towards relationship among African American youth. *The Journal of Black Psychology*, *34*(3), 356–380. doi:10.1177/0095798408314141

Burns, J. (2002). *Web design. Navigare, creare, gestire la rete*. Milano, Italy: Jackson Libri.

Busacca, B. (1994). *Le risorse di fiducia dell'impresa* (pp. 73–74). Turin, Italy: UTET.

Butcher, K., Sparks, B., & O'Callaghan, F. (2001). Evaluative and relational influences on service loyalty. *International Journal of Service Industry Management, 12*(4), 310–327. doi:10.1108/09564230110405253

Buti Bandini, L., Cosenza, G., & Massarutto, L. (2002). *Ergonomia del web. Gli utenti, la rete, i contenuti, i siti e le pagine.* Milano, Italy: Il Sole 24 Ore Ed.

Butler, P., & Collins, N. (1999). A conceptual framework for political marketing. In Newman, B. I. (Ed.), *Handbook of political marketing* (pp. 55–72). Thousand Oaks, CA: Sage Publications.

Buttle, F. (2009). *Customer relationship management: Concepts and techniques*. Oxford, UK: Butterworth-Hinemann.

Calder, B. J., Malthouse, E. C., & Schaedel, U. (2009). An experimental study of the relationship between online engagement and advertising effectiveness. *Journal of Interactive Marketing, 23*(4), 321–331. doi:10.1016/j.intmar.2009.07.002

Caldwell, N., & Friere, J. R. (2004). The differences between branding a country, a region and a city: Applying the brand box model. *Journal of Brand Management, 12*(1), 50. doi:10.1057/palgrave.bm.2540201

Calegari, R. (2000). Aspetti psico-sociali della rivoluzione comunicazionale. *Congresso Divisione Psicologia Sociale.* Associazione Italiana di Psicologia, (Parma, 25-27 Settembre 2000).

Cantoni, L., Di Blase, N., & Bolchini, D. (2003). *Comunicazione, qualità, usabilità*. Milano, Italy: Apogeo.

Castells, M. (2001). *Internet galaxy*. Oxford, UK: Oxford University Press.

Castells, M. (1996, 2000). *The rise of the network society.* Oxford, UK: Blackwell.

Chang, W.-L. (2008). *Using multi-attribute utility theory to rank and select co-branding partners*. Eighth International Conference on Intelligent Systems Design and Applications (pp. 195–200). IEEE.

Chao, P. (1993a). Partitioning country-of-origin effects: Consumer evaluations of a hybrid product. *Journal of International Business Studies, 24*(2), 291–306. doi:10.1057/palgrave.jibs.8490851

Chao, P. (2001). The moderating effects of country of assembly, country of parts, and country of design on hybrid product evaluations. *Journal of Advertising, 30*(4), 67–81.

Chaplin, L. N., & Roedder John, D. (2005). The development of self-brand connections in children and adolescents. *The Journal of Consumer Research, 32*(1), 119–129. doi:10.1086/426622

Chaudhuri, A. (2006). *Emotion and reason in consumer behavior*. Amsterdam, The Netherlands: Butterworth-Hinemann.

Chebat, J.-C., Davidow, M., & Codjovi, I. (2005). Silent voices: Why some dissatisfied consumers fail to complain. *Journal of Service Research, 7*(4), 328–342. doi:10.1177/1094670504273965

Chen, Y.-H., Wu, J.-J., & Chung, Y.-S. (2008). Cultural impact on trust: A comparison of virtual communities in China, Hong Kong and Taiwan. *Journal of Global Information Technology Management, 11*(1), 28–48.

Chernatony, L. d., Harris, F. J., & Christodoulides, G. (2004). Developing a brand performance measure for financial services brands. *The Service Industries Journal, 24*(2), 15–33. doi:10.1080/0264206041233l301232

Chevron, J. R. (1998). The Delphi process: A strategic branding methodology. *Journal of Consumer Marketing, 15*(3), 254–264. doi:10.1108/07363769810219125

Clark, T., Rajaratnam, D., & Smith, T. (1996). Toward a theory of international services: Marketing insights in a world of nations. *Journal of International Marketing, 4*(2), 9–28.

Clarkson, M. B. E. (1995). A stakeholder framework for analysing and evaluating corporate social performance. *Academy of Management Review, 20*(1), 92–117.

Clott, C. B. (2004). Perspectives on global outsourcing and the changing nature of work. *Business and Society Review, 109*(2), 153–170. doi:10.1111/j.0045-3609.2004.00189.x

Collins, D. (2001). The branding of management knowledge: Rethinking management fads. *Journal of Organizational Change Management*, *16*(2), 186–204. doi:10.1108/09534810310468152

Comolli, F., & Condello, C. (2000). *Note sulla creazione di siti web.* Retrieved May 23, 2010, from http://www.manuali.it

ContactBabel. (2004). Finding the balance: The effect of offshore customer contact on profit and brand. Retrieved June 1, 2009, from http://www.contactbabel.com/

Corbett, M. F. (2003, June 18). Outsourcing's future. *Fortune*, S1–S6.

Corbett, M. F. (2002). *Outsourcing's next wave*.

Cornell, C. (2004). Offshore options: Outsourcing operations to overseas providers can save you money or cause you pain. The choice is yours. *Profit*, *23*(4), 87–88.

Coulter, R. A., Feick, L., & Price, L. L. (2003). Rethinking the origins of involvement and brand commitment: Insights from post-Socialist Central Europe. *The Journal of Consumer Research*, *30*(2), 151–169. doi:10.1086/376809

Cox Edmondson, V. (2008). A preliminary review of competitive reactions in the hip-hop music industry – Black American entrepreneurs in a new industry. *Management Research News*, *33*(9), 637–649. doi:10.1108/01409170810898536

Crié, D. (2003). Consumers' complaint behaviour. Taxonomy, typology and determinants: Towards a unified ontology. *Database Marketing & Customer Strategy Management*, *11*(1), 60–79. doi:10.1057/palgrave.dbm.3240206

Cunningham, R. M. (1956). Brand loyalty-What, where, how much? *Harvard Business Review*, *34*(1), 116–128.

Cunningham, R. M. (1961). Customer loyalty to store and brand. *Harvard Business Review*, *39*(6), 127–137.

Curtis, J. (2001). Branding a dtate: The evolution of brand Oregon. *Journal of Vacation Marketing*, *7*(1), 75–81. doi:10.1177/135676670100700107

Czellar, S. (2003). Consumer attitude toward brand extensions: an integrative model and research propositions. *International Journal of Research in Marketing*, *20*, 97. doi:10.1016/S0167-8116(02)00124-6

Dahrendorf, R. (1958). Homo sociologicus: On the history, significance, and limits of the category of social role. In Dahrendorf, R. (Ed.), *Essays in the theory of society*. London, UK: Routledge and Kegan Paul.

Dailey, L., Demo, L., & Spillman, M. (2005). The convergence continuum: A model for studying collaboration between media newsrooms. *Atlantic Journal of Communication*, *13*(3), 150–168. doi:10.1207/s15456889ajc1303_2

Data-Monitor. (2004). *Axa/Abbey: A passage to India.* MarketWatch: Financial Services.

Daugherty, T. M., Li, H., & Biocca, F. (2001). Consumer learning and 3D ecommerce: The effects of sequential exposure of a virtual experience relative to indirect and direct product experience on product knowledge, brand attitude and purchase intention. In F. Biocca, (Ed.), *Proceedings of the Experiential E-Commerce Conference* (CD-ROM). East Lansing, MI: Michigan State University.

Davis, L., & Thornton, C. (2005, December 11-14). *You are not my type!! The influence of stereotypes in the service encounter.* Paper presented at the 11th Cross-cultural Research Conference, Puerto Rico.

Dawkins, R. (1976). *The selfish gene*. Buckingham, UK: Open University Press.

de Chernatony, L. (2001). A model for strategically building brands. *Brand Management*, *9*(1), 32–44. doi:10.1057/palgrave.bm.2540050

de Chernatony, L., & McDonald, M. (2003). *Creating powerful brands* (3rd ed.). Elsevier Butterworth Heinemann.

de Chernatony, L. (1998). *Brand management*. Aldershot, UK: Ashgate Publishing Limited.

de Chernatony, L. (1998). Developing an effective brand strategy. In Egan, C., & Thomas, M. (Eds.), *The CIM handbook of strategic marketing*. Oxford, UK: Butterworth Heinemann. doi:10.1016/B978-0-7506-2613-2.50012-6

de Rosa, A. S. (1990). Per un approccio multi-metodo allo studio delle Rappresentazioni Sociali. *Rassegna di Psicologia*, *3*, 101–152.

de Rosa, A. S. (1993). Social representations and attitudes: Problems of coherence between the theoretical definition and procedure of research. *Papers on Social Representations, 2*(3), 178–192.

de Rosa, A. S. (1995). Le "réseau d'associations" comme méthode d'étude dans la recherche sur les représentations sociales. *Cahiers Internationaux de Psychologie Sociale, 28*, 96–122.

de Rosa, A. S. (2002). The associative network: A technique for detecting structure, contents, polarity and stereotyping index of the semantic fields. *European Review of Applied Psychology*, 181–200.

de Rosa, A. S. (2006). The boomerang effect of radicalism in discursive psychology: A critical overview of the controversy with the Social Representations Theory. *Journal for the Theory of Social Behaviour, 36*(2), 161–201. doi:10.1111/j.1468-5914.2006.00302.x

de Rosa, A. S. (Ed.). (2012forthcoming). *Social Representations in the "social arena."*. New York, London: Routledge.

de Rosa, A. S., & Bocci, E. (2002). E-branding strategies and development of the e-commerce and tourism: The case of Italian tour operators. *International Business & Economics Research Journal, 1*(10), 11–24.

de Rosa, A. S., & D'Ambrosio, M. (2005). L'Union Européenne de 15 à 25: Représentations, projections et previsions des jeunes étudiants de neuf nationalités un an avant l'Elargissement. *Connexion, 84*(2), 129–146. doi:10.3917/cnx.084.0129

de Rosa, A. S., & Losito, G. (1996). E' bianca o nera? Interpretazioni conflittuali e atteggiamenti contrastanti nei confronti della comunicazione pubblicitaria "ambigua" di Benetton. *Rassegna di Psicologia, 2*(13), 75–117.

de Rosa, A. S., & Smith, A. (1997a). Strategie comunicative da minoranza attiva nello scenario dei pubblicitari: il caso Benetton-Toscani. *Micro & Macromarketing, 1*, 99–126.

de Rosa, A. S., & Smith, A. (1997b). Cmpameruu obujehuk akmubhoro mehumuhcmba b peknamhon cujehapuu: Benetton-Toscani. *Psychological Review, 1*(4), 39–55.

de Rosa, A. S., & Smith, A. (1998b). Représentations sociales polémiques et styles d'influence minoritaire: Le cas Benetton-Toscani en tant que 'minorité active' dans le scenario des publicitaires. *Bulletin de Psychologie, 51*(436), 399–416.

de Rosa, A. S. (1990). Per un approccio multi-metodo allo studio delle Rappresentazioni Sociali. *Rassegna di Psicologia, 3*, 101–152.

de Rosa, A. S. (1993). Social representations and attitudes: Problems of coherences between the theoretical definition and procedure of research. *Papers on Social Representations, 3*(2), 178–192.

de Rosa, A. S. (2003). Le réseau d'association. Une technique pour détecter la structure, les contenus, les indices de polarité, de neutralité et de stéréotypie du champ sémantique liés aux représentations sociales. In Abric, J. C. (Ed.), *Méthodes d'étude des Représentations Sociales* (pp. 81–117). Ramonville Saint Agne, France: Erès.

de Rosa, A. S., & Farr, R. (2001). Icon and symbol: Two sides of the coin in the investigation of social representations. In Buschini, F., & Kalampalikis, N. (Eds.), *Penser la vie, le social, la nature. Mélanges en hommage à Serge Moscovici* (pp. 237–256). Paris, France: Les Editions de la Maison des Sciences de l'Homme.

de Rosa, A. S. (2000). North-South-East-West: The four points of the compass in the European skies. A comparison of views from different latitudes in the social representations of young people in ten European Countries. In Chaib, M., & Orfali, B. (Eds.), *Social representations and communicative processes* (pp. 51–91). Jönköping, Sweden: Jönköping University Press.

de Rosa, A. S. (2012in press). Place-identity and Social Representations of historical capital cities: Rome through the eyes of first-visitors from six nationalities. In de Rosa, A. S. (Ed.), *Social Representations in the "social arena": the theory in contexts faced with "social demand"*. New York, London: Routledge.

de Rosa, A. S. (2001). The king is naked. Critical advertisement and fashion: The Benetton phenomenon. In Deaux, K., & Philogène, G. (Eds.), *Representations of the social* (pp. 48–82). Oxford, UK: Blackwell.

de Rosa, A. S. (2002). Le besoin d'une théorie de la méthode. In Garnier, C. (Ed.), *Les formes de la pensée sociale* (pp. 151–187). Paris, France: P.U.F.

de Rosa, A. S. (2006). From September 11 to the Iraq War. Shocking images and the polarization of individual and socially negotiated emotions in the construction of mass flashbulb memory. In Gertz, S., Breaux, J.-P., & Valsiner, J. (Eds.), *Semiotic rotations: Modes of meaning in cultural worlds* (pp. 137–168). Greenwich, CT: Information Age Press.

de Rosa, A. S., & Mormino, C. (2002). Au confluent de la mémoire sociale: Etude sur l'identité nationale et européenne. In Laurens, S., & Roussiau, N. (Eds.), *La mémoire sociale. Identités et Représentations Sociales* (pp. 119–137). Rennes, France: Les Presses Universitaires de Rennes.

de Rosa, A. S., & Bocci, E. (2001a). Sul potere persuasivo della comunicazione via Internet: E-commerce e turismo. In Olivetti Belardinelli, M. (Ed.), *Orientamenti della ricerca in Italia sullo sviluppo e l'adattamento psicosociale. Valentini Day 12 Gennaio 2001* (pp. 378–387). Roma, Italy: Edizioni Kappa.

de Rosa, A. S. (2005). A Rede Associativa: Uma técnica para captar a estrutura, os conteùdos, e os ìndices de polaridade, neutralidade e estereotipia dos campos semànticos relacionados com a Representações Sociais. In Paredes Moreira, A. S. (Ed.), *Perspectivas Teorico-metodològicas em Representações Sociais* (pp. 61–127). João Pessoa, Brazil: Editora Universitária – UFPB.

de Rosa, A. S. (1998). How to sell pullovers by provoking discussion on social issues. The role of the advertising for activating and diffusing controversial social representations. In Rigas, V. (Ed.), *S.R. and contemporary social problems* (pp. 228–277). Athens, Greece: Ellinika Grammata Publisher.

de Rosa, A. S., & Bocci, E. (2005). Rappresentazioni Sociali e turismo: Canali tradizionali e nuovi media a confronto nella ricerca di pacchetti di viaggio. In Sangiorgi, G. (Ed.), *Turista e turismi. Contributi psicologici allo sviluppo del settore* (pp. 173–190). Cagliari, Italy: Cuec.

de Rosa, A. S. (2006). "¿Por qué es importante?" Notas inspiradas en una Mirada reflexiva a la teoria de las representaciones sociales. In Valencia Abundiz, S. (Ed.), *Representaciones sociales. Alteridad, epistemologia y movimientos sociales* (pp. 79–173). Guadalajara, Mexico: Universidad de Guadalajara.

de Rosa, A. S. (1995). Psicologia del turismo: Per una psicologia sociale dell'ambiente applicata. In Zani, B. (Ed.), *Le dimensioni della psicologia sociale* (pp. 153–186). Bologna, Italy: Il Mulino.

de Rosa, A. S., Bocci, E., & Saurini, S. (2006). Risk perception as a motivational barrier for on-line purchasing. In Zappalà, S., & Gray, C. (Eds.), *Impact of e-commerce on consumers and small firms* (pp. 235–248). London, UK: Ashgate.

de Rosa, A. S., Bocci, E., & Saurini, S. (2006). Risk perception as a motivational barrier for on-line purchasing. In Zappalà, S., & Gray, C. (Eds.), *Impact of e-commerce on consumers and small firms* (pp. 235–248). London, UK: Ashgate.

de Rosa, A. S. (1994). From theory to meta-theory in S.R.: The lines of argument of a theoretical-methodological debate. *Social Science Information, 33*(2), 273-304. ISSN: 0539-0184

de Rosa, A. S. (1997). Turisti di sei nazionalità per la prima volta nella città eterna: Place identity e rappresentazioni sociali di Roma e del suo centro storico. In A. Nenci (Ed.), *Conoscere e rappresentare la città* (pp. 149-214). Padova, Italy: ed. Cedam. ISBN: 8813200935

de Rosa, A. S. (2003). The social representations "of" and "within" the changing organizational contexts: The case of the Italian National Institute for Social Provisions and Pensions (INPS). In M. Lavallée, S. Vincent, C. Ouellet & C. Garnier (Eds.), *Les représentations sociales. Constructions nouvelles* (pp. 683-715). Montréal, Canada: Groupe d'étude sur l'interdisciplinarité et les representations socials. Retrieved from http://www.unites.uqam.ca/geirso/livre_repres_sociales/ index_livre.htm de Rosa, A. S. (2006). Paris – Rome: Contexts transformations, dynamics images and identity continuity of the twin capitals in people and media. *Proceedings 8th International Conference on Social Representations: Media and Society. Key Lecture Thematic Area: Social Representations, National and Supranational Identity in the Media and Society* (p. 437). (Roma, 28th August – 1st September 2006).

de Rosa, A. S., & Bocci, E. (2006). Social representations and enterprise communication: Profile of the Benetton galaxy between organizational dynamics and featured representations in the target sample. In A. S. de Rosa (Ed.), *8th I.C.S.R. Proceedings, Rome: Rocografica, 2006*, (p. 115).

de Rosa, A. S., & Bocci, E. (2009). Représentations sociales et communication de l'entreprise: Profil de la galaxie Benetton entre la dynamique organisationnelle et les représentations présentes dans l'échantillon cible. *Special Issue of Revue leti im on Les Représentations Sociales et Communication*, 301-342.

de Rosa, A. S., & Bocci, E. (2001b). E-commerce e turismo: Comprare pacchetti di viaggio su Internet o in Agenzia? In L. Greco (Ed.), *Accessibilità e turismo: problemi e metodologie di analisi* (pp. 85-106). Collana di Pubblicazioni – Ricerche Università di Siena /n° 1-2001.

de Rosa, A. S., & Bocci, E. (2002). E-branding strategies and development of the e-commerce and tourism: The case of Italian tour operators. *International Business & Economics Research Journal, 1*(10), 11-24. ISSN: 1535-0754 E187253

de Rosa, A. S., & D'Ambrosio, M. L. (2009). *Universi semantici tra luoghi immaginati e luoghi esperiti: first visitor italiani in sei capitali europee.* V Congresso ARIPT Psicologia, ambiente e salute per un turismo di qualità, (Viterbo-Tarquinia, 15-17 Ottobre 2009).

de Rosa, A. S., & D'Ambrosio, M. L. (2010). *First-visitors in European Capitals: Imagined and experienced places before and after their first visit.* Paper presented at Symposium Social Representations of Urban Places: Images, Memory and Identity organised by Annamaria de Rosa. 10th International Conference on Social Representations: Representations, Knowledge Transmission and Social Transformations, (Tunis, Tunisia 05th - 8th July 2010).

de Rosa, A. S., & Picone, M. (2007). The European Ph.D. on social representations and communication: Integrating virtual and physical mobility via the European Ph.D. Web-auditorium. In A. Boonen, & W. Van Petegem (Eds.) *European networking and learning for the future.* Antwerp, Belgium: Garant. (pp. 147-159). ISBN: 978-90-441- 2256-5

de Rosa, A. S., & Smith, A. (1996a). Tecnica retorica e pubblicità: il caso Benetton. *Informazione Radio TV, 2.*

de Rosa, A. S., & Smith, A. (1996b). Discourse and image: Two sources and ways for expressing social representations. In J. C. Abric (Ed.), *Acts of the 3rd International Conference on Social Representations* (Aix-en-Provence, France 27-30 September 1996). Paris, France: Harmattan.

de Rosa, A. S., & Smith, A. (1998a). Retorica pubblicitaria e rappresentazioni sociali. La comunicazione Benetton come caso esemplificativo. *Ikon, Forme e processi del comunicare, 37*, 173-208.

de Rosa, A. S., Antonelli, T., & Calogero, A. (1995). Roma immaginata e Roma vissuta nelle rappresentazioni sociali di turisti di sei nazionalità. In V. Cinanni, R. Virdi & G. Fumai (Eds.), *Ambiente, Salute, Cultura* (pp. 137-155). Roma, Italy: Kappa ed. ISBN: 8878901733

de Rosa, A. S., Ardone, R. G., & Bonnes, M. (1987). Rappresentazione dell'ambiente urbano e 'place-identity'. In V. Mayer & R. Meran (a cura di), *Il Laboratorio e la città.* Milano, Italy: Guerini & Associati. (vol. I, pp. 519-527). ISBN: 8878020494

de Rosa, A. S., Bonaiuto, M., Calogero, A., & Antonelli, T. (1992a). Imaginary and experential levels in social representations of Rome in people coming from six countries: Empirical approach to the place-identity theory. *Joint Meeting of European Association of Experimental Social Psychology and the Society for Experimental Social Psychology,* (Belgium, Leuven, 15-18 July 1992).

de Rosa, A. S., Bonaiuto, M., Calogero, A., & Antonelli, T. (1992b). Place-identity and social representations of Rome in people coming from six countries. *Joint Meeting of Association pour la Recherche Interculturelle (IV International Congress)* and *IACCP (XI International Congress)*, (Belgium, University of Liège, 15- 18 July 1992).

de Rosa, A. S., Bonaiuto, M., Calogero, A., & Antonelli, T. (1992c). *Social representations of Rome and its historic centre in people coming from six countries: Place-identity and social identity*. 1st International Conference on Social Representations, (Ravello, 3-5 Ottobre 1992).

de Rosa, A. S., Calogero, T., & Antonelli, T. (1992). Rome through the eyes of tourists from six nationalities. *Proceedings of the International Conference of IACCP*, (Liege, July 1992).

de Rosa, A. S., D'Ambrosio, M., & Bocci, E. (2005). EuroSKYcompass: Nation, Europe, world, social representations systems in action and construction. *Psihologia Sociala. Buletinul Laboratorului Psicologia câmpului social, 15*, 47-81.

de Rosa, A. S., Nenci, A., & Testa, G. (1995). L'esperienza del quartiere di residenza nelle rappresentazioni degli abitanti: il caso di tre quartieri di Roma. In V. Cinanni, R. Virdi & G. Fumai (Eds.), *Ambiente, salute, cultura* (pp. 156-171). Roma, Italy: Kappa ed. ISBN: 8878901733

Deese, J. (1965). *The structure of associations in language and thought*. Baltimore, MD: John Hopkins Press.

Dereli, T., Ar, A. A., & Durmosoğlu, A. (2006). *Branding and technology management* (pp. 1757–1763). PICMET 2006: Istanbul, Turkey. IEEE.

Devasagayam, R., Aurand, T., Judson, K., & Buff, C. (2010). Building brand community membership within organizations: A viable internal branding alternative? *Journal of Product and Brand Management, 19*(3), 210–217. doi:10.1108/10610421011046184

Devasagayam, R., & Van Den Heuvel, D. (2008). Building brand communities on the Internet: GeoFree BrandComm. *DIAS Technology Review: The International Journal for Business and IT, 4*(2), 10–16.

Diamond, N. (2009). American Girl and the brand gestalt: Closing the loop on sociocultural branding research. *Journal of Marketing, 73*, 118–134. doi:10.1509/jmkg.73.3.118

Dick, A. S., & Basu, K. (1994). Customer loyalty: Toward an integrated conceptual framework. *Journal of the Academy of Marketing Science, 22*(2), 99–113. doi:10.1177/0092070394222001

Distance Education Report. (2009). Marketing online programs in a recession. *Distance Education Report, 13*(7), 1 – 3.

Donbavand, R. (2007, June). Brands need to get emotional. *Brand Strategy, 36.*

Donnelly, V., & Merrick, R. (2003). *Community portals through communitization. CUU '03* (pp. 9–14). Vancouver, British Columbia, Canada: Association for Computing Machinery.

Douglas, M., & Isherwood, B. (1996). *The world of goods: Toward an anthropology of consumption*. New York, NY: Routledge.

Dubin, J. A. (1998). The demand for branded and unbranded products: An econometric method for valuing intangible assets. In Dubin, J. A. (Ed.), *Studies in consumer demand: Econometric methods applied to market data* (pp. 77–127). Norwell, MA: Kluwer Academic Publishers. doi:10.1007/978-1-4615-5665-7_4

Durkheim, E. (1895). *Les règles de la méthode sociologique, 18*. Paris, France: Presses Universitaires de France.

Dwyer, F. R., Schurr, P. H., & Oh, S. (1987). Developing buyer-seller relationships. *Journal of Marketing, 51*(2), 11–27. doi:10.2307/1251126

Eco, U. (1975). *Trattato di semiotica generale*. Milano, Italy: Bompiani.

Eco, U. (1990). *I limiti dell'interpretazione*. Milano, Italy: Bompiani.

Economist. (2001, May 3). *India, back office to the world*. Retrieved June 1, 2009, from http://www.economist.com/

Editors of Advertising Age. (1988). *Proctor & Gamble: The house that ivory built*. Lincolnwood, IL: NTC Business Books.

Ehrenberg, A. S. C. (1988). *Repeat buying: Facts, theory and applications* (2nd ed.). New York, NY & London, UK: Oxford University Press & Griffin.

Ellen, P., Wiener, J., & Cobb-Walgren, C. (1991). The role of perceived consumer effectiveness in motivating environmentally conscious behaviors. *Journal of Public Policy & Marketing, 10*(2), 102–117.

Ericsson, K., & Simon, H. (1993). *Protocol analysis: Verbal reports as data* (2nd ed.). Boston, MA: MIT Press.

Ericsson, K., & Simon, H. (1987). Verbal reports on thinking. In C. Faerch & G. Kasper (Eds.), *Introspection in second language research*. Clevedon, Avon: Multilingual Matters. (pp. 24–54).

Fan, Y. (2000). Strategic outsourcing: Evidence from British companies. *Marketing Intelligence & Planning, 18*(4), 213–219. doi:10.1108/02634500010333398

Farquhar, P. (1989). Managing brand equity. *Marketing Research, 1*(3), 24–33.

Farr, R. M., & Moscovici, S. (Eds.). (1984). *Social representations*. Cambridge, UK: Cambridge University Press.

Farr, R. M., & Moscovici, S. (Eds.). (1989). *Rappresentazioni sociali. Problemi e prospettive*. Bologna, Italy: Il Mulino.

Farr, R. (1993). The theory of social representations: Whence and whither? *Textes sur les Représentations Sociales, 2*(3), 130-138.

Fassott, G. (2004). CRM tools and their impact on relationship quality and loyalty in e-tailing. *International Journal of Internet Marketing and Advertising, 1*(4), 331–349. doi:10.1504/IJIMA.2004.006328

Favero, G. (2005). *I colori del successo*. Milano, Italy: EGEA.

Feick, L. F., & Price, L. L. (1987). The market maven: A diffuser of marketplace information. *Journal of Marketing, 51*(January), 83–97. doi:10.2307/1251146

Ferguson, R., & Hlavinka, K. (2007). *Quo Vadis: Sizing up the U.S. loyalty marketing industry.*

Fiedler, L., & Kirchgeorg, M. (2007). The role concept in corporate branding and stakeholder management reconsidered: Are stakeholder groups really different? *Corporate Reputation Review, 10*(3), 177–188. doi:10.1057/palgrave.crr.1550050

Fiocca, R., & Corvi, E. (1996). *Comunicazione e valore nelle relazioni d'impresa*. Milan, Italy: EGEA.

Fischer, E., Bristor, J., & Gainer, B. (1996). Creating or escaping community? An exploratory study of internet consumers' behaviors. In Corfman, K. P., & Lynch, J. (Eds.), *Advances in consumer research* (*Vol. 23*, pp. 178–182). Provo, UT: ACR.

Fodor, J. A. (1998). *Concepts: Where cognitive sciences went wrong*. UK: Oxford University Press.

Formenti, C. (2000). *Incantati dalla rete*. Milano, Italy: Raffaello Cortina Editore.

Forrester Research. (2003). Forrester's consumer technographics Q2 2003 North American study and Forrester's consumer technographics 2003 retail and media online study.

Fournier, S. (1998). Consumers and their brands: Developing relationship theory in consumer research. *The Journal of Consumer Research, 24*(March), 343–373. doi:10.1086/209515

Foxall, G. R. (1999). The substitutability of brands. *Managerial & Decision Economics, 20*(5), 241–257. doi:10.1002/(SICI)1099-1468(199908)20:5<241::AID-MDE936>3.0.CO;2-U

Foxall, G. R. (2008). Reward, emotion and consumer choice: From neuroeconomics to neurophilosophy. *Journal of Consumer Behaviour, 7*(4/5), 368–396. doi:10.1002/cb.258

Francese, P. A., & Renaghan, L. M. (1990). Data-base marketing: Building customer profiles. *The Cornell Hotel and Restaurant Administration Quarterly, 31*(1), 60–63. doi:10.1177/001088049003100116

Franzen, G., & Bouwman, M. (2001). *The mental world of brands – Mind, memory and brand success*. NTC Publications.

Freeman, R. E. (1984). *Strategic management: A stakeholder approach*. Boston, MA: Pitman.

Freeman, R. E., & Reed, D. L. (1983). Stockholders and stakeholders: A new perspective on corporate governance. *California Management Review, 25*(3), 93–94.

Freud, S. (1924). *Collected papers*. London, UK: Hogarth.

Frost & Sullivan. (2007). Global outsourcing market to be worth $1,430bn by 2009. *Computer Business Review*. Retrieved from http://cbr.co.za/article.aspx? pklArticleI d=4714&pklCategoryId=404

Fyall, A., & Leask, A. (2006). Destination marketing: Future issues — Strategic challenges. *Tourism and Hospitality Research*, *7*(1), 50–63. doi:10.1057/palgrave.thr.6050029

Galton, F. (1880). Psychometric experiments. *Brain*, *2*, 149–162. doi:10.1093/brain/2.2.149

Gardner, B. B., & Levy, S. J. (1955, March-April). The product and the brand. *Harvard Business Review*, 33–39.

Garsten, C., & Hasselström, A. (2004). Homo mercans and the fashioning of markets. In Garsten, C., & de Montoya, M. L. (Eds.), *Market matters: Exploring cultural processes in the global marketplace*. New York, NY: Palgrave Macmillan.

GfkAmerica.com. (2009). *The Anholt-GfK Roper nation brands index*. Retrieved July 19, 2009, from http://www.gfkamerica.com/practice_areas /roper_pam/nbi_index/index.en.html/

Gibbons, W. C. (2007). A librarian's guide to hip-hop culture. *Collection Building*, *26*(7), 119–126. doi:10.1108/01604950710831924

Gibson, J. J. (1977). The theory of affordances. In Shaw, R., & Bransford, J. (Eds.), *Perceiving, acting and knowing: Toward an ecological psychology* (pp. 67–82). Hillsdale, NJ: Lawrence Erlbaum Associates.

Gilbert, D., & Hewlett, J. (2003). A method for the assessment of relative brand strength: A UK tour operator example. *The Service Industries Journal*, *23*(2), 166–182. doi:10.1080/02642060412331300942

Gioiosa, C., de Rosa, A. S., & D'Ambrosio, M. (2005). Exploring the structure of social representations of the Euro via facet theory approach and WSSA1. In Bilsky, W., & Elizur, D. (Eds.), *Facet theory: Design, analysis and applications* (pp. 57–64). Prague, Czech Republic: Agentura Action M.

Godelier, M. (1999). *The enigma of the gift*. Chicago, IL: University Of Chicago Press.

Gold, J. R., & Ward, S. V. (1994). *Place promotion: The use of publicity and marketing to sell towns*. Chichester, UK: Wiley.

Goldsmith, R. E. (2000). Characteristics of the heavy user of fashionable clothing. *Journal of Marketing Theory & Practice*, *8*(4), 21–28.

Goldsmith, R. E., Flynn, L. R., & Korzenny, F. (2010). Brand engagement and consumer innovativeness. *Proceedings of the Association of Marketing Theory and Practice*.

Govers, R., & Go, F. M. (2004). Cultural identities constructed, imagined and experienced: A 3-gap tourism destination image model. *Tourism Interdisciplinary Journal*, *52*(2), 165–182.

Granitz, N. A., & Ward, J. C. (1996). Virtual community: A sociocognitive analysis. In Corfman, K. P., & Lynch, J. (Eds.), *Advances in consumer research* (*Vol. 23*, pp. 161–166). Provo, UT: ACR.

Gregory, A. (2007). Involving stakeholders in developing corporate brands: The communication dimension. *Journal of Marketing Management*, *23*(1-2), 59–73. doi:10.1362/026725707X178558

Gronhaug, K., & Gilly, M. C. (1991). A transaction cost approach to consumer dissatisfaction and complaint actions. *Journal of Economic Psychology*, *12*(1), 156–183. doi:10.1016/0167-4870(91)90048-X

Gronroos, C. (1999). Internationalization strategies for services. *Journal of Services Marketing*, *13*(4/5), 290–297. doi:10.1108/08876049910282547

Grundey, D. (2002). *Partnership marketing: Present and future reviews compilation: Marketing methods and theories*. The 4th International Conference Marketing Methods and Theories, (pp. 153-161). ISBN 9986-19-516-0

Gupta, S., & Kim, H. W. (2007). Developing the commitment to virtual community: The balanced effects of cognition and affect. *Information Resources Management Journal*, *20*(1), 28–45. doi:10.4018/irmj.2007010103

Gurhan-Canli, Z., & Maheswaran, D. (2000). Cultural variations in country of origin effects. *JMR, Journal of Marketing Research*, *37*(August), 309–317. doi:10.1509/jmkr.37.3.309.18778

Hall, E. T. (1969). *The hidden dimension*. Garden City, NY: Anchor Books.

Han, C. M., & Terpstra, V. (1988). Country-of-origin effects for uni-national and bi-national products. *Journal of International Business Studies, 19*(Summer), 235–255. doi:10.1057/palgrave.jibs.8490379

Hankinson, G. (2004). The brand images of tourism destinations: A study of the saliency of the organic images. *Journal of Product and Brand Management, 13*(1), 6–14. doi:10.1108/10610420410523803

Hannu, K., & Pallab, P. (2000). A comparison of concurrent and retrospective verbal protocol analysis. *The American Journal of Psychology, 113*(3), 387–404. doi:10.2307/1423365

Hansen, R. S., & Hansen, K. (2007). The student experience in speed teaming: A new approach to team formation. *Journal of College Teaching and Learning, 4*(7), 69–78.

Harrison-Walker, L. J. (1995). The relative effects of national stereotype and advertising information on the selection of a service provider. *Journal of Services Marketing, 9*(1), 47–59. doi:10.1108/08876049510079880

Hartmann, J., Sutcliffe, A., & De Angeli, A. (2008). Towards a theory of user judgment of aesthetics and user interface quality. *ACM Transactions on Computer-Human Interaction,* 15(4), 15:1–15:30.

Hass, V. (2004). Les cartes cognitives: un outil pour étudier la ville sous ses dimensions socio-historique et affectives. *Bulletin de Psychologie, 474*, 621–633.

Hass, V., & Jodelet, D. (2000). La mémoire, ses aspects sociaux et collectifs. In Roussiau, N. (Ed.), *Psychologie sociale* (pp. 121–134). Rennes, France: P. U. de Rennes.

Heding, T., Knudtzen, C. F., & Bjerre, M. (2009). *Brand management – Research, theory and practice*. New York, NY: Routledge. doi:10.4324/9780203996171

Heitmann, M., Prykop, C., & Aschmoneit, P. (2004). Using means-end chains to build mobile brand communities. *Proceedings of the 37th Hawaii International Conference on System Sciences* (pp. 1–10). IEEE.

Henderson, J. C. (2007). Uniquely Singapore? A case study in destination branding. *Journal of Vacation Marketing, 13*(3), 261. doi:10.1177/1356766707077695

Henion, K., & Wilson, W. (1976). *The ecologically concerned consumer and locus of control. Ecological Marketing* (pp. 131–144). Chicago, IL: American Marketing Association.

Henneberg, S. C. (2004). The views of an Advocatus Dei: Political marketing and its critics. *Journal of Public Affairs, 4*(3). doi:10.1002/pa.187

Henneberg, S. C., & O'Shaughnessy, N. J. (2002). *The idea of political marketing*. Praeger.

Herman, E. S., & Chomsky, N. (1988). *Manufacturing consent: The political economy of the mass media*. New York, NY: Pantheon Books.

Hesmondhalgh, D. (2008). Towards a critical understanding of music, emotion and self-identity. *Consumption Markets & Culture, 11*(4), 329–343. doi:10.1080/10253860802391334

Hill, J. (1996). Keeping customers loyal at Liverpool Victoria Friendly Society. *Managing Service Quality, 6*(4), 27–31. doi:10.1108/09604529610120258

Hill, S., & Rifkin, G. (1999). *Radical marketing*. New York, NY: HarperBusiness.

Hirschman, E. C., & Thompson, C. J. (1997). Why media matter: Toward a richer understanding of consumers' relationships with advertising and mass media. *Journal of Advertising, 26*(1), 43–60.

Holt, D. B. (2002). Why do brands cause trouble? A dialectical theory of consumer culture and branding. *The Journal of Consumer Research, 29*(June), 70–90. doi:10.1086/339922

Holt, D. B. (2004). *How brands become icons*. Boston, MA: Harvard Business School Press.

Holt, D. B. (2005). How societies desire brands: Using cultural theory to explain brand symbolism. In Mick, D., & Ratneshwar, S. (Eds.), *Inside consumption*. Routledge.

Hong, S.-T., & Wyer, R. S. Jr. (1990). Determinants of product evaluations: Effects of the time interval between knowledge of a product's country of origin and information about its specific attributes. *The Journal of Consumer Research, 17*(December), 277–288. doi:10.1086/208557

Houston, M. J., & Rothschild, M. L. (1978). Conceptual and methodological perspectives in involvement. *Research Frontiers in Marketing: Dialogues and Directions, Conference Proceedings*, (pp. 184-187).

Huang, W.-Y., Schrank, H., & Dubinsky, A. J. (2004). Effect of brand name on consumers' risk perceptions of online shopping. *Journal of Consumer Behaviour*, *4*(1), 40–50. doi:10.1002/cb.156

Hussaini. (2009). *Website*. Retrieved from http://www.political-marketing.net

IBM Global Services. (2006). CRM: The myth vs. The new agenda. Executive Brief. In C. K. Yim, et al. (Eds.), Strengthening customer loyalty through intimacy and passion: Roles of customer-firm affection and customer staff relationships in services. *Journal of Marketing Research, 45*, 741-756.

ISO. (2010). *ISO 9241-10: Ergonomic requirements for office work with visual display terminals (VDTs) – Dialog principles.* Retrieved May 23, 2010, from http://web.tiscali.it/userware

Jacoby, J., & Chestnut, R. (1978). *Brand loyalty: Measurement and management*. New York, NY: John Wiley.

Jain, P. (2006). Offshore outsourcing "India vs China:" An empirical investigation. *Business Review (Federal Reserve Bank of Philadelphia)*, *6*(2), 316–324.

Jansen, B. J., Zhang, M., Sobel, K., & Chowdury, A. (2009). Twitter power: Tweets as electronic word of mouth. *Journal of the American Society for Information Science and Technology*, *60*(11), 2169. doi:10.1002/asi.21149

Jansen, B. J., Zhang, M., Sobel, K., & Chowdury, A. (2009). Micro-blogging as online word of mouth branding (pp. 3859–3864). CHI 2009: Boston, Massachusetts. Association for Computing Machinery.

Jodelet, D. (Ed.). (1989). *Les representations sociales*. Paris, France: Presses Universitaires de France.

Jodelet, D. (1982). Les représentations socio-spatiales de la ville. In Derycke, P. H. (Ed.), *Conception de l'espace, recherche pluridisciplinaire de l'Université Paris X.* Nanterre.

Johnson, C. (2007, August 15). *Managing brand in the shifting media landscape*. Retrieved from http://www.odwyerpr.com/members /0815johnson_oped.html

Jones, R. (2005). Finding Sources of brand value: Developing a stakeholder model of brand equity. *Brand Management*, *13*(1), 10–32. doi:10.1057/palgrave.bm.2540243

Jones-Lee, M., & Loomes, G. (2004). *Eliciting measures of value for health and safety* (pp. 49–58). 9th Australian Workshop on Safety-Related Programmable Systems, Brisbane, Australia.

Junglas, I. A., Johnson, N. A., Steel, D. J., Abraham, D. C., & Loughlin, P. M. (2007). Identity formation, learning styles and trust in virtual worlds. *The Data Base for Advances in Information Systems*, *38*(4), 90–96.

Kant, A. (2009). *Branding India: An incredible story*. Noida, India: Collins-Business.

Kant, I. (1977). *Prolegomena to any future metaphysics. (P. Carus, Trans., J. W. Ellington, Rev.)*. Indianapolis, IN: Hackett Publishing Company, Inc.

Kapferer, J. N. (2008). *The new strategic brand management* (4th ed.). London, UK: Kogan Page.

Kapferer, J.-N. (1997). *Strategic brand management*. Great Britain: Kogan Page.

Kasser, T. (2002). *The high price of materialism*. Cambridge, MA: The MIT Press.

Kaynak, E., & Kara, A. (2002). Consumer perceptions of foreign products: An analysis of product-country images and ethnocentrism. *European Journal of Marketing*, *36*(7/8), 928–949. doi:10.1108/03090560210430881

Kaynak, E., Kucukemiroglu, O., & Kara, A. (1994). Consumer perceptions of airlines: A correspondence analysis approach in an airline industry. *Management International Review*, *34*(3), 235–254.

Keller, K. L. (2003). *Strategic brand management: Building, measuring and managing brand equity*. Upper Saddle River, NJ: Prentice-Hall.

Keller, K. L. (1993). Conceptualizing, measuring and managing consumer-based brand equity. *Journal of Marketing*, *57*(1). doi:10.2307/1252054

Keller, K. L. (2001). *Building customer-based brand equity: A blueprint for creating strong brands*. Marketing Science Institute, (Working Paper 01-107).

Kennedy, C. (2002). Name and shame: If you outsource, beware. Your brand may be in tatters through appalling customer service - And you may never know it. *Director (Cincinnati, Ohio)*, *56*(5), 23.

Kim, M.-K., Park, M.-C., & Jeong, D.-H. (2004). The effects of customer satisfaction and switching barrier on customer loyalty in Korean mobile telecommunication services. *Telecommunications Policy*, *28*(2), 145. doi:10.1016/j.telpol.2003.12.003

King, P., & Tester, J. (1999). The landscape of persuasive technologies. *Communications of the ACM*, *42*(5), 31–38. doi:10.1145/301353.301398

Kinnear, T., Taylor, J., & Ahmed, S. (1974). Ecologically concerned consumers: Who are they? *Journal of Marketing*, *38*(2), 20–24. doi:10.2307/1250192

Kirchler, E., & de Rosa, A. S. (1996). Wirkungsanalyse von Werbebotschaften mittels Assoziationsgeflecht. Spontane Reaktionen auf und überlegte Beschreibung von Benetton-Werbebildern. *Jahrbuch der Absatz und Verbrauchsforschung*, *1*, 67–89.

Klaassen, A. (2006). This is the Avon lady... on steroids. *Advertising Age*, *77*(36), 1–39.

Klein, N. (2000). *No logo*. London, UK: Flamingo.

Konecnik, M., & Go, F. (2008). Tourism destination brand identity: The case of Slovenia. *Journal of Brand Management*, *15*(3), 177–189. doi:10.1057/palgrave.bm.2550114

Kostakos, V., & Oakley, I. (2009). *Designing trustworthy situated services: An implicit and explicit assessment of locative images' effect on trust* (pp. 329–332). CHI 2009: Boston, Massachusetts, USA. Association for Computing Machinery.

Kotler, P., Haider, D., & Rein, I. (1993). *Marketing places: Attracting investment, industry, and tourism to cities, states and nations*. Oxford, UK: Free Press.

Kotler, P. (1997). *Marketing management casi*. Torino, Italy: ISEDI.

Krause, R. D. (2003). Managing higher ed web sites: Balancing the need for timely updates, the requirements of institutional marketing, and the development of content. In the *Proceedings of the Special Interest Group on University and College Computing Services* (SIGUCCS '03) (pp. 139–141). San Antonio, Texas, USA. ACM.

Krishnamurthy, S., & Kucuk, S. U. (2009). Anti-branding on the Internet. *Journal of Business Research*, *62*(11), 1119. doi:10.1016/j.jbusres.2008.09.003

Krotoski, A. (2010, February 2). The virtual revolution: The great levelling? *BBC News Online*. Retrieved May 31, 2010, from http://www.bbc.co.uk/worldservice / documentaries/2010/02/100128 _the_virtual_revolution_part_one.shtml

Krugman, H. E. (1965). The impact of television advertising: Learning without involvement. *Public Opinion Quarterly*, *29*(3), 349–356. doi:10.1086/267335

Krugman, H. E. (1966). The measurement of advertising involvement. *Public Opinion Quarterly*, *30*(4), 583–596. doi:10.1086/267457

Laaksonen, P. (1999). Involvement. In Earl, P. E., & Kemp, S. (Eds.), *The Elgar companion to consumer research and economic psychology* (pp. 341–347). Cheltenham, UK: Edward Elgar Publishing.

Landi, P. (1993). *News*. Treviso, Italy: Colors Pubblications.

Landi, P., & Pollini, L. (1993). *Cosa c'entra l'aids con i maglioni?* Milano, Italy: Arnoldo Mondadori Editore.

Lebart, L., Morineau, A., & Becue, M. (1989). *SPADT: Système portable pour l'analyse des Données textuelles, Manuel de l'utilisateur*. Paris, France: Cisia.

Lees-Marshment, J. (2001). Marketing the British Conservatives 1997-2001. *Journal of Marketing Management*, *17*(9-10), 929–941. doi:10.1362/026725701323366674

Lees-Marshment, J. (2001). The product, sales and market-oriented Party and how Labour learnt to market the product, not just the presentation. *European Journal of Marketing*, *35*(9/10), 1074–1084. doi:10.1108/EUM0000000005959

Lees-Marshment, J. (2001). *Political marketing and British political parties: The party's just begun*. Manchester University Press.

Lees-Marshment, J. (2001). Let's go comprehensive: Reaching the full potential of political marketing. *Proceedings of The Political Marketing Conference*, Dublin (September).

Lees-Marshment, J. (2001). Comprehensive political marketing: What, how and why. *Proceedings of The Academy of Marketing Conference*, Cardiff University (2-4 July).

Lehmann, D. R., & Meslin, S. A. (2003). Revenue premium as an outcome measure of brand equity. *Journal of Marketing*, *67*(3), 1–17.

Leuthesser, L. (1988). *Defining, measuring and managing brand equity*. (Working Paper No. 88-104). Cambridge, MA: Marketing Science Institute.

Lévy, P. (1996). *L'intelligenza collettiva. Per una antropologia del cyberspazio*. Milano, Italy: Feltrinelli.

Lévy, P. (1997). *Il Virtuale*. Milano, Italy: Raffaello Cortina Editore.

Lévy, P. (2000). *WorldPhilosophie*. Paris, France: Éditions Odile Jacob.

Lévy, P. (2002). *Cyberdémocratie*. Paris, France: Éditions Odile Jacob.

Levy, S. J. (1986). Meanings in advertising stimuli. In Olson, J., & Sentis, K. (Eds.), *Advertising and consumer psychology* (*Vol. 3*, pp. 214–226). New York, NY: Praeger Publishers.

Lewis, D., & Bridger, D. (2000). *The soul of the new consumer*. London, UK: Nicholas Brealey Publishing.

Lewis, C. H. (1982). *Using the thinking aloud method in cognitive interface design*. (Technical Report IBM RC-9265).

Lewis, C., & Rieman, J. (1993, 1994). *Task-centered user interface design: A practical introduction*. Retrieved May 29, 2010, from http://grouplab.cpsc.ucalgary.ca/ saul/ hci_topics/tcsd-book/ chap-1_v-1.html

Li, Z. G., Murray, L. W., & Scott, D. (2000). Global sourcing, multiple country-of-origin facets, and consumer reactions. *Journal of Business Research*, *47*, 121–133. doi:10.1016/S0148-2963(98)00061-7

Li, C., & Bernoff, J. (2008). *Groundswell: Winning in a world transformed by social technologies*. Boston, MA: Harvard Business Press.

Li, H., Daugherty, T., & Biocca, F. (2002). Impact of 3-D advertising on product knowledge, brand attitude, and purchase intention: The mediating role of presence. *Journal of Advertising*, *31*(3), 43–57.

Li, X.-W., & Zhang, M.-L. (2008). *Relationship benefit in consumer markets and its role in brand image-brand loyalty in chain* (pp. 578–584). 2008 International Conference on Management Science and Engineering, Long Beach, USA. IEEE.

Limone, D. A., Preite, G., & Mancarella, M. (2008). *Turismatica. Un nuovo paradigma della società dell'informazione*. Trento, Italy: Uniservice.

Lindstrom, M. (2005). *Brand sense: How to build powerful through touch, taste, smell, sight and sound. London, UK & Sterling*. VA: Kogan Page.

Lippman, W. (1965). *Public opinion*. New York, NY: The Free Press.

Liu, Y., & Yang, R. (2009). Competing loyalty programs: Impact of market saturation, market share, and category expandability. [American Marketing Association.]. *Journal of Marketing*, *73*, 93–108. doi:10.1509/jmkg.73.1.93

Lorusso, M. (2007). *Italia in svendita: la privatizzazione delle aziende statali: politica, impresa, etica*. Milano, Italy: Il sole 24 ore.

Losito, G. (1993). *L'analisi del contenuto nella ricerca sociale*. Milano, Italy: Franco Angeli.

Losito, G. (1994). *Il potere dei media*. Roma, Italy: Nuova Italia Scientifica.

Luo, W., & Najdawi, M. (2004). Trust-building measures: A review of consumer health portals. *Communications of the ACM*, *47*(1), 109–113.

Lynd, R. S. (1939). *Knowledge for what? The place of the social sciences in American culture*. Princeton, NJ: Princeton University Press.

MacDonald Report, M. (2007). *Evaluation study of rural tourism scheme*. Retrieved October 18, 2009, from www.tourism.gov.in/survey /RuralTourism.pdf

Maio, E. (2003). Managing brand in the new stakeholder environment. *Journal of Business Ethics, 44*(2-3), 235–246. doi:10.1023/A:1023364119516

Maldonado, T. (1997). *Critica della ragione informatica*. Milano, Italy: Feltrinelli.

Mantle, J. (2000). *Benetton: The family, the business and the brand*. London, UK: Little Brown & C.

Mantle, J. (2002). *Benetton*. London, UK: Penguin Books.

Mantovani, G. (2000). *Ergonomia*. Bologna, Italy: Il Mulino.

Maranda, P. (1990). *DiscaAn: Users manual*. Quebec, Canada: Nadeau Caron Informatique.

Marsden, P. (2002). Brand positioning: Meme's the word. *Marketing Intelligence & Planning, 20*(5), 307–312. doi:10.1108/02634500210441558

Marx, K. (1967). Commodities. In *Capital: A critique of political economy, vol 1. The process of capitalist production*. (S. Moore & E. Aveling, Trans.). New York, NY: The International Publishers Co.

Marzano, G., & Scott, N. (2009). Power in destination branding. *Annals of Tourism Research, 36*(2), 247–267. doi:10.1016/j.annals.2009.01.004

Mason, K., & Bequette, J. (1998). Product experience and consumer product attribute inference accuracy. *Journal of Consumer Marketing, 15*(4), 343. doi:10.1108/07363769810225984

Mauss, M. (1924). *The gift - The form and reason for exchange in archaic societies*. London, UK: Routledge.

Mayer, K. J., Bowen, J. T., & Moulton, M. R. (2003). A proposed model of the descriptors of service process. *Journal of Services Marketing, 17*(6), 621–639. doi:10.1108/08876040310495645

Mayer, R. C., Davis, J. H., & Schoorman, F. D. (1995). An integrative model of organizational trust. *Academy of Management Review, 20*(3), 709–734.

Mc Luhan, M. (1989). *The global village*. Oxford, UK: Oxford University Press.

McAlexander, J. H. (2002). Building brand community. *Journal of Marketing, 66*, 38–54. doi:10.1509/jmkg.66.1.38.18451

McAlexander, J. H., Schouten, J. W., & Koening, H. W. (2002). Building brand community. *Journal of Marketing, 66*(1). Chicago.

McCartney, L. (2003). A shore thing. *CFO-IT Magazine*, Spring, 60–63.

McCaskey, D., & Symes, S. (2004). Travel Inn: Everything you want for a good night's sleep - 100 per cent satisfaction guarantee or your money back. *International Journal of Contemporary Hospitality Management, 16*(3), 166–174. doi:10.1108/09596110410531159

McClure, S. M., Li, J., Tomlin, D., Cypert, K. S., Montague, L. M., & Montague, P. R. (2004). Neural correlates of behavioral preference for culturally familiar drinks. *Neuron, 44*(2), 379–387. doi:10.1016/j.neuron.2004.09.019

McConnell, B., & Huba, J. (2003). *Creating customer evangelists: How loyal customers become a volunteer sales force*. Chicago, IL: Dearborn Trade Pub.

McCracken, G. (1986). Culture and consumption: A theoretical account of the structure and movement of the cultural meaning of consumer goods. *The Journal of Consumer Research, 13*(June), 71–84. doi:10.1086/209048

McCracken, G. (1990). Culture and consumer behavior: An anthropological perspective. *Journal of the Market Research Society. Market Research Society, 32*(1), 3–11.

McEwen, W. (2004, November 11). Why satisfaction isn't satisfying. *Gallup Management Journal*. Retrieved February 17, 2009, from http://gmj.gallup.com/content/14023/why-satisfaction-Isnt-Satisfying.aspx

McIntosh, N. (2003, February 18). Google buys blogger web service. *The Guardian*. Retrieved from http://www.guardian.co.uk/business/ story/0,3604,897610,00.html

McKnight, D. H., Choudhury, V., & Kacmar, C. (2002). Developing and validating trust measures for e-commerce: An integrative typology. *Information Systems Research, 13*(3), 334–359. doi:10.1287/isre.13.3.334.81

McNally, D., & Speak, K. D. (2003). *Be your own brand - A breakthrough formula for standing out from the crowd*. Berrett-Koehler Publishers.

McWilliam, G. (2000). Building strong brands through online communities. *Sloan Management Review*, *41*(3), 43–54.

Memmi, D. (2006). The nature of virtual communities. *AI & Society*, *20*(3), 288–300. doi:10.1007/s00146-005-0020-7

Menon, A., & Menon, A. (1997). Enviropreneurial marketing strategy: The emergence of corporate environmentalism as market strategy. *Journal of Marketing*, *61*(7), 51–67. doi:10.2307/1252189

Meyer, C., & Schwager, A. (2007). Understanding customer experience. *Harvard Business Review*, *85*(February), 117–126.

Meyer-Waarden, L. (2007). The effects of loyalty programs on customer life time duration and share of wallet. *Journal of Retailing*, *83*, 223–236. doi:10.1016/j.jretai.2007.01.002

Mick, D. G. (1986). Consumer research and semiotics: Exploring the morphology of signs, symbols and significance. *The Journal of Consumer Research*, *13*(September), 196–213. doi:10.1086/209060

Middleton, V. T. C., & Clarke, J. R. (2001). *Marketing in travel and tourism*. Oxford, UK: Butterworth-Heinemann.

Miles, M., & Covin, J. (2000). Environmental marketing: A source of reputational, competitive, and financial advantage. *Journal of Business Ethics*, *23*(3), 299–311. doi:10.1023/A:1006214509281

Miles, M. P., Munilla, L. S., & Darroch, J. (2006). The role of strategic conversations with stakeholders in the formation of corporate social responsibility strategy. *Journal of Business Ethics*, *69*, 195–205. doi:10.1007/s10551-006-9085-6

Mintel (2007). Call centres: Offshoring vs onshoring in the United Kingdom. Retrieved June 1, 2009, from http://www.mintel.com/

Mitchell, R. K., Agle, B. R., & Wood, D. J. (1997). Toward a theory of stakeholder identification and salience: Defining the principle of who and what really counts. *Academy of Management Review*, *22*(4), 853–886.

Mitchell, W. J. (1999). *E-topia: Urban life, Jim - But not as we know it*. Cambridge, MA: MIT Press.

Mittal, V., & Kamakura, W. A. (2001). Satisfaction, repurchase intent, and repurchase behavior: Investigating the moderating effect of customer characteristics. *JMR, Journal of Marketing Research*, *38*(2), 131–142. doi:10.1509/jmkr.38.1.131.18832

Mittal, B., & Lee, M.-S. (1989). A causal model of consumer involvement. *Journal of Economic Psychology*, *10*, 363–389. doi:10.1016/0167-4870(89)90030-5

Moliner, P. (1996). *Images et représentations sociales*. Grenoble, France: Presses.

Montoya, P. (2005). *The brand called you: The ultimate personal branding handbook to transform anyone into an indispensable brand*. Peter Montoya Pub.

Morgan, N., Pritchard, A., & Pride, R. (2001). *Destination branding: Creating the unique destination proposition*. Oxford, UK: Butterworth-Heinemann.

Moscovici, S. (1961). *La psychanalyse son image et son public. Etude sur la répresentation sociale de la psychanalyse*. Paris, France: Presses Universitaires de France.

Moscovici, S., & Duveen, G. (Eds.). (2000). *Social representations. Explorations in social psychology*. Cambridge, UK: Polity Press.

Moscovici, S. (1984). The phenomenon of social representations. In Farr, R., & Moscovici, S. (Eds.), *Social representations*. Paris, France & Cambridge, UK: M.S.H. & Cambridge University Press.

Moscovici, S. (1989). Des représentations collectives aux représentations sociales: éléments pour une histoire. In Jodelet, D. (Ed.), *Les représentations sociales* (pp. 62–86). Paris, France: Presses Universitaires de France.

Mossberg, L., & Getz, D. (2006). Stakeholder influences on the ownership and management of festival brands. *Scandinavian Journal of Hospitality and Tourism*, *6*(4), 308–326. doi:10.1080/15022250601003273

Mulas, A. (2004). *Architettura per Benetton*. Milano, Italy: Skira.

Muniz, A. M., & O'Guinn, T. C. (2001). Brand community. *The Journal of Consumer Research*, *27*, 412–427. doi:10.1086/319618

Muniz, A.M., Jr., & O'Guinn, T. C. (2001). Brand community. *Journal of Consumer Research, 27*(4). Gainesville.

Murphy, P., Kangun, N., & Locander, W. (1978). Environmentally concerned consumers-racial variations. *Journal of Marketing, 42*(4), 61–66. doi:10.2307/1250087

Murray, K. B., & Schlacter, J. L. (1990). The impact of services versus goods on consumers' assessment of perceived risk and variability. *Journal of the Academy of Marketing Science, 18*(1), 51–65. doi:10.1007/BF02729762

Nail, J. (2006). *The 4 types of engagement*. Retrieved from www.imediaconnection.com.

Nardin, G. (1987). *La Benetton Strategia e struttura di un'impresa di successo*. Roma, Italy: Edizioni Lavoro.

Nenci, A. M., de Rosa, A. S., Testa, G., & Carrus, G. (2003). Social and architectural legibility of the city. In Moser, G., Pol, E., Bernard, Y., Bonnes, M., Corraliza, J. A., & Giuliani, M. V. (Eds.), *People, places and sustainability* (pp. 25–37). Gottingen, Germany: Hogrefe & Huber Publishers.

Netemeyer, R. G., Krishnan, B., Pullig, C., Wang, G., Yagci, M., & Dean, D. (2004). Developing and validating measures of facets of customer-based brand equity. *Journal of Business Research, 57*, 209–224. doi:10.1016/S0148-2963(01)00303-4

Ngyuyen, L., Torlina, L., Peszynski, K., & Corbitt, B. (2006). Power relationships in virtual communities: An ethnographic study. *Electronic Commerce Research, 6*, 21–37. doi:10.1007/s10660-006-5986-9

Nielsen, J. (2000). *Web usability*. Milano, Italy: Edizioni Apogeo.

Nielsen, J., & Loranger, H. (2006). *Web usability 2.0. L'usabilità che conta*. Milano, Italy: Edizioni Apogeo.

Nielsen, J., & Tahir, M. (2002). *Homepage usability*. Milano, Italy: Edizioni Apogeo.

Nielsen, J. (1994). Heuristics for users interface design. In Nielsen, J., & Mack, R. L. (Eds.), *Usability inspection methods*. New York, NY: John Wiley & Sons.

Nielsen. (2009). *Nielsen global online consumer survey: Trust, value and engagement in advertising*. Retrieved from http://blog.nielsen.com/nielsenwire /wp-content/uploads/2009/07 /trustinadvertising0709.pdf

Nöth, W. (1988). The language of commodities: Groundwork for a semiotics of consumer goods. *International Journal of Research in Marketing, 4*(3), 173–186. doi:10.1016/S0167-8116(88)80003-X

Obama, B. (2007). *The change we need*. Retrieved February 10, 2008, from http://www.barackobama.com/2007 /10/08/remarks_of_ senator _barack_obam_28.php

O'Brien, L., & Jones, C. (1995). Do rewards really create loyalty? *Harvard Business Review, 73*(3), 75–82.

Onkvisit, S., & Shaw, J. J. (1994). Standardization versus localization: The need for the compromising perspective. In Hassan, S. S., & Blackwell, R. D. (Eds.), *Global marketing: Perspectives and cases*. Forth Worth, TX: Dryden Press.

Ooi, C. (2004). Poetics and politics of destination branding: Denmark. *Scandinavian Journal of Hospitality and Tourism, 4*(2), 107–128. doi:10.1080/15022250410003898

Osgood, C. E., & Tannenbaum, P. H. (1955). The principle of congruity in the prediction of attitude change. *Psychological Review, 62*(1), 42–55. doi:10.1037/h0048153

Osgood, C., Suci, G., & Tannenbaum, P. (1957). *The measurement of meaning*. Urbana, IL: University of Illinois Press.

Osgood, C. E., May, W. H., & Miron, M. S. (1975). *Cross-cultural universals of affective meaning*. Urbana, IL: University of Illinois Press.

Osterhus, T. (1997). Pro-social consumer influence strategies: When and how do they work? *Journal of Marketing, 61*(4), 16–29. doi:10.2307/1252084

Ouwersloot, H., & Schroder, G. O. (2008). Who's who in brand communities and why? *European Journal of Marketing, 42*(5-6), 571–585. doi:10.1108/03090560810862516

Pagnucco Salvemini, L. (2003). *Benetton/Toscani. Storia di una avventura, 1984-2000*. Azzano San Paolo, Italy: Bolis.

PaidContent.org. (2003, September 25). *Bourland*. Retrieved from http://www.paidcontent.org/ stories/ bourland.html

Palacio, A. B., Meneses, G. D., & Perez, P. J. (2002). The configuration of the university image and its relationship with the satisfaction of students. *Journal of Educational Administration*, *40*(4/5), 486–505. doi:10.1108/09578230210440311

Park, S., & Petrick, J. F. (2006). Destinations' perspective of branding. *Annals of Tourism Research*, *33*(1), 262–265. doi:10.1016/j.annals.2005.10.007

Park, H., & Rabolt, N. (2009). Cultural value, consumption value, and global brand image: A cross-national study. *Psychology and Marketing*, *26*(8), 714. doi:10.1002/ mar.20296

Paswan, A. K., & Ganesh, G. (2005). Cross-cultural interaction comfort and service evaluation. *Journal of International Consumer Marketing*, *18*(1/2), 93–115. doi:10.1300/J046v18n01_05

Payne, A., Ballantyne, D., & Christopher, M. (2005). A stakeholder approach to relationship marketing strategy: The development and use of the six markets model. *European Journal of Marketing*, *39*(7-8), 855–871. doi:10.1108/03090560510601806

Pekala, N. (2009, June 26). The age of the 24/7 consumer creates emergence of customer engagement agencies. *Marketing Matters Newsletter*.

Pennington, R. (2000a). Brands as the language of consumer culture. *Journal of Global Competitiveness*, *8*(1), 318–329.

Pennington, R. (2001a). Signs of marketing in virtual reality. *Journal of Interactive Advertising*, *2*(1). Retrieved from http://jiad.org/vol2/no1/pennington.

Pennington, R. (2005). Affording cultural and social presence in e-marketing. In Gao, Y. (Ed.), *Web systems design and online consumer behavior* (pp. 305–318). Hershey, PA: The Idea Group Inc.

Pennington, R. (2004a). Brands, culture and semiotics (revisited) in creative strategy development. In Ribeiro Cardoso, P., & Nora Gaio, S. (Eds.), *Publicidade e Comunicação Empresarial: Perspectivas e Contributos* (p. 29043). Porto, Portugal: Edições Universidade Fernando Pessoa.

Pennington, R. (2006). A cultural framework for studying youth, brands and lifestyles. In Ribeiro Cardoso, P., Nora Gaio, S., & Pérez Seoane, J. (Eds.), *Jovens, Marcas e Estilos de Vida* (pp. 15–24). Porto, Portugal: Edições Universidade Fernando Pessoa.

Pennington, R. (2004b). Revising a psycho-linguistic application of information theory for the consumer psychology of brands. In Williams, J. D., Lee, W.-N., & Haugtvedt, C. P. (Eds.), *Diversity in advertising* (pp. 201–214). Hilldale, NJ: Lawrence Erlbaum Associates, Inc.

Pennington, R. (2000b). *The theory is the press: A view of the press as developer of informal theory*. Association for Education in Journalism and Mass Communication Annual Convention (Communication Theory and Methodology Division). Phoenix.

Pennington, R. (2001b). The conceptual definition of culture in advertising, marketing and consumer research literature. In M. Roberts & R. L. King (Eds.), *Proceedings of the 2001 Special Asia-Pacific Conference of the American Academy of Advertising* (pp. 34-40). Gainesville, FL: The University of Florida.

Pentina, I., Prybutok, V. R., & Zhang, X. (2008). The role of virtual communities as shopping reference groups. *Journal of Electronic Commerce Research*, *9*(2), 114–136.

Penz, E. (2006). Researching the socio-cultural context: Putting social representations theory into action. *International Marketing Review*, *23*(4), 418–437. doi:10.1108/02651330610678985

Peppers, D., & Rogers, M. (1993). *The one-to-one future: Building relationships one customer at a time*. New York, NY: Currency Doubleday.

Peppers, D., & Rogers, M. (2008). *Building equity through the customer experience*. White Paper.

Persky, J. (1995). Retrospectives: The ethology of Homo economicus. *The Journal of Economic Perspectives*, *9*(2), 221–231.

Peters, T. (2007). *Personal branding blog spotlight: Tom Peters brand talent*. Retrieved from http://personalbrandingblog.wordpress.com /2007/10/17/personal-branding-spotlight-tom-peters-brand-talent/ 03

Petrillo, G., & Lionetto, S. (1996). Spot anti-Aids e rappresentazioni sociali. *Ikon*, *32*, 289–320.

Phillimore, M., & Wilson, J. A. J. (2010). *Social media newsrooms: Exploring identity through user generated comment*. Euprera Spring Symposium, 25th-27th February 2010, University College Arteveldehogeschool, Ghent, Belgium.

Picone, M. (2006). Interview. In M. Armemi (Ed.), *Communicating physics*. (pp.173-174). Roma, Italy: 2adigroma Editore.

Pike, S. (2005). Tourism destination branding complexity. *Journal of Product and Brand Management*, *14*(4), 258. doi:10.1108/10610420510609267

Pinker, S. (1997). *How the mind works*. Penguin.

Pinker, S. (1994). *The language instinct*. New York, NY: William Morrow and Company, Inc.

Pitt, L. F., Watson, R. T., Berthon, P., & Zinkhan, D. W. G. (2006). The penguin's window: Corporate brands from an open-source perspective. *Journal of the Academy of Marketing Science*, *34*(2), 115–127. doi:10.1177/0092070305284972

Polanyi, K. (1944). *The great transformation*. New York, NY: Rinehart.

Polonsky, M. J., & Hyman, M. R. (2007). A multiple stakeholder perspective on responsibility in advertising. *Journal of Advertising*, *36*(2), 5–13. doi:10.2753/JOA0091-3367360200

Porra, J., & Parks, M. S. (2006). Sustainable virtual communities: Suggestions from the colonial model. *Information Systems and eBusiness Management*, *4*(4), 309-341.

Prahalad, C. K., & Ramaswamy, V. (2004). Co-creation experiences: The next practice in value creation. *Journal of Interactive Marketing*, *18*(3), 5–14. doi:10.1002/dir.20015

Preece, J. (2000). *Online communities: Designing usability, supporting sociability*. New York, NY: John Wiley & Sons.

Prideaux, B., & Cooper, C. (2002). Marketing and destination growth: A symbiotic relationship or simple coincidence. *Journal of Vacation Marketing*, *9*(1), 35–51. doi:10.1177/135676670200900103

Proshansky, H. M., Fabian, K., & Kaminoff, R. (1983). Place-identity: Physical world socialization of the self. *Journal of Environmental Psychology*, *3*, 57–83. doi:10.1016/S0272-4944(83)80021-8

Qiu, X., Hu, S., & Zhao, P. (2007). *The effect and strategy of high-priced level premium brand products price reduction: An empirical research to auto industry* (pp. 4181–4184). IEEE.

Quelch, J. A., & Jocz, K. E. (2009). How to market in a downturn. *Harvard Business Review*, *87*(4), 52–62.

Quinn, J. B. (1997). *Innovation explosion: Using intellect and software to revolutionize growth strategies*. New York, NY: Free Press.

Ramirez, E., & Goldsmith, R. E. (2009). Some antecedents of price sensitivity. *Journal of Marketing Theory and Practice*, *17*(3), 199–213. doi:10.2753/MTP1069-6679170301

Rampersad, H. K. (2008). *Authentic personal branding*. Charlotte, NC: Information Age Publishing.

Rao, A. R., & Ruekert, R. W. (1994). Brand alliances as signals of product quality. *Sloan Management Review*, *36*(3), 87–97.

Reed, J. (2008, March 25). REM launch new album on the web. *BBC Radio 1*. Retrieved September 29, 2009, from http://news.bbc.co.uk/newsbeat /hi/technology/newsid_7312000 /7312288.stm

Reeves, P., & de Chernatony, L. (2003). *How voters choose political brands*. U K: Seminar Series at School of Public Policy, University of Birmingham.

Reeves, P., DeChernatony, L., & Carrigan, M. (2006). Building a political brand: Ideology or voter driven strategy. *Journal of Brand Management*, *13*(6). doi:10.1057/palgrave.bm.2540283

Reeves, P., & DeChernatony, L. (2003). Political brand choice in Britain. In *6th Annual Political Marketing Conference, University of Middlesex, Thistle Hotel/ House of Commons*, London, UK.

Reichheld, F. F. (1996). *The loyalty effect*. Boston, MA: Harvard Business School Press.

Reilly, P. (1997). Outsourcing: Employers becoming cautious. *Management Services*, *41*(6), 9–11.

Reinert, M. (1992). *Logiciel ALCESTE pour l'analyse des données textuelles (version 2.0)*. Université de Toulouse-Le Mirail C.N.R.S.

Reprise Media. (2004, December 16). *SEMPO talks brand, generic terms score big and Sullivan on search*. Retrieved June 24, 2009, from http://www.searchviews.com/index.php/archives/2004/12/sempo-talks-brand-generic-terms-score-big-and-sullivan-on-search.php

Reynolds, T. J., & Gutman, J. (1984). Advertising is image management. *Journal of Advertising Research*, *24*, 27–37.

Rheingold, H. (2002). *Smart mobs: The next social revolution*. Cambridge, MA: Perseus Books Group.

Rheingold, H. (1993). *The virtual community: Homesteading on the electronic frontier*. New York, NY: Harper Collins.

Richardson, T. (2002, April 12). NTHellworld.com founder takes job with NTL. *The Register.* Retrieved from http://www.theregister.co.uk

Riegelsberger, J., Sasse, M. A., & McCarthy, J. D. (2003). Shiny happy people building trust? Photos on e-commerce websites and consumer trust. CHI 2003: Ft. Lauderdale, Florida, USA. *CHI Letters*, *5*(1), 121–128.

Ries, A., & Trout, J. (1982). *Positioning: The battle for your mind*. New York, NY: Warner Books.

Rigopoulou, I., Siomkos, G., Kehagias, J., & Vassilikopoulou, A. (2007). *Brand equity elements and crisis management*. Academy of Marketing Conference, 2007, 4-6 July, Kingston University, Surrey – UK.

Ritchie, J. R. B., & Ritchie, J. B. R. (1998). The branding of tourism destinations: Past achievements and future challenges. *Proceedings of the Annual Congress of the International Association of Scientific Experts in Tourism (AIEST)*. Marrakesh, Morocco, (pp. 89-116).

Ritson, M., & Elliott, R. (1999). The social uses of advertising: An ethnographic study of adolescent advertising audiences. *The Journal of Consumer Research*, *26*(December), 260–277. doi:10.1086/209562

Roberts, J. (1996). Green consumers in the 1990s: Profile and implications for advertising. *Journal of Business Research*, *36*(3), 217–231. doi:10.1016/0148-2963(95)00150-6

Robinson, S., & Etherington, L. (2006). *Customer loyalty*. Houndmills, UK: Palgrave Macmillan.

Roggeveen, A. L., Bharadwaj, N., & Hoyer, W. D. (2007). How call center location impacts expectations of service from reputable versus lesser known firms. *Journal of Retailing*, *83*(4), 403–410. doi:10.1016/j.jretai.2007.03.008

Romano, D. (1988). *Immagine Marketing e Comunicazione*. Bologna, Italy: Il Mulino.

Rondeau, D. B. (2005). For mobile applications, branding is experience. *Communications of the ACM*, *48*(7), 61–66. doi:10.1145/1070838.1070867

Rood, V., & Bruckman, A. (2009). Member behavior in company online communities (pp. 209–218). GROUP '09: Sanibel Island, Florida, USA. Association for Computing Machinery.

Roper, S., & Davies, G. (2007). The corporate brand: Dealing with multiple stakeholders. *Journal of Marketing Management*, *23*(1-2), 75–90. doi:10.1362/026725707X178567

Ross, C. F., Temkin, B., & Herbert, L. (2003). *Can outsourcers really transform IT?* Boston, MA: Forrester Research Inc.

Roy, M. (2003, November 7). Outsourced call centres damage long-term effort. *Precision Marketing*, 14.

Rozanski, H. D., Baum, A. G., & Wolfsen, B. T. (1999). Brand zealots: Realizing the full value of emotional brand loyalty. *strategy+business*, *17*, 51-62.

Russell, D. W., & Russell, C. A. (2006). Explicit and implicit catalysts of consumer resistance: The effects of animosity, cultural salience and country-of-origin on subsequent choice. *International Journal of Research in Marketing*, *23*(3), 321–331. doi:10.1016/j.ijresmar.2006.05.003

Ruyter, K. d., Birgelen, M. v., & Wetzels, M. (1998). Consumer ethnocentrism in international services marketing. *International Business Review*, *7*, 185–202. doi:10.1016/S0969-5931(98)00005-5

Ruyter, K. d., & Wetzels, M. G. M. (2000). The impact of perceived listening behavior in voice-to-voice service encounters. *Journal of Service Research*, *2*(3), 276–284. doi:10.1177/109467050023005

Sabbadin, E. (1997). *Marketing della distribuzione e marketing integrato: I casi Marks & Spencer e Benetton*. Milano, Italy: Egea.

Sahlins, M. (1972). The original affluent society. In Sahlins, M. (Ed.), *Stone age economics* (pp. 1–39). New York, NY: Aldine.

Sauer, P. L., Young, M. A., & Unnava, H. R. (1991). An experimental investigation of the processes behind the country-of-origin effects. *Journal of International Consumer Marketing*, *3*(2), 29–59. doi:10.1300/J046v03n02_04

Saviane, S. (1998). *Il miliardario: La vita segreta di Luciano Benetton*. Venezia, Italy: Marsilio.

Schultz, D. E. (2007). Focus on brand changes rules of engagement. *Marketing News*, *41*(13), 7–8.

Schultz, D. E., Barnes, B. E., Schultz, H. F., & Azzaro, M. (2009). *Building customer-brand relationships*. Armonk, NY: M. E. Sharpe, Inc.

Schultz, D. E., & Barnes, B. E. (1995). *Strategic advertising campaigns* (4th ed.). Lincolnwood, IL: NTC Business Books.

Scotexchange.net. (2009). *About us*. Retrieved June 21, 2009, from http://www.scotexchange.net/about_us /vision_priorities_and_objectives.htm

Scott, C. (1977). Modifying socially-conscious behavior: The foot-in-the-door technique. *The Journal of Consumer Research*, *4*(3), 156–164. doi:10.1086/208691

Scutchfield, F. D., Ireson, C., & Hall, L. (2004). The voice of the public in public health policy and planning: The role of public judgment. *Journal of Public Health Policy*, *25*(2), 197–205. doi:10.1057/palgrave.jphp.3190018

Selnes, F. (1993). An examination of the effect of product performance on brand reputation, satisfaction and loyalty. *European Journal of Marketing*, *27*(9), 19–35. doi:10.1108/03090569310043179

Semprini, A. (1993). *Lo sguardo semiotico*. Milano, Italy: Franco Angeli.

Semprini, A. (1994a). *Marche e mondi possibili*. Milano, Italy: Franco Angeli.

Semprini, A. (1994b). Benetton: dalla missione all'azione. *Micro & Macro Marketing*, *2*, 157–173.

Semprini, A. (1997). *Analyser la communication. Comment analyser les images, les médias, la publicité. Paris, France: L'Harmattan, 1996; tr. it. Analizzare la comunicazione. Come analizzare la pubblicità, le immagini, i media*. Milano, Italy: F. Angeli.

Sentinelli, M. (2003). *Usabilità dei nuovi media*. Roma, Italy: Carocci Editore.

Sha, Z., Wen, F., Gao, G., & Wang, X. (2009). *Antecedents and consequences of flow experience in virtual brand community*. IEEE.

Shannon, C., & Weaver, W. (1949). *Mathematical theory of communication*. Urbana, IL: University of Illinois Press.

Sharma, P., Mathur, R., & Dhawan, A. (2009). Exploring customer reactions to offshore call centers: Toward a comprehensive conceptual framework. *Journal of Services Marketing*, *23*(5), 289–300. doi:10.1108/08876040910973404

Sharma, P., Tam, J. L. M., & Kim, N. (2009). Demystifying intercultural service encounters: Toward a comprehensive conceptual framework. *Journal of Service Research*, *12*(2), 227–242. doi:10.1177/1094670509338312

Sharma, S., Shimp, T. A., & Shin, J. (1995). Consumer ethnocentrism: A test of antecedents and moderators. *Journal of the Academy of Marketing Science*, *23*(1), 26–37. doi:10.1007/BF02894609

Sharma, P., Mathur, R., & Dhawan, A. (2008b). Understanding consumer reactions to offshore outsourcing of customer services (Reprint). In Bandyopadhyay, S. (Ed.), *Contemporary research in e-branding* (*Vol. 1*, pp. 228–240). Hershey, PA: Information Science Reference. doi:10.4018/978-1-59904-813-0.ch015

Sharma, P., Mathur, R., & Dhawan, A. (2008a). Understanding consumer reactions to offshore outsourcing of customer services (Reprint). In Becker, A. (Ed.), *Electronic commerce: Concepts, methodologies, tools and applications* (*Vol. 1*, pp. 92–104). Hershey, PA: Idea Group Inc.

Sharma, P., Mathur, R., & Dhawan, A. (2006). Understanding consumer reactions to offshore outsourcing of customer services. In Kehal, H., & Singh, V. P. (Eds.), *Outsourcing and offshoring in the 21st century: A socio-economic perspective* (pp. 326–340). doi:10.4018/978-1-59140-875-8.ch015

Sharma, P. (2010). Offshore outsourcing of customer services - Boon or bane? *Working Paper*.

Shimp, T. A. (1984). Consumer ethnocentrism: The concept and a preliminary empirical test. *Advances in Consumer Research. Association for Consumer Research (U. S.)*, *11*, 285–290.

Shimp, T. A., & Sharma, S. (1987). Consumer ethnocentrism: Construction and validation of the CETSCALE. *The Journal of Consumer Research*, *24*(August), 280–289.

Siems, T. F., & Ratner, A. S. (2003). Do what you do best, outsource the rest. *Southwest Economy*, *6*, 13–14.

Simon, H. A. (1996). *Sciences of the artificial* (3rd ed.). Cambridge, MA: MIT Press.

Singh, J., & Wilkes, R. E. (1996). When consumers complain: A path analysis of the key antecedents of consumer complaint response estimates. *Journal of the Academy of Marketing Science*, *24*(4), 350–365. doi:10.1177/0092070396244006

Sizoo, S. (2007). The effect of intercultural sensitivity on cross-cultural service encounters in selected markets: Hawaii, London, and Florida. *Journal of Applied Management and Entrepreneurship*, *12*(1), 47–66.

Slater, S. F. (2009). Know your customers. *Marketing Management*, *18*(1), 36–44.

Slouka, M. (1995). *War of the worlds: Cyberspace and the high-tech assault on reality*. New York, NY: Basic Books.

Snodgrass, R., & Brucks, M. (2004). Branding yourself. *SIGMOD Record*, *33*(2), 117–125. doi:10.1145/1024694.1024722

Solomon, M. R. (2003). *Conquering consumerspace: Marketing strategies for a branded world*. New York: AMACOM.

Song, J., & Kim, Y. J. (2005). Social influence process in the acceptance of a virtual community service. *Information Systems Frontiers*, *8*, 241–252. doi:10.1007/s10796-006-8782-0

Spilman, M. (2006). *Cracking the engagement code*. Retrieved from www.imediaconnection.com

Sprott, D., Czellar, S., & Spangenberg, E. (2009). The importance of a general measure of brand engagement on market behavior: Development and validation of a scale. *JMR, Journal of Marketing Research*, *46*(1), 92–104. doi:10.1509/jmkr.46.1.92

Stockman, S. (2009, March 13). *Personality branding defined*. Retrieved from http://www.customproductions.tv/2009 /03/personality-brand-defined.html

Stokinger, P. (2002). *La description-évaluation de sites web*. Séminaire dans la cadre du DESS Webmestre Editorial à l'UFR Sciences humaines et Arts de l'Université de Poitiers.

Straczynski, S. (2009, September 3). *Social network branding fails to sway female purchasing*. Retrieved from progressivegrocer.com

Strauss, R. E., Schoder, D., & Gebauer, J. (2001). The relevance of brands for electronic commerce results from an empirical study of consumers in Europe. *Proceedings of the 34th Hawaii International Conference on System Sciences* (pp. 7064–7072). IEEE.

Stringfellow, A., Teagarden, M. B., & Nie, W. (2008). Invisible costs in offshoring services work. *Journal of Operations Management*, *26*(2), 164–179. doi:10.1016/j.jom.2007.02.009

Sullivan, A. (2002, October 13). An honest blogger will never make a quick buck. *Sunday London Times*.

Susman, W. I. (1985). *Culture as history: The transformation of American society in the twentieth century*. New York, NY: Pantheon Books.

Sutton, D., & Klein, T. (2003). *Enterprise marketing management*. Hoboken, NJ: John Wiley & Sons.

Swartz, N. (2004a). Much more than jobs being outsourced. *Information Management Journal, 38*(3), 3.

Swartz, N. (2004b). Offshoring privacy. *Information Management Journal, 38*(5), 24–26.

Tafani, E. (2006). Image and social representations: Conceptualization and perspectives of application in the fields of marketing, advertising and communication. In A. S. de Rosa, (Ed.), *8th I.C.S.R. Proceedings,* Rome: Rocografica, (pp. 112-115).

Talukder, M., & Yeow, P. H. P. (2007). A comparative study of virtual communities in Bangladesh and the USA. *Journal of Computer Information Systems, 47*(4), 82–90.

Teevan, J., Cutrell, E., Fisher, D., Drucker, S. M., Ramos, G., Andre, P., & Hu, C. (2009). *Visual snippets: Summarizing web pages for search and revisitation* (pp. 2023–2032). CHI 2009: Boston, Massachusetts, USA. Association for Computing Machinery.

The Bay Charles Consulting Company. (2009). *Experiential branding: An introduction.* Retrieved July 16, 2009, from http://www.baycharles.com/images/ BC3%20 %20Experiential%20Branding %20White%20Paper.pdf

The Economist. (2003, March 13). The revenge of geography. *The Economist Magazine.*

The Times. (2009, March 8). EMI has a new spin on record market. *The Times Online.* Retrieved October 12, 2009, from http://business.timesonline.co.uk/tol /business/ industry_sectors/media /article5864044.ece

Thurston, P., Buff, C. L., & Devasagayam, P. R. (2009). Participation preferences and brand community integration: An empirical investigation. *Review of Business Research, 9*(2), 34–44.

Times Online. (2008). *Barack Obama looks to green jobs to save the planet and economy.* Retrieved from http://www.timesonline. co.uk /tol/news/world/us_and_ americas/article5349809.ece

Tobias, P., & Spiegel, D. S. (2009). *Is design the preeminent protagonist in user experience? Ubiquity, 10(6).* Association for Computing Machinery.

Todreas, T. M. (1999). *Value creation and branding in television's digital age* (p. 175). Westport, CT: Quorum Book.

Tönnies, F. (1957). *Gemeinschaft and Gesellschaft. (C. P. Loomis* (Trans, A., Ed.). East Lansing, MI: Michigan State University Press.

Torres, A., & Bijmolt, T. (2009). Assessing brand image through communalities and asymmetries in brand-to-attribute and attribute-to-brand associations. *European Journal of Operational Research, 195*(2), 628. doi:10.1016/j.ejor.2008.02.020

Toscani, O. (1995). *Ciao Mamma.* Milano, Italy: Mondadori.

Trapp, R. (1999). Blunder boss. *British Journal of Administrative Management,* (July/August): 12–16.

Tse, D. K., & Lee, W.-N. (1993). Removing negative country images: Effects of decomposition, branding and product experience. *Journal of International Marketing, 1*(1), 57–75.

Tsiotsou, R., & Goldsmith, R. E. (2011). Exploring the formation process of brand love: a comparison between goods and services. Presentation 2011 Academy of Marketing Science World Marketing Congress, Reims, France July 19-July 23.Uncles, M. (2008). Know thy changing consumer. *Journal of Brand Management, 15,* 227–231.

Tsygankov, V. (2004). *Evaluation of website trustworthiness from customer perspective, a framework* (pp. 265–271). Sixth International Conference on Electronic Commerce, ICEC '04. Association for Computing Machinery.

Turkle, S. (1985). *Il secondo io.* Milano, Italy: Frassinelli.

Turkle, S. (1995). *Life on the screen. Identity in the age of the Internet.* New York, NY: Simon & Schuster.

Turkle, S. (1996). Virtuality and its discontents: Searching for community in cyberspace. *The American Prospect, 7,* 24.

Turner, A. M., Liddy, E. D., & Bradley, J. (2002). *Breathing life into digital archives: Use of natural language processing to revitalize the grey literature of public health* (p. 411). JCDL '02: Portland, Oregon, USA. Association for Computing Machinery.

Usunier, J.-C., & Lee, J. (2009). *Marketing across cultures.* Canada: Financial Time Prentice Hall.

Vargo, S. L., & Lusch, R. F. (2004). Evolving to a new dominant logic for marketing. *Journal of Marketing*, *68*(1), 1–17. doi:10.1509/jmkg.68.1.1.24036

Vaucelle, C., Bonanni, L., & Ishii, H. (2009). Design of haptic interfaces for therapy (pp. 467–470). CHI 2009: Boston, Massachusetts, USA. Association for Computing Machinery.

Venables, M. (2006). Final say: Outsourcing falls short of expectations. *Manufacturing Engineering*, *85*(3), 48. doi:10.1049/me:20060315

Verlegh, P. W. J., Steenkamp, J.-B. E. M., & Meulenberg, M. T. G. (2005). Country-of-origin effects in consumer processing of advertising claims. *International Journal of Research in Marketing*, *22*(2), 127–139. doi:10.1016/j.ijresmar.2004.05.003

Visciola, M. (2000). *Usabilità dei Siti Web*. Milano, Italy: Edizioni Apogeo.

Wæraas, A., & Solbakk, M. N. (2009). Defining the essence of a university: Lessons from higher education branding. *Higher Education*, *57*, 449–462. doi:10.1007/s10734-008-9155-z

Walker, R. (2008). *Buying in*. New York, NY: Random House.

Walton, D. A., Farmer, P. E., Lambert, W., Leandre, F., Koenig, S. P., & Mukherjee, J. S. (2004). Integrated HIV prevention and care strengthen primary health care: Lessons from rural Haiti. *Journal of Public Health Policy*, *25*(2), 137–158. doi:10.1057/palgrave.jphp.3190013

Wang, H. X., Chen, J., Hu, Y. C., & Ye, M. (2008). *The consistency of product design and brand image* (pp. 1142–1144). IEEE.

Wang, M. (2009). *Research on the innovation mechanism of digital brand in enterprise* (pp. 728–732). 2009 International Conference on Networks Security, Wireless Communications and Trusted Computing. IEEE.

Washburn, J. H., Hill, B. D., & Priluck, R. (2004). Co-branding: Brand equity and trial effects. *Journal of Consumer Marketing*, *17*(7), 591–604. doi:10.1108/07363760010357796

Watzlawick, P., Bavelas, J. B., & Jackson, D. D. (1967). *Pragmatics of human communication*. New York, NY: W. W. Norton & Company.

Webopedia. (2003, October 1). *What is a blog?* Retrieved from http://www.webopedia.com/ TERM/B/blog.html

Webster, F. Jr. (1975). Determining the characteristics of the socially conscious consumer. *The Journal of Consumer Research*, *2*(3), 188–196. doi:10.1086/208631

Weed, D. L. (2002/2003). Is the precautionary principle a principle? *IEEE Technology and Society Magazine*, *21*(4), 45–48. doi:10.1109/MTAS.2003.1166567

Williamson, J. (1978). *Decoding advertisements: Ideology and meaning in advertising*. London, UK: Marion Boyars.

Wilson, J. A. J., & Liu, J. (2009). The Pinocchio effect – When managing the brand creation process, across cultures. *TMC Academic Journal*, *4*(1), 45–58.

Windsor, D. (1992). Stakeholder management in multinational enterprises. In S. N. Brenner and S. A. Waddock (Eds.), *Proceedings of the Third Annual Meeting of the International Association for Business and Society* (pp. 121-128). Leuven, Belgium.

Wolfe, R. A., & Putler, D. S. (2002). How tight are the ties that bind stakeholder groups? *Organization Science*, *13*(1), 64–80. doi:10.1287/orsc.13.1.64.544

Wolton, D. (1999). *Internet et après. Une tbéorie critique des nottveaux medias*. Paris, France: Flammarion.

Wong, A. (2004). The role of emotional satisfaction in service encounters. *Managing Service Quality*, *14*(5), 365–376. doi:10.1108/09604520410557976

Wong, A., & Sohal, A. (2003). Service quality and customer loyalty perspectives on two levels of retail relationships. *Journal of Services Marketing*, *17*(4/5), 495–511. doi:10.1108/08876040310486285

Wu, H., Fan, Q., & Wang, X. (2008). *The design of university image and construction of brand strategy* (pp. 874–876). IEEE.

Yagy, T. (1993). *United colors of Benetton: A global vision*. Japan: Robundo.

Yohn, D. (2008). The brand ultimatum. [The American Marketing Association.]. *Marketing Management, 17*(4), 34–38.

Yoo, B., & Donthu, N. (2001). Developing and validating a multidimensional consumer-based brand equity scale. *Journal of Business Research, 52*(1), 1–14. doi:10.1016/S0148-2963(99)00098-3

Youngdahl, W., & Ramaswamy, K. (2008). Offshoring knowledge and service work: A conceptual model and research agenda. *Journal of Operations Management, 26*(2), 212–221. doi:10.1016/j.jom.2007.02.007

Zabieglik, S. (2002). The origins of the term Homo economicus. In *Economics and values*, (pp. 123-130). Gdansk.

Zahra, A., & Ryan, C. (2007). From chaos to cohesion - Complexity in tourism structures: An analysis of New Zealand's regional tourism organizations. *Tourism Management, 28*(3), 854–862. doi:10.1016/j.tourman.2006.06.004

Zaltman, G. (2003). *How customers think*. Cambridge, MA: Harvard Business School Press.

Zaltman, G., & Puccinelli, N. (2001). *Strategic use of music in marketing, a selective review*. (Harvard Business School Note, 9- 501-056).

Zhang, Y., Yan, D., Chen, Y.-D., Chen, H., Thurmond, M., & King, C.-C. … Larson, C. A. (2008). BioPortal infectious disease informatics research: Disease surveillance and situational awareness. *Proceedings of the 9th Annual International Digital Government Research Conference. Association for Computing Machinery* (pp. 393 – 394).

Zhu, D.-H., & Chang, Y.-P. (2009). *The influence of knowledge sharing in virtual communities on consumers' brand trust: An empirical study* (pp. 580–583). 2009 International Conference on Networks Security, Wireless Communications and Trusted Computing. IEEE.

Ziethaml, V. A., Bitner, M. J., & Gremler, D. D. (2006). *Services marketing: Integrating customer focus across the firm*. London, UK: McGraw-Hill.

Zimmerman, D. (2003, July 7). Mix DM, branding online? Just do it. *DM News,* (p. 20).

Zipf, G. K. (1965). *Psychology of languages*. Cambridge, MA: MIT Press.

About the Contributors

Avinash Kapoor received the PhD in Management and MBA from the R.A. Podar College at University of Rajasthan, Jaipur, India, and the MA and BSc from University of Rajasthan. He has been recipient of National Scholarship Award. He has more than fifteen years of industry, teaching, training, and research and consultancy experience to his credit. He was former Dean in JIMS, Jaipur and is currently Faculty of Marketing and Chair Person PGPIM, at MDI, Gurgaon, India. He is author of textbook on "Marketing Research" and his forthcoming textbook is on "Marketing Management" published by Cengage publishing (formerly Thompson publishing group). He has several research papers, articles published and presented in reputed refereed international journals and research conferences.

Chinmaya Kulshrestha received the PhD in Management and MBA from the R.A. Podar College at University of Rajasthan, Jaipur, India, and the BA from University of Rajasthan. She has been recipient of National Scholarship award. She has more than ten years of teaching, training, and research and consultancy experience to her credit. She was former Dean BBA, Bradford University; IILM Jaipur, and Programme Head MBA, BBA at JIMS, Jaipur. She is currently Faculty of Marketing at MDI, Gurgaon, India. She is author of textbook on "Marketing Research" and her forthcoming textbook is on "Management" published by Cengage publishing (formerly Thompson publishing group). She has several research papers, articles published and presented in reputed refereed international journals and research conferences.

* * *

Elena Bocci obtained her PhD in 2006 on Social Representations and Communication. In the course of the same year, she collaborated on one of the research projects on social representations funded by the International Foundation Balzan. In 2007 she was awarded a post-doc fellowship at the Department Psychology of Developmental and Socialization Processes – Faculty of Psychology 2 - 'Sapienza' University of Rome. Since 2008 she is a full time researcher at the Department Psychology of Developmental and Socialization Processes – Faculty of Psychology 2 - 'Sapienza' University of Rome. Among other areas related to social psychology, she currently works on the following research fields: social representations and enterprise communication strategy, analysis of the behaviour of potential e-commerce clients, social representations of Internet, and risk.

Raj Devasagayam, PhD, is Professor and Chair, Marketing Department in the School of Business of Siena College in Albany, NY. Dr. Raj's teaching interests include: marketing strategy, marketing research, sales and sales management, business statistics, and international business. He has received awards for excellence in teaching from peers as well as students. He received the Jerome Walton Excellence in teaching award from Siena College in 2007 and the Ladvina excellence in teaching award from the St. Norbert College, Green bay, WI in 2003. Most recently he was honored with the Hormel meritorious teaching award at the Marketing Management Association 2008 annual meeting in Chicago. Dr. Raj has published his research in the areas of dispute resolution mechanisms in customer/firm conflicts, not-for-profits, channels, brand strategies, sports marketing, marketing pedagogy, and corporate social responsibility. He has several publications in leading journals such as *Journal of Brand Management, Journal of Product and Brand Management, Marketing Management Journal, Journal of Financial Services Marketing,* and *Sport Marketing Quarterly*. Raj serves on the board of the Marketing Management Association and is the vice-president of publications of the Marketing Management Association.

Ronald E. Goldsmith, PhD, is the Richard M. Baker Professor of Marketing in the College of Business at Florida State University where he teaches consumer behavior and marketing research. Most of his research focuses on personality's role in consumer behavior and measurement issues, especially in the areas of diffusion of innovations, consumer involvement, and services marketing. Since 1991 he has been a co-editor (North America) for *The Service Industries Journal*. He has published over 140 articles in such journals as *The Journal of Services Marketing, The Journal of Consumer Behaviour, The Journal of Advertising, The European Journal of Marketing, The Journal of Social Psychology, The Journal of the Academy of Marketing Science,* and the *Journal of Business Research*. His book co-authored with Gordon Foxall entitled *Consumer Psychology for Marketing* was first published in 1994 and appears in Chinese, Polish, Russian, and Korean editions.

Shalin Hai-Jew works as an instructional designer at Kansas State University. She has worked on several public health projects related to online learning. Currently, she is working on designing short courses and creating e-learning faculty support modules for the university. She has BAs in English and psychology, and an MA in English from the University of Washington; she has an EdD in Educational Leadership from Seattle University (2005). She teaches for WashingtonOnline (WAOL) in Washington State. She is interested in the role of human perception in e-learning.

Dana VanDen Heuvel is the founder of the marketing consulting firm, The MarketingSavant Group. An award-winning marketing blogger, Dana is also the author of the American Marketing Association's "Marketech Guide to Marketing Technology" and their "Guide to Social Network Marketing" and the creator of the AMA's TechnoMarketing training series, Advanced Social Media training series and B2B Social Media training series. Dana is a widely recognized expert on thought leadership marketing, social media, blogging, podcasting, RSS, Internet communities and interactive marketing trends, and best practices and speaks at over 50 events each year on these and other marketing topics at industry and private client events. Dana consults with dozens of clients each year on social media and marketing strategy. Recognized as one of the "50 People You Should Know" by the Green Bay Chamber of Commerce, Dana serves on several advisory boards for nonprofits and community organizations in and around Wisconsin. Dana is a member of the National Speakers Association (NSA), the leading organization for professional speakers. Dana is also an Adjunct Professor at St. Norbert College and teaches a course on social media and thought leadership marketing.

Omkumar Krishnan, PhD is Associate Professor and Area Chair- Marketing at the Institute of Management Technology, Ghaziabad. A PhD from IIT, Bombay, he specializes in the area of qualitative and quantitative market research and has worked with Drishti Strategic Research Services and Lowe Lintas, Bombay. Omkumar has publications in refereed journals and has presented a number of conference papers at national and international forums and is responsible for conceptualizing and designing the International Conference on Brand Management. Over the last ten years he has been conducting training programmes in SPSS at various business schools and research organizations in the country. Omkumar regularly holds long term and short term Management Development Programmes for corporate executives of some of the top-rated public sector and private firms in India and offers consultancy in the areas of marketing, quantitative and qualitative research, and entrepreneurship. He teaches courses on Market Research and Marketing Management and heads the Entrepreneurship Development Program funded by AICTE at IMT.

Lubna Nafees, PhD, is Assistant Professor of Marketing at the Institute of Management Technology, Ghaziabad. Lubna specializes in the areas of brand management, visual and verbal marketing communications, advertising, and consumer behaviour. She has published several research papers, articles, and case studies in various national and international journals and has worked on projects funded by Ministry of Human Resource Development, European Union, and the AICTE. She has co-authored a book on Family Managed, Multinational and Public Sector Enterprises: The strategic choices for global competitiveness and co-edited Brands Rising.....as Products Fall and Brand Research. Lubna teaches courses on Strategic Brand Management, Integrated Marketing Communications and Marketing Management at IMT. She conducts corporate trainings and consultancy in the area of marketing communications, brand strategy, and customer value management with some of the globally renowned national and international brands.

Piyush Nangru is currently working as an Area Manager in Great India Rural Tours, a rural tourism company based out of Jaipur. He did his Post Graduate Diploma in Management from Institute of Management Technology, Ghaziabad majoring in Marketing. He has been associated with Karnataka State Tourism Development Corporation (KSTDC) for marketing of three rural sites in Karnataka. Before IMT, Piyush worked with Tata Consultancy Services, Mumbai for two years. His interest areas include destination marketing, destination development and marketing of services.

Manish Makhija is currently working in the Retail and Consumer Goods consulting practice at HCL Technologies, Noida. He did his Post Graduate Diploma in Management from IMT Ghaziabad, majoring in Marketing. Previously he was working with ITC Ltd. in the Tobacco Division and was looking after Operations in the primary module of the Bangalore Cigarette Factory. He did his BE in Electronics and Telecommunications from Pune University. Manish's interests lies in branding, trade marketing and distribution, and Six Sigma.

Margherita Pagani is Assistant Professor of Management at Bocconi University (Milan), and Affiliate at MIT Massachusetts Institute of Technology. She is Member of Lorange Institute of Business (Zurich) Executive Faculty. She was Visiting Professor at Redlands University, California (2004) and Visiting Scientist at MIT's Sloan School of Management (2008 and 2003). She serves as Associate Editor for the Journal of Information Science and Technology. Her current research examines mobile marketing, consumer technology acceptance models, consumer behavior in social networks and system dynamics models for assessing the leverage among the various components in IT value networks. She published several books (published in US, Korea, Italy) two encyclopedias and articles in leading international journals, such as *Information & Management, Journal of Business Research, Journal of Interactive Marketing, Technology Analysis and Strategic Management, The International Journal on Media Management, Technological Forecasting and Social Change, International Journal of Mobile Marketing, Revue Français du Marketing* and a variety of other publications. For her research activity and publications in the mobile marketing field, she won the 2009 Mobile Marketing Association Global Award "Academic of the Year." She also got the award for distinctive academic research from Bocconi University for the results achieved during the periods 2004-2006.

Robert Pennington earned his PhD in Mass Communication Research at the University of Wisconsin. He is on the faculty of Fo Guang University, Taiwan, where he teaches in the Department of Communication, the Department of Management, and the Department of Foreign Languages and Cultures. He specializes in the cultural development implications of communication technology. His general interest concerns consumption and marketing communication as cultural processes. He has written previously about marketing communication development, advertising and brands within consumer culture, the meanings of consumer brands, and psycho-linguistic methodology. In addition, he is a respected photographer.

Massimiliano Picone is the IT Manager of the European PhD on S. R. & C., University of Rome "La Sapienza." He planned the Apple-based IT infrastructure of the European PhD on Social Representations and Communication Research Centre and Multimedia Lab and implemented various services like the video conferencing system from Marratech (now Google), where the software whiteboard is combined with a hardware SMART board to provide distance learning and collaboration. He is also the founder and creator of "La mela di Newton" (http://lameladinewton.it), a website about science and technology for which he won several prizes including three international awards: the Pirelli International Award in 2001, the Global Junior Challenge in 2002 and the Cable & Wireless Childnet Academy in 2004. Since 2003 he is an international juror of the Pirelli International Award (http://www.pirelliaward.com/ch3_jur-2.html), and member of the ICT panel together with Walter Bender (MIT Media Lab Executive Director) and Pasquale Pistorio (Vice President of Confindustria).

Annamaria Silvana de Rosa has a PhD in Psychology. She is Professor of Attitudes and Social Representations and of Communication and New Media, Faculty of Psychology2, University of Rome "Sapienza." She is creator of the first EU-approved international joint doctorate (http://www.europhd.eu) and of the SoReCom Thematic Network. She is Director of the European PhD on Social Representations and Communication Research Centre and Multimedia Lab and of Sapienza Co-ordination Program for Joint International Doctorates. Author of more than one hundred publications - inspired by the unified paradigm of Social Representations and Communication and characterized by a variety of thematic topics and multi-methodological approach - she was awarded a Doctorate Honoris Causa by the University A.I. Cuza, Iasi. She is often invited to review manuscript proposals for international journals and publishers and to evaluate research programmes by the European Science Foundation, the Belgian Federal Science Policy Office, FCAR in Québec, the Qatar National Research Fund, and the Italian Ministry of Scientific Research.

Vaibhav Rustagi basically belongs to the national capital city of New Delhi. He did his schooling from Delhi Public School, Mathura Road. He has a Bachelor's Degree in Electrical and Electronics Engineering from MIT Manipal, Karnataka. He had a brief stint of about two years with Tata Consultancy Services as a software developer, but found that his interests lie in marketing, so he pursued his PDGM from Institute of Management Technology (IMT) Ghaziabad with Marketing as his major specialization. He is presently working with ITC Ltd in the Trade Marketing & Distribution function of their FMCG business. His key interest areas are brand management, new product development, marketing research, and distribution management. He is an avid traveler, and it is this interest in exploring new places that inspired him to research on this present work on destination branding.

Piyush Sharma is an Associate Professor in the Department of Management and Marketing at The Hong Kong Polytechnic University (PolyU), Hong Kong. He is also the Deputy Program Director for the Hong Kong MBA Program at PolyU. Dr. Sharma earned his BE (Electrical) from Delhi University and MBA (Marketing) from Indian Institute of Management Bangalore. He worked for almost 15 years in various industries including consumer products, healthcare, and financial services, before earning his PhD in Marketing at Nanyang Business School, Singapore in 2006. Dr. Sharma's research interests include cross-cultural consumer behavior, services and international marketing, offshore outsourcing of customer services, inter-cultural service encounters, self-regulation, and self-regulatory failure. He has published his research in the *Journal of the Academy of Marketing Science, Journal of International Business Studies, Journal of Service Research, Journal of Services Marketing, Journal of Business Research, Journal of Marketing Management,* and *Journal of International Consumer Marketing*, among others. He has also presented papers at major marketing conferences all over the world.

Index

A

abracadabra approach 153
accessible site 221
advertising 3, 19-20, 23, 25, 28, 30, 32, 41, 49, 60-61, 63, 66-67, 69-74, 76, 78, 82-90, 93-95, 113, 121, 123-125, 127-128, 130-133, 143, 147, 149, 151-152, 158, 165, 167, 169, 190, 204-206
affordance 198-199
Analysis of Lexical Correspondence (ACL) 81
artefact 141
artefacts 160
associative networks 78, 81-85, 90, 141
astroturfing 32, 40
Attitude toward Offshore Outsourcing (AO) 11
attraction sector 48
avatars 31, 202-203
awareness aggregate 63
ayurveda 161-163

B

Benetton Group 70, 74, 76
brand architecture 141, 159
brand awareness 25, 58, 68, 104, 186
brand-centric 147, 149
brand cognition 146
brand commitment 121, 132, 134, 186
Brand Communication Tools 66, 68
brand community 39, 147, 149-150, 155, 158-160, 177-181, 183, 185-188
brand competence 166
brand culture 109, 160, 167
brand culture approach 160
brand engagement 121-123, 125-126, 129-132, 134
Brand Engagement in Self-Concept (BESC) 121, 125-126, 134
brand equity 55, 58, 67-68, 96, 98, 113, 118, 121, 125, 133, 139, 151, 155, 157, 159, 164, 178, 186
brand evangelist 125
brand identity 2, 36, 50, 52, 54-55, 58, 68, 96, 98, 102, 107-108, 113, 118, 123, 147, 163-164, 166, 168, 210
brand image 3-7, 10-11, 13-17, 23, 34, 39, 48, 52-54, 58-59, 68, 89, 97-98, 107, 111, 114, 164, 167-169, 181
branding elements 50, 54
branding experience 25, 66
Branding Implications 185
brand life-cycle 65
brand loyalty 4-6, 10, 13-17, 23, 31, 53-54, 58, 64, 121-123, 125, 127-129, 131, 133-134, 148, 178-179, 182-183, 186
brand personality 67, 96, 98, 107, 110, 114, 118, 163, 165-169, 171, 174
brand positioning 34, 72, 158
brand promise 1, 3, 102, 114
brand promotion 118
brand relationship 160, 167
brand stakeholder 136-138, 143-144, 154, 160
brand stakeholder analysis 137, 143, 154
broad view 137, 140, 143, 146, 154, 160

C

Canadian Institute for Distance Education Research (CIDER) 28
cause-related marketing 123, 127, 134-135
chain competition 61
channels for specific viewer-groups 59
Children's Online Privacy Protection Act (COPPA) 35
click-through 32, 40
Colleague to Colleague (C2C) consortium 28
collective individualism 160
company-initiated communication 179
Computer-Assisted Design (CAD) 202
condition of normal daily exposure 78-79

Connective Web 31
conservatism 6-7, 10, 17
consumer culture 157, 189-190, 192, 196-200, 202-203, 205
consumer culture values 199
consumer ethnocentrism 4, 6-7, 10-17, 21-23
consumer perception 96, 111, 163-164, 168
consumer reflection 107, 109, 167
consumer self-image 167
consumption objects 197, 201
context of communication 190
core personality parameter 111
Corporate and Social Responsibility (CSR) 138
corporate profile 75
country of origin (COO) 6-7, 18-20
cross-media communication 240
crossover competition 61
Customer-Based Brand Equity (CBBE) 58, 67-68, 125, 133, 164
Customer Experience Management (CEM) 123, 128
customer reflection 167
Customer Relationship Management (CRM) 7, 123, 126-128, 131-132, 135, 148-149, 157
customer satisfaction (SAT) 4-6, 10-18, 20, 23, 128, 186
Customer Service Representative (CSR) 5, 9-10, 14-15, 17

D

daisy wheel 142, 149
decentralization 71, 225, 227, 240
desi 154
destination branding 47-56
Destination Marketing Organizations (DMO) 47, 52-53
destination organization sector 48
differentiating element 50
digital governance 40
digital television 57-60, 66-68
DiscAn 80-82, 85-86, 95
discursive dynamic 78, 81, 87
Distance Education Online Symposium (DEOS) 28
donership 143, 154

E

eBranding 189
e-branding strategy 91, 242, 244
e-culture 192, 195, 197
Edinburgh Tourism Action Group (ETAG) 51
e-Gemeinschaft 194
Electronic Word of Mouth (EWOM) 38, 40
email marketing 32
e-marketing 32-33, 205
emotive effect 2
Endogenous Tourism Projects (ETP) 51
engagement 24, 31, 73, 121-134, 136-137, 144, 148, 152
environmental scan 24, 26, 28-29, 40
error prevention 211, 237
e-updates 179
evoked aggregate 63

F

fabrica 75
face-to-face interaction 195
feedback loop 40, 186
free text 81

G

Gandhi, Rahul 96-98, 103-111, 117-118
general channels 59
generational revolution 104
GeoFree BrandComms 177-180, 182-187
Geographic Information System (GIS) 26
Geoinformatic Hotspot Systems (GHS) 40
geolocation metadata reportage 26
Gesellschaft 194, 206
global branding 24-25, 27-29, 36-37, 41-42, 45
global communication strategies 71, 76
global financial management 71
globalization of labor force 5, 15
global product 71
Gold Coast Airport (GCA) 52
Gold Coast Tourism (GCT) 52
green business 1
grey literature 36, 39

H

Harley Davidson Owners' Group (HOG) 179
herd medicine 25
homo economicus 137-138, 158-160
homo sociologicus 137-138, 156, 160

I

identity management 24, 41
image building choices 96, 118
Indian Political System (IPS) 97, 104
information architecture 40

Instructional Design Open Studio (IDOS) 28
Interactive Distance Education Alliance (IDEA) 29
interactivity 40, 61, 73, 136, 192-194, 201-202, 208, 212, 221, 240
inter-cultural interactions 12
inter-cultural service 12
interrelationships 30, 178, 192, 196
intersectorial competition 61
involvement 16, 49, 51, 99, 103, 109, 123-126, 129, 132-133, 135, 142-143, 162

K

Kapferer brand identity prism 166

M

macro 83, 93, 137, 141, 143, 146, 154, 160
Marketing Science Institute (MSI) 2, 67, 133
market mavenism 124-126, 135
Member Implications 186
membership newsletters 179
memetics 141, 160
microblogging 33, 40
micro perspective 160
mobile marketing 32
morphemes 199
narrow view 137, 140, 146, 160
National Rural Employment Guarantee (NREG) 104
network society 208, 243
niche channels 60

O

Offshore Call Center (OCC) 11, 15
Offshore Customer Service Center (OCSC) 9
offshore outsourcing 4-18, 20, 22-23
online branding 24, 156
online experience 193
online marketing 32
online services 222
organizational dynamics 69, 91

P

Panchayat Raj Institutions (PRI) 51
paradigm classes 197
perceived product importance 124
perceived service quality (SQ) 4, 6, 12, 14-18, 23
Personal Balance Scorecard (PBSC) 102
personal brands 96, 102, 117
personality branding 97-98, 100-101, 103, 119
personality facet 111
Personally Identifiable Information (PII) 33-34
persuasive technology 37, 40
physical appearance 107, 166
physical environment 191, 196, 199, 201
political marketing 96-101, 118-119
political marketing management 99
presence 7, 28, 51, 72, 82, 106, 144, 147, 151-152, 165, 189, 192-196, 200-205, 212, 218, 224, 233, 237, 241
Primary Documents (PDs) 229, 231-232, 234-235
product involvement 124-126
pseudo-environment 192-193, 198, 200
public health 24-30, 32-34, 36-37, 39

Q

qualitatively analyzed 228

R

refurbishing brand 115
relationship marketing 121, 126-127, 131, 135, 158
representational value 198
repurchase intentions 5, 15, 23
Return on Investment (ROI) 33

S

sampling 160
Scottish Enterprise Edinburgh and Lothians (SEE & L) 51
semiotics 192, 199, 205
service firm 5-6, 11, 13, 15-16
Severe Acute Respiratory Syndrome (SARS) 53
social objects 189, 193, 195, 198-199, 202
social representations 69, 76-78, 87-93, 207-209, 243-246
specific brand 64, 110, 121, 125-126, 129
stake 54, 143, 147, 154
stakeholder analysis 137, 139-143, 151, 154-155
stakeholder gains 137
Stakeholder Relationship Management (SRM) 150
stakeholder typology 140
state of the system 237
sustainability 1-2, 6, 165, 246
sustainable competitive advantage 57, 96, 131
sustainable synergy 96, 118
symbolic distinction 197
symbolic representations 190, 193, 195-198

T

target audience 34, 59, 66, 83, 87, 98, 101-102, 107, 109-111, 154, 163
themed channels 59-60
transport sector 48
travel and tourism marketing 48-49, 53
trendlining 26
triadic relationship 199
TV branding channel strategy 68
TV channel logo 68

U

usability 31, 206-212, 216, 218, 224-228, 233, 240, 246-247
usability test 207-209, 224-228, 233
Useful Links 218, 221
user-friendly 210
US Patent and Trademarks Office (USPTO) 34, 43

V

viral marketing 32, 40, 184
Virtual Brand Communities 39, 177, 180
Virtual Communities (VCs) 26, 31-32, 40, 179, 187, 189-190, 192-195, 198, 200-206
visiting card 207, 242
visual display terminals (VDTs) 210, 245
vividness 192-195, 200-203
Voice-Over-Internet Protocol (VOIP) 194

W

Washington Online (WAOL) 28
Web Based Logs (Blogs) 28, 30, 42, 101, 113, 139, 151, 177-178, 180-187

Y

yoga 161-165, 168

CPSIA information can be obtained at www.ICGtesting.com
Printed in the USA
BVOW042146250312

285865BV00008B/8/P

9 781613 501719